# PRINCIPLES OF
# NON-PHILOSOPHY

## ALSO AVAILABLE FROM BLOOMSBURY

# PRINCIPLES OF NON-PHILOSOPHY

**François Laruelle**

**Translated by Nicola Rubczak and Anthony Paul Smith**

B L O O M S B U R Y
LONDON • NEW DELHI • NEW YORK • SYDNEY

**Bloomsbury Academic**

An imprint of Bloomsbury Publishing Plc

50 Bedford Square
London
WC1B 3DP
UK

175 Fifth Avenue
New York
NY 10010
USA

**www.bloomsbury.com**

First published 2013

Originally published in French as *Principes de la non-philosophie*
© Presses Universitaires de France, 1996

This English translation © Bloomsbury Publishing Plc, 2013

**British Library Cataloguing-in-Publication Data**
A catalogue record for this book is available from the British Library.

ISBN: HB: 978-1-4411-7756-8
ePub: 978-1-4411-4993-0
ePDF: 978-1-4411-4214-6

**Library of Congress Cataloging-in-Publication Data**
Laruelle, François.
[Principes de la non-philosophie. English]
Principles of non-philosophy / François Laruelle ; translated by Nicola Rubczak and Anthony Paul Smith.
p. cm.
Includes bibliographical references and index.
ISBN 978-1-4411-7756-8 (hardcover)– ISBN 978-1-4411-4214-6 (ebook pdf)–
ISBN 978-1-4411-4993-0 (epub)  1. Philosophy. 2. Methodology. I. Title.
B77.L36613 2013
101–dc23
2012034664

Typeset by Fakenham Prepress Solutions, Fakenham, Norfolk NR21 8NN
Printed and bound in India

# CONTENTS

## 3 UNIFIED OR "NON-CARTESIAN" THEORY OF THE SUBJECT: DUALITY OF THE EGO AND THE SUBJECT 79

## 4 DETERMINATION-IN-THE-LAST-INSTANCE: TRANSCENDENTAL THEOREM OF THE FORCE-(OF)-THOUGHT 121

## 5 THE METHOD OF DUALYSIS: (PERFORMATION, CLONING, A PRIORI) 163

## 6  THE CONSTITUTION OF THE NON-PHILOSOPHICAL ORDER  231

# CLONING THE UNTRANSLATABLE: TRANSLATORS' INTRODUCTION

*There is an absolute untranslatable—the Real—before every translation, condemned moreover by the Real to its foreclosure.*
**FRANÇOIS LARUELLE**

Something happens after one first falls in love with philosophy. One's love for a lived experience, an experimental way of moving through an alienating world, gets confused with a faith in some reified object, a discipline, and from there a duty to uphold that faith comes. And what used to be a love becomes redoubled, a love for the love of wisdom takes on an economy, a law of a household one is trapped in. It is not just in politics that human beings are in chains, but also in their heads, and responding to our yearning to be free, François Laruelle tells us: you always have been. Responding to our alienation from ourselves and to the love and joy found in thinking at first, Laruelle fashions tools and weapons to dis-alienate ourselves, to see that in the very force of thinking, the very moment it is lived, we never were alienated and that our love for theory, for its practice taking place in our bodies, can be reclaimed and refashioned. That we know, as Human-in-person, an inalienable Real that we are, to which philosophy is foreclosed.

The above may seem a strange claim for a book of abstract philosophy, rooted very profoundly in the history of Continental philosophy. But, the reality is that whatever text or conversation first made you fall in love with thinking in the first place seduced you, not with the words of a pedant, comforting your common sense or reassuring you of whatever notions you already held. But there was something else. Call it wonder, or even annoyance, but at bottom it was the experience of something stranger, a Stranger, that spoke so that you could understand, but always with something hidden, something alluring. This character is present in Laruelle's writing, and perhaps no more so than in *Principles of Non-Philosophy*, where Laruelle speaks to us in language that feels so familiar, but so strange at the same time. And with an utter respect for his reader, attempting to practice theory, not through metaphor or the empirical example, but trusting that his reader will see that here Laruelle says what he does and does what he says. And that is, quite simply, to think and create theory for human beings, to practice a love that has been lost. It does this not by destroying philosophy, but by recasting the relationship completely, of thinking its practice under different axioms (hence the analogy made in the name non-philosophy, as is now well-known, is non-Euclidean geometry, which of course did not destroy Euclidean geometry).

*Principles of Non-Philosophy* has a special place in the development of Laruelle's non-philosophy. It fits securely in the phase he calls Philosophy III. Smith has explained at length the periodization of works that Laruelle has given to the development of non-philosophy elsewhere, but in short what it represents are phases, or what Laruelle also calls waves, that represent changes in axioms and in the regional materials (philosophical and extra-philosophical) he engages with, but with the same general form and guiding problems.[1] In this regard, *Principles* represents the first truly mature phase of non-philosophy and the most rigorous explication of the underlying method used in future works. Laruelle is perhaps best known for his global critique of the form of philosophical practice, represented in English by the 2010 translation of his 1987 book *Philosophies of Difference*. But this work, one of the most important of Philosophy II, acted in a polemical and antagonistic manner towards standard philosophy. In short, what marks this work and the others of Philosophy II is a subjection of philosophy to science as practices in the scientific posture or stance. Laruelle came to see this as a simple inversion of philosophy's own sense of self-importance, its sufficiency, and a repetition of philosophy's tendency to overdetermine everything it claims to give an account of through whatever Philosophy of X, and came to think that rejecting this simple inversion in favor of a "democracy (of) thought" or "unified theory of philosophy and science" (or art, or religion, or ethics, etc.) was necessary in order to truly achieve a non-philosophy.

And that is the goal in *Principles*, mainly through an engagement with science. However, this is not science as represented by a particular empirical form, or what Laruelle would call "regional", but science in the large sense as a represented, albeit in an overdetermined way, by

epistemology. So the task in *Principles* is to deal with some of the foundational questions that abide for philosophers of science and scientists in the
field, like the relation between subject and object, the question of the ability
of thought to represent what we might call "complex objects", causality,
and the relationship between a part of reality, reason, and reality itself (or
what Laruelle calls the Real, to differentiate it from a reality made all-too
mundane and worldly). And through this engagement, Laruelle is able to
rethink some of the underlying aspects of non-philosophy, most notably
perhaps we see his theory of Philosophical Decision, begun in earnest in
*Philosophies of Difference*, find its mature and complete form here.

Out of this method came a number of other important works dealing
with art, religion, and ethics (many which have or are set to be released in
English translation in the coming years). And so *Principles* stands as an
operating manual, relatively unchanged, that outlines the most important
concepts and method of non-philosophy. Its only rivals for this status
would be the earlier *Philosophy and Non-Philosophy*, though this work is
tainted by its simple inversion of the standard philosophical overdetermination of science, and the more recent 2010 *Philosophie non-standard.
Générique, quantique, philo-fiction*, which claims to have completed
non-philosophy in bringing this more abstract development of method
together with the concrete though no less abstract practices provided by
quantum mechanics. Yet, *Philosophie non-standard* is a clear development
from *Principles* in so far as this work completes Laruelle's science of
philosophy, making philosophy truly a simple material for the use of new
theories combined with a regional knowing (the gerund is intentional) like
quantum mechanics. Here the democracy-(of)-thought remains, but given
a Marxist turn analogous to the Marxist understanding of the relationship
between forces of production and the means of production, whereby
thinking the relationship of science and philosophy as "underdetermined"
by science, meaning that philosophy "goes under" the scientific posture
in the same way that one may "go under" anesthesia, where the relative
autonomy of philosophy continues but changed in a vital way.

A word on the French context of the book will help bear out the general
relationship of non-philosophy to standard philosophy. *Principles of
Non-Philosophy* was published in France in 1996 by Presses Universitaires
de France (PUF) in the *Épiméthée* series. *Épiméthée*, originally edited by
Jean Hyppolite (who took the secret behind the name of the series, French
for Epimetheus, the foolish brother of fellow titan Prometheus, to his grave)
and since the early 1980s by Jean-Luc Marion, had been home to a number
of important twentieth century philosophical texts, including the majority
of French translations of Edmund Husserl and some of Martin Heidegger's

most influential texts, as well as major works by Jacques Derrida, Gilles Deleuze, and Michel Henry, while also publishing reprints of important works from the history of philosophy prior to the twentieth century. As a series it has quite simply been the standard-bearer of an important tradition in philosophy, and as such exhibits some of philosophy's dual nature. While the series is ostensibly concerned with phenomenology, it publishes both works that might be considered establishment-style philosophy, a kind of history of philosophy confusing itself with philosophy in flesh and blood, and books that had and perhaps continue to have the possibility of breaking apart and constructing anew the very practice of philosophy.

And so it is somewhat strange to find here one of Laruelle's most important texts in the construction of his non-philosophy since he is self-proclaimed non-philosopher, once accused by Jacques Derrida of being a terrorist within philosophy. And for the Anglophone philosophical establishment if someone is a terrorist to Jacques Derrida, then they must be the devil incarnate for "proper philosophy" of the English sitting-rooms of Oxbridge and depopulated American university towns. What the reader will find here is a work of a contemporary thinker, one who perhaps rightly passes for a philosopher, that draws from those established schools before him, both from when they were themselves young and radical, and from their nadir as custodians of what became an establishment. He does not take their lives from them, like a terrorist, but instead Laruelle practices a form of thought more akin to dumpster diving or gaming the system. While, as he says in the pages that follow, every new philosophy has tried to succeed another one only to become precisely a repetition of *Philosophy* or philosophy qua philosophy, Laruelle aims to experience life outside of this repetition using the means provided to him by human theories and practices. The great deconstructive rebels of what had become a moribund phenomenology ended up in their later years trying to protect the dignity of philosophy, taking on the tradition (in the sense of a fight) only to end up taking on the tradition (in the sense of carrying it and bearing the burden of homage to it). Laruelle instead picks at philosophy or cons it, not for mere survival, but in order to carve out a life and a defense against the system of philosophy itself. Non-philosophy truly does exist outside the system of philosophy and the appearance of this text in such a prestigious series speaks only to Laruelle's status as a kind of Marrano, one who practices their true faith in secret, using the tools of those who would oppress them.

For this is a common claim of Laruelle, that non-philosophy is a weapon, a tool that is lived out in the defense of human beings. While some of the early Anglophone reception of Laruelle has misunderstood him as a scientistic thinker or one who has nothing but contempt for human beings in the name of some impersonal Real, the truth is that non-philosophy is "non-humanist" theory. The meaning is, of course, that what we find here is not typical philosophical humanism, represented in everyday culture as a privileging of some claimed universal human being that is in reality taken as a heteronormative, white, healthy male. But instead the question of the human is open in non-philosophy, even as the human or what he comes to call Human-in-person is also the name of the Real. It is not the Real that is impersonal, but rather the Real is foreclosed to philosophy, represented not in some anti-humanist hatred or indifference towards human beings, but in the maxim that, "Philosophy was made for man, not man for philosophy." While throughout the history of philosophy there is no lack of definitions for human beings, they always *represent* or overdetermine the human in or under some other phenomenon under or beyond it, whether it be "rational animal", "thinking subject", "overman", "Dasein", "desiring machine", to say nothing of the more insidious "common sense" notions like "free individual". Non-philosophy is in part the attempt to think what philosophy and science, theory and practice generally, can do for human beings without attempting to dominate them or accept the common, nearly unconscious, everyday notions of what exactly a human is, does, or means, and *Principles* is the handbook for that practice.

While in *Principles* the reader will find only a single original footnote by Laruelle, and this only to signal the work of his friend Serge Valdinoci called *europanalysis*, there are still clear concepts and images freely taken and used from a plethora of establishment and radical philosophers: Plato, Spinoza, Kant, Heidegger, Wittgenstein, Derrida, Deleuze, Badiou, and even Gödel and Lacan. Perhaps though, the two most important reference points are Marx and Husserl, alongside Fichte whose *Wissenschaftslehre* is explicitly adapted and mutated. For, to Laruelle, these are the thinkers who have taken the notion of a scientific philosophy the furthest. Both err in their own way; Marx goes too far towards empiricism and Husserl too far towards transcendentalism, but their efforts, even as philosophers, have to be respected even if through a non-philosophical indifference, and that respect takes the form of drawing materials from both that come to form the core concepts of non-philosophy, albeit in mutated form: namely the Husserlian question of what a subject is alongside the question of phenomenology's Transcendental Ego (and the related question of the "givenness" of phenomena) and the development of the Marxist concept of determination in the last instance, alongside a development of Fichte's radicalization of Kant's *Critique of Pure Reason* in his philosophy of a priori knowing. The development of these notions forms the bulk of *Principles* and so we will not subject the reader to a representation of what they can read for themselves directly, but we will say that these notions are surrounded by constructions native to Laruelle's corpus as well, namely cloning, First Science, Philosophical Decision, and perhaps most importantly force-(of)-thought.

Laruelle's work is not easy to translate and *Principles* is no exception. While his French is relatively simple, sometimes ambiguities do arise through his reliance on interrogative pronouns and demonstrative pronouns in the course of his long sentences. Laruelle will often playfully ape the style of some other philosopher and in some ways *Principles* does that by drawing on the German thinkers Kant, Fichte, and Husserl, whose eighteenth and nineteenth century Germanic styles are taken up into Laruelle's experimental use of French. Trying to balance these constant (and unspoken) references with Laruelle's own experimental *and* rigorous use of language has at times proven a challenge. Yet, it exposes and undermines what we might name a Principle of Sufficient Translation that itself lies at the heart of the standard philosophy of translation.

*Principles* is a text that is itself concerned with the issue of translation, though from the language of one particular philosophy to another, with something untranslatable in-the-last-instance that allows the very possibility of such a translation. Consider, in addition to the epigraph opening this introduction above, these remarks from *Principles:*

> It is thus in this theoretical usage, in this transcendental theory of private philosophical languages (at once general and total), from this non-linguistic identity of language, that the problem arises of a translation of philosophies "into" one another, which is to say in-One-in-the-last-instance, rather than an inter-philosophical translation under the ultimate authority of philosophy. Non-philosophy is this translation of Kant "into" Descartes, of Descartes "into" Marx, of Marx "into" Husserl", etc. That is to say under the condition of the vision-in-One as un-translatable Real. To put it more rigorously, no more than it is im-possible or un-symbolizable, the Real is not un-translatable, but is rather that which renders the possibility of translation real-in-the-last-instance, the Real itself being foreclosed, without negation, to any translation and not becoming the untranslatable other than as force-(of)-thought or, in this instance, force-(of)-translation. It is in this manner, through a translation of philosophical decisions or through solely transcendental equivalents of their respective identity, that a democracy that is not a simple transcendental appearance can be introduced into philosophy and between philosophies in place of their conflictual and hierarchical multiplicity.

There is no contradiction here; the Real is untranslatable in the sense of its foreclosure (as the epigraph says), but this is not a negation of the fact of translatability, but instead a kind of manifestation of the superlative character of the Real. The Real cannot be captured by philosophy, but instead authorizes the equivalency of all philosophies, all knowings, as relative before the Real. Or, in other words, the Real is not ineffable, but infinitely effable.

While Laruelle is here speaking of his own translation of, say, Husserl into Marx (or vice versa), we can see how this applies to the translation of French philosophy into English. Anyone who has ever struggled with thought in another language can see the truth here and may even see the freedom from the Principle of Sufficient Translation offered here. All too often one thinks there may be some strict equivalent word in English for whatever language one is working with. But the reality is that in each language something is always at play, something is always lived (as Laruelle will say), that simply is not captured in the movement from one language to another. In many ways, in flagrant disregard for the desire of translators, the practice of translating already manifests this in-the-last-instance as one has to make a decision for what word to use from English when dealing with (in this case) a French word that has very different resonances, multiple senses, sometimes related etymologies but with very different contemporary implications, etc. And these decisions, just like particular philosophical decisions, are not arbitrary (none of this is an apology for simple errors that can creep into the translation process), but they are also not nearly sufficient.

So in the spirit of non-philosophy, we consider this translation a *clone* of the original French. A clone in the non-philosophical sense is not a simple representation, presenting again the original, nor is it a copy of the original. But it carries within it the underlying code of the original. And so in that spirit we have stuck, as earlier Smith did in *Future Christ*, to a relatively literal translation, for a few reasons. First, Laruelle's style in the French has a very particular feel, playing with syntax in a way that intentionally brings attention to it. Since syntax is the stuff of communication, bringing such attention to bear can have the effect of making it, in everyday terms, "awkward" but such awkwardness has a specific intention here and the best way to capture that tone is to stick with it in the English—that is to say, the English is (or at least ought to be) no more awkward than the French, and vice versa. Second, Laruelle makes the claim that non-philosophy has a quality of saying what it does and doing what it says, or of carrying forth its theory through a specific practice of writing that is also theorized at the same time in the carrying out of its practice. Thus, owing to the close relationship of French and English linguistically, it seemed to us best to tend towards this literal approach. But another clone would have been possible! The important thing here is that the translation carries forth the code of non-philosophy, allows it to manifest in English in flesh and blood, real-in-the-last-instance but without any claim to being sufficient in itself to the Real as such.

Still, a few remarks on specifics related to the translation. First, the multitude of philosophical vocabularies plus the challenges posed by Laruelle's own French, confirmed our decision to undertake this translation as two, combining our various skills to provide the best translation we could. In general, to the best of our abilities and combined knowledge, we have tried to stick with established translations of terms from the various philosophical vocabularies Laruelle works with in *Principles*, largely for the sake of familiarity so that readers conversant with the history of philosophy can recognize these instances.

Following discussions with Robin Mackay we have translated *force (de) pensée*, and other constructions that take this form, as force-(of)-thought, hyphenated to highlight the unified, or "in-One" character of the idea, with the parenthetical suspension of the possessive as in the French. Some constructions have been rendered with a different formulation of the possessive, for example Real('s)-essence, so that they can be read in the same way as, for example, "force-thought" (still with the possessive "of" visible but suspended), in this case "Real-essence".

As Laruelle engages with phenomenology throughout *Principles* while also engaging with the empirical sciences, he has seen fit to use the English word data when he means the sense of *datum* or variables given and used in scientific discourse. The typical French word for this is *donné*, but because of its use in phenomenology and emphasis on the "givenness" of objects we have translated this consistently as "given".

Another linguistic tussle was presented in the form of the translation of *connaissance* and *savoir*, both usually translated as "knowledge". Here, we have translated *connaissance* as "knowledge" and *savoir* as "knowing", the gerund form intending to imply the wider and more abstract notion.

We have also translated *la-philosophie* and similar forms by capitalizing and italicizing the word (i.e. *Philosophy*), which marks a difference from the translation of *Future Christ* where it was translated as the-philosophy. This form taken here matches how a similar formulation in Lacan's French is translated in English.

The planned work on this translation took a very different shape than we originally planned, after Anthony was forced to leave the UK under new immigration rules upon finishing his PhD. So, aside from the usual arguments (mostly friendly) that co-translators have, we also had to navigate the antagonisms of our different software packages which broke our hearts more than once. We were able to work together in flesh and blood as well thanks to a number of people who financially helped us. A special thank you goes to John Mullarkey, who supported this project with Continuum and organized two events in London with Laruelle which allowed us to meet and work together on the translation. Thanks also to Marjorie Gracieuse and Iain Campbell for housing us during these two trips. Anthony would like to thank the many supporters and readers of his group blog An und für sich who donated money, as well as the participants who paid to take part in his para-academic on-line seminar on Laruelle's non-philosophy. The money raised by these endeavors allowed us to spend four weeks together in Dundee, Scotland over the course of June and July of 2012 working over and finishing the translation. An extra special thank you goes to Nova Rubczak who, during this time, furnished us with coffees, teas, entertainment, and other provisions. We would also like to thank each other, however indulgent that may appear, for each supporting the other where one or the other felt deficient. Finally, our sincere thanks and admiration to Anne-Françoise Schmid and François Laruelle, for their hospitality and continued friendship. While friendship is lived and never merely a reciprocal exchange we hope that the labor undertaken here is a sign of profound gratitude for what remains unspoken.

# PREFACE

One philosopher does not succeed another without claiming to succeed philosophy itself as a whole. This is how, without knowing it, they renew the original or grounding philosophical gesture. As for non-philosophy: which philosophy does it succeed? Does it wish to replace philosophy, or simply to accompany it, as knowing accompanies its object? Non-philosophy only claims to succeed the faith and authority of philosophy, never to deny its reality, nor to refuse it at least a "relative" autonomy. The unconscious has long since found its controls against the myths of philosophy; what remains is for thought (which is to say science and philosophy) to find its own discipline against the myths of philosophical sufficiency. Inevitably, philosophy poses the greatest and wiliest resistance to an enterprise of this nature. But it is equally inevitable that knowing triumphs over spontaneous representations of its object, whatever that may be, and that this object has its own complexity with a particularly intimidating power of resistance. The preceding essays on the constitution of this new discipline (*Une biographie de l'homme ordinaire, Philosophie et non-philosophie*) and on its investment in the classical problems of philosophy such as man, other, and unconscious (*Théorie des étrangers*), have shown the complexity of the situation and the difficulty in circumventing the authority of philosophy, which is to say the spontaneous representation that it has of itself. The originality and specificity of this object—the "Philosophical Decision"—demand a cross-rewriting and a new usage of the traditional theoretical approaches given by philosophy itself (in order not to become a simple meta-philosophy), and of science (in order not to become a simple positive science of philosophy). In *Principles*, these endeavors find their systematic completion, the implementation of their problematic, and a more just appreciation of non-philosophy's objectives.

In particular, it is worth signaling that non-philosophy was born on a terrain already dominated by philosophy—that of "radical immanence", of the One, if you will, but of the One insofar as it succeeds Being as well as the Other and Difference as the principal theme of thought—but signaling too that it has laboriously extricated itself from here, through its own "analysis" and self-education, discovering the insufficient nature of this theme remaining in all its users under the ultimate authority of philosophy. It is insufficient if its radicality of the "real" is not taken seriously and if it is not accompanied by a very particular scientific and philosophical elaboration of thought and the discourse it uses. Originally thematized as such as a "thinking from the One" and the philosophical forgetting of the One, non-philosophy is realized rigorously, in a precise manner, as thought in-One or according-to-the-One. Radically immanent identity, or the Real, is the "form" of thought such that, refusing to turn itself toward the One as if toward a first or last object, it is necessarily turned toward philosophy and science. This impossibility of turning toward the One is not attributable to an insufficiency or forgetting of thought; it is rather a constraint that the One imposes upon thought, the grounding axiom of non-philosophy being that the One or the Real is foreclosed to thought and that this is of its own accord rather than owing to a failure of thought. This is moreover to renounce the last metaphysical mirage, that of a "science of the One" opposed to metaphysics as "science of Being". Non-philosophy is a "first science", but this is because it is *according-to-the-One* rather than *of-the-One*. A "science of the One", like that of Being, albeit more subjective, continues to be taken in its transcendental appearance which nourishes philosophical sufficiency and is nothing but an abstraction of the complex it naturally forms with that of Being. Renouncing and overcoming this frustration is the condition for positing a real thought *according-to-the-One* which could relate, as to its object, to philosophy thought *according to Being*, which is to say in and for itself.

The treatise is organized as follows:

- The introduction undertakes a first synoptic tour of the variety of themes, objects, syntaxes and objectives of non-philosophy.

- The first chapter recalls the broad origins of the problematic. This is a brief reminder of what has been established previously and a first idea of certain new assets, like the theory of transcendental cloning of the real One. A short history of non-philosophy through the various stages of our research (Philosophies I, II and III) closes the chapter.

- The second chapter describes the general form of non-philosophy as non-epistemology, as *identically* scientific and philosophical thought or, more precisely, as thought identically for science and for philosophy. It seeks to avoid any epistemological synthesis and to renounce the authority of philosophy over science, to use these two equally; to practically introduce a certain democracy in the very essence of thought and to abandon the vanity of philosophical discourse over democracy.

- The third chapter examines the problem of beginning non-philosophy and introduces the unilateral distinction of the Ego and the subject, the duality of the Real and the force-(of)-thought. The invalidation of Cartesian amphibologies, and those that follow, confusing the Ego and the subject of thought, render possible a "non-Cartesian" theory of the subject and turn non-philosophy into a pure or first transcendental thought, but first-without-primacy, primacy being reserved for the Real or the One alone.

- The fourth chapter examines the most fundamental problems, the relations of the Real as One or vision-in-One and the syntax of thought which thinks according-to-the-One. It takes up the essential theory of cloning and moves to the intersection-theme [*thème-carrefour*] of the force-(of)-thought which is the subject of a transcendental theorem based on the axioms which describe the Real as One. To this end it sketches a parallel with the first three principles of Fichte's 1794 *Wissenschaftslehre*.

- The fifth chapter describes the theoretical style of non-philosophy from the point of view of the themes which clearly distinguish it from philosophy (cloning contra model/copy system, performation contra objectification,[1] dualysis contra analysis, non-conceptual symbolism contra concept, words-without-language contra rational narrative, real critique of reason contra philosophical critique, etc.).

- The sixth chapter, the most complex in its combinatory aspects and double-pronged techniques (philosophical, non-philosophical and their relation), explicitly or thematically investigates the non-philosophical enterprise in its philosophical material. It posits numerous non-philosophical theorems of the usage of philosophy, posing the identity of the fundamental and the regional and transforming the philosophical resolution of antinomies and mixtures into a soluble problem, opposing their explication to their interpretation.

- Finally we suggest that the way non-philosophy does not define itself by its objectives comes through reducing the signification rather than still describing it under the etiquette using "theory of philosophy": it is identically a thought of science, a thought for philosophy as much as for science, and moreover, in its other aspect or its transcendental beginnings, it touches on the vision-in-One, on the ultimate essence of the phenomenon, and affects the oldest claims of metaphysics since it makes its start in the mystical core of the One.

These *Principles* are only a treatise on the non-philosophical method, an introduction—Kant would say a "critique" or still a method—to an unpublished work, "Science première", which constitutes the realization of non-philosophy in traditional and scientific philosophical material, but whose amplitude and difficulty render its publication problematic in the current situation of publishing, and especially of philosophical readership.[2] In this uncertain waiting for better times and more favorable conditions, these *Principles* will hold the place of the most complete introduction to non-philosophy, for want of its realization.

# INTRODUCTION

Which philosophers do not ask, to end or to begin: what is philosophy? Those who now do not claim to advance their concept of a "non-philosophy?" Some nonetheless most often ignore the problem of Philosophy [la philosophie], of its identity as much as its multiplicity, and circularly practice its auto-legitimation. And others—the same really—establish an *ad hoc* non-philosophy conforming to their own claims and re-integrate non-philosophy into philosophy. It is thus urgent to put forward a "non-philosophical" thought and to dissipate the ambiguities. Under the perhaps too classical title of "Principles" we will find a program of research defined by a problematic; by a form of work called a "unified theory of science and philosophy"; by an inaugural theorem called the "force-(of)-thought" connected to "determination in-the-last-instance"; by a description of the acts of thought and the essential structures of the theoretical and pragmatic "non-philosophical" field.

"Non-philosophy" is the generic term for an enterprise which takes on other names locally according to the materials to which it relates. Most generally, it concerns an elaboration of the theoretical and pragmatic status of Philosophy, of the *identity* it has, even when considered in its diversified practices and in its relation to regional knowings, a radical identity or an identity of performance that philosophy itself refuses or does not recognize: a problem directly linked to "non-philosophy" and its status.

Of course, the expression "non-philosophy" has several meanings and a history. From the end of the eighteenth century, Kant sought the conditions of possibility of philosophy, and philosophy, at the turn of the 18th and 19th centuries, used this term to designate its "Other". Between Kant, Fichte, Hegel and Feuerbach, philosophy endeavors to systematically reflect on itself: on its limits and its abilities [*puissance*], on its activity and its object, on its relation to "collective consciousness". "Non-philosophy", then, designates the pre-speculative state or the absence of philosophy, the ignorance where natural, popular consciousness inheres; a momentary ignorance, destined to be overtaken or substituted, "superseded" in philosophy itself which nonetheless does not suppress it without taking into account its own virtue; but also a healthy innocence, not speculative and not merely pre-speculative. From there a dialectical reconciliation of these two states sometimes follows; the equality of collective and philosophical consciousnesses. In this case, "non-philosophy" designates a post-philosophical innocence or an over-philosophical state, an overvalorization of the non-philosophical which forms a system with its possible devalorization under other conditions or in other systems. Later, it will concern an alterity, a peripheral residue or an external-internal condition of philosophical activity.

Each philosophy defines then a non-philosophical margin that it tolerates, circumscribes, reappropriates, or which it *uses* in order to expropriate itself: as beyond or other to philosophical mastery. So its concern is with a "non" whose content and means of action [*agent*] are ontic or empirical, ontological in the best of cases, but whose reach is limited by this mastery.

This tradition of non-philosophy has not stopped and probably never will. Still recently, Deleuze evoked a certain "plane of immanence"—his concept of Being—and defined it as anti-philosophical and unable to be grasped except by a "non-philosophy". Thus he brought about the interiorization into the philosophical of the powers [*puissances*] of its surroundings, margins and other alterities. This is in fact all contemporary thought, substituting Being with the Other and Identity with Difference as the linchpin of thought, which welcomes *this* restraining concept and *this* secondary non-philosophical experience which continues to revolve around the philosophical. It undoubtedly generalizes the philosophical beyond pre-philosophical innocence in terms of the effects of the Other; including it, as excluded, in the philosophical and thus causing the philosophical to pass from its modern to its postmodern state. However, the non-philosophical is left in its state of marginality, of minority, as an adjacent phenomenon, thus reinforcing the superior ability or the sufficiency of the philosophical, reaffirming its capacity to dominate and to rule over the non-philosophical in the ultimate manner: the moment of its triumph over the philosophical scene is the moment of its burial. This is all philosophy was able to do for and with the non-philosophical: at best, sometimes, with Deconstruction, it could form a certain balance of the philosophical and non-philosophical which resists philosophical mastery and constitutes a symptom.

Given what we hear by "non-philosophy", giving it an autonomous consistency of thought and ordaining it now as the philosophical, it is evidently about something other than these concepts and this tradition. When "non-philosophy" ceases to designate a simple philosophical relation to the extra-philosophical in order to designate a relationship to the philosophical itself in its identity and ceases to be an attribute in order to become "a subject", it speaks of a thought which, without being subsumed again into philosophy, is no stranger to it; of a new relationship to this thought and of a new practice of philosophy. It is philosophy which then becomes an "object" of non-philosophy, of a pure and no longer metaphysical or ontico-ontological "non" transcendental. We will speak of a *material* rather than an *object*, an *occasional cause* rather than a *margin*. Even historically, we do not hold onto the usage of this word of the philosophies of Collective Consciousness or even of Differ(e/a)nce and Deconstructions, the effects of ethnology and of psychoanalysis on philosophical centrism, of the contemporary pathos of alterity in general but of another "tradition", this one scientific, by way of a reference to a "non Euclidean" style of certain geometries. It concerns a new practice of philosophy, more universal than philosophy because it liberates itself from some of its postulates—in particular that of its correspondence to the Real, of its convertibility with the Real. Indeed, it does not reduce itself to being a mere non Euclidean *type* of generalization of philosophy. Some much more contemporary scientific styles and other "revolutions" like that of Gödel for example are included and show its plasticity and openness. But it is from the former type that it takes its name.

Still more fundamentally, the reference to the non Euclidean revolution was only itself possible in the context of a radical critique of the whole of or the identity of philosophy and not only philosophies of Difference and Deconstruction (Wittgenstein, Heidegger, Derrida) as being the philosophies of our times, which is to say the newest and most emergent, and of their experience of the non-philosophical. A radical critique: in this we hear the search for an instance at once more real and more immanent than Difference or the Other, and one that we have found in the "One" or "vision-in-One", heard in a "non philosophical" sense and with precisely "non philosophical" means. It is toward a global change of terrain that we must proceed, abandoning that of Being then that of the Other for a terrain of the One or of radical immanence that has shown us the Real itself.

On this new basis, it is the whole continent of thought, particularly but not only the relationships of science and philosophy, that is re-organized. Philosophy has lost its sufficiency or no longer satisfactorily fulfills its claim, in one manner or another, by idealism or realism, etc., to the Real: it is now nothing but a simple field, undoubtedly necessary, of "phenomena", "objects" or of *data*. Why, for what or for whom? Not for the One or the Real itself, which will no longer have a meaning here, but for the new experience of thought that the vision-in-One allows beyond itself and which we call "force-(of)-thought" precisely because it now maintains starting from the One a new and more universal relationship to *Philosophy* taken "globally". It is about practicing and proposing a new usage under this term, a true pragmatic, though with a theoretical essence, of the philosophical tradition. It is up to us to show the consistency of this thought which is no longer "before" or "after" philosophy, which is no longer the celebration of its death or that of its historical re-affirmation, which is no longer a simple rebellion from its margins, of the Other-than-philosophical against philosophy, but an autonomous discipline which possesses its principles, its rules, its norms of validity, its positivity, its objects (philosophy) and its ultimate experience of the Real (the One). It must in effect possess the means for a consistent and autonomous thought: a specific experience of the Real, a universal syntax, rules and procedures for the transformation of philosophical material, objectives, etc. The problem is of inventing and discovering, undoubtedly simultaneously, a thought which, without negating philosophy, without wishing for its death, without subordinating it once again, merely suspends its claims over the Real and makes a new usage of philosophy with a view to constituting an order of thought more rigorous and more real than philosophy itself. What experience of the Real can *determine* thought in this way?

The most universal invariant trait of philosophy is a fractional matrix in 2/3 terms: it gives itself an interiority and an exteriority, an immanence and a transcendence *simultaneously*, in a synthetic or hierarchal structure, the one overcoming the other in turn. This matrix of "Philosophical Decision" can be read as the identity of a double relation of philosophy to itself. First, an identity of 2/3 (insofar as the third term, synthesis, is immanent to the dyad, philosophy being in need of itself). Second, a 3/2 identity (insofar as the term of synthesis is transcendent to the dyad, philosophy being in excess of itself). Through this structure, philosophy claims to determine itself beyond all its empirical determinations which it only calculates in order to prescribe it in an *auto-position* in which it is titular, an auto-comprehension or auto-legislation, auto-naming, etc. In this formal trait the circularity of philosophical argumentation takes root along with its procedures of auto-validation. Furthermore this trait is not purely formal or syntactic, it is in and for it that philosophy claims to reach the Real and thus to at least partially constitute it. Auto-Position (and auto-givenness) is not a simple syntactic trait whose effects it would be possible to limit: it is identically the claim of philosophy to be able to co-determine the Real in this way. It suffices then to postulate—through a thought adequate to the Real—a type of experience or of Real which escapes auto-positioning, which is not a circle of the Real and thought, a One which does not unify but which remains in-One, a Real which is *immanent (to) itself rather than to a form of thought*, to a "logic", etc., or which is given without-position and without-givenness in order to refuse philosophy its principal pretension and to be entitled to say that it does not reach the Real, even if necessarily maintaining certain relations with it. In order to find our feet within the scholastic and mystic tradition, we will distinguish between the transcendental One, proper to philosophy; the transcendent One, proper to historical and religious mysticism; and finally from these two "Ones"—and this is what will distinguish non-philosophy from philosophy and from philosophico-mystic mixtures—the simply real One, which is only immanent (to) itself, for which immanence is real essence or "substance" rather than relation or ownership. The One through immanence distinguishes itself as much from the transcendent One as from the transcendental One: on the condition that it is radical immanence, without the smallest fragment of transcendence within it, of exteriority, of scission, of negativity, or of nothingness. We call this One-in-One rather than One-in-Being or as-Being; One which is real as One rather than as it is or would be; we can equally say "vision-in-One", and better still, "seen-in-One".

Non-philosophy lets itself be given *minimal or phenomenal immanence*: that which can only be given before all givenness; which is given obligatorily and which alone is possible; it examines every experience of transcendence which presents itself and describes every experience of transcendence under the conditions of this immanence. Therefore it is a thought which remains within the limits of the most radically "internal" experience but as immanence of phenomenal being-given, even when the layers of transcendence arise and implicate different modes of givenness and in general a givenness or a position that this immanence then reduces, and which gives their content in reality. Exercising within the limits of phenomenal immanence, of being-given or manifested, it is a real "thought", but we will outline an important nuance: "in-the-last-instance" or transcendental; a thought *according to* real experience, which reduces objectivity itself, rather than *of* possible experience. When it comes to thought, for the *auto-position* of possible experience it substitutes the *simple or axiomatic (but transcendental) experience*; the real or phenomenal experience can no longer be posed or thought other than through axioms and "first terms"—we will explain why—rather than through concepts, categories and philosophical theses.

This matrix is no longer that in 2/3 terms of philosophy and its ultimately circular causality; it is not even that of 1/2 (= Difference) and still less of the metaphysical 1 which is merely an artifact of the 1/2. It is not fractional since it is that of the 1 which is only 1, equally it is not that of the 2 which, as irreducibly 2, is however 2-in-1 in-the-last-instance or 1-(of)-2, but not 1/2.

It seems to contain three terms: a real or indivisible identity—the Real one; a term = X, strictly speaking, received from transcendence and which is thus not immanent; and thirdly a term called "Transcendental Identity", a true clone of the One which the term X extracts from the Real. In reality, the One is not a "term", not being identifiable in transcendence and being nothing but an identity-without-synthesis; the term X, "added" to the Real, does not form a dyad and fails to form a dyad with the One which refuses to be counted in the structure. On the other hand, it resolves its desire in extracting from the One an image-(of)-the One where the One does not alienate itself; thus a purely transcendental image, but with which it forms a duality or a dual wherein the transcendental is only counted from the point of view of X: a duality called "unilateral" for this reason. This transcendental cloning of the Real represents a simplification and a radical minimalization to the "naturals" of the matrix of Philosophical Decision. This syntax has received a name in the history of philosophy; a surprising name but of which we believe—though this is not important—that it is indeed this very logic that it designates; logic that is not philosophical, but is nonetheless still interior to philosophy. This name is that of "Determination-in-the-Last-Instance" whose sense the philosophers have barely been able to grasp as a result of their desire to re-dialecticize this form of causality. From the Real to philosophy and consequently from radical immanence to transcendence, there is this relation of causality that we will take up again in the idea of a certain blend of Identity and Duality; a blend that is not philosophical or not mixed, where Identity is undoubtedly that of a Duality, but a *unilateral* one: outside-Identity or without synthesis or division in terms of Duality, but in-Identity despite everything, precisely "in-the-last-instance". Duality is relatively autonomous, distinct *qua* duality but at the same time, or rather under a different reason, identical to Identity. For its part, Identity, that of the Real, is untransformable or unconstitutable by Duality, which is rejected from it; which cannot really penetrate it. Duality has its cause in Identity, but does not divide it like philosophy does for an analysis and a synthesis: Identity and Duality are no longer contemporaneous or simultaneous as they are in Difference, nor even *de jure* shifted back or differentiated. This is a radical duality: rather than a still-philosophical dualism reabsorbable in an ultimate synthesis, it *remains* a duality even when it takes root in the Identity of the One. The One no longer shuts Duality or multiplicity into the circle of a synthesis or an encyclopedia, and Duality for its part does not undermine the Real; does not intervene here. Every horizontal teleology; every difference, is thus finished. This matrix is not and has never been philosophical even if it has worked inside philosophy. Marxism partially discovered it without being able, because of Hegelianism and as such philosophy, to give it its transcendental sense and efficacy. This is the causality of *real identity* and of the Real as identity. And this "logic" puts an end to the privileges and domination not only of the dialectic or of differ(e/a)nce, but of all philosophy. Finally considered in its concreteness, determination-in-the-last-instance will take the form of a transcendental organon, the "force-(of)-thought" which is the heart of non-philosophy and its work.

It now suffices to take a dyad of terms from philosophy, a contrasted couple like "philosophy and science", in order to transform it according to this Identity-(of)-Duality. This syntax—really this *unitax*—is inferred on its part of duality from radical immanence as that which applies itself to philosophical or another transcendence and conditions it. It subsists within these final limits but from real experience and consequently within the limits of this experience in-the-last-instance. *Non-philosophy is the object of a transcendental induction and deduction from the real-One (or the force-(of)-thought) in the field of experience insofar as it is constituted from now on by philosophy and regional knowings.* These operations determine a new conditioning or usage of philosophy itself: it can no longer be considered as in itself or as real, which is to say as auto-positional, but it is treated as the material of non-philosophy, from whose point of view non-philosophy in turn is a phenomenon-in-the-last-instance. Philosophy and science, art, ethics, etc., do not come into non-philosophy as such or as themselves, but as *provisions* whereby they are simple provisions, which is to say in-the-last-instance simple phenomena.

The status of philosophy is thus overturned. Spontaneously, philosophy enters into competition with regional knowings, the sciences in particular, because it claims to determine equally, like these but otherwise than them, the same objects or experience. It postulates a double discourse for a single experience. Non-philosophy abandons this project and raises its object up a notch or a degree. This object is no longer experience "in itself" but the group of constituted knowings to which it gives place, regional *and fundamental* knowings. It presents itself, then, as transcendental thought, relating itself to these knowings rather than to their objects. The assumed sameness [*mêmeté*], the accepted analytic or synthetic identity of the scientific object and the philosophical object: this is the alleged "Real" or "common sense" which determines the enterprise of legislation of philosophy and the war it wages everywhere. Let us assume now that the Real is not this objective identity, this sameness, but that it is Identity in flesh and blood, Identity as such in its in-objective immanence; this is the sole Real which can undo the claims of philosophy and determine non-philosophy as a transcendental thought which relates itself to philosophies and to sciences rather than to their objects. The type of identity that grounds philosophy presents in effect an unthought and artificial character which comes from is nature as *black box* or from a connection of a *technological type* and turns philosophy into a transcendental technology. We can equally describe it as the postulation of a "miracle", *common sense* or *pre-established harmony*, which dedicates philosophy to begging the question. Non-philosophy can only ground itself in the instance of a real identity which excludes common sense, pre-established harmony, technological causality and its modes (analysis, synthesis, difference, dialectic) and which establishes pure thought within its rights and its element. What we call "transcendental cloning" is the remainderless destruction of this common sense or of this postulated harmony and the affirmation of a "real" or transcendental causality which pushes technology outside of thought. If it can seem that transcendental cloning remains mysterious, this mystery is in any case simpler than the mystery of Philosophical Decision and forms its real core, that which philosophy represses or ignores on principle and to which it adds the mystery of this repression. Kant, as we know, discovered the brilliant principle according to which the conditions of experience and those of the object of experience are the same. But this principle turns out to be strictly within philosophy and to have a restrained form here, from which we give it its optimal or radical form: *the real conditions of experience and those of the object of experience are identical-in-the-last-instance*. This is the base from which non-philosophy is deployed outside any speculative "miracle".

Why a transcendental knowing? In one sense, philosophy has wanted to cumulate or blend two operations which are rather distinct in the sciences: 1) the acquisition of "naive" knowing over experience; whence its obliged reference to the sciences, arts, technologies, etc., stems, as much as its competition with these regional knowings; 2) the universalizing, quasi-formalizing thought, of these regional knowings, a task which it keeps to itself but which is not unique and consequently not pure. Non-philosophy, for its part, first renounces these tasks that it abandons to that which *de jure* can fulfill them: precisely the sciences, arts, ethics, etc., without claiming, then, to compete with regional knowings on their own terrain. It keeps for itself their purely transcendental formulation, which is to say the constitution with their provisions of an order of pure thought, as usage (and) theory identically. The acquisition of knowing is necessary but not sufficient if its generalization or its formalization are not appended. But this does not need to interiorize the naiveté of the acquisition nor to reproduce it in itself. Non-philosophy proposes the universalization of all knowings, including fundamental and philosophical knowings, in order precisely not to proceed in the same manner as those which blend acquisition and formalization. But generalize them how? By allocating a supplement of auto-positional reflexivity or indeed alterity? This would be to return to the mistakes of philosophy which universalizes insufficiently and still too empirically just as it roots this universalization in the first acquisition of knowing. The only rigorous formalization of which thought will be capable *insofar as it is thought* is necessarily pure-transcendental rather than empirico-transcendental. Thus non-philosophy treats all knowings without exception, regional and fundamental, as simple a prioris for experience; a priori without auto-reflection (auto-position, auto-givenness), and as such without a transcendental aim that would be able to account for them. Non-philosophy instates an equality of the regional and the fundamental, but not without conserving their qualitative heterogeneity which is, however, henceforth deprived of any hierarchical or inegalitarian outlook. The transcendental reduction of philosophy to the status of simple materials, which is to say phenomenal objectives, clears an infinite, really universal field of possibilities from any philosophical closure.

We posit that, within the tradition—whereby any philosophy must be replaced if it does not, as non-philosophy does, relate to its own identity—all philosophies play for some other the role of meta-philosophy. This role, with its adopted claims of authority, comprehension and critique, recasts the most general philosophical project and does not constitute a science or a true theory of philosophy. Non-philosophy denounces, in all its practices, the failure and the compulsive character of this meta-philosophical claim with wishes to assume any sort of philosophy with regard to others, and in particular, to their multiplicity. This is a claim which adopts the ideal of the "death-of-philosophy". Thus the question is of inventing a thought which is undoubtedly more powerful [*puissante*] than philosophy but which is not a meta-philosophy. More "powerful" in the sense of a theoretical domination of philosophy, rather than a political domination. Non-philosophy is liable to be the object of a new type of transcendental induction and deduction, which is to say an "application" within experience now extended to philosophy and science; philosophy and art; philosophy and ethics, etc. If non-philosophy is grounded on the renouncing of the meta-philosophical ideal, then it is all the more exercised as a *unified theory—unified rather than unitary—of philosophy and science*, philosophy and art, ethics, etc.; a theory which brings both the fundamental *and* the regional under the reason of immanence and no longer under that of transcendence (*meta*-philosophy). A "science of philosophy" and a "philosophy of science" are no longer possible as species of a philosophy that is at once meta-science and meta-philosophy (but for a positivist reversal), but rather in the form *of a unification through identity of immanence or through determination-in-the-last-instance of the provisions of philosophy and of science*. Non-philosophy, then, is neither a so-called "positive" science of philosophy, nor an "absolute" or "rigorous" science, which is to say still a philosophy. Non-philosophy excludes the positivist reduction of philosophy (of which it is the transcendental reduction) to its meta-philosophical death which can disguise itself—and this is not the only instance—under the guise of a "philosophy as rigorous science". As for the relations that it establishes between philosophy and science, non-philosophy notes the Gödelian limitation and marks, in its transcendental and complex manner, a generalized blow to the programs of the philosophical grounding of the sciences, substituting in place of the meta-philosophical project a project we will call the *unified theory of science and philosophy*. In a general sense, in place of metaphysical or transcendental auto-position or auto-grounding which regulates the relations of philosophy and science in a regime that itself is precisely philosophical, non-philosophy substitutes the transcendental organon (the "simple" position) of the *force-(of)-thought* and relates it to these two disciplines. This is how it makes sense of the multiplicity of philosophical decisions and their non-domination over experience.

When it is situated on the margins of philosophy and under the *ultimate* authority thereof, the non-philosophical remains an object or a metaphysical thesis, directly or indirectly (as the deconstruction of metaphysics) a supplementary hypothesis on the essence of the Real and of philosophy. On the other hand, it stops being such a philosophical hypothesis on essence or the "in itself", that is, it stops being a thesis, when as "non-philosophy" it takes on the status of a "simple hypothesis", operatory and theoretical; a scientific as much as a philosophical hypothesis, identically one and the other. Here we are faced with the antinomy of science and philosophy, and non-philosophy is the *real* resolution of this antinomy, without synthesis or a still philosophical supplementary decision. The concept of non-philosophy is in effect not only descriptive but equally (in its intrinsic identity) theoretical; capable, through an original reduction and deduction, of explaining philosophical-and-scientific efficacy and not only of under-standing it. Furthermore, it is not purely and solely theoretical, but also, intrinsically, practical and capable of transforming and not only inter-preting the efficacy of knowledges. The problem to which non-philosophy responds is that of the type of reality, not of the object, ("philosophy", "science", "art", etc.) but of the knowledge of the object—a transcendental problem. And this response is that of a transcendental organon destined to replace, *for* the thought of philosophy and of science, the organon of logic which is only viable *for* philosophical thought of experience. Why such an organon?

Non-philosophy must remain an explicative theoretical hypothesis: it does not confuse itself with its object, with experience; the theory of philosophy is no more philosophical than the idea of a circle is circular. Furthermore, it must not simply content itself with explaining effective reality, but it must rather contribute to transforming it, or at least to making a new usage for it, if not directly then at least through and within the limits of its power of knowledge and of explication, and as such to be more than a verifiable or falsifiable hypothesis which we realize or abandon under the pressure of experimentation [*experience*]. Verified or falsified, a hypothesis disintegrates; disappears under the form of sanctioned knowledges, and non-philosophy must not stop being a hypothesis. On the other hand, even as a simple hypothesis, it must—this is our second demand—contribute to transforming the reality of philosophy and science, rather than just having knowledge of it. In effect, the hypothesis of non-philosophy can neither be empirically justified nor invalidated through comparison to experience; it must at least also transform experience. What is the name of the device [*dispositif*] that identifies in itself these two functions? An *organon*. To make non-philosophy a universal organon of thought, more than a simple hypothesis, less than a closed system or a theoretical thing: this is the objective. In one sense, this type of theoretical instrument never encloses itself in definitive knowings; it is in a perpetual state of producing novelty; of opening and rectifying a specific space of knowing without confusing itself with the reality to be described. In another sense, it is capable of penetrating reality sufficiently to promote not necessarily an internal transformation of the effective course of the philosophy of history, or politics, of science, which would be an illusion, but rather a transformation of their usage precisely within the limits of theoretical knowledge; a "transcendental" usage since the sciences and philosophies serve as its materials and field of objects.

This would be the means of assuring for non-philosophy—this concept that is meanwhile so indeterminate and an object of such incalculable stakes—a double fecundity: theoretical and practical. The ransom for this fecundity is the abandonment of unilateral and opposed decisions, and of determinations of its concept as simply descriptive in terms of philosophical thought, or perhaps simply theoretical, or deconstructive. In other words: in one sense it takes on a universal function, as a theoretically operative concept capable of explaining, eventually in a predictive manner, the functioning and the dynamic of a philosophy or the philosophical tradition. In another sense, if it is perhaps not a *direct* means of intervention *in* philosophy and science, except for the distant cultural effects; it intervenes in knowledges already constituted by the sciences and philosophies, using and orienting them differently: a transcendental *organon* is a tool for modifying the course not of the object itself but of the knowing of the object, and an immanent usage of this knowing.

It is tricky to define objectives or stakes of non-philosophy without giving rise to new misunderstandings. Finality having ceased to be determining for non-philosophy, such objectives are not absent; rather they are now secondary in relation to the Real whose radical autonomy is liable to determine thought in-the-last-instance, and so without return. There are no objectives nor stakes other than for thought so-limited by the Real, not for the Real: moreover they result in a certain transformation of the very idea of teleology that philosophy carries. Non-philosophy is not the thought which must succeed philosophy, pronounce it dead or reassemble its *membra disjecta*, reviving it for a less metaphysical task and a "re-commencement". It is the thought for philosophy, but which philosophy does not want, and which it resists *de jure*. It relies on this thought to make something other than a simple transcendental illusion which is ignorant of itself, or in order to be able to know that it is necessarily foreclosure of the Real. It is the thought which relates to philosophy as to a new type of "object", and which can do so without destroying it through positivism. Anything, in or outside of the World, is subject, if not to a science and a philosophy separately, at least to a science-thought where philosophy has a role to play: why not philosophy in turn which is the very World? Philosophy presents itself as the highest thought. But is it perhaps not the most universal form, but rather only a still restrained and authoritarian form which has concealed another possibility from us? Why would philosophy have straight away achieved the most universal form of thought whereas everything in its behavior shows its spontaneous origins, its "state of nature", its savage and uncivilized passions?

Thinking in terms of the "death of philosophy", including the painless death of domination, and the attempted parricide, is what all philosophy wants and practices, even when it manifests for philosophy, which is to say for its own death rather than for others. Understood in this way, the "death of philosophy" is the "principal affect" proper to philosophy itself. This is not an intra-philosophical pathos like anxiety, doubt or astonishment; it is the pathos which grasps the relation of whichever philosophy to the multiplicity of others. We must stop posing this problem in a general and abstract manner, which is to say from the point of view of such a determined philosophy which is necessarily blind to the others, and pose it concretely as an internecine war proper to the multiplicity of philosophical decisions, ignorant though of itself. Neither a foreign nor a guerilla war, but a civil war of all against all, "civil" which is still to say "natural". The order of thought is in reality doubly shared: between the multiplicity of concurrent philosophies, between philosophy and sciences, philosophy and art, philosophy and ethics, etc. It is a hierarchical order, inegalitarian and authoritarian, an order without democracy which speaks of democracy without doing what it says, and which is moreover conflictual in its essence. Non-philosophy is the attempt to edify, on behalf of philosophical nations and empires, on the real base of a universal language, a *new democratic order of thought* which excludes the conflictuality between philosophies and between philosophy and regional knowledges, and which exclude it by the process of a "transcendental" democracy which assumes the irreducibility of the *real identity* and of its own type of multiplicity or of "multitudes". Non-philosophy conserves the heterogeneity of realms of experience, gives way to their relative autonomy, which is to say to their identity, against the unitary and often totalitarian claims of philosophy, or the sciences when they try to assume a philosophical role. But it sets, between these realms, a minimal *order* which we call "unilateral", which excludes every hierarchy of identities without however positing their unitary leveling or even an anarchizing multiplicity which is always the residue of the decomposition of authoritarian forms. It distinguishes between order and domination; between priority and primacy. Hence the idea of a transcendental and no longer transcendent order of thought, which only appears to be trans-philosophical and trans-scientific because it is, at base, *the democratic order of identities recognized first and foremost as such*.

If philosophy has only been and only ever will be an opinion and a poorly thought out passion, then the question is of passing from its state of war and of competition, a state of exploitation of thought and as such of man, to its civil state, which we want to call human and democratic. This democratic humanization is one of the objectives—if there are any—of non-philosophy and perhaps even the only objective, if we decide to put the Real at the heart of man or man at the heart of the Real rather than one at the periphery of the other as philosophy itself does. The *tradition* has up to the present been the universal element of philosophical decisions: a true *Kampfzeit* as much as a *Kampfplatz*. To the tradition as this space-time of philosophical combat, we will oppose the *non-philosophical translation of philosophies* in a new universal outlook, in an egalitarian order, as far from "difference" as from nihilism which is its residue. There is an absolute untranslatable—the Real—before every translation, condemned moreover by the Real to its foreclosure. But for all that, it allows the translation of philosophies through their transcendental equivalence or their relative autonomy, non-philosophy itself, outside of which the philosophical statements remain that which they are, but within which they are translated together in "equivalent" statements with regard to the Real. Non-philosophy is the universal dictionary of philosophies; the transcendental idiom in terms of thought which relates to them. A pragmatic of the translation of philosophical decisions, it looks to discover and invent all the conditions of universal peace: rather than through treaty, through the constitution of an idiom of the identity of thought. Only a "language" capable of this feat of positing the multiplicity *de jure*, non-empirically, of philosophies, can also introduce peace into thought by means of democracy.

Do we fight here against the presumption of philosophy by that which will be taken as a new presumption, to know that *non-philosophy is the thought that philosophy merits and that philosophy cannot find in itself, or in its own resources*? Philosophy has become a new gamble between… philosophy and non-philosophy; between itself and the Real. We know the question: who will educate the educator? It is an infinite regress: who philosophizes philosophy? But philosophy cannot really and rigorously think itself; it can reflect upon itself, meta-philosophize itself, it cannot invent a totally other thought which would not be to some extent a double or a reflection of itself. It goes as far as dialectic or deconstruction, which is to say as far as these absurdities: post-philosophy, post-metaphysics, but it never renounces its ultimate authority over the Real, even when it accepts limiting and sometimes deconstructing this authority. The problem is formulated thus: what should we do not philosophically (a *not* more or a *not* less…)—with a philosophy, through the eventual means of such an other, but what should we make *of Philosophy* itself? Not philosophy taken "globally", "generally" or "totally"—we do not claim here to leave it, but rather never to have entered into it—but of *Philosophy* related to its identity? Who can determine it; who can make a good use of it if it is no longer the philosopher himself? Who posits the multiplicity of philosophical decisions given that the philosophers most enamored with multiplicity, that of Being or even that of Becoming, are wary of positing a multiplicity of philosophies themselves, which will no longer be cloistered by their philosophies, but which include multiplicity in a general manner. Non-philosophy is not exactly the educator of philosophy; it is the "subject" who receives it and transforms it, the force-(of)-thought as subject *of* non-philosophy and *for* each philosophy. What is the subject of the reception of philosophies if not every man, as in, each-and-every? Furthermore too often, philosophy looks to impose itself authoritarianly over man (through a so-called philosophical education) who it claims to transform with a view to adapting them to this reception. To this selection of man by the philosopher, and of the philosopher by philosophy, we oppose the induction and deduction of non-philosophy between the real-Man and philosophy: either real man given as "first term", abstracted from its philosophical condition, or as untransformable through philosophical technology—what will result of this for philosophy itself, which is transformable? Rather than modifying man, non-philosophy modifies philosophy. Rather than giving itself philosophy and authoritarianly subsuming man, it does the opposite, and more than the opposite: do we not leave man as being-given, that is, deduced for philosophy?

# 1 PROBLEMATIC OF NON-PHILOSOPHY

## The "first names" that distinguish non-philosophy from philosophy

How can non-philosophy be presented according to its circumstance, without exhausting its essence? The philosophical field has its own way of moving and redistributing itself; of reorganizing itself incessantly around new front lines. Actually, the principal axis of sharing is that of "immanence" (for certain philosophers, as radical as possible) and of "transcendence" (for certain philosophers, as exacerbated as possible). This demarcation has replaced others to which it is no stranger, and which it recoups: those of Consciousness and the Object; Being and the essence of Being; Identity and Difference; Logocentrism and the Other, etc. Let us say that for us this is symptomatic and can define the circumstance. The pole of transcendence allies a certain number of philosophers who are more or less neighbors or strangers; very different in some ways (Heidegger, Levinas, Derrida, Badiou); that of immanence brings together others (Nietzsche, Deleuze, Henry), who are also very different. One such line of demarcation quite evidently is all too simple and does not do justice to anyone. The philosophers distinguish between themselves by *a system of diversely measured mixtures of immanence and transcendence,* by these infinitely varied twists and interlacings. Even non-philosophy appears in the first place to be a neighbor of these philosophers: it asserts immanence like the second group above, but also a certain relative autonomy of transcendence and a refusal to sacrifice it, a little like the first group. However, with non-philosophy as an autonomous discipline, it is the very nature of immanence and that of transcendence which have changed at the same time as their relation: the field of philosophical mixtures is thereby globally displaced; its authority suspended. Its novelty, its heterogeneity with philosophy holds to four tenets which seem only to make one. These tenets are in reality, following the theoretical style of non-philosophy, really *first terms*; we prefer to call them "first names".

1) Immanence of the Real, undoubtedly, but moreover as *effectively* "radical", blended without a single morsel of transcendence (of the World, language, movement, topology, set theory, etc.)—of philosophy. It is what it names, according to the circumstance, the first terms of the "One", "One-in-One", "vision-in-One" or "seen-in-One", "Performed-without-performation", etc. It is as such an *autonomy through radicality* in relation to every form of transcendence. Phenomenally, it is a "Given-without-givenness", and from this point of view, non-philosophy formulates the following axioms, rather than principles: a) there is a radical given, and from its very essence it excludes givenness, which is to say the fold of the given and the givenness; b) Because it is in-One, the One does not unify, in or outside of itself.

2) Equally an autonomy, but only *relative,* of the realm of transcendence. "Relative autonomy" is an expression which must be nuanced; it signifies as much, no longer opposing itself to "radical autonomy": a) when it concerns philosophy, or the data that philosophy provides, it too is "absolute", but for the sole reason of its spontaneous or given existence, becoming relative when thought in relation to non-philosophy properly so-called, whereas the real-One remains radically autonomous, whether it is thought or not, thought neither adding to it, nor subtracting anything from the real; b) when it concerns this very thought, which is to say non-philosophy in the strict sense of the term which has its cause in the One, it is relatively radical in relation to philosophy, and radically relative to the real-One.

This system of double autonomy is not what we will come call the "mixture"—the essence of philosophy—which is only autonomous in relation to its terms, but what we will call "unilateral duality" or "deter-mination-in-the-last-instance". It is the "syntax" which must necessarily accompany, from our point of view at least, immanence when it is only (in) itself, effectively radical and presented as the definition of the Real. For want of this double autonomy, which reserves the unilat-eralizing causality of the real-One, immanence remains blended with transcendence and "radical immanence" proclaimed wrongly by thoughts which no longer want to be philosophies, but are. Hence a new axiom: If immanence is radical, transcendence is autonomous and consistent and cannot be denied. It suffices to set out this "syntax", this order rather, of determination-in-the-last-instance in order to discover that in effect most "philosophies of immanence" (Spinoza, Leibniz, Nietzsche and now Deleuze and also Michel Henry in another altogether less evident fashion) devote themselves more or less surreptitiously to transcendence, after having denied its consistency, according to this logic of mixture, and as such reinstate philosophical authority and not that of "non-philosophy".

3) When it is effectively "radical", immanence does not exclude philosophy's authority without calling for and rendering possible a new style of thought—non-philosophy in the strict sense. We will again call it a "unified theory" rather than "unitary". This style is identically—and this is its novelty—*theoretical (and) pragmatic*. Measured in terms of its data or material—science and philosophy—this thought is exercised under a first form for which we recover the ancient term of "first science", a thought which is in-the-last-instance in-One or through-the-One rather than an Aristotelian "science of the One" or a science *in* the One, and whose object consists in determining the identity of science and philosophy in terms of their data. The vague concept of "non-philosophy" is as such given content in a precise, positive manner and is torn from philosophy, as much from its material aspect as from the aspect of its cause and form.

4) As for the discipline which is meant to be dominant and which is known under the name "philosophy", non-philosophy holds to: 1) the destitution of its sufficiency and its authority (of the "Principle of Sufficient Philosophy"); b) the affirmation of the equivalence of every philosophical position before the Real; c) a reevaluation of the *identity* (if not of the "whole") of philosophy as simple a priori of a "field of phenomena" or objects for the new discipline; d) more generally, a theoretical usage (a philosophically contradictory expression which is no longer resolved within a supplementary mixture) of philosophy's identity (and) of any field of regional experience, a usage which thus falls outside of every philosophical or other teleology.

Non-philosophy entails putting an end to the spontaneous and naive practice of philosophy, incapable of a real critique of itself. This is not, however, a second order thought, a meta-philosophy. It is a unique usage or a transcendental thought *for* philosophy and equally for science, ethics, art or any other region of objects. Nothing here, then, signifies a superior capacity of philosophy; the empowering [*potentialization*] of its tradition. To the contrary: a disempowering [*dépotentialization*], something altogether other than its "superior form" or a "metaphysics of metaphysics", rather *the identity of philosophy* and consequently also that, for example, of science; of each of the experiences of thought. A democratic identity, "contemplated" in an immanent manner.

# The three discoveries which ground non-philosophy

Three problems are fundamentally revealed for the constitution of an autonomous non-philosophy insofar as, tangled up according to a law of essence, they have received solutions that were disjointed in time but undivided in their theoretical pertinence. These solutions were proposed each time with the status of *discovery* rather than the status of *philosophical decision*: we will soon see why. We stop asking: what is the capability of, say, a Hegel, a Nietzsche, a Heidegger; how far does it extend, and how do we "break" with it? This is a problem for the heirs of the tradition; heirs of grand philosophies, and it at once forms a system with philosophical sufficiency and with the question of the "death of philosophy" which is latent in every demand for philosophical sufficiency. We ask: what is to be done with philosophy, what theoretical or pragmatic use of it is still possible, that we had not imagined? It is not the question of the end and the ends of philosophy, but *that of a non-philosophical discovery that we would not yet have made and which would change the face of philosophy*. This discovery, probably, cannot be made without the renunciation of the question of its death, a question which is moreover that of its sufficiency to be adequate to the Real, the real of death. It comprises three facets:

- The essence of the One as radical immanence or vision-in-One, correctly understood, is the first discovery; that of the conditions that must be realized in order that immanence can be effectively "radical"; or, again, the concept of Given-without-givenness.

- The causality of the real-One as determination-in-the-last-instance, which is first made concrete on the occasion of organon that is the force-(of)-thought.

- The form of thought adequate to the radical autonomy of the One, the form of an organon which works through hypothesis or axiomatic yet "real" decision rather than through a thesis or philosophical decision; as such the abandonment of the thematic of "thought" in lieu of an organon of thought, and the distinction between the two absolutely heterogeneous concepts of decision.

## 1

The discovery of the autonomy of the One as Real or of its essence of radical immanence: *Philosophie et non-philosophie*,[1] among other previous works, gives a dozen possible descriptions or formulations of this essence of the One—we will not go back to this. We must add the first name of Given-without-givenness. By this we mean, then, the type of given that is *radically* given (to) itself rather than to a subject or to any other form of transcendence, and which is thus given without an operation of assumed givenness "behind" it, a background of the given. Instead of givenness determining the given under a quasi-objectifying mode, it is rather the given that determines the givenness, but in-the-last-instance only, and as such outside of any objectifying form. The Given-without-givenness is the first name of phenomenological extraction for the Real; another means of thinking radical immanence. It entails the non-philosophical usage and critique, among others, of the phenomenological concept of givenness, its continuity and its difference from the given, of the fold that is givenness and which still structures the phenomenological concept of "given". The radical autonomy of the One—its real indifference with regard to Being and thought, of their blend (the "same", the ultimate object of philosophy) which has only relative autonomy—invalidates a major ontological thesis: that of its convertibility with Being, convertibility of their *logos aside*, and limits the supposedly primary pertinence of the thesis of this other convertibility; the *Ontological Difference* of Being and beings. It is no longer a case of thinking the One beyond Ontological Difference; of positing a parallel *Henological Difference*, but rather of proceeding with a reorganization of the economy of the great moments: One, Being, Other, Being, beginning with the *first discovery* of the non-convertibility of the One with Being (the ontology of the Ancients), or with the Other (contemporary deconstructions of ontology); or moreover of its incommensurability with Being-without-One (ontology of Being-as-Multiple). All of these positive or negative forms of convertibility are from now on eliminated by the One which entails if not the pure and simple dissolution of these amphibologies (One-Beings, One-Being, One-Other), then at least their non-pertinence in terms of the Real.

Heidegger attributes the confusion of Being-presence with beings to "metaphysics"; someone else attributes the confusion of Being as empty with being-One [*étant-Un*] to "being-presence" [*être-présence*]; someone else attributes the confusion of Multiplicities (of the One-Multiple) with the duality of the One and the Multiple to "representation", and someone else again attributes the confusion of Logos and the Other taken as Other, etc., to "logocentrism". They all do the work of philosophy which cuts its own body into a dead part and a healthy part. But confusing in their turn the malady and the medicine, they chase confusion away only to reestablish it elsewhere. The critical auto-denunciation of these amphibologies leaves intact that upon which they all feed: the confusion of One and of Being (of the Other; of Beings). No philosopher can effectively suspend authority effectively without a remainder, since only the One can absolutely undo it on its own terms without resuscitating it elsewhere. It is not that the One is foreign to philosophy; it is that it renders itself foreign to it and condemns it to its own foreclosure, specifically the foreclosure of the Real. If it is absolutely indifferent to Being, this is because it not only has an absolutely distinct essence (radical immanence, the given-without-givenness), but also an original causality precisely over Being. The One is necessarily, as we will show, One-in-the-last-instance and thus force-(of)-thought, if at least Being and thought are also in play when the question is only to think and to carry out critiques of these confusions; to enter into non-philosophy. With this thematic, we have already entered the terrain of other discoveries, but it must suffice to distinguish the One-in-One from the transcendental figures it receives within philosophy and with which the philosophers are forced to *recognize* the One-in-One (eventually suppressing or believing themselves able to suppress it) and to reappropriate it—to normalize it: Parmenides' "spherical" One-Being, Heraclitus' One-All, Plotinus' One-in-procession-conversion, Spinoza's Unity-God of substances and attributes, Fichte's I = I, Wittgenstein's "Internal Relation" and its immanence, etc.

In comparison to the transcendentals of ontology and mysticism, the One taken up by non-philosophy is neither transcendent nor transcendental; it is only immanent or real, immanent through-and-through; an immanence (to) itself rather than just *to* itself; rather than to Being, to the Ego, to Life, to Substance, etc. This is its action or its causality called "transcendental". Furthermore, this transcendental trait roots itself, through *cloning* as we will say, in real immanence on the *occasion* of transcendent entities, instead of grafting itself over them in the manner of philosophy's "transcendentals". The One itself cannot then be called "transcendental"—a central axiom against the still philosophical interpretations of radical immanence, as we will see—no more than it could be said, without reference to Being or to thought, "in-the-last-instance". Here we distinguish the One which is only seen-in-One and the concrete form of its causality, force-(of)-thought or noetic function "of" the One. This precisely does not add anything nor remove anything (of the real) to or from the One. We will avoid, then—concerning vision-in-One, which is to say the Real—evoking a "transcendental realism", an old formula for rather scholastic philosophies, inadequate in this circumstance. If there is realism it is of-the-last-instance and consequently there is a Real-without-decision-of-realism, realism being nothing but one philosophical position among others. The force-(of)-thought accords radical primacy of the Real over thought with the relative autonomy of thought.

# 2

The discovery of determination-in-the-last-instance operating in the force-(of)-thought is, with vision-in-One, non-philosophy's heart. It determines non-philosophy (which is important given the philosophical circumstances) as a positive practice of philosophy rather than as something that would subtract itself from philosophy's self-sufficiency. Sometimes we speak, too, of *unilateral duality* or of *dual*, a syntax or general order implicated by vision-in-One, and condensed or concentrated in the force-(of)-thought. This type of duality must, from our point of view, substitute itself for all types of distinction or philosophical difference, but not in their place, if it is to respect a triple condition.

This must be a question of a true duality, as we said in the preface—not resulting from a division and without any possible synthesis—with the radical autonomy of the one term and the relative autonomy of the second; not a philosophical *dyad*, or a *unity-of-contraries* or Unity-synthesis; the mixture is absolutely autonomous or concrete and both its terms are relatively autonomous or abstract. The One as vision-in-One does not exclude duality; it tolerates it without needing it. The belief in this exclusion, which is to say *the confusion of the One with a new type of unity, either exclusive or inclusive of Being or of transcendence*, is an effect of the being-foreclosed of the One, and the source of philosophical normalizations of non-philosophy.

This duality of terms or of autonomies, radical and relative respectively, integrates with the *unilateral* character of the causality of the first over the second, or, more precisely, with a duality of the types of causality that replaces the four intra-ontological forms of metaphysical causality (form, matter, agent, end). This duality is one of a first causality (transcendental or "of" the Real) which operates in an irreversible manner, without sharing, without reciprocity, of the One over the sphere of transcendence; and of a secondary causality, heterogeneous with the former, which is as such no longer a part of or a residual "return" to it, but an original causality belonging to the sphere of transcendence (to philosophical *dat*a) and which is only *occasional*. The divided unity of the "unitary" causality of Being, whose types metaphysics establishes, is dismissed and replaced by the discovery of the specific causality of the One, which is to say of the Real, when it is thought in relation to Being but is all the same absolutely outside-Being or outside-thought.

This duality is only unilateral if it receives a *transcendental* essence, that is, an essence with a real or immanent (in-One) essence, but which for this very reason, if radically thought, adds nothing of the real to its cause (it does not modify the One) and nothing of the effective to its effective material (it does not modify science or philosophy from inside, or does not pretend to intervene in them); it leaves the extreme spheres of the "given" intact in their respective autonomies.

# 3

The discovery of a thought adequate to vision-in-One is the final and most complex step in non-philosophy. The One, the given-without-givenness, is not by definition a problem. On the other hand, if is there is now a crucial problem, it is that of the form of a thought, of a givenness, or of a position that would be adequate to being-radically given and to the "solitude" of the One. Philosophy can no longer be the *presupposition* (in the traditional sense) of this thought; it is only its presupposition without auto-position, itself being relative to the Real. It is a material or a configuration of *data* in terms of its elaboration or its knowledge: *given that* the One is absolutely indifferent to Being and to thought; not convertible with them, *what does this mean for them* when the question is of "seeing"-them-in-One? If it is no longer a question of philosophy, is it then a question of science? How can this avoid returning to a certain scientism and positivism? The One cannot accept a simple reversal of the philosophy/science hierarchy, nor an all-too immediate and rigged reprisal of the Aristotelian motif of a "science of the One". Rather it entails—and this is precisely its causality as "determination-in-the-last-instance"—an identity, without difference and without synthesis but not without transcendental priority or duality, of philosophy and of science for example—not against all their possible relations, but against the unitary spirit of philosophical and epistemological hierarchy in these relations. This transcendental identity, then, is the object of a "*unified theory*" which first operates like that of science and philosophy. Far from simply being a passive given or a lazy thought, it demands interminable work on philosophical representations of philosophy and science, that is, on meta-sciences. The One opens up a new field of research, not at the borders of non-philosophical and philosophical alterity, but rather at the very heart of thought *before* its disjunction into science and philosophy.

What are the instruments of this thinking *in*, *through* but not *from* or *within* the One? The main organon is the force-(of)-thought, which will be the object of a transcendental theorem in this treatise. More concretely, non-philosophy is realized first as a unified theory of philosophy and science; as such its tools will be *hypothesis* and *axiom* in as much as they define only a rigorous or non-circular thought. But axiom or hypothesis as real in-the-last-instance, and as such transcendental rather than transcendent and ideal objects of an epistemology, like *hypothesis-form* or *axiom-form* which draw their transcendental identity ("-form") from the One, rather than philosophical argumentation and thesis. The *One('s)-decision* or force-(of)-thought no longer implicates, in its essence, its hypothesis-form, nor its axiom which here would be the mode of effectuation, but this formula assumes *exclusion at the very same time as the One is the object of a decision and that decision is an operation external or transcendent to the One*. It signifies that the decision is the internally obligated form of thought which has the One as its immanent cause ("by immanence"). Let us compare philosophy and non-philosophy from this point of view. The philosophical economy is not reducible to a simple decision but to the decision as first *and* assumed real, which is to say as essence or determining; furthermore it only exists as enveloped by and overcome by the undecidable. This, then, is its identity type, the mixture or the blend, which defines philosophy and this is another facet of its identity, purely transcendental and without synthesis such as it conditions "unilateral duality", which defines and delimits the force-(of)-thought as organon of non-philosophy. In the first case the decision is primary and thought consists in the auto-cutting [*auto-découpage*] of this mixture with the help of and necessary reference to the sciences, art, history, politics, which sketch or draw a dotted line for the future philosophical cut. In the second case, the decision is equally requisite, but it is no longer primary or determining; it is instead unilaterally directed by a now radical Undecided—a given-without-givenness—and is no longer blended with it; "first" Undecided or already-manifest. So we will call *Discovery as such*—whether hypothesis or axiom—that decision-(of)-thought determined in-the-last-instance by the already-Discovered or the real-One that determines it in an immanent manner. Understood in a real and no longer logico-epistemological manner, Discovery is the principal operation of thought in the regime of "unified theory".

We will also carefully distinguish the "Philosophical Decision"—a mixture of decision *and* the undecidable, concrete in 2/3 terms—and the "decision-in-One", also called force-(of)-thought. Decision and Undecidable either form a philosophical duality, mixing a unity-of-contraries, in reality a triad, or they form a simple duality which never gives rise to a triad, where the undecided (of the) Real determines the decision without being otherwise identified or synthesized with this decision. This, then, is the concept of "determination-in-the-last-instance", a concept of the specific causality of the One, which unifies the-One-as-not-convertible-with-Being and decision as the internal form of Being and of thought internally or in an undivided manner, in the principal process, or the organon of the force-(of)-thought, or "force-(of)-decision". The three discoveries are actually only one, even though in the long process of research, working through philosophical hesitations and temptations, the first has preceded the second and the second the third, as has long since been expressed throughout philosophy.

# What would "thinking (from) the one" mean? A solution to a non-philosophical problem

Being that the One-in-One, given as the mode of the One in itself, is given independent of any givenness and of any thought of itself: what will be the result of this for the position of thought in relation to the One? What would it mean to say that thinking is "thinking (from) the One" and, more fundamentally, what does "as One" signify? First, it signifies that it is given—thought or not—only from the point of view of the One in-itself, that it is *as it is* or One-in-One. This radical autonomy, not relative to Being, to the Other, or to thought, does not follow from an essence distinct from and higher than itself; radical autonomy is its essence; *if* it must be described, it will be described starting from itself in-the-last-instance. Radical immanence amounts to more than a "transcendental fact": more than a fact, it is the given (in) itself before every transcendental givenness; more than transcendental: it is the Real which "precedes" every description of itself or every usage of transcendence.

Furthermore, *if* "qua" [*en tant que*] signifies "thought as One" [*pensé comme Un*], *if* then the One itself is thought, then this thinking is (though in-the-last-instance) itself "in-One" or a participle of the One in its mode, immanent and not reflected or circular: it is the force-(of)-thought. Through this the in-One is the cause which transforms philosophical statements that have claimed to bear on itself. So it can eventually be described and defined by recourse to *data* and models of very diverse philosophical origins which are re-worked not just according to this immanence but from the thought that it so determines. For example, according to the original philosophical statements, the One is described as inherent (to) itself; as non-decisional and non-positional immanence-(of)-itself; as One-without-Being; as vision-in-One; as 'seen' or "lived" from its own grounding, outside of every perspective and without passing through an ontological panorama, etc.

If the One is in-One, then it is so first by its essence and not as thinking the Real (from the One)—it is the suspension of every idealism at the heart even of thought. *If* there is a thought or a representation of the One, it can only follow from the One or be determined by it, but irreversibly. Thinking the One qua One is thus thinking the radical precession, of the given-without-givenness, over thought, and thinking always the One itself or in-One. Thought is knowing-(of)-itself, undoubtedly, but-(of)-itself as determined in-the-last-instance by it; the effect is knowing-(of)-itself as effect-(of)-its cause: but because it is first knowing of its cause "in" its cause. So, thinking thinks itself without contradiction (in-One, from its cause) as "second". Its comprehensive existence, undivided, is the already-manifest Real('s)-very manifestation, which is yet not alienated in this operation. So, still more radically than Aristotle assumed, a thought can think itself and recognize itself but as second and not as first (real), and think itself as necessary contingency without necessarily presenting itself as auto-position. This is the philosophically unintelligible paradox of non-philosophy. It is resolved by the fact that thought thinks itself in a manner that is ultimately in-One in-the-last-instance, and not through idealist auto-position of itself, therefore assumed real by abstraction. Philosophical idealism abstracts knowing or thought from their second-arity and asserts them as first *and* real. In spite of the distinction of order included within determination-in-the-last-instance or *because of it*, thought is "(of) itself" without being auto-reflection or an Idea of the Idea, but only by its cause or by non-decisional and non-given immanence.

So without still worrying ourselves with philosophy and what it believes to be able to do through thinking, we practically "assume" (within a certain kind of posture—it is at least an appearance—similar to that of every scientific kind) that thought, being in-One, thinks itself and practices with philosophical material without needing this operation of philosophy's authority. We can always make the One qua One either a problem or an *object* of this thought—this is philosophy—spontaneously assuming at least, without wanting to take a new "position", its posture and its practice with regard to philosophy and science. This immanence being taken for an immanent guiding thread itself, it suffices to elaborate its consequences and its theoretical means in terms of necessary *data* (scientific-and-philosophical, for example). So we freely call on a variety of materials: not just the "hermeneutical" system and operations of philosophy, but equally those of art, technology or "true" sciences; not just ontological (the "sought after science", a failure in principle), but the model by example of "the sciences themselves", independently not of their philosophical or epistemo-logical images, but of the authority of these. Giving science and philosophy a usage and authentic thought (a relation to the Real as it knows itself from positive foreclosure), pulling them from their antiquated submission to philosophy's authority and the transcendental illusions that this authority engenders, this is the work of thought which thinks contingent on the One or *according to* the One and this maybe gives itself a chance, hereafter, of thinking the One itself.

# On non-philosophy as thought-in-cause (without-object) and in-support (without subject)

"One qua One": what would it mean to say "qua One" from the point of view of causality? Within philosophy and within non-philosophy?

This formula is at first evidently received with a philosophical sense: the One = a subject is thought qua One = an attribute or even a predicate. "Qua" is then a copula in the manner of the verb "to be", and the One is divided or crossed out by the Being that divides it according to the classical philosophical hierarchy of the determinable subject and the determining attribute; of the empirical subject and the attribute = essence or of the predicate = event. The judicative and predicative structure, linguistic in general and in origin (subject-copula-attribute or even subject-verb-complement) is thus reflected in the form of an ontologico-linguistic mixture, without relevance in rigor and reality. It affects from the exterior, in a transcendent way, the One('s)-identity (the *Being-One-(of)-the One*). It places a blank (the "Being of the One") in place of this identity and divides the One from what it can do or from its essence; also dividing causality itself by casting it into transcendence, here of form (in a complementary manner, into the transcendence of matter, finality and efficiency).

Within non-philosophy, this indicative formula loses its relevance and becomes a simple material and so a *support* for new a priori structures, in the sense that this word's new usage will offer the program for philosophical statements; or an experimental datum, equally demanded by non-philosophy. So, treated as a transcendental axiom rather than as a philosophical injunction, the formula "qua" is first displaced in this one: the One-in-One or as such. It designates the cause but returned to its immanence; delivered from the ontologico-predicative structure; returned to its essence and thus to its ulterior functions of determination-in-the-last-instance. The "cause" is no longer by nature predicative but real or undivided, and the "subject" is no longer an empirical given, but an occasional material. From there, a new distribution of the "subject" and the "attribute", that is of the One itself: it distinguishes the One-cause and the One-support ( = the One of/within philosophy).

The old attribute or predicate ("qua One") becomes the cause-by-immanence, a radical cause or *being-cause-(of)-the cause*, such that it ceases to be divided by Being and projected under the quadruple transcendent form. The One is a cause by immanence, so without transcendence: without the ideality of form, without the materiality of matter, without the finality of the end, and without the efficiency of the agent it is "cloning".

The One-cause becomes really first—in the sense of primacy, that of the Real—and ceases to be second or an "attribute". It becomes absolutely autonomous or indifferent to an occasion, even though it needs one, but only for its representation. Unlike Being or Grounding, which form a circle with what they ground, it neither posits nor repositions the subject or the act of givenness—there is none behind it—on which it would reposition itself partially in its essence if it were the One-of-philosophy or a given-by-givenness. It frees the subject in its supporting functions at the same time as it undercuts its importance, reducing it to the role of an occasional and no longer determinant cause. If the attribute, ontologically interpreted, becomes the *object* in the philosophical sense of the word, then non-philosophy is a *thought-without-object* but *in-cause* [à-cause].[2]

As for the 'subject', it ceases to be the *subordinate* [suppôt] of the One (what we mean when we say "qua One"), a subordinate empirically given from the attribute which repositioned itself or grounded itself partially upon this subordinate. It becomes—like the set of transcendent ontological statements on the One—the *occasional cause*, with the supporting and material functions, of thought which finds its real cause, real and not occasional, within the One-in-One.

Passing from the subordinate/substance to simple support, the ontological One changes in theoretical status: released from the yoke of predicative ontological relation, it becomes an empirical datum and so a support; it ceases to be given within transcendence, but it now *represents*, by way of a relation to the One-cause, transcendence itself, given in general as material, support and occasion. It changes then within the order of priorities and functions: the philosophical 'subject' and its primacy of "first-given" becomes this support made contingent by the One-cause but necessary for its very representation. So non-philosophy is a *thought-without-subject* but *in-support*. So it changes extension; these are now globally philosophy and its statements, whatever they may be, and which always relate to the One with more or less mediation, which constitute the universal (but not unique) content of the support. This is the whole theory to come of philosophy as simple a priori giver of experience and so also the non-philosophical theory of the subject.

# Theory of cloning

With a few exceptions, what follows is essentially a reminder of what non-philosophy has previously established. But another theory belongs to its problematic and its internal architecture; a theory that completes and explains "determination-in-the-last-instance". The possibility of a "unilateral duality" in effect rests on a mechanism called "cloning", which must turn out to be an essential piece of non-philosophy. Let us begin again from the general form of the One's causality. Take the One or real identity, given and only given by definition, and a term = X from an empirical or transcendent origin, and which will be "filled out" by philosophy and by science, by their philosophical relations. This relation passes through three stages.

First, a state we call spontaneous or sufficient where philosophy claims to encompass, or at least to think and to interpret the One: this state is the "dyad" itself, a philosophical appearance of relation, an absolute appearance identical to the negation of the being-foreclosed or indifference of the Real which, by definition, is only "given" but does not "exist" nor is thought.

Second, a state we call "transcendental" where we see the resolution of the quasi-contradiction between the dyadic appearance and the Real that is inaccessible and inalienable within that appearance, between philosophical calculation and the One that refuses to let itself be counted and thought within a relation. This aporia must be resolved since we think within the thought-outside-immanence through the immanence of the vision-in-One (by initial definition) and moreover since philosophy, and so thought, is relatively autonomous. It is resolved by the production of a clone of the real-One, a clone twice identical: as clone and as clone of identity par excellence. This clone is the transcendental identity which, if we can put it this way, "is" the Real or is given in its immanent mode but which brings nothing of the real to Real, no predicate, just a function. This function of the Real in relation to its empirical "occasion" is not the Real "itself" but a consistent order, with its own kind of autonomy and complexity; it is the pure-transcendental order of non-philosophy, the transcendental essence of thought. Cloning is the result of an empirical term = X which as "occasion" or "occasional cause" extracts from the Real a simply transcendental identity by way of a mechanism that is no longer that of the double or philosophical reflection (this will be examined in Chapters 4 and 5). "Transcendental" cloning is the phenomenal content of the circle of "empirico-transcendental" doublet.

Third, a stage called "aprioristic" where the transcendental essence "extracts" an a priori from an empirical datum, in the non-philosophical occurrence and applicable *to* philosophy and *to* science, reducing the "sufficient" datum or the datum qua philosophical to the state of a simple empirical "support". This is a true "transcendental reduction" operating under non-phenomenological conditions.

The non-philosophical process thus connects to four instances: Real, Empirical, Transcendental, A priori. Or moreover: One, Mixture, Transcendental Identity, Unilateral Duality. This last expression is plurivocal and certainly seems to be able to speak of the Real/Empirical relation, the Transcendental/Empirical relation, the A Priori/Empirical relation, and the Transcendental/A priori relation. But we principally specify it through this last relation within which unilaterality (as relative autonomy of the empirical and the unilateralization of the empirical, as support, by the transcendental clone) is recovered in order to define the a priori and its double origin. The real-One is not a term, barely an instance and in no way composes a duality with any term whatsoever, not even with its transcendental clone. On the other hand, this clone, together with the aprioristic structures of which it is the essence and which claims to be, it forms one such duality—not a dyad but precisely the a priori duality *of* (for) the dyad—first with the empirical, that it rejects or brings to the state of a simple support, not constitutive of itself. And secondly, it forms one with the a priori itself that it also distinguishes, following the empirical, from itself or that it unilateralizes. "Unilateral duality" strictly speaking claim to be of the absolute non-relation or absolute appearance of relation between the Real and philosophy, or even that of its being-foreclosed to its clone. But it can by way of empirical effect and by way of transcendental cause claim to be of the relation of the transcendental or of the a priori.

A few points of terminology to return to later. The spontaneous empirical or empirical in the state of philosophical sufficiency is "occasional cause", but not support of the in-One, of the causality of the One or the process of cloning. The invalidated or suspended empirical in its sufficiency (but not destroyed) is a "support" of the a priori that the transcendental extracts from it. As for the a priori, we will be able to say strictly speaking that it is the support of a transcendental clone in the sense of its "vehicle" (not of its occasional cause), but it does not follow that this is the occasion nor the support in the precise and rigorous sense of these words.

The theory of cloning is of course fundamental within a thought which is nonetheless not one of identity in the philosophical and intentional sense, but a thought *by* and *according to* identity. More exactly, a thinking *in-identity*. Indeed, the formula "in-One" which we use in order to shorten the radical non-philosophical phenomenalization of every philosophy datum, of every representation, and which finds itself within the expression "in-the-last-instance", above all does not designate an effective inherence in the Real and still less a process within the Real, a "becoming-immanent" or an "im-manenting" under some form that a philosophy of immanence may imagine. "In-One" identically means the transcendental clone as received by way of the One but not constitutive of it. Only transcendental identity can be called "in-One" and also "real in-the-last-instance", and the other (aprioristic) representations are only such insofar as the transcendental clone is their essence, under threat of inherence of an irreality in the Real. The a priori non-philosophical representations thus are not in-One except in-the-last-instance. The latter, the Real itself, is not a hinter-world [*arrière-monde*], a hinter-instance [*arrière-instance*], but the non transcendental given from which we transcendentally accede to the World and philosophy which is the World's form. "Being-seen-in-One" signifies being given rather than thought, or thought but insofar as thought must be also given, that is given in-the-last-instance-in-One. The formula can claim to be of the One itself that is, by an initial "axiomatic" definition, "in-One", but this formula is then only redundant and repeats radical immanence or being-given. However, for a representation, or more rigorously for its a priori structure, it indicates its transcendental state, at once an ultimate being-given and a non-cobelonging to the Real: more than a unilateralization by the latter, a radical indifference. Non-relation but non-confusion, precisely a "relation" of cloning, which will be decisive in order to understand the status of the organon of the force-(of)-thought. "Determination-in-the-last-instance" means the only possible relation of the empirical or of philosophy to the Real which is not a refusal or a "forgetting" of being-foreclosed of the Real but a thinking based on that "criterion" of foreclosure.

Similarly, if the transcendental order *is* not the One but the in-One, the a priori will neither be in-transcendental, nor the empirical in-a priori. Unilateral duality expresses itself in the "for": the transcendental *applies* to or *for* the a priori, and above all the a priori *for* the empirical, but of course the Real is not *for* its transcendental clone.

Transcendental cloning is understandable within a thought of the double given, given-without-givenness (the Real) and given-by-givenness and position (philosophy, experience, and their relations).

The One or *radical* immanence (without any transcendence, thought, movement, etc.) excludes division, the production of the doublet or the philosophical kind of reflection, always double and divided, we will say more on this later, but not at all excluding a phenomenon of cloning that is no longer a process of scissiparity. The transcendental clone is the true minimal phenomenal essence or *identity of the double*, its identity without synthesis or its being-in-One-in-the-last-instance. It is the *real* critique of philosophical specularity and speculation.

# History of non-philosophy: Philosophies I, II, and III

The problematic, as outlined in broad strokes within its internal architecture before being developed and demonstrated, has been the object of a patient elaboration punctuated by advances and repentances, slowed by philosophical resistance which we have first experimented with and combated—this is not over...—in us before grasping it in the works of other philosophers. We tell this story of three epochs within our research: Philosophies I, II, and III. This triplicity has a necessity and a precise meaning: it responds to the triadic or tri-fold structure of philosophy itself, that is to say of the material that non-philosophy requires and that it has not managed to attain by radically posing it as simple material except in the third and final stage. Having covered these three moments, the elaboration of non-philosophy is essentially complete. Philosophy I placed itself under the authority of the Principle of Sufficient Philosophy but already sought to put certain themes to work; themes that would only find their definitive form, a transformed form, in Philosophy III: the individual, its identity and its multiplicity, a transcendental and productive experience of thought, the theoretical domination of philosophy, the attempt to construct a problematic rivaling that of Marx, though mainly on Nietzschean terrain and with Nietzschean means. Philosophy II marks the break with this philosophical sufficiency. But it is more than break or a new first decision, it is the subordination of the non-philosophical to its immanent cause, the vision-in-One, discovered in *La principe de minorité* and put to work in a more rigorous way, less equivocal, in *Une biographie de l'homme ordinaire*, a work that contains a sketched form of all the future themes and later developments to the point of giving the impression that Philosophy III is only a new "version", a game organized differently and a useless replica. In reality, Philosophy III gives the preceding break its true sense and impact. The latter was still equivocal. All in all, Philosophy II was grounded on two axioms assumed to be complementary: 1) The One is immanent vision in-One. 2) There is a special affinity between the vision-in-One and the phenomenal experience of "scientific thought", so much so that non-philosophy certainly realized itself no longer in a naively philosophical manner, but by reversing the epistemo-logical hierarchy, within the privileged element of science, thus by an ultimate ruse of philosophy that refused to "lays down arms" before the Real, that is to recognize the foreclosure of the Real in which the Real as vision-in-One constrained it. Philosophy III begins, then, with these *Principles* (and with *Théorie des étrangers*, published prior to but depending upon this work) by and with the suspension of this second axiom, already partially felt to be useless for non-philosophy, and which had even prevented it from being deployed in its liberty and plasticity. With this principle discovery of the radical autonomy of the Real (against every metaphysical "absolute") and of its being-foreclosed which induces philosophical sufficiency within all its forms and even within its scientistic avatars, it becomes possible to better define what distinguishes Philosophy II and II, these two stages within non-philosophy's elaboration.

If Philosophy I is intra-philosophical and if II marks the discovery of the non-philosophical against philosophy and to the benefit of science, III frees itself from the authority of science, that is in reality from every philosophical spirit of hierarchy, and takes for its object the whole of philosophical sufficiency. So, it paradoxically corresponds to the philosophy's affirmation of the self, but "negatively" or in order finally to suspend it globally.

From now on we distinguish the material of objects, operations and scientific theories, always utilizable by non-philosophy, and the scientific codetermination of the essence of its "non-" which becomes a very limited phenomenon. On the one hand this non- is now determined integrally and positively by the One or the Real rather than by the thought that leaves it partially undetermined. On the other hand the assumed affinity of the vision-in-One and the scientific experience of beings (their opacity, their unreflected character) is dissolved or, better still, *dualyzed*, and consequently any scientific theory can serve as material to non-philosophy.

Philosophy III sees two major concepts appear beside the One, though they were already sketched but poorly elucidated in II:

- The concept of the *force-(of)-thought* as transcendental organon of the Real. The One and the force-(of)-thought are distinguished like, for example, the radically immanent *Ego* and the *subject* which takes root in the Ego but "overcomes" it or adds to it the aprioristic dimension of transcendence or decision. In concrete terms we distinguish, against their modern philosophical confusions, the *Ego* and the *Subject* by way of a unilateral duality— this is a "non-Cartesian" theory of the subject.

- The concept of a *unified theory* (of science and philosophy, of ethics, of psychoanalysis, etc., and philosophy). Non-philosophy is fulfilled under the form of these unified theories, each time according to regional materials. The unified theory replaces the affinity of the One and science with the unilateral equality of philosophy and science, philosophy and art, ethics, etc., with regard to the One and introduces the "democratic" theme within thought itself rather than as a simple object of thought.

Philosophy III contains—this is a consequence—a revalorization of the function of philosophy whose relative autonomy it affirms. This point is crucial for what is to come: non-philosophy will distinguish itself from "philosophies of radical immanence" (Michel Henry, but there are some others in the process of forming)[3], by the radical autonomy of the Real *and thus* by the (relative) autonomy of philosophy or of the "empirical" sphere of effectivity. Philosophy, far from being dissolved, forgotten or critiqued and hastily rejected, and consequently its resistance increased, is the object of a theoretical posture and very positive pragmatic, albeit transcendental. Philosophy II, all in the pursuit of liberation and the specification of the originality of non-philosophy, surrendered itself to an excessive critique of philosophy in the name of the primacy of science. With science finally abandoned, the right of philosophy—at the same time its resistance—can be recognized and its process driven at last without passion… at least a philosophical one. The most radical critique of philosophical sufficiency is made only in the name of the Real rather than of philosophy or science, etc.

Philosophy III elaborates three other fundamental concepts:

- The clear distinction of the Real and the transcendental, then of the One and the force-(of)-thought as aprioristico-transcendental structure. The confusion of the Real and the transcendental within "Life" the "Internal Impression", or the transcendental "Ego" is typical of the philosophies of immanence and *misses* the radicality of immanence due to philosophical sufficiency still operating.

- Philosophical resistance and its cause and the philosophical foreclosure of the Real imposed by the Real itself (transcendental foreclosure) are finally located as constitutive of an autonomous non-philosophy.

- Transcendental cloning, of which we will present an outline, and which was not present in Philosophy II except under barely drafted and inadequate forms (theory of "non-thetic reflection").

Lastly, concerning the realization of non-philosophy's "machinery", all the pieces of the puzzle scattered here and there within the preceding works have taken the "good form" or their "pregnant form", abandoning the over-privileged landscape that some of them demanded because of their isolation and their state of abstraction (for example the themes of the three a priori constituents of "non-thetic Transcendence"). We hope that with these *Principles* the problematic, progressively completed and "filled out", has crossed over a threshold of reality or existence; of coherence, too.

Of course, within the detail of texts and formulations, the preceding distinctions are less clear and even the statements of I and above all of II imposes the idea of a continuous and teleological development or more subtly a retroactive reading from this constraint. However, if this is just a local "impression" grounded upon an objective appearance, it can only once again miss non-philosophy's specificity and bring it back to a philosophy of immanence, under the authority of the Principle of Sufficient Philosophy.

# 2 "FIRST SCIENCE" AS UNIFIED THEORY OF SCIENCE AND PHILOSOPHY: OR, DEMOCRACY WITHIN THOUGHT

## The concept of "First Science"

Non-philosophy whose major lines and stakes we are going to trace can receive various effective realizations in terms of its regional material or its *data*. We call *First Science* or *Unified Theory of Science and Philosophy* its realization, the first possible one, through the data of these two disciplines. This program of research intends to *determine the identity of science and of thought such that this identity is in-One-in-the-last-instance*. It comes together in a unique Idea: 1) a thought of *the One qua in-One* rather than a thought of Being or Difference; as such it distinguishes itself from the kinds of contemporary philosophies of Difference or Multiplicities and more generally from every ontology as from every deconstruction of ontology; 2) a thought that is also a science and not only a philosophy or a mysticism of the One: a *science-thought*, the pragmatico-theoretical thought adequate to the One such as it is *according to* the One. Under these two headings, non-philosophy distinguishes itself from a philosophy or even from a simple science without ceasing to maintain certain precise relations with them.

Although our guiding formulas come from a philosophical or ontological origin, here they take on a sense that is philosophically unprecedented, both in terms of the ultimate "object" of non-philosophy (the One as in-One and not as Being or as convertible with it) and in terms of "method" (also a science rather than a philosophy alone). Equally, a sense that is scientifically unprecedented by its cause (the One) which is rather "philosophical" by its tradition and does not find itself within the being and its properties which comprise the theme of existing sciences; and which neither finds itself in solitude in the "science of Being" or ontology.

It is, though, a science-thought that is instituted, and the ultimate objective is to create a new discipline rather than a supplementary philosophy that would be more critical, for example, than deconstructions; and whose aspect of "science" would be more "empirical", but always ontic or even ontological. We could say: a *first science* for which the priority is consequently of a different nature, without primacy or hierarchy, than that of *first philosophy*. Or moreover: a *theory, unified-in-One, of science and philosophy that is in its essence as much a science as a philosophy*, which is different than an enriched philosophy as in Husserl. Unlike Husserl, in effect, and ultimately unlike nearly all philosophers, we do not first continue to assume philosophy as valid in order to correct it in the sense of rigor, in order to critique traditional ontology with a view to transforming it from within its proper *telos* into a "science". Not philosophy-as-rigorous-science, not even a positive rigorous science of philosophy (of philosophical statements on the One or of ontology), but a science-thought identically, something other than their synthesis. Not a reform, but a new usage of philosophy and science deduced from the unseparated identity of the Real.

We know that no philosophy begins without demanding the moving duality of names that designate it: of "general metaphysics" and "special metaphysics"; of "ontology" and "theology"; of "metaphysics" and "philosophy"; of "system" and "existence"; of "philosophy" and "thought"; of "logocentrism" and "deconstruction"; of "philosophy" and "science", etc.—often in order to critique the first by the second, substituting the second for the first or sometimes vice versa. Nonetheless, these are the hierarchical carvings on the unique body of philosophy; these dualities are in reality trinities, philosophy returning a second time as instance of ultimate synthesis. Invariably subsisting in a certain connectivity of first terms to second terms, a sort of enigmatic identity of the two states of thought, it must share in two absolutely unequal halves. If we demand a "non-philosophy", something other than the edification of a new system, of a new epoch, of a new philosophical science too, and furthermore, all things being unequal, then we oppose to all these solutions which never cease to traverse the orb in 2/3 terms or philosophy's world, the simple unilateral duality: *the Real determines the whole of thought without reciprocity, science and philosophy in their pre-nodal identity*, or moreover the theorem: *the Real and philosophy are only identical in-the-last-instance*. If "non-philosophy" is an old name which has given place to recent philosophical reclamations, it receives from this transcendental theorem a new sense, a heterogeneous usage in philosophy as much as in science. It traces the field of a "first science" which is the real content of the non-philosophical Idea. Without the incessant return to this theorem, the expression of "first science" gives place to the fantasy of a new synthesis of philosophy and science through a third term, "return to the things" of philosophy rather than departing *in* the Real. It posits the point and the type of identity of science and philosophy before their philosophical disjunction and poses it as function of the real-One which is never synthesis since it only acts under the form of this identity in-the-last-instance. First science abolishes the authority of philosophical or assumed first ontology, and does so without remainder, but not every ontology: this identity-without-synthesis of science and philosophy will be equivalent to a new ontology, but second, absolutely ordered by the real-One. Taking from the One its being-determined-in-the-last-instance, it presents itself under the form of a theoretical discipline which must be as much science as philosophy without being either one or the other, nor their assorted blendings (philosophy-as-science, philosophy-of-science, philosophy-in-science, science-of-philosophy); and of a *pragmatic* which only considers them from the side where they are transcendentally determinable by the One. Hence its object, an identity that we will call "science('s)-essence" and which is at once the object and the essence of first science.

Externally, non-philosophy, in this first effectuation, is thus a method for dealing with philosophical statements and scientific knowledges which brings together in this way the two intersections: philosophy/philosophy and philosophy/science. Precisely without falling into these or recovering them, it is from an inspiration that is *identically* and thus also *dually* scientific and philosophical in its procedures, its objects and its operations, in its ambitions. In one of its aspects, it is in a sense a scientific discipline of philosophy, a neighbor of its "history" and its deconstructions but distinct from them through its refusal to continue to treat philosophy philosophically. This treatment is never simple, but non-philosophy is something altogether different than one of its nuances. On the other hand, it no longer reproduces the classical relation of the authority of philosophy over science and its positivist and scientist inversions, philosophy-of-sciences, philosophy-in-science, epistemology and pragmatism, science of philosophy, etc., but delivers this relation from any hierarchy. This concerns constituting the datum "philosophy-of-sciences" in the domain of identically fundamental and regional objects for a theoretical and pragmatic discipline to be invented. This discipline must be sufficiently powerful to be able to "dominate" philosophy theoretically and science pragmatically, but it must also be sufficiently transcendental in order to respect and not dismember or "reduce" the one and sufficiently positive to respect the other.

This first science thus redistributes in this way the science/philosophy relations without being a simple scientistic and dogmatic reversal of their traditional relations which are globally those of ontological domination of philosophy over science, even when they are for example of deconstruction of the former by the latter, or with the aid of the latter. Science as we make a *theoretical usage* of it is neither a deficient mode or an ontological project, nor the Other of metaphysics, it is saved as such at the heart of unified theory, and saved from its philosophical servitude as much as philosophy itself is.

We will find a counter-proof to the validity of this project and its non-contradictory character in an interpretation/generalization of Gödel's enterprise *subject to its insertion as simple datum in the transcendental problematic of the One-of-the-last-instance and unified theory.* Among the possible interpretations of Gödel's enterprise, maybe this is not the most orthodox, but it is the least negative or least Kantian: *the problems of metascience* (that of arithmetic) *can be resolved but within the limits of science, inside of an effective practice of science.* Yet what we call first science is particular science, science-thought adapted to the treatment of philosophical discourse as metascientific. If we treat *all* philosophies, and not only epistemologies, as programs-of-grounding for science, moreover more generally than logistic and formalist programs, it is possible to discover a discipline that converts them in scientific terms and projects them in scientific problems, excepting their insertion, into a unified theory, and finally procures for them a solution that philosophies themselves cannot bring, being given over to an infinite "metascientific" drift. It is possible to consider philosophical statements: 1) as metascientific; 2) as objects inside a scientific practice to come; and 3) as destined to elaborate a knowledge of the science('s)-essence that evidently substitutes itself for the philosophical grounding of science (the grounding and its various historical modalities).

We do not doubt that this problem offends the sensibility of philosophers—first here we mean our very own...—since it creates a certain "resistance". But it has historical forms of realization that are more (Gödel) or less (Leibniz) scientific, thus more (Leibniz) or less (Gödel) philosophical. These "examples" suffice to justify within certain completely exterior limits this project and to show its viability. Resistance is included in the scientific relation, and more so within the non-philosophical relation, to philosophy. Non-philosophy is *de jure* badly formed, interpreted sometimes as a positivist and scientistic negation of philosophy, and sometimes as a new "philosophy of no" [*philosophie du non*], and even sometimes as a Spinozism (the misinterpretation which confuses the One-of-the-last-instance, as we develop it, with Spinoza's One-All). In reality it responds—this is the sense of the "non-Euclidean metaphor" to which we regularly return—to the following problem: to invent *and* discover a form of thought that is more universal than "Philosophical Decision" which will be what we agree to call, a little quickly, a "particular case", and also, perhaps more rigorously, a "model".

# When is "First Science" first? On priority-without-primacy

What does the One-in-One result in for the relation of the One, or better still of science-thought that is in-One, to philosophy? That the given One is also thought as given implies that thought is in-the-last-instance-in-One. In this thought at least and for it, for its immanence, the One thus absolutely precedes, without reserve or return, thought and philosophy *a fortiori*, and this thought in turn precedes, but less absolutely than the One itself, philosophy which cannot justify it, ground it or relate it itself to the Real. Non-philosophy nevertheless uses philosophy, but according to a certain order, assigning it functions from the outset as non-constitutive, occasional and second. Science-thought in its essence is a thought of order and by order, a "qualitative" discipline that denies nothing: it neither destroys nor nihilates [*néantise*], it identifies-in-the-last-instance science and philosophy, affecting the philosophy of the (non-)One rather than of not-ing [né-ant] or non-being.

The term "first" is not univocal and changes its meaning in passing from philosophy to science-thought. In "first philosophy" priority is also a primacy, hierarchy or domination, as such susceptible to a reversal and dis-order [*dés-ordre*]. "First science" retains only the *irreversible order, that is the order of the "last instance", in order to define Being in its relation to the One*. The term "first" can always be ontologically understood, first arithmetically then according to a theory of ontologically assumed numbers.

But its "ordinality" is no longer mathematical and regional here, or even ontologico-mathematical and fundamental: it is purely "transcendental" insofar as it deduces the immanent Real and adds nothing of the real to it.

In reality, "first" designates here the primacy-without-priority of the One over Being or thought, the fact that the One is radically autonomous and Being relatively autonomous. This character of the One's primacy, however, only receives its true sense in "determination-in-the-last-instance" as a concept of the causality of radical immanence and must be elucidated in this way. It gives its radical or unreserved sense to the term "precession", if not ambiguous and philosophically shared according to a reciprocal precession of the One and Being. "The One determines-in-the-last-instance Being or thought in general" signifies, we will say, 1) that being absolutely immanent to itself or in-One, 2) it precedes, not *within* the Real but *as* the Real itself, irreal Being or thought, transcendence in general, which is also in-One but which is no longer so in-the-last-instance (this is the organon of the force-(of)-thought), 3) without at all alienating itself in it or identifying itself with it, 4) but in being given just as it is (in-One) up to the most distant experience of Being.

The One thus inaugurates a transcendental order within which it does not alienate itself, an irreversibility into which it does not fall and which itself does not become again a reversibility. This order is *order-for…* Being, thought, etc.; but an immanent order that no longer *dominates* what it orders. The One is not "first", in the sense where it would itself be included in an order superior to it, a third and transcendent order that would overhang the Real. Because then it would be shared: half-first half-second with and by relation to Being; reciprocally first one in relation to the other and so sharing the priority, the One recognizing Being by its claim. It possesses *primacy* insofar as it immediately determines Being or thought in being *first*; but this determination itself is only transcendental, it is not real. Saying that it is first in relation to Being should not therefore here have a meaning for itself or for thought—here it is indifferent. There is only primacy *on the occasion* of Being and thus for science-thought of which it is the real cause: *if* Being presents itself to itself, the One has primacy in relation to it, but on the determinant basis of its essence. As for Being and its modes: Subject, *Dasein*, Givenness, etc., they are unilateralized by the One and forced to abandon their claim to be first (dominant in a circular hierarchy). *Science-thought is Commencement or is "first" in relation to "first philosophy" thanks to this primacy-without-priority of the Real.*

We are going to penetrate further into the structure of the unified theory of science and philosophy by describing their different aspects.

# Unitary theory and unified theory

Since this concerns two regions of objects, that is, philosophy and a region or all regions of knowing, unifying or reassembling these is a specifically philosophical task. Since it concerns a synthesis, or a system, or a resolution of antinomy or of an encyclopedia, unifying in these different modes belongs to the most constant teleology of philosophy—this is teleology itself. We will describe the invariant formal properties of this teleology under the name of "unitary theory" in the following way.

Synthesis, system, encyclopedia, gathering, all envelop the simultaneity of a circle or a reciprocal determination, which is more or less distended, slowed, differentiated, it matters little since here we are looking for invariants and they all come under the primacy of transcendence. The circle is the telos, sometimes broken, sometimes sketched out, of philosophy. Unity is the ongoing end, even under the form of a becoming, of a unity-becoming. Philosophy must become science (absolute, rigorous), science must let itself be determined, grounded, limited by philosophy.

This simultaneity assumes a duality of terms, a dyad or a contrasted pair (a philosophy and a region, two regions, etc.). The adverse parties are different in simultaneity: how to resolve this contradiction that is at the heart of the Philosophical Decision? Through hierarchy, difference of sense, of truth, of reality and of value. The philosophical dyad is *de jure* hierarchical or auto-positional, it is in a state of overseeing in relation to itself.

Philosophy holds the dominant place, science the dominated place. In positivism or scientism, the hierarchy is reversed or inverted; but it is still philosophy that dominates in anti-philosophy. The superior or dominant place is in effect always occupied by philosophy: within the unification or intersection of two regions, it is still philosophy as over-dominant, if we can put it this way, that triumphs, the satisfaction of the need to philosophize; the synthesis is made to the benefit of philosophy and this is what consummates the encyclopedia and enjoys it.

There is no unitary unification by philosophy or of philosophy with a regional knowledge without philosophy partially excepting itself from this synthesis, without it being an over-science rather than an ordinary science, an over-artistic or over-religious activity, etc. There is a scientific exception of philosophy which makes philosophy into this or into a science, not positive, not empirical, an absolute science through its object, its method, and theory of sciences. There is an ethical exception of philosophy which makes of it an over-ethics, an imperative superior to the categorical imperative itself, etc.

Philosophy thus leads to a double politics with regard to every regional knowledge and in particular to science. It manifests a *claim* to domination, legislation, grounding, critique; a claim under the form of a teleological project or *horizon*. But it must recognize the weakness of this claim which is always in the process of realization, because it must *receive* the regional given of science and because this reception is synonymous with finitude. Claim and finitude form a system and explain the anguish and precariousness of philosophy, its infinite pursuit of scientific naivety that it repels and which fascinates it.

Finally, it maintains with regional knowledges an invariant relation of difference *and* identity whatever the definition of these is, according to this system or that, be it rationalist, dialectical, differential, structural, reflexive—it matters little. Rather, what matters is that this relation be a blend, a mix or an amphibology and be, as synthesis of two contraries, *of a simple assumed and so unintelligible identity*. In spite of its rationalizations, at the heart of the relation of philosophy to itself or to science, there is a *black box*, an *unthought identity*, a technological, incomprehensible relation for which only the effect counts. Philosophy is neither a theory nor a practice, it is a technology—admittedly a transcendental technology—with theoretical and practical *aspects*. This could explain Heidegger's thesis on "techne" as the interminable fulfillment of metaphysics.

We will bring together all of these formal traits in a matrix, which will formalize them a bit more. We have said that Philosophical Decision is a matrix not in 2 terms nor 3 terms but in 2/3 terms; the 2 of the Dyad and the 3rd of the One (Unity of synthesis or of system); but the 3rd is divided or intervenes 2 times: it is identical to one of the terms of the dyad and distinct from it and from the Dyad. As such 2/3 or even 3/4 terms, the fractional if not fractal character of the dimensions of Philosophical Decision indicating that every term is divided here and here intervenes twice. *Auto-Position, auto-givenness or auto-nomination* (according to the idealist or phenomenological context, etc.): this is what we call the general and formal property of philosophy dividing/differentiating itself from itself and to relate itself or identifying itself with itself, of being in a fixed state of overseeing in relation to itself. This matrix explains *all* the preceding properties, particularly the traditional relations of philosophy and the sciences, whether that be philosophy-of-sciences, theory-of-science, philosophy-in-science, epistemology. We call this mode of unification by this matrix *unitary*. Philosophy is a *unitary theory* of knowing, whatever the dispersion or dissemination that it offers and that it sometimes opposes—this is "critique" and "deconstruction"—to the heavy identities of metaphysics. We have in effect defined the unitary matrix insofar as, if it no longer completely envelops deconstructions, it is still assumed by them, simply repressed, sometimes "broken" but always conserved under the form of debris. The auto-(position, givenness, nomination) signifies that philosophy poses or reposes as assumed in themselves, or the Real itself, philosophy, science and their relations. Therefore it subtracts them from the real-One phenomenon—through this claim.

Let us now describe all other relations of philosophy and science according to a "dual" matrix (not binary, not ternary or trinitary, that is philosophical, mixed or fractional).[1] Rather than a *unitary* theory, we will say *unified* theory: this formula signifies first that philosophy itself is integrally unified (by the Real) without being still unifying in the sense philosophical idealism wants; a party without being still and once again judge and exception; a simple "phenomenon" and no longer "in itself"; reduced and no longer real. The relations of philosophy and science will be shattered; this other logic, with its own transcendental reduction, will have the effects (produced rather than researched) that we will describe in this way.

Science and philosophy do not stop being what they are, each in turn and for its own part, as autonomous practices and such that they give themselves with their respective claims always considered here as reduced phenomena. Effectively, they stop being "in themselves" or philosophically blended, denatured and compromised the one by the other: not a becoming-philosophy of science, not a becoming-science of philosophy; not a grounding of the one and a pollination of the other, all operations that form themselves in the element of auto-position (etc.). Generally, there is no pretension to intervention of one into the other; so no longer hypotheses on their essence or on what they are "in themselves".

More positively, they simultaneously enter into another usage, a usage that is not philosophical, that prohibits their intervention in their efficacy and their assumed "essence". This concerns making a usage of *simple phenomena*, under the conditions of phenomenal immanence, with the aim of constituting, with their provisions and with what remain simple provisions, the new order of science-thought or first science. It entails a pragmatic of science and of philosophy that takes them in an equal or equivalent manner, because it takes them insofar as they are simple phenomena after bracketing them from their real claims and so from their conflicts. Of course we have to determine who, what is the "subject" that can make this pure transcendental usage, without teleology, of philosophy and science.

Evidently, the structure of hierarchy, domination and philosophical benefit, the structure of teleological horizon, of the horizontal type of opening and closure, finite and infinite, are invalidated and no longer enclose thought. Philosophy and science are only its provisions, not determinations of thought's essence. On this basis, we introduce democracy between philosophies and between philosophy and the sciences, arts, ethics, etc., and we give a democratic solution and an a priori universal peace to the "conflict of the faculties". The absolute condition for democratic peace in the sciences is the abandonment of philosophical sufficiency or claim, of auto-sufficiency, for their heteronomous or "non-philosophical" usage.

These are the invariants of these new relations. We know the non-philosophical matrix, that of determination-in-the-last-instance or identity of unilateral duality, is capable of realizing them. What are the forms this syntax now takes concretely; 1) from the point of view of or according to the One or Identity?; 2) from the point of view of or according to, on the other hand, Duality, which is to say the philosophy/science given? The vision-in-One does not think by itself, it does not act directly on philosophy and science, but only by the means of an organon that is a realization of this syntax from the perspective of Identity. This organon is the force-(of)-thought, which is to say the identity in-One of unilateral duality or moreover the clone of radical immanence and the element where transcendence moves itself. In fact this too is equally radicalized or reduced to its core of pure exteriority. The force-(of)-thought is the means by which the real-One can act on philosophy, and is as such an aprioristico-transcendental function which takes root in the real without itself being a real property susceptible to enriching or modifying the One. It is transcendence "inside" [*dans*] immanence or rather "in" [*en*] immanence, which is to say in the mode of immanence rather than in that which would still be a quasi-internal space.

Now from the perspective of material, which is to say given "philosophy/science" opposite the One, this couplet takes the form of Duality. This duality proper to material is a mode of determination-in-the-last-instance. 'science" and "philosophy" are no longer considered "in themselves" but in terms of themselves each as *provisions* of the order of thought. They remain qualitatively distinct, precisely no longer blending or denaturing each other without however giving rise to an atomization, a simple disconnection or anarchy. They are now linked in what we call a *uni-lation* which does not make a synthesis, system or encyclopedia. These relations are precisely no longer hierarchical: that philosophy as provision is absolutely autonomous (to simplify this) and that science as provision is relatively autonomous is no longer a relation of domination or of primacy, but rather the condition for an equal but heterogeneous usage, heterogeneous in democracy, of philosophy and of science.

We call "non-philosophy" that usage according to the force-(of)-thought and no longer philosophy, a usage that is consequently not auto-philosophical, not auto-positional, of the provisions of philosophy and science or any other region. Because the philosophical synthesis of philosophy and science is the material of non-philosophy, this is non-philosophy-of-sciences rather than simply "non-science". Of course, non-philosophy is concretely a work of transforming philosophical statements, and the scientific statements they contain, according to the force-(of)-thought which suspends or brackets their auto-positional aspect. It consists in establishing, everywhere there is a circular synthesis, which is to say everywhere, such a relation of determination-in-the-last-instance and consequently modifying, at the risk of evident contradiction, the concept of philosophy, of such a philosophy, and that of science, of such a science or such a theory.

The benefit of this "method", of this thought rather, is to deprive philosophy of its transcendental claim over the Real and to tightly fasten it to experience; to transform it into a simple a priori (itself non-philosophical since it is a priori *for* philosophy…) of every possible experience. Philosophy and science, fundamental and regional, are *identical without confusion*, in the respect of their own autonomy, they are *identical in unilateral duality*. We will not say, then, that the regional is immediately identical to the fundamental but that it is so in-the-last-instance and that it is the relation of duality of the regional to the fundamental, a relation which assures the relative autonomy of the regional, which is identical to the fundamental *within* transcendental identity. Philosophy—to simplify here—is a simple a priori for science, but this is now a priority without primacy or domination. In what is no longer a new alliance of philosophy and science, philosophy is no longer judge and party, but simply a party like science, and yet this democratization is not confusion nor abstract equalization. Philosophy has stopped auto-positing and overseeing itself; but in the same blow its connection to experience is stricter. It no longer has the claim of dominating or transcending science, but it is assured that, for this thought at least, non-philosophy, that *if* there is science, *then* its identity with it is determined-in-the-last-instance. It captures a universality or a generality that it did not spontaneously have. On its part, science is assured, in spite of its usage or because of it, its relative autonomy or its irreducibility to philosophy. Determination-in-the-last-instance grants relative autonomy, this is a syntax of liberation, of unchaining regional knowledges, and a term given to philosophical anguish and single-mindedness, to its triumphalism for which it pays with the permanent pathos of "essential" failure.

Every unitary theory will be utilized, and utilized by a unified theory rather than by a new unitary theory.

Every synthesis will be downgraded, and downgraded by determination-in-the-last-instance rather than by a new synthesis.

Every encyclopedia will be dispersed, and dispersed by a chaos of identities rather than disseminated or differed by a new encyclopedia.

# Introducing democracy into thought

A thousand solutions—as many philosophies—can be brought to the problem of the relation of philosophy and science. But a great distinction traverses them and distributes them into two groups according to the predicables of "difference" and "identity". Of course the majority of these solutions blend difference and identity according to diverse and singular propositions but it is precisely these blends that we will regroup under the invariant of *epistemological Difference*. Sometimes, difference is simply dominant here; identity determinant, but an identity itself penetrated by difference (most classical and modern philosophies of sciences, philosophies-in-science and epistemologies of all types—reflexive, idealist, realist, empiricist, etc.). Sometimes difference is determinant and identity is simply dominant, here again in assorted ways (philosophy and science according to Nietzsche, Bergson, Wittgenstein, Deleuze, etc.).

The other invariant, that of determinant identity without difference but not subsequently without duality, knows three main types of realization. A weak type, where the identity of philosophy and of science is again penetrated by difference and which thus partially overcomes the preceding invariant (Schelling and, among recent and contemporary philosophers, Meyerson and Thom). Then, a strong and strict type in which philosophy or one of its parts immediately and strictly identifies itself, without difference, with science or with a science par excellence (mathematical equation = ontology). In the case of this figure (Badiou), difference disappears in general, and first under the "ontological" form (being is reabsorbed into Being and gives place to a materiality of the idea or an idealization of the material, the mathematical being the science which allows it to be thought possible to posit Being without object, without particular ontic reference); but a residue of difference reappears outside of the identity of science and philosophy under the form of a cut between ontology and philosophy, a cut that gives place to the projection of philosophy as "meta-ontology".

Finally a third type, the purest, is possible, posing that the strict identity-(of)-the duality of science and philosophy is not really radical and egalitarian, forbidding that philosophy recapture science beyond this identity and only surreptitiously reconstitutes difference if, instead of doing so to benefit Being at the expense of beings—and thus finally of science—it does not identify itself with Being but remains in itself as pure transcendental, and overcomes the Difference of Being and beings in its two senses and consequently overcomes epistemo-logical Difference. An identity which, as transcendental, claims itself univocally to be of Being and beings, and of philosophy and science, and of the fundamental and the regional. It annuls the persistent privilege of Being or of philosophy (even as simple "meta-ontology") or the hierarchy of philosophy and science in some sense in which the philosophers overturn or invert it. In a comple-mentary manner, philosophy ceases to legislate over science (to ground it, reflect on it, critique it, legitimate it, etc.) and science symmetrically ceases to count for philosophy as model or transcendent norm of rigor, but also of reality or of the representation of the Real (whether ontic or ontological). However, a supplementary condition is necessary, rendering this solution admissible: precisely a condition of reality such as it prevents the transcendental identity of science and philosophy from sinking into one another then into their relations of difference and antinomy, but also such that it gives this identity a transcendental function of the relation to these terms—relation to… but without blending with…—a non-mixed relation to science and to philosophy, without reciprocity. Only an identity that is real this time, the very instance of the Real that is neither beings or Being but One-without-Being, can bring together these two demands. We will call this third solution, the most radical, the "unified theory" of science and philosophy.

A concept of democracy which would not already be political and so philosophical, which would apply to thought itself and to all its givens—not theoretical democracy but democracy of theory itself—would allow a new manner of "resolution" of the traditional antinomies of philosophy with experience, art, ethics, technology, mysticism, science, etc. What could an *equality* for example of philosophy and science which is not a mode of their philosophical hierarchization or an avatar of epistemo-logical Difference mean? Philosophy assumes, from the sole fact of its existence, this problem to have been resolved but contents itself to redivide the hierarchy or to reduce the antinomy, to fill it with itself with a view to its implosion. It empirically gives itself philosophy and science in a confrontation of disciplines "in themselves" or auto-posited and separated (whether exclusively or inclusively), a duality that it has already overseen—at once judge and party, so much so that it reproduces the antinomy and reroutes it to a difference and a synthesis that is not a *concession* made to experience, to science for example. It only considers itself equal with science in order to except itself too from their relation and in order to posit itself as legislator or founder of the other term and of its assumed relation to the Real, a relation which it claims to own. For one level, inferior to and productive of itself (the production of knowledges), it is co-determined by science, but for another (sense, truth, the value of knowledges), it is the superior synthesis, by itself, of itself and of science. On the other hand a "unified theory" is egalitarian, of an equality definitively without difference but through identity of-the-last-instance.

Negatively, this is not, though, a question of coming back to philosophy under science, as a direct object of a positive science either given or still to come and manifesting a special affinity with the real One. The works comprising my "Philosophy II" assume a privileged affinity of radical immanence and science, inverse and complementary to the thesis of the affinity of radical immanence and philosophy (Michel Henry) which casts science out from itself. These two theses remain, the latter, resolutely philosophical, the former impregnated in spite of itself with philosophical sufficiency. The same principle, the Real as radical immanence, is still here—perhaps always—consequently interpreted in both cases as transcendental and thus claiming to be reciprocally either from philosophy or from science. *Théorie des étrangers* on the other hand inaugurates a rectification of the non-philosophical problem, outlined here, where the vision-in-One is indifferent—but without exclusion—to science as much as to philosophy, without however being "non-science" in the spontaneous philosophical sense of this expression, but simply *non-philosophy (-of-science)*.

Positively, this is a question of coming back to philosophy *with* science as an equal partner, within the transcendental order of non-philosophy which no longer recognizes hierarchy or difference. The democratic equality we are looking for is neither difference as such of these two terms nor the residue of equality which the leveling of this difference or this hierarchy could give objective appearance, an equality which remains in itself an inequality. More generally non-philosophical democracy can no longer be a *principle* or a *telos*, a *first equality*, which is to say auto-positional, and finally an equality of essence or which returns to philosophical difference. Equality is only realized as such, conserved too, if it is an effect rather than a principle; an effect of a radical identity rather than an auto-positional principle. The true equality, that which does not return to difference, is the equality of transcendental identities which each claim to be terms of an antinomy. Neither egalitarian politic of thought nor political pragmatic of thought, equality here is a non-political concept because it is first non-philosophical. This transcendental politic of science and of philosophy, that is to say philosophy, must cede to a pure transcendental pragmatic of their relations.

Not philosophy of science, of philosophy, of their relations; not science of philosophy, of science of their relations: their unified theory begins with the renunciation of forming hypotheses on their essence in itself as separate experiences of thought, exclusively or inclusively, but in each case included in a relation giving place to antinomy, and with the symmetrical renunciation the imagining of a science taking them as its object. "In itself" designates here the assumed real independence, by auto-positioning, of philosophy, of science, of epistemo-logical Difference. Non-philosophy opposes this to the reduction of these transcendent positions to radical phenomenal immanence in which the force-(of)-thought spontaneously replaces itself and abandons the assorted experiences of thought to their "private" delirium. Radical phenomenality can no longer be codetermined by its essence either by philosophy or by science, nor by their spontaneous or unitary relations. However, the force-(of)-thought, when it would only be for thinking itself and forming statements of knowledge over immanent structures, is condemned to return to two sole experiences of thought which we dispose of, philosophy and science, and to return to these in an equal manner, having renounced the respective privileges each is assumed to have over the other.

Non-philosophy as first science is the manifestation of the essence-(of)-philosophy of philosophy and identically of the essence-(of)-science of science, which is to say the aprioristico-transcendental identity of each of these opposing terms, through which they are truly equal and escape from the antinomy or the war in which they both serve. "Non-philosophy" does not denote a refusal of philosophy in favor of science—because in effect *from this point of view* non-philosophy must also be non-science—but the just denomination of a discipline where the "philosophy" side *will have* wanted to dominate the "science" side, thus the *objective appearance* of a reversal of domination which is not constitutive of the essence of the force-(of)-thought but outside of the sphere of the material. The true content of non-philosophy is rather the unified theory *for* philosophy and *for* a region = X, for the fundamental and the regional.

From a terminological point of view, "unified theory" designates, then, the new regime of philosophy torn from its "fundamental" domination over the regional; its "regionalization" or its "localization" through its identification (to) regions of beings, its specification, its quasi intuitive materialization, then. Materializing philosophy through experience, but transcendentally, in a manner that is ultimately non empirical or philo-sophical: this is the sense of a unified theory that introduces the possibility of generalizing equations of the mathematical = ontological type beyond these last two alone. As for "non-philosophy", this term indicates rather the fully fledged regime, universalized or generalized without reserve, which is to say aprioristico-transcendental, which is where philosophy, too, enters, though not pragmatically, and in the order by which its statements serve to produce more universal statements. They are in effect delivered here from the philosophical postulate which claims that to every real = transcendent X, meaning to that which is postulated as the Real by philosophy, corresponds one and only one adequate thought (called "philosophy"), such that the Real itself, now defined as immanent throughout, does not correspond to any adequate philosophy within thought and does correspond to an infinity of statements which are adequately non-philosophical by definition. This is the order of non-philosophical a prioris, manifested by the aprioristico-transcendental force-(of)-thought, an order in which philosophy is radically universalized outside of itself.

# Sense and limits of this formula: "New Science" rather than "New Philosophy"

Why should we label "science" rather than "non-philosophy" a discipline which claims to identify, in-the-last-instance only, science and philosophy and sets between them an equality that the tradition of their conflictual relations has regularly refuted? Why keep the term "science" if the vision-in-One effectively adds nothing to its concept and to that of philosophy, if by their identity it undifferentiates them before dualyzing them? Why does thinking from the One, which can call itself "non-philosophy", not accompany a "non-science"? In order to justify that it could give place to a formula like "new science" rather than to a new philosophy *despite* the inclusion of "essence" in the very object of this discipline, let us go back to what is given: from the One of course, but above all from the material, from the region of "objective phenomena" of the new theory. Moreover, these *data* are generally given under the form of the philosophical kind of discourses, and these discourses relate themselves in a privileged or constitutive way to science, this being as to their repression. The general structure of these *data* is the *mixed-form* of Philosophical Decision (Dyad + One), but co-determined by the science that philosophy itself allows first as its Other. From there follows the general relation of conflictual hierarchy that it maintains with this Other, where philosophy takes the dominant place, menaced by the metalanguage of science. It could be that this concerns an already philosophical interpretation of this relation, perhaps: this is the indication or symptom that is given to us outside of the One which, from itself, brings no such thing, no material. Philosophy is not a formal guise thrown over science; it is rightfully *philosophy-of-science* and *philosophy-in-science*. Even as "first" and as "fundamental" ontology, philosophy maintains here a relation of essence or a constitutive relation, epistemology being only a supplementary folding of this relation. Non-philosophy only gives itself science through the medium of philosophy-of-sciences, it does not hypothesize (still philosophically…) on its pure "essence" or its "in itself": this is why it is non-philosophy and not "non-science" in the same way.

On this basis, three interpretations can be imagined which we must be careful to avoid.

A simple reversal of philosophical hierarchy, the dominant place passing from philosophy to science. This inversion of the primacy conserves the hierarchy or mixture, the determinant essence of philosophy, even when science becomes dominant, as in logical or sociological positivisms. Moreover, the One-of-the-last-instance by definition excludes this solution which autonomizes the philosophical type of reversal, assumes it constitutive and returns to a positivist metaphysic still present in the formula: a science-of-philosophy, as it is spontaneously interpreted.

A logical identification of science and philosophy, the One being understood, in its effect, as a formal identity of the A = A type, apparently opposing itself to hierarchy and effacing all difference. The theme of equality or peace between science and philosophy always risks being interpreted in terms of an equality through logical identity simply abstracted—but thus dismembered—from the mixture of the Philosophical Decision, which is the sole concrete. In a first science, to the contrary, hierarchy is undoubtedly raised from the One or "unilateralized", but the residue left by the mix is not simple identity, still from a mixed origin, of terms (their logistic reduction), this is their transcendental "Unidentity". Moreover, this is not a real but a transcendental clone of the One in as much as the One itself does not provide any material (nor any form), but for this it must completely rely on philosophy. So it is not an empty form for philosophy, since a form is never as indifferent to its matter as the One can be—this is not a formalism. Unidentity integrates with the suppression of the nature of the auto-positional double that philosophy gives to its relations to science.

The synthesis of these two preceding solutions is "deconstruction", a general title for great contemporary philosophies (Wittgenstein, Heidegger, Derrida). Their principle is as follows: the reversal of philosophical hierarchy does not remain in state (metaphysics of logical and sociological positivisms); it is included in and limited by an identity that is undoubtedly not only logical but real and metaphysical (nonetheless it interiorizes or "overcomes" logical identity). What distinguishes these from one another is the acuity of alterity given to differ(e/a)nce until it is forced to protrude from unity, but always in or as a margin of unity, and the corresponding destruction of metaphysical unity. But they doubly conserve philosophy's authority: through the reversal, always assumed real or constitutive of its primacy, and through the still metaphysical and transcendental unity in which they include and limit this inversion. They remain on this side of the promised land of the One-of-the-last-instance and only glimpse it from afar.

Unified theory poses and resolves the problem by other means, no longer philosophical or even deconstructive of philosophy. The vision-in-One of the philosophy/science hierarchy simultaneously gives place to a "unilateralization" and a "unidentification" of this hierarchy always considered in these two terms, the only materials upon which its transcendental effects are exercised, rather than a term by term reversal inside the mix. They both act on the hierarchical relation rather than on the supposedly separate terms. However, the problem of conservation arises again in this operation of a relation, if not a difference at least of a certain relative heterogeneity of the status of science and philosophy (without still being constitutive of the identity of the real-One). Insofar as the One is no longer logical identity and no longer either its interiorization in the very concept of philosophy, this difference would have to take another form and receive another status. Undoubtedly the two transcendental effects together bear on the mix itself, but this formula remains ambiguous and undetermined. The mix does not only put philosophy and science into an objective relation of dyad, it is under the authority of philosophy which returns as One-of-the-Dyad, so much so that philosophy's function is itself divided: it allows science to govern, it says, but pretends to reign over it and, as Principle of Sufficient Philosophy, "posits" the whole of the mix. However, if its unilateralization really affects this very claim or the philosophical authority of the mix, it still can only conserve the two terms and their necessary relation, albeit a new one, such that this unidentification can only equalize them through the materials of a philosophy/science hierarchy *by allowing a reversal of science/philosophy from now on in the state of objective appearance bound to the material and projected as support of the new relation.* Since transcendental causality only has this hierarchy as material, it extracts from it only an essence-(of)-science whereby science seems to be the orienting, polar object of the whole. It also brings with it an objective appearance of the inversion of authority, and of the only authority, of philosophy in favor of that of science.

So "identity" and "reversal" no longer blend as in deconstructions; nor do they balance or hierarchize themselves. The unidentity and unilaterality that are substituted for them form the real core of the operation and of its outcome but it is as having enveloped this objective appearance since the One only exercises transcendental causality and does not *effectively overcome, which is to say in its effectivity*, the philosophical hierarchy but only "reduces" its validity. This appearance reflects or redoubles itself, under the effects of this transcendental reduction, the reversal of its contents. Determination-in-the-last-instance was never a philosophical causality, by first or constitutive reversal and displacement, but it pushes them back to the furthest periphery of the process in the name of objective appearance.

So it is not without reason, it is only through simplification, that we speak of non-philosophy, in its first application, as a new science rather than a new philosophy. Far from proceeding to a reversal of philosophical authority, still internal to the Principle of Sufficient Philosophy, a positivist reversal, it only inverts and simultaneously displaces the philosophy/science hierarchy on the new basis of their identity-in-the-last-instance. This is the real and theoretically valid content of one of the initial guiding ideas of this research: *a science or a theoretical domination of philosophy*, a project that had to be detached in this way from its philosophical interpretation.

# The philosophical, scientific, and mystical

How, these principles put forward, is the problem of philosophical, scientific, and mystical relations resolved?

We distinguish mystique and the mystical [*la mystique et le mystique*].[2] Mystique is an experience of the soul's identity with transcendence. It therefore entails transcendence *within* a certain immanence, a mix of the two; it does not separate the soul from transcendence through a real mode but rather ties it to transcendence; finally it makes immanence a property or attribute of the relation of the soul and of God rather than a subject-essence as such. On the other hand, we call the mystical a real and actual essence, an already-performed-without-performation as we will call it, an absolutely autonomous instance rather than an attribute, property, event or relation. This essence therefore no longer involves transcendence, rather it excludes it absolutely. The "reduction" of the soul is confused with this essence; it is not immanence to transcendence, to a subject or a substance, to the Soul or God, but (to) itself. So much so that the mystical is never an *on this side or a beyond*, a phenomenon of frontier or limit, or even of the beyond of the limit as it is in Wittgenstein. The mystical is a "subject", more rigorously still: it is the real content of the Ego and that which determines the subject that is the force-(of)-thought in-the-last-instance.

The mystical is not in front of us, far from us, or close behind, virtual or potential, demanding reversal, conversion, return or turn. It is in-us or rather it is us who are actually in it, in-mystique or in-One as the One itself. Moreover immanence (to) itself, not being a property or a relation, is the Real itself insofar as it is absolutely distinct from and even indifferent to empirico-ideal reality, which is to say to what we call effectivity. Vision-in-One is a radically unreflected experience-(of)-itself, not even an "auto-affection" but the Affected-before-all-affection, the Given-before-all-givenness, the Manifested-before-all-manifestation. In contradistinction to mystique, here we postulate an absolute autonomy, the Real itself, of the mystical experience in the sense whereby it is the mystical that is the core-in-the-last-instance of all possible experience. Conceived thus, the Real radicalizes the famous mystical indifference to the World which it takes as indifference to philosophy and to science and which it gives, as we will see, a transcendental bearing. This indifference alone can explain cloning and determination-in-the-last-instance and this curious logic of unified theory, unified rather than unitary, this new relation to science and to philosophy.

The mystical in effect does not act directly on science and philosophy but acts through its organon, the force-(of)-thought. Through this, it does not determine them in-the-last-instance separately, as we have said, but does so in their relation, itself unilateral. It grounds another usage here; another pragmatic which in particular avoids their confusion or blending and which recognizes their relative autonomy in heterogeneous practices. In determining the philosophical and the scientific *only in-the-last-instance*, the mystical destroys mysticism [*le mysticisme*] in general and that which, much the same, is at the base of this amphibology, the philosophies-of-science, epistemologies, programs of the grounding of science, and finally, "encyclopedic" type projects which we know to be the telos of almost all philosophies. The work of the mystical is a solely "transcendental" work; that of mystique is a "metaphysical" one, which claims to modify the essence of the Real through thought. This solely transcendental and not real usage of the mystical as being, the only Real, allows the elimination of the voluntary idealism of philosophy, the secret or more or less spontaneous positivism through science, but also, the mysticism of immediate philosophical and scientific collisions.

If the mystical does not operate directly on a new synthesis, if it does not join ranks with the philosophical and the scientific, no more so than One with Duality, if it is not "in play" in what it renders possible, *if there is nothing* of the One in this pragmatic, then it destroys every teleological horizon of synthesis, every philosophical and encyclopedic closure, and opens for us a new infinite dimension of thought. In any case it entails a practice generalizing the philosophical and scientific styles, a thought using, as its "logical" form, the essential means provided by science and philosophy (axioms and hypotheses, induction and deduction), and *the force-(of)-thought rather than logic* as transcendental organon. So much so that non-philosophy has its own "transcendental logic" and this is no longer the interiorization of logic in the transcendental—this mixture is dissolved—but the usage, purely transcendental in origin, of the instruments and logic provided by sciences and philosophies.

# Philosophy as resistance and as necessary reference of non-philosophy

The exposition of non-philosophy's givens and principal procedures necessarily returns to the philosophy from which it deduces, according to its needs, the "first names" (and identically, "first terms" and "proper names") and a priori structures. But this approach cannot be correctly conceived without the status of philosophy at the heart of non-philosophy being thematized for itself. Non-philosophy risks running aground once more on a "philosophy of radical immanence" when it makes use of philosophy with a view to formulating it without looking into the possibility of a thought in a theoretico-pragmatic mode, and without problematizing the necessary return to philosophy and its relative autonomy. Hence a double antinomic objection arises from philosophical resistance, insufficiently analyzed: 1) philosophy would be useless to non-philosophy which does not know how to get rid of it; 2) non-philosophy would still be a philosophy and consequently a contradictory project. In order to defeat both of these contrary objections together, we must recognize and elaborate *the relative autonomy* of philosophy and its material and to that end describe its auto-presentation (the Principle of Sufficient Philosophy) and the new type of "transcendental reduction" to which it is subjected in order to become non-philosophy's object, and finally—but later—the aprioristic knowledges extracted from this material. That an object be necessary to non-philosophy that will not have produced but will have received it, that non-philosophy precisely excludes philosophical idealism and is identically a science and a philosophy: these demands are contained within the idea of a *relative autonomy* of philosophy correlating to the *radical autonomy* of the vision-in-One, and posit that philosophy does not dissolve itself as if by magic in radical immanence—to be reborn surreptitiously as "philosophy" from this immanence. Non-philosophy provides the means of analyzing philosophical resistance and reality without simply denying them.

How is the non-philosophical problem of philosophy posed if, moreover, it must now start over in the philosophical and scientific resistance to the vision-in-One? It suffices to posit the double antinomy, variously acute, of science and philosophy and to make it a project or guiding thread: how are a science of philosophy and a philosophy of science possible, meaning how are they identically possible in a single gesture? How does thought come to science, how does science come to philosophy? Through a process of philosophical auto-reflection taking over science; through a transfer of the techniques of positive knowledge over philosophy? But such "solutions" to an antinomy, such limited objectives (give to science the thought it needs and to philosophy the science that it deserves) remain caught in the general antinomy of the epistemo-logos, complexify and divide it but do not invalidate it. In order to free itself from antinomies, thought must return to another operation that is invisible within the philosophico-scientific horizon of epistemo-logical Difference, so invisible that its place is occupied and concealed, rendered doubly invisible by the philosophies of the sciences, with their epistemological sub-products, and symmetrically by the attempts of "rigorous philosophy". When we pose the problem starting from science or philosophy, when we take a *theory of philosophy* or a *philosophy of science* as our directing thread or as a guideline, each time we must not content ourselves with problematizing the antinomy starting from itself, in the manner of philosophical "resolutions" that only comment on or interpret philosophy, but rather we must include not only its aspects but the antinomy itself within non-philosophy's transcendental identity, in a single and indivisible operation, a clone of the vision-in-One, without forgetting that this, on account of its radical immanence, frees in itself a relative autonomy of the antinomy. This is the principle of a *real solution* to antinomies, meaning the phenomenal filling of these "partially" empty guidelines: a *theory of philosophy*, a *philosophy of science*.

# How science comes to philosophy: The non-Husserlian paradigm

## 1

So let this be the first guideline, a *theory of philosophy*, a general demand inscribed within the most traditional philosophical sufficiency. The following are its philosophical and, "beyond" this, non-philosophical requisites:

a) The theory of philosophy must be taken from the sciences and not itself be a mode of philosophy, which excludes the well-known solutions which apply philosophy to itself by repeating its circle with the exception of a few mediations (meta-philosophy, metaphysics of metaphysics, doctrine of science, philosophy as rigorous science, philosophy of the history of philosophy, etc.).

b) However it must, although theoretical, not dismember or destroy the unity of its objects, its specific and original phenomenal characteristics irreducible to material, social, psychological, etc., objects; a "fundamental" object of Being which cannot be pulled down onto its regional objects (beings). Philosophy demands a science which is itself identically philosophical. Moreover, philosophy's identity is special; it takes the original form of repetition as *same* or *qua* and we will call "philosophy" every thought having the form of repetition or of the same and which auto-represents itself in the form of *auto-position* or *auto-givenness*; that which does not think itself according to radical identity but which directs it or intends it through repetition (transcendence, difference, distance, nothingness, etc.) and in this way divides it.

c) Consequently the identity of theory and philosophy within the theory of philosophy cannot be philosophical identity since it must also be a science of repetition or theory of the "qua". If this object is a *cogitable* being, the *cogitatio* that will think it will no longer be simple philosophical thought or scientific theory assumed in themselves and separated (exclusively or inclusively, either way, this is always about the antinomy). Correlatively the essence of philosophy will no longer be philosophical or scientific—this will be non-philosophizable or non-theorizable. In a general way, the real solution of the antinomy demands abandoning every thesis on the essence or the in itself of philosophy, or even science (every philosophy of philosophy, philosophy of science, science of science, science of philosophy), a thesis which would only be a hypothesis taken within the antinomy, and reproducing it. The idea is beginning to emerge that we cannot "exit" the philosophical antinomy except on the condition of having never entered into it. On what condition would the antinomy no longer be the element or principle of its solution, would it be pushed back from a single side of a new distribution? On what condition would, whatever their meaning, the hierarchy or difference of philosophy and science now be ordered according to the radical identity of the vision-in-One?

One possible solution, already itself at the limit of philosophy, would be the epistemological *deconstruction* of philosophy (if it had existed) but this is equally eliminated. It would effectively give a *determinant* function to *reverse* philosophy/science into science/philosophy; it would take its departure from within philosophy and would posit science (both result and motor of the reversal) as being the Real under the form of the Other, thus it would attribute to it a pure function of identity and alterity, not from One but from Other(-as-One), without having elucidated the One within its source and transforming it into a simple function of synthesis, admittedly empty of Being. The solution projected here is not this deconstruction positing the Other as *first* and so ordering itself in a simple reversal of the classical hierarchy. To the contrary, it lets itself be given identity as real and first and as unilaterally ordering, without reciprocity, every possible hierarchy and its reversal, the two antithetical solutions of the philosophy/science difference. *Non-philosophical identity is identity of science and philosophy but such that their distinction is not itself reflected in non-philosophy*. The phenomenal fulfillment of the injunction: a *theory of philosophy* thus passes through this *transcendental identity*, an identity which claims to be of science and philosophy, of their antinomy, without the second conditioning the first, comes to open it up and differentiate it [*différer*]. And so, along with a philosophy of philosophy, we avoid a positive science of philosophy, but also a simple deconstruction of philosophy.

d) A supplementary step in the research on conditions of the radical realization of a theory of philosophy must be made. Effectively, identity, radical as it is, is a transcendental identity because it claims an object and it surpasses this object's division. It therefore remains an ambiguous concept: in a philosophical regime a transcendental identity undoubtedly surpasses and overcomes a division, an opposition; but since it has no meaning or possibility except *through a relation* and *in relation* to that division, it does not surpass the division without still being secretly affected and determined by it, within which it finds more than a simple support. If we remain in the science/philosophy identity (or whatever other dyad, for example of the thinking thought and the thought thought), this dyad would always co-determine the identity which would still be *traversed* or struck by an ultimate cleaving, or which would immediately integrate with this divide, that being without reflection or reciprocal penetration: a kind of overwriting itself of the dyad, and of identity onto the dyad. Is this a type or figure of philosophy—still of philosophy—that effectively exists? In effect, it is the figure of philosophy that takes shape between Descartes and Michel Henry with the idea of transcendental identity of an Ego as auto-affection. The philosophical triad is still assumed to be constitutive through its immediate negation: valid or sufficient as immediately negated universal horizon. It is modified by its identification not with an extra-territorial *Other* (decon-struction), but with a radical *Identity* though still given in relation to the dyad, and so within transcendence: immanent, undoubtedly, but treated as an object, so not conforming to its essence of radical immanence. So then this Identity too quickly called "real" is only transcendental; integrates with a division which certainly does not reflect it in itself but which continues to constitutively or reciprocally adhere to it. Radical immanence remains deter-mined by a dyad or transcendence, and so by thought; it is then posited as opposed or in a restrictive way as *feeling* (of thought), as immediate reflection of thinking thought and thought thought, as auto-affection (Henry), so charged anew, as in all philosophy, with *grounding* transcendence and being in its service. This is a practice of *identity as overwriting of the dyad*: in place of the deconstructive ripping apart of the dyad, Descartes and then Henry proceed to its overwriting under the form of an Ego, but retain all the traits of the philosophical matrix (Dyad, One, or Identity at once internal and external to the philosophical matrix). What has changed? It is that within traditional philosophy, above all in the German tradition from Kant to Nietzsche and Heidegger, the philosophical triad is grounded on a division that is not simple or pure and abstract but on a "phenomenological distance" (reflection, intentionality, representation) which is *reflected* or *split in two*, where the terms and distance, inseparable, reciprocally mediate themselves (division as nothingness, nihilating [*néantir*], objectification, etc., as *mediate* negation). On the other hand Descartes and Henry de-mediatize or "immediatize" distance as pure distance or formal difference, abstract, without content; as *identity-(of)-division* or-(of)-phenomenological distance. So they do not exceed the level of a transcendental identity, they do not clear away the division or remain within the philosophical horizon—this is a "semi-philosophy"; this radical identity of philosophy is such that it is still philosophy itself which can think it rather than a non-philosophy. The theme of radical immanence is then nothing if it is not accompanied by the radical distinction of the Real and the transcendental.

If we eliminate these antithetical semi-solutions again—that of radical semi-immanence as much as that of deconstruction through transcendence—what is then possible? *To think radical immanence as the autonomous Real or as preceding transcendental identity itself, and not only every dyad and every phenomenological distance, even "reduced"*; to think it as already given on the mode of its own nature, thus without objectifying it by relating it to the support of distance however reduced; to think it as already given in its own mode and not in the mode of the dyad/duality. It must let itself be given a real Identity, not transcendental, not mixed, and think transcendental identity starting from itself. This is the theory of cloning.

# 2

Whether and how this solution is possible is still to be determined, along with what this question could intend to signify here. It alone can abandon philosophical circularity, whether naive, deconstructed, overwritten, and then radical identity could be given in-the-last-instance in its own mode instead of being taken in service of the Philosophical Decision again. As such it determines a theory—neither philosophical nor scientific separately or antinomically—a unified theory where the sides, the philosophical and scientific aspects, are unified in-the-last-instance by the Real rather than claiming to reunify a divided real in an idealist manner. If the scientific aspect, the aspect of knowledge, can be condensed in *theory* and the philosophical aspect in that of *usage* (as circular transcendental relation to experience or to things), two traits which are in extremity opposed in their phenomenal characters, we will say that non-philosophy is a *theoretical usage, a theoretical pragmatic*, which relates itself to the antinomies of philosophy and science. *What theoretical usage should we make of the epistemo-logical relations of philosophy and science*, and not only of philosophy or only of science separately? This is the formula which expresses the phenomenal replenishing of the old philosophical indications from which we have departed: "science of philosophy", "philosophy of science", etc. The state of things designated by these indications appears to be much more complex than these old formulations allow us to think philosophically. A certain type of analysis has shown that we must combine science and philosophy otherwise than according to the relations of epistemo-logical Difference. These old relations are nothing more than the materials of a new thought determined now through the vision-in-One. The first indications belong, through their evident sufficiency, to a transcendental appearance which is that of philosophy and had to be "overcome" and "critiqued" through their phenomenal fulfillment that finally causes the appearance of the blank and the repressed (repression of their foreclosure of the Real, if we can put it that way) which has given them this appearance of sufficiency. This repression is altogether *the non-philosophical essence of philosophy and of science*. Philosophy, the first to be questioned here, is in effect spontaneously *meta-philosophy*, philosophy *qua* philosophy, *identity directed by auto-position and auto-donation*. There is a form of non-phenomenological intentionality but widened to or co-extensive with every philosophy and with all of philosophy, an intention of identity which is at the same time the repression of transcendental identity and, more profoundly still, which explains this, is the negation of the philosophical foreclosure of every real Identity. Non-philosophy is, then, the radical phenomenal fulfillment of intra-philosophical maxims or injunctions, a fulfillment that rejects philosophical intentionality within the material or object and which, consequently, cannot appear as the achievement of a telos or a repetition. In a general way we will define unified theory, from this perspective of a being-science of philosophy, through the idea of a *non-Husserlian paradigm*, an allusion to the Husserlian solution whereby a philosophy would have to become a "rigorous science". "Non-Husserlian" signifies that the Husserlian paradigm is integral to the non-philosophical project and is consequently transformed under the conditions of "unified theory".

# How thought comes to science: The non-Gödelian paradigm

The second indication, antinomic to the first: how does thought come to science? Underlying this: how can philosophy, which auto-presents itself as titleholder of thought, speak of science without giving place to the traditional philosophy of science or to epistemology, and without reforming a philosophical antinomy out of these givens. If the traditional distribution of the relations of philosophy and of science is made under the ultimate authority of philosophy even when it concerns transforming philosophy into "rigorous science", if consequently philosophy always takes itself as having the position of meta-science, another economy of their relations is possible which equally admits an autonomy of thought for science and a rigor for philosophy without returning once again to the predominantly philosophical forms of their blends. As before, however, we can and in this sense must move on from these hierarchies and their reversals then, once again, posit the radical identity of science and philosophy in order to infer the intrinsically thinking character of science or of what it becomes within this new sphere, non-philosophy. Why this apparent detour? The initial or symptomatic indication of "philosophy-of-science" must also, and in whatever way, be phenomenally fulfilled or "performed". But it is possible still to reverse the normal sense of epistemo-logical Difference, to posit in an autonomous manner, which is to say from science, the specific problem of a thought belonging to science and which consequently begins by limiting the traditional project of philosophy-of-science. To this end, we use the Gödelian model, transposing it onto our more general problem, that being the idea of a particular science which takes as its materials these traditional relations between philosophy and science, or their canonical form, that of epistemo-logical Difference wherein philosophy presents itself as foundational meta-science, thus making meta-science into the object of a new science. Now, this is only the first step in the construction of a so-called "non-Gödelian" paradigm which, instead of annulling its Gödelian form, includes it under the radically transcendental conditions of the unified theory. In one sense, we generalize Gödel's enterprise under the form of a telos defined as that of a science of meta-sciences in order to be able to apply it or to transfer it onto our problem. In another way, we give it a radical and purely transcendental reality by inserting it into the cadre of a unified theory of science and of philosophy. The constitution of a non-Gödelian theory of philosophy has in mind not only the project of a "science of philosophy" but also the phenomenal performing of the other indication, that of a thought belonging to science and which makes use of philosophy without being immediately and banally a mere form of epistemo-logos.

How does philosophy auto-present itself in terms of our new problem? Every philosophy presents itself as meta-philosophy or philosophy of an other or for an other. Claiming to be sufficient to the Real, it represents the Real for another philosophy, and consequently it is equally sufficient to other philosophies. This Principle of Sufficient Philosophy includes a modality under which a philosophy presents itself as meta-science or absolute science (real and authentic) of the "positive" and "ontic" sciences. This relation of auto-hetero-interpretation is the philosophical tradition itself. The Gödelian model allows us not only to treat this claim as the object of a science and to undertake here a critique of a scientific and no longer philosophical type, dissipating the confusion of meta-philosophy with a theoretical knowledge of philosophy itself, but demonstrates that this knowledge and this critique of philosophy and its foundational project is the work of thought rather than of science. To this end, it suffices to project philosophy as a meta-science within the space of the procedures of a science adequate to this type of object and simultaneously to include this enterprise under the condition of a radical identity or to relate it to the specific "subject" of a unified theory, the force-(of)-thought.

Let us then call *metascience* the philosophical or grounding type of discourse on science, and *metascientific* the set of statements of epistemologies, philosophies-of-science but also philosophies-in-science. In this manner we generalize a fundamental distinction of scientific practice, that of language-object and metalanguage; of arithmetic for example and metamathematics. Meta-scientific statements are characterized by their project of elucidating the essence of science, but first by their assumed power which is that of a relation of auto-objectifying what they speak about, statement-objects. This concerns philosophical transcendence: the correlation of the *meta* of meta-physics and the *object* objectified by it. We will call "epistemo-logical distance" the formal trait of "meta" or of objectification through which these statements articulate with the language-object and give it a spontaneous philosophical interpretation. The language-*object* here is finally—under forms more or less transformed or masked by scientific content—the correlate of *meta*-language. Meta-scientific discourses are thus structured by *epistemo-logical Difference*, by the reciprocal or reversible play of the *episteme* and of *logos*. Even under its logico-mathematical form, this distinction and this correlation appeared quite quickly under the form Hilbert and Russell gave them as formalist and logicist *foundational programs* of science, and then their "critique" by Gödel, as mixtures of science and philosophical decision, as programs of philosophical inspiration bringing epistemo-logical Difference into play.

Given this situation, to what does the constitution of a non-philosophy that *indicates* the keyword for a philosophy of science or epistemology, without completely thinking it, respond? Is the usage of epistemo-logical Difference not sufficient to the task of rendering science thinking—and rendering philosophy rigorous? One of the positive effects of Gödel's proofs was to cause the metascientific to appear as generally incapable of correctly posing the problem of science's essence and the necessity of "inverting" the operation. Instead, then, of assuming alongside all philosophies-of-science (including formalism and logicism) and philosophies-in-science around which all sciences revolve with more or less independence from the metascientific point of view, let us form the inverse hypothesis and posit that the army of metascientific discourses revolve around science or rather, that failing to revolve around them—itself a metascientific gesture—they unilaterally depend on it as simple phenomena for a new science to be constituted. Instead of making science into a philosophical *object* of the *meta*-scientific, let us make the metascientific into a new scientific object, a phenomenon for a science that will be adequate to it. In other words, let us constitute the epistemo-logical Difference, meaning the reciprocal hierarchy of science and philosophy, through a simple object or *datum*, a new science devoted to the essence of science.

Nonetheless analyzing and positing all the requisites of such a program—a science of meta-sciences—is sufficient to noticing that the Gödelian inversion, if it gives a certain chance to quasi-reflexivity or properly scientific thought, not philosophical but relating itself to philosophy, is itself only a possibility of the epistemo-logical antinomy and cannot be "overcome" unless this antinomy is destroyed, at least in its claims, by a radical identity, without analysis or synthesis, of philosophy and science which transforms this antinomy and its Gödelian version itself into material or *data* for a discipline *according to* this identity. Hence the idea of a non-Gödelian thought universalizing the Gödelian paradigm under the conditions of a radical identity and radical duality for philosophy and science and which would not be affected by their *relations*, their opposition and correlation—their antinomy. Science itself only thinks its essence of science if it can transform philosophy and meta-science into its object, but then it does not only include (by identity) science within philosophy (this is the route of philosophy to the theory of philosophy); it equally includes philosophy within science: this is what signifies essence, that is, what we call the *essence-(of)-science* or the *identity-(of)-science*, following the *essence-(of)-the philosophy of philosophy* or the *identity-(of)-philosophy*.

The "theoretical-unified" new world freed up in this way is thus that of the *identity-(of)-science*. It must constitute itself between the theoretical emergence of a new object—the *essence-(of)-science* (rather than that of Science or the sciences)—and the collapse of the claims of epistemo-logical Difference that structures meta-scientific statements. Another way of saying that non-philosophy, when it takes science itself and not only philosophy for its object, pronounces the theoretical invalidation of philosophy as auto-grounding and auto-position of *constituted knowing*, and of its epistemological byproducts. The criteria of science have never been and will never be philosophical, and the epistemological works of Popper and Kuhn join with those of Russell or Wittgenstein in order to constitute the meta-scientific "reserve" that non-philosophy exploits.

This is a new science because it has a new theoretical object: the identity-(of)-*Science*, the *essence-(of)-science* (which does not confuse itself with the invariant properties and operations of scientific practices) next to the identity-(of)-*Philosophy* or the essence-(of)-philosophy of philosophy. This no more concerns a science of existing sciences or scientific knowledge, which to this end would seek their essence, than a philosophy of science, but rather concerns a theory of this essence itself, a theory identically philosophical and consequently altogether non-philosophical. Philosophy gives itself Science/sciences under the form of local forms of knowledge or completed theories, of their end products, and infers from them, half-empirically half-aprioristically, their essence. This reflection on theories, methods, or forms of knowledge treated and posited by epistemology as empirical "fact" (*datum*) and/or rational "fact" (*faktum*) is excluded by non-philosophy; or moreover posited as "text" of the history of science assumed to be finished and sedimented. So a science of the *essence-(of)-science* rather than of scientific *knowing*, just as the identity-(of)-philosophy is not the whole set of the invariants of philosophical systems. If the real object of this science is "science itself" and no longer the scientific knowing produced and ready for consumption, this essence can itself no longer be of a kind philosophically assumed to be separate, an *eidos* or an Idea of the Platonic-Husserlian type, an a priori system of the Kantian type, a game of knowledge-power [*jeu de savoirs-pouvoirs*] of the Nietzschean type, a blend of sensible experience and logic of the Wittgensteinian and Carnapian type, etc.

Let us imitate for a moment the philosophies that love to identify the *telos* of science: what is the *telos* of science according to Gödel and moreover according to a non-Gödelian paradigm rather than according to Husserl? Gödel's major *theoretical* discovery is not in his theorems as results (a limitation of logicism) that philosophers hasten to capture and to fetishize, thus restraining its reach, but in the hypothesis—entirely positive—that a science can be really exercised over meta-scientific "phenomena". He discovers a new type of scientific quasi-reflexivity, precisely not reflexive in the philosophical sense, or those derived from it. This is a first form of science-thought, and it limits the metascientific (or meta-mathematic, structuralist, etc.) type of reflexivity. More universally still, and this is non-Gödelianism, science-thought as such, non-philosophy does not return to a Greco-occidental decision, but only to identity or to the intrinsic finitude of science as capable of thinking itself, and moreover, of philosophy as capable of becoming the object of a rigorous knowing. That science be *index sui* is the positive side of Gödel's genius such that we make use of it in the non-philosophical pragmatic, from which the "theorems of impossibility" at the encounter of the grounding of sciences take not only their exact range, which is to say scientific rather than philosophical, but more profoundly still, a universal range of real impossibilization of the relations of philosophy and science, of epistemo-logical Difference, in the name of the Real. No new "return"… a return to sciences against philosophy: this would be a new philosophical decision. But a departure within the actual or "performational" practice of the identity-(of)-science and-(of)-philosophy, in the discovery and invention of a new discipline which has the identities "science", "philosophy", etc., as its object. We will object that this type of project was precisely condemned by Gödel and his theorems. But what Gödel condemned was the claim of metascience, the philosophical type of grounding of the sciences. What he himself really practiced alongside this "condemnation" of any philosophy-of-science, philosophy-in-science and epistemology was the science of metascience, an effective science no longer using these metascientific formations other than with a view to describing the essence of science. What he did not do but left open is the constitution of a non-Gödelianism grounded on transcendental identity, which is to say the unilateral duality of science and metascience. And non-Gödelianism is not the simple prolonging of Gödel's work that would continue to determine it beyond itself: it is the identity of thought such as it determines a philosophical usage of Gödel, but a usage that is occasional and without philosophical appropriation.

Analyzed within this horizon, the formula "science of science" shows that which, as spontaneous meta-scientific statement, it dissimulates or represses: an absence, a *blank* identifiable not from the instance of science or of philosophy separately, which is to say antinomically, but from the instance of non-philosophy, specifically the instance of the Real. The repression of the philosophy of sciences and of the science of philosophy is evidently not knowing, it is their essence in as much as it signifies their transcendental identity and does not confuse itself with philosophical auto-position of complete knowledges. Philosophy seems to give way to essence, in effect positing the *Being* of science, but it bars science's phenomenal identity or splits it off from the auto-positional decision inherent in being. The *Being*-of-science is a manner of denying its identity or of subsuming it into exterior and transcendental forms: logico-formal (identity Principle) or logico-real (I = I). What thus is lacking in the indicative formula "philosophy of science" in order for it to be torn away from philosophical authority and its resistance is *the identity-(of)-science* or, more rigorously, the *Being-science-(of)-science*. These new formulas, entirely incomprehensible for philosophy and for that matter for epistemology, describe rather the point of departure of non-philosophy and the object in light of which it must operate as whatever discipline. We can formulate our project more clearly: *it concerns practicing a science of metascientific statements such that, on their part, inversely, they aim for—without reaching—the essence of identity-(of)-science*; thus treating them as the region of phenomena taken as object by non-philosophy. This is from two angles: limiting or inhibiting metascientific hubris, the philosophical idealism of any epistemology as inversely the positive treatment of philosophy; treating them also as materials in the production of knowledges relating to the essences-(of)-science and-(of)-philosophy.

All things considered, philosophy is much more and much less than a presupposition, it is a necessary object for science first of all, for science-thought next, but one which resists the rigorous knowledge we take from it; the complex object (as philosophy-of-science) whose occasion constitutes a theoretical new world. Only science-thought manifests the full extension of idealism attached to philosophy, a *hallucinatory idealism*—a sanction of the philosophical foreclosure of and by the Real—that defines a new variety, alongside "dreamer" and "visionary"... Our problem is not the traditional one: giving science the philosophy it deserves and giving philosophy the science it deserves, but giving philosophy the only science that is useful and necessary to it and which it nonetheless refuses. It is giving the antinomy of science and philosophy the treatment that really resolves it.

# Processes of unified theory

## Hypothesis and first names

A unified theory is always expressed in the identity of a so-called transcendental equation, not a mathematical one, which nonetheless is a quasi-scientific object. A philosophy on the other hand is expressed in a tautology or a repetition, for example the Cartesian and Husserlian ideal of "philosophy *as* rigorous science" and in general the "qua". In one case, identity is constitutive or given, in the other it is targeted or sought. The Platonic-Cartesian ideal is equivalent to a unified theory of science and philosophy only on the condition of being transformed and understood otherwise than it has been within the cadre of metaphysics as science.

Let us recall the facts of the problem. Two apparently contrary relations, but which form a system, the one not annulling the other, rule the globally philosophical relations of philosophy and science: 1) their alternative and thus reciprocal hierarchization or domination; consequently their status of exception for itself from their discourse "over" the other term: the philosophical exception of (to) science; the scientific exception of (to) philosophy—hence a reversible antidemocracy; 2) their reciprocal or circular conditioning, some gap or difference aside—hence an equality or democracy that is altogether "apparent", the objective appearance of a democracy of thought. This is the logic that the unified theory strives to eradicate by rendering it scientific, theoretical and experimental, in a manner intrinsic to philosophy, and rendering it philosophical, transcendental and pragmatic in a manner intrinsic to science, outside of their external and internal conditionings or epistemo-logics. Instead of the hierarchy of philosophy and science, and its various reversals, they must enter *together (on the basis of or from the materials of their philosophical hierarchy)* but outside of themselves into a relation of identity that is not synthetic but dual-unilateral. Philosophy cannot except itself from its discourse on science, and nor can science except itself from its theorization of philosophy. This will thus not be a blend of the two, a becoming-science of philosophy and a reciprocal becoming-philosophy of science, but rather what becomes here their antinomy: their transcendental equation philosophy = science, which generalizes this for example: ontology = mathematics. An equation that is philosophically and scientifically unintelligible and absurd, which assumes a particular "syntax" of the equation and a regulated transformation of its terms.

A unified theory being a philosophy just as much as it is a science must thus have the essential traits of a science. In particular it must without a doubt have a transcendental type of thought (or one which relates not to empirical objects but to Being or existence as a priori giver of objects), but such that it does not form a circle with the a priori or moreover with its objects, and such that it does not belong to the corpus of its objects, either. A science is not a dependent party of its objects and just as the idea of a circle is not circular, a science-(of)-philosophy cannot itself be simply "philosophical" without risking a vicious circle. A unified theory would be, then, as a science, a non "philosophy" in this sense whereby its statements do not obey the philosophical decision, always more or less circular. The theoretical demand in effect signifies that the unified theory must be *explicative* of epistemological Difference and must proceed by axiomatized hypotheses and by operations of induction and deduction of knowledges over this Difference.

But such a unified theory is only a science in as much as it is identically a philosophy, thus precisely a *transcendental* science that relates itself to knowledges of objects rather than to objects themselves. These hypotheses and these operations bear on the a priori structures relevant for epistemo-logical Difference. If these objects are precisely here science and philosophy as given in their blend, then this transcendental science will no longer hypothesize either philosophically or scientifically on this blend nor on its assumed terms in this state of "difference".

Based on these conditions, we are going to have to "construct" non-philosophical thought by using science and philosophy without purporting to say what they are in themselves.

Thought must have the nature of a hypothesis as much as a thesis, which is to say here (not *within* science) of a true theoretical organon susceptible to being verified or falsified, in various proportions, as field of experience or as *data*, but only in its empirical aspect or that of experimental hypothesis. It must itself be formed and induced starting from this field but all the same exceeding it absolutely as a discovery can do. Such a hypothesis is produced starting with the *data* of experience through an induction; but it must remain irreducible to these *data*, or implicate their transformative usage in a theory that really modifies the given theoretical field, or the field anterior to the formation of the hypothesis, which is to say always here the epistemo-logical field. It must be able to be transformed—verified and falsified—through a part of itself alone, and not as much by the experimental data as in their "occasion". Verification and falsification cannot touch the essence of this hypothesis, which is to say its nature of organon or its *hypothesis(-)essence*, since these two relations to experience, which thus form an epistemo-logical circle, belong to this essence and must thus be posited here as non-determining. Being verified and falsified by new epistemo-logical *data* can only happen on a superficial level, of support or of overdetermination only of the hypothesis, but not the fact that this is *by essence* a hypothesis. In a unified theory, there will be first and foremost the essence of hypothesis of hypotheses, of its transcendental identity, not of any particular or regional hypothesis of an exclusively scientific type, whose validity is strictly limited to a sole region of phenomena. Nor a dogmatic hypothesis, a philosophical *thesis* that certainly likes to think itself "fundamental" but that continuously modifies itself not only in its content but in its very essence of hypothesis, ceasing to be one in order to become an auto-confirmed totality (and for us, a simple datum to explain), and this is as a function of its contents or materials. In philosophy, the hypothesis is always annulled whether by verification or indeed falsification or philosophically by their system, while the hypothesis sought here never ceases to keep the hypothesis-form. It does not only form a circle, partial and relative, with its *data*, but remains *de jure*, as organon, a hypothesis in excess of these data and, as such, is neither verifiable nor falsifiable by them. It is in effect constitutive of an aprioristico-transcendental structure and of its aprioristic specifications which indeed refer themselves to experience but find there only a simple support or a necessary "occasion". Consequently, this relation to the empirical as support also excludes the simple unilateral (though direct) verification/falsification, term by term, of the regional scientific hypothesis through experiment [*expérience*], as such a relation of adequation or of contradiction; as well as the relation of conditioning reciprocal with the experience [*expérience*] proper to the philosophical hypothesis. The necessary reference to a simple empirical support is neither scientific nor philosophical separately. It intrinsically makes philosophy into a science (the reference to experience already given and not co-produced by the philosophical circle is constitutive here); and intrinsically makes science into a philosophy insofar as only essence or the force-(of)-hypothesis of hypotheses can reduce the empirical unilateral conditioning of thought—proper to science—to the universal form of a function of "occasion" and of "support".

The statements of a unified theory, then, will be constituted from terms taken from philosophy, the only means of assuring them a hold over the philosophical domain or experience, but these terms will be stripped of their philosophical dimension or sense; consequently, it will consist of terms that are philosophically indefinable and indemonstrable, and definable only "implicitly" through the system of their axioms. This is the only means of retaining their character of irreducible hypothesis. This form of "first names" is the equivalent, at the level of terms, to the hypothesis previously defined at the level of the organon of thought. A unified theory, then, will have an axiomatic *aspect* without being an axiomatic as such. As hypothesis, these first names are concurrent with the explication—rather than interpretation—of the properties of an object just as they are not a dependent part of that object or a specular reflection of it (the empiricist theory of *abstraction*). Nonetheless, a nuance arises between the hypothesis and the terms or rather their designations, between the organon and the vocabulary, from the viewpoint of their relation to experience. 1) Between the structures of philosophy or of epistemo-logical Difference and the "corresponding" structures that the force-(of)-thought frees up (even its own), there is no specular continuity but only a relation of "support". 2) Between the terms (in the sense of content, not of vocabulary) of philosophy and those of non-philosophy, there is the same relation, philosophical terms serving equally as support for non-philosophical terms. 3) On the other hand, between the linguistic *significations* of terms and structures, there is undoubtedly *at the same time* this sort of relation and a certain irreducible continuity. 4) Between the philosophical and non-philosophical designations, there is no rupture, but a *symbolic* or *signifying* continuity, which can without doubt be varied and enriched.

*Remarks*: a) in a general and vague manner, we can say that a symbol serves as signifying support to a relation or a structure; philosophically or non-philosophically, a structure requires this general function of signifiers, even if it is not the only one; b) the concept of support that the unified theory assumes is different; it is a condition and an effect of the transcendental work of the force-(of)-thought; c) really, symbols here have a continuity which exceeds the simple relation of support; we call *overdetermination* the continued role of philosophical signifiers in non-philosophy—overdetermination of structures by symbols; d) this symbolic continuity between philosophy and non-philosophy is the occasional cause or from the effective order, non-real cause, of the transcendental appearance that affects philosophy and that, itself, has a real cause (the being-foreclosed of the Real that forbids philosophy from being able to know it).

# Transcendental induction and deduction

If philosophy enters into a unified theory insofar as it is intrinsically a science, it must be able to operate through induction and deduction—rather than through interpretation—but transcendental induction and deduction, or relating to a priori knowledges on the very mode where induction and deduction relate to the objects of knowledge. If science enters into a unified theory insofar as it is intrinsically a philosophy, it must be able to operate through and on the a priori knowledges, by *universal* "condition" or "conditioning" rather than by general and regional laws; equally through transcendental operations which are ultimately operations of the *usage* of these universal knowledges.

It is the force-(of)-thought that represents and operates this "identification" without synthesis of the two possibilities of thought, this double "theoretical" possibility, but it does not represent it under the form of their blend but under the form of their *unilateral* duality. The force-(of)-thought is the transcendental identity which, through the a priori organon called non-phenomenological or abstract Distance—universal a priori—is declared univocally to be of science and of philosophy. However, it does not speak of these in their unitary spontaneity or their sufficiency or in their empirical blends, on pain of being another philosophical "in itself" or even a scientific "in itself" (like the logico-mathematical organon for the sciences). It purports to be for and by only the non-philosophy *of* essence or of the a priori of science and of philosophy identically. The force-(of)-thought is cause or agent, but transcendental, of the scientific type of operations like induction and deduction: against any epistemological, idealist and/or positive spirit, induction and deduction, experimentation and the axiomatic are in effect themselves "transcendental" here.

In a unified theory, an induction is carried out on the epistemo-logical mix, an induction motivated by the independence and the contingency of this empirical given, but this is paradoxically a transcendental induction in the sense that as transcendental (and universally aprioristic), the force-(of)-thought frees up or manifests the modes of itself starting from this given of experience, thus of the a prioris which are by definition non-auto-positioning/-giving. A philosophy (Kant's for example) refuses the a priori as its inductive object. Why? Precisely because it puts between them an antinomy and thus a quasi-unity or a co-determination rather than a real independence of the a priori in terms of experience; it attributes to experience a causal function other than occasional, or other than simple necessary support of the a priori, and assumes it co-determinant of this, which in reality does not autonomize it but threatens it with absorption by the a priori. It is upon the presupposition of this co-determination of the essence of the a priori by experience, thus of the non-independence of experience that is more or less reappropriated by the a priori, that it can now oppose the a priori to experience *as it does* and make it the object of a metaphysical "exposition" or "deduction" rather than of a true transcendental induction through its cause. This necessarily demands the given of experience but in its relative autonomy, so without making this into a circular co-determining of the a priori but rather its 'simple support" or "occasion" that it evidently only is in terms of identity of the fundamental and the regional, but not as experience opposed to theory or to understanding and to the a priori.

In a unified theory, a deduction is carried out on the a prioris obtained through induction by means of the force-(of)-thought that deduces from them, conforming to its identity or its rigorous immanence, other a prioris. This concerns a transcendental deduction but of the axiomatic type. Kant's "transcendental deduction" is not a true scientific deduction nor one of theoretical validity, but a judicial "deduction", *de jure*, and ultimately philosophical; it proves the validity of the a prioris even more *intuitively* through the relation assumed to be essential or constitutive to the experience charged with verifying it or refilling it—to the experience as philosophy posits it as simply opposed to the a priori. It is not a "formal" validity but a half-metaphysical, half-psychological enterprise. It is not a pure-transcendental deduction whose transcendental identity is recognized, but a semi-transcendental, semi-empirical deduction, undoubtedly according to "possible experience", but this is nothing other than this mixture. A transcendental deduction in a theoretico-scientific and no longer a philosophical or epistemological spirit does not form itself "with a view to experience", were that possible; it eliminates this experimental finalization. This is the meaning of the distinction of the two orders, the order of the identity of the fundamental and the regional, and the theoretical order of a prioris as produced through the force-(of)-thought which, far from assuring them a transcendent validity with a view to experience, assures them one that is immanent or that it alone can produce without constitutive appeal to experience. The validity of the non-philosophical a prioris *for* experience is all the more assured.

From its perspective of "simple" or non-autopositional transcendental identity, determining-in-the-last-instance, the force-(of)-thought represents the transformed "philosophical" aspect or the residue of philosophical power, which is to say the *possibility* for transcendence or non-autopositional distance of which it is constituted to relate itself to: a) the empirical through the mode of a simple support; b) to the empirical which is constituted by "real" knowledges, meaning to the a prioris of the philosophical type; c) transcendentally to the a priori of a non-autopositional or more universal type than the philosophical a priori—the non-philosophical knowledges.

From its perspective of non-autopositional transcendence, determined in-the-last-instance by transcendental identity, the force-(of)-thought represents the transformed scientific aspect or the residue of scientific power, meaning the possibility for transcendental identity to act, by this organon, through the mode of a (transcendental) induction and deduction of the a priori; for example, through an extraction, necessarily from contingent experience, of the a prioris that assume the variety of experience in order to be manifest but which constitute an order other than the experimental one. On the one hand, they maintain in experience (contingent and renewed) a relation of reference *de jure*, necessarily stronger than that which always somewhat tolerates philosophy *de facto*; and at the same time a more radical heterogeneity than that which assures them the force-(of)-thought, without specularity or blend with experience. The a prioris are at once more "empirical" and more "theoretical" than they are in philosophy where their blending causes them to lose the specificity of this double origin, where they are pervaded by empiricism without being experimental a prioris; they are abstract without being truly heterogeneous to experience, and possess a theoretical and explicative pertinence. So much so that non-philosophy represents the *equivalent* of an experimental regionalization of philosophy and at the same time a true "theory" of the a priori, which ceases to be meta-physical. The gain is at once experimental and theoretical, explicative while being proper to the a priori and not to the generality of empirical laws.

These two operations take as their object epistemo-logical (in the most extended sense) mixtures and as their end goal, providing an explication (through aprioristico-transcendental induction and deduction) and a critique of these representations of the essence-(of)-science and -(of)-philosophy that are epistemological relations.

We will not think that what is not a theory of science, but a unified theory of philosophy and science as a discipline of a new type, actually tells us those things that are truly the essence of science, its operation and its categories (as hypothesis, induction, deduction), or the essence of philosophy (its origin, status, etc.). It contents itself with a minimal program of making usage—under new conditions, foreign [*étrangères*] to philosophy and science—of these disciplines such that they present themselves randomly with their tenses [*temps*], claims and illusions. We do not put non-philosophy's operations and style together here with those of philosophy and science assumed "in themselves" and/or "mixed" in epistemo-logical Difference. The ontological auto-grounding of a science and its ontological, domain-centric [*domanial*] project themselves are used by non-philosophy—under its conditions—such that they give themselves, and non-philosophy frees in them, a priori structures which are not an epistemological thesis on the in itself of the sciences, but are identically philosophical/scientific operations. We deal with the characteristics generally assumed to belong to science "in itself", through a transcendental exigency, without the mixture of epistemo-logical Difference, without being able to know if it truly concerns the essence of science. It is the same for philosophy's assumed essence, of which we can only know the already philosophical. This is why we have used the scientific hypothesis, the axiomatic method, induction and deduction, but also the transcendental and philosophical a prioris, in order to construct the proper instruments of non-philosophy, i.e. of a discipline that does not yet exist, which thus had to be discovered and some of whose tools we have tried to gather.

Clarified in this way, the meaning of the axiomatic reference must be understood. We are not adding to philosophy (taken as a naive and intuitive domain) an axiomatic procedure destined to render rigorous or deductive the metaphysical knowledges that would merely be still empirically determined abstractions. Or more exactly, indeed, this operation is effective here, but it is no longer *first*, or does not exhaust the sense of a unified theory, being rather a consequence of such a project which is at once certainly a rigorous enterprise at the very heart of philosophy and not appended to it, and an enterprise of the usage of philosophy and science. This particular statute of the first possible relation of non-philosophy to philosophy is thus equally that of philosophy's axiomatization and that of science's pragmatic: they are radically immanent and *consequently* heteronomous to philosophy and science. So they do not at all prolong themselves, one within the other, through the mode of their blend. We will say, then, that non-philosophy has only a transcendental axiomatic *aspect* or *side*, the *aspect* being the correlate of a reduction. This is why it cannot, in place of interpreting, only deduce, but as much induces non-philosophical knowledges from its materials. And it cannot, in place of explaining regional or positively scientific essence through hypotheses, only use knowledges, but equally positions them already as a priori and universal. We will say that this is a reformulation of the concept of "transcendental science" or *mathesis transcendentalis*. But more rigorously than a reformulation or a "recasting", it is the discovery of the grounding concept of transcendental science through its integration into its true element which is admittedly not its native element.

# 3 UNIFIED OR "NON-CARTESIAN" THEORY OF THE SUBJECT: DUALITY OF THE EGO AND THE SUBJECT

## From the dialectic of the subject to the unified theory of the subject

"Theories of the subject" do exist in the history of thought, but under the philosophical form of "theory". Here, the subject is in reality a wheel or a function of the philosophical machinery, a quasi-object. We will treat these philosophies of the subject as simple materials, as givens for a scientific as much as a philosophical discipline.

These historico-systematic formations are predominantly Cartesian in origin. Even though equivalent forms or primers had preceded the Cartesian form of the subject, Descartes guaranteed the subject a reality and an autonomy of *principle* that distinguish it from these prior forms (Aristotle, St Augustine), and that he bequeathed to his descendants as both a resource and a problem. The Cartesian galaxy is well known for its thematic filiations and its structural invariances, its continuities and its problematic divergencies, not to mention, each time, the historico-political and "ideological" overdetermination of the motif of the subject. A series of bifurcations weaves a complex web between Descartes on one side and Kant, Fichte, Hegel, Nietzsche, Husserl, etc. on the other. But contemporary thinkers are directly interested in the Cartesian subject and in its "supersession" [*dépassement*] (Lacan, Henry, Badiou, Marion and, earlier, between Marxism and psychoanalysis, Althusser) following the critiques of the "cogito" (by Kant, Nietzsche, Husserl, Heidegger). From this point of view, we discern a major disjunction on the synchronic plane that we will take as object, a disjunction initiated by Descartes himself, either toward a *theory of the subject* whose culmination is in Lacan, Althusser and their successors, particularly under the form of an "unconscious subject", or toward a *philosophy of the subject* from diverse and original figures (Husserl and then Michel Henry under the form of an immanence of life and affectivity). The first branch is that of a scientifically skewed treatment—mathematico-psychoanalytic here—of the subject by means of mathematical techniques which always culminate in objectifying it, dividing it and dispersing it to the brink of the void. The second, on the contrary, orients itself toward an undivided immanence of the Ego and toward its purely philosophical treatment, in any case an absolutely not scientific and not "objectifying" treatment of its consistency, and sometimes toward a version of the Ego in quasi romantic terms of affectivity and of life. These two branches form a new antinomy, *the antinomy of the philosophical subject*, which is the situation we are in. This antinomy which is on the road to shattering philosophy and which works to surpass it is as much the subject as the Ego, each one of these, and their blends. It in effect reduces itself to other antinomies sketching out a generalized "transcendental dialectic" of the modern and postmodern subject. For example:

- Between real and logic (substance/reflection; *jouissance/* unconscious; lived/thought or objectification; affect/ representation, etc.);

- Between intuition and inference (or reasoning = deduction); between affective intuition and intellectual intuition; intuition and performativity;

- Between subjectivity and objectivity; immanence and transcendence; givenness and position, etc. (these pairs in fact never overlap);

- Between immanence and division or alterity (psychoanalytic "splitting" by the signifier, deconstructive dissemination, Nietzschean intensification, etc.);

- Between identity and multiplicity;

- Between its internal constitution and its situation or its function within a philosophical system, etc.

These various antinomies, more or less "softened" and nuanced, overdetermine each other or intersect in a network that indefinitely develops them. Beyond isolated names, we must theoretically explain the reasons that philosophies of the Ego and of the subject form a network. These are the antinomies that a unified theory of the subject strives to resolve through their "a priori explication", taking them for a domain of phenomena or of givens but never—as is the case in philosophies of the subject—for a viewpoint over themselves. The philosophical auto-representation of the subject is only a given to work on, no longer bringing with it its own theory. We give ourselves philosophical antinomies, we do not discuss them, we do not contest any conception of the Ego in the name of another: this would be a philosophical type of *hypothesis* that would remain within the antinomy, structured by and reproducing it. But taken as such in its scientific meaning, "theory" also receives, as we have said, a transcendental reach, or a function adequate to this special object (not natural/social, not positive and finally not ontic), insofar as it is a "real" or ontological object. In fact, this concerns a *theory of the subject qua subject*: moreover, scientific theory does not tend to bear on the *qua*, a uniquely philosophical theme, and it is necessary that it be identically philosophical in order to be adequate to its object. It operates then under the form of a radical *identity* (not antinomically divided...) of these two postures of thought and, according to its object, takes philosophical antinomies as a field of properties and phenomena. This posture, in as much as it truly accomplishes the phenomenal Idea of a "theory of the subject", is more complex than the initial antinomy of philosophy, since it rejects this in the simple *data* and turns out to be *identically theoretical and pragmatic* (philosophy being in general a problem of usage rather than of knowledge, of pragmatics of things and of knowledge rather than of theory and of the production of knowledges).

The sense of the enterprise is outlined as follows: in the name of the "cogito", its philosophers and its critics, neither the Ego, first, nor *consequently* the subject are thought for themselves. In particular, the Ego is not thought in its identity and in its primacy of Real over thought and over Being, which is to say over the subject, but in terms of a universal philosophical apparatus valid for whatever object, too large and too strict for it, too general and transcendent in any case, and which "blends" it with the subject. The "cogito" to which the sense of the Ego is suspended— that is, the identity-(of)-ego of the Ego, which it carries and circulates through other transcendent notions—undoubtedly "turns" around an Ego toward which it directs identity, but precisely without being able to seize it otherwise than as an object or a "noema" since it mediatizes this identity of its structure and its movement. It turns around an impossible identity, only assumed and suppressed, which conceals a "blank" under its name. Posited by the Philosophical Decision as substance and consequently divided in its immanent essence, the Ego is alienated from its identity. Thinking thought, the *cogitatio* generally intends "thought thought" and in this way aims for a vanishing point that is the Ego, not as simple intersection of these two thoughts but moreover as identity susceptible to explicating the possibility of this intersection. But the "existing" Ego is also a simple conclusion of the argument: even if it cannot concern a reasoning in form but a simple representation or reflection (in its dominant interpretations), since it is simply *presupposed* in the origin of the inference without giving itself radically as given-without-givenness and as "first name", it can only *claim* to demonstrate—only claim and only demonstrate—its existence. In other words, even if it really "demonstrated" its existence, it would only demonstrate a borrowed and secondary reality, a reality of substance or of principle cut from the Real and within which it is divided and given behind a variety of masks. The amphibology of heterogeneous natures like the Ego and the subject is not only the host of blends between being and thought, Ego and being, Ego and thought, but more generally the continuation of the confusion of the Ego and philosophy. The philosophy of the Ego has taken the place of the Ego, and of the philosophy-in-Ego that the Ego "unilateralizes". The passage to a unified and non-Cartesian theory of the Ego simultaneously assumes a modification of the content of the three basic terms and a new economy of their relations, such that the primacy of the Ego becomes the real origin and no longer an assumed priority; such that its structure radically excludes the auto-reflection of thought and becomes capable of explicating and critiquing its philosophical auto-representations. The paradigmatic example of Descartes shows that a philosophy of the subject as Ego situating itself within the apparatus of a "cogito" assumes a certain amphibology of the Ego with the *cogitatio* (thought) and the *esse* (being). This intrication of the Ego and the subject must be undone by a theory that gives itself the Ego as in-Ego [*en-Ego*] or as Ego-without-subject and thus can *demonstrate* that the subject only assumes the Ego in order to "clone" it in the manner whose properly transcendental identity is added to the Real. A theory of the subject is only possible on the basis of the invalidation of the confusion of the Ego with the subject or with the structure of the Philosophical Decision: the Ego is no longer subject but Real, and the subject too is "devoid" [*vide*] of its blends with the Ego (not of the Ego itself). As such, we must define and redistribute these three terms (Ego, thought, being), to make a new philosophical usage of them outside of the structure of the Philosophical Decision, rendering them philosophically indefinable and indemonstrable in a "cogito". Abandoning the egological style is the first condition through which, on the other hand, the theory of the subject demonstrates that the subject is unilaterally distinct from the Ego and can form the object of a scientific type of thought as much as a philosophical one.

The principle of "Modernity", of the "spirit", is the amphibology of the Ego and the subject, their reduction to one another. The interpretation of man's essence in terms of the subject has succeeded its interpretation in terms of the individual, disseminating into multiple figures of the subject. This subject is the synthesis, although more or less immediate or mediatized then differed, of being and thought. In philosophy, the unity of being and thought is a universal and first principle, it is as such determinant of the real of the Ego or carries itself out as this; it is presupposed here without being elucidated, and carried out or carries itself out through and in its elucidation only as being and thought. So much so that the Ego is manifested or given as divided, as enveloped in the depths of a universal onto-cogitative plane and re-enveloped or re-deployed by this plane. Yet, this amphibology is also the "principle of philosophy" (Feuerbach), as we suspected. For non-philosophy, which is neither modern nor post-modern but non-modern, the human essence of man or of the Ego implies in itself and on its account the dissolution of this amphibology, the Ego separating itself out from the "unilateral" subject or giving it unilateral leave—from itself or from philosophy—but thus disposing of it for a new science.

A theory (of the subject), such as that whose requisites we have proposed at the beginning of this research, is a transcendental science. This term, "transcendental", signifies in any case that it bears on *real* objects. But all science bears on the real, ontic the majority of the time, which is to say on beings and their regions. "Real" then must designate here the specifically philosophical objects and above all the philosophical object par excellence, Being rather than beings. Yet, Being is not an objectified object; it is an "object" in idea or in action and by definition universal: it confuses itself, through an essential trait of itself, with knowledge, not "empirical" but "a priori" or absolutely universal and necessary, given independently of ontic experience although relating to it. If we call transcendental any knowledge that in general concerns itself not with objects but with our means of knowing objects in as much as this mode of knowledge is possible a priori (Kant), a transcendental theory thus takes for its "object" a priori knowledge—which is the true real—of objects (of experience). As such, we transpose this definition onto our problematic which, as we have seen, gives itself the philosophies of the subject themselves as data-objects and, in some sense, steps up a gear or raises itself up a notch through relation to philosophy itself since this must be a "unified theory" of science and philosophy—a theory of the object "philosophy" and not a philosophical theory of empirical objects. Consequently a theory of the subject in our sense will be concerned less with the objects of the philosophy and sciences of the subject than with our manner of knowing a priori these new "objects", these philosophies and these sciences themselves.

A *unified theory* assumes the following conditions:

- A cause of theory that assures, through a transcendental identity, the *unified* character of theory, identically philosophical and scientific; this cause is the real-One or the Ego, and this will be posited as term or first name in the axioms of this theory.

- A field of phenomena or a material—here the philosophies of the subject, for example those of the "cogito" or of psychoanalysis, etc.

- A universal organon—precisely the subject insofar as it presupposes itself without auto-positing itself—capable of elaborating its a priori structures, transcendental organon, or real only in-the-last-instance.

- Scientific operations of this subject which free up the aprioristic structures through which it precisely can access the *data* that are those philosophies and sciences directed at the subject. We have already hinted at these operations and we will elucidate them further here. But we necessarily exercise them and point them out—without "reflecting" them—in that which precedes and in that which follows, rather than from the theory of the Ego, from the subject, the force-(of)-thought or auto-affection; we use terms and relations taken from philosophical materials in order to treat them through operations that are precisely operations of the subject of non-philosophy or of the force-(of)-thought.

# Egology as the philosophical decision of the "cogito"

The system of statements summed up by the "Cogito", in whatever philosophical interpretation we choose from among Descartes and his interpreters puts three terms into reciprocal circulation: *ego, cogitation, esse*, and circularly exchanges them. This is the philosophical construction of the subject; it gives itself these terms and thus assumes the Ego itself, which it thus must codetermine through the dyad of the *cogitatio* and the *esse*. The Ego is taken in a structure that surpasses it and envelops it, the Philosophical Decision, which includes a dyad (the *correlation* of two terms) and a unity of synthesis, an immanent and transcendent One according to the various proportions of the dyad.

*The dyad of the "cogito".* This is the dyad of thought (*cogitatio*) and of being (*esse*), of their necessary liaison: if I doubt (= think), then I am; or, if I am wrong, I am, so I am not wrong about my being, etc. Here, under this form, as we know, is a reputedly "facile" and "common" inference (Descartes), or historically "banal" (St Augustine and others), a sort of common philosophical place or "axiom", a common notion, but one to which Descartes gave a new sense and a principle [*principielle*] usage within philosophy. In reality, this "facility" is that of the structure of the Philosophical Decision dyad, philosophy "facilitating" the liaison of opposites and this liaison being the common sense *of* or proper to philosophy. The content of the axiom is a reflexive or reciprocal inference between being and thought, such that it follows from the no less "facile" axiom of Parmenides: for thought and being are the Same. In any case, the Ego is divided by philosophy itself and, *qua* philosophical object, enters into being and thought to the benefit of thought and its privilege over being (the Moderns) rather than of being over thought (the Ancients). *Ego cogito, ego sum*, the "same" Ego is affected by this antinomy, even if it reconciles itself with itself in the statement of the "cogito".

*The One or the synthesis of the dyad.* In the preceding dyad, the Ego is already implicit or insinuated but is never explicitly posited. The dyad is thus in fact already a triad but the Ego, the third term and consequently the triad, no longer appear as such. Thus, the Ego itself must appear as such in what we presuppose in order to be able to be associated with the *cogitatio* first of all, but also with *esse*. That the Ego proves to be immanent to itself as a substance or a principle (Descartes) or even that it returns to God and is simply an image of God (St Augustine), either way, it must functionally have a specific, original nature that it must now posit by drawing it out of its essence as philosophy has traditionally formulated it. We know that philosophy in effect contains another common axiom, another "banality" concerning the Ego itself but always in relation to thought. This is Aristotle's axiom in the *Nicomachean Ethics*: the "thought of thought", a common statement that Descartes re-actualized in his own way. "One who sees is conscious that he sees", "one who hears is conscious that he hears";

"one who walks is conscious that he walks", "we are conscious that we are conscious and think that we think": this is auto-reflexivity as essence of the Ego and of thought. Indeed the Ego and *cogitatio* are inseparable here or form a mixture. The Ego is thought as having an affinity with thought (and sensation: knowing in general) rather than with being, it is in some sense already divided by thought or by the thought/being couplet. The Ego takes the place of and actualizes the function of the *One*, so much so that throughout it as throughout all philosophy the One is divided between opposites and thought simply as the "same" or as One-which-unifies. Auto-reflexivity is an ambiguous term which returns to the Ego ("auto-") and to the *cogitatio*.

*The unity of the two preceding moments or the philosophy of the subject.* Philosophy itself is the setting in motion of the structure of the triad (Dyad + One) which combines the three terms (*ego, cogitatio, esse*) or what Descartes calls the simple or primitive natures (indivisible into others): existence, doubt, thought, ego. This is the equivalent of the *first terms* of an axiomatic, but the Cartesian egology is woven only from "philosophical" and intuitive axioms, never scientific. This is an ontological rather than a transcendental-pure axiomatic (like unified theory, including a scientific dimension). These assumed "first terms" are susceptible here to an inter-pretation or a reciprocal or circular "hermeneutic", so much so that the necessary relations between any two of the three terms close themselves off into a circle (of circles) or into an egological system under the form of a substantial principle or a substance. The thought of existence must in any case fold in on itself, existing in turn as thought and not being only a thought oriented toward an object. Thought overcomes itself in existence, existence in the Ego and the auto-reflection of being (*se existere, se cogitare*). Of course, there is a *primacy* of the Ego over the *cogitatio* and *esse* but it remains a reflexive operator or, more widely beyond this reflection, a dependant of thought. *Cogito sum = Cogito me cogitare* (Heidegger) is the most German of the interpretations of the "cogito", perhaps not the most "Cartesian", but it bears witness to a structural and thus universal triad. Descartes himself supersedes his first usage (cf. *Regulae*) of these simple natures, which were epistemic or scientific, which juxtaposed them without coordinating or fixing them through and in terms of the Ego, without hierarchizing them (he is thus closer to a true theory of the subject), toward a philosophical and hermeneutic usage, where these primitive notions are hierarchized, where the Ego certainly has primacy over thought and being but *reciprocally*, so all of the philosophical structure over the Ego itself. The passage to philosophy properly termed of the Ego, to egology, happens when the reflection comes onto the scene, when the circle of auto-reflection of the Ego joins up with being or the *sum* and when the Ego is posited as self-sufficient substance and principle. In Descartes, there is already the sketch of an antinomy of the science and the philosophy of the Ego, which is our material for a "non-Cartesian" theory of the subject.

# Typology of philosophical critiques of the "cogito"

The so-called "formal" [*protocolaire*] statement, the syntagm or philos-opheme, of *cogito ergo sum* must be, in its philosophical usage in Descartes, interpreted/effectuated with a metaphysical aim in order to produce it as "the first principle of my philosophy" (Descartes). But beyond Descartes, the critical rethinkings of the "cogito" for the most part reiterate, with some slight adjustments, the same operation. It always concerns dividing, nuancing and complexifying this amphibology that concentrates in itself the whole of the structure of the Philosophical Decision recast in this way. This is what the critics of the "cogito" do; they content themselves with diversifying it, displacing it, pulling it apart or differing it toward another declared instance whether of thought or of being; thus decon-structing its metaphysically "heavy" sense of *substance* (*res*) but conserving the structure of the Philosophical Decision for the most part. In this history of the "cogito", we can distinguish five key stages, including the Cartesian, which accentuate its philosophical future and which are, *already* in Descartes, its critique. If "cogito" is a statement subject to philosophical interpretation, its "authentic" sense can be grasped on the levels that define the different philosophies and the different critiques of the "cogito". We will recount them schematically and as a matter of interest:

1) That of the *statement* [*énoncé*] or of thought thought, of the result or of the exterior sign, such that it absorbs the enunciation or refuses the distinction of the *I* of the statement [*énoncé*] and the *I* of the enunciation. A rather "Cartesian" stage where the difference of the statement [*énoncé*] and the enunciation, the signified and the signifier, are reabsorbed into the transparency of auto-reflection or auto-diction. Due to this transparency, this stage remains the object of the following interpretations which critique it, repress it, or truncate it but conserve the matrix in any case. But this is already a first critique (metaphysical, principle [*principielle*]), of the *cogito* as banal statement [*énoncé*] given within history.

2) That of the *act* of thinking or of reflection: "The indubitable reality (*Realität*) of spirit—but not qua statement [*énoncé*] or dogma; to the

contrary as effective act, as this *act* of thought through which *I* differ from everything sensible and know myself in this difference—this is the principle of philosophy" (Feuerbach). Rather, the act is generally interpreted in the manner of Descartes where pure understanding, freed and separated from the sensible and the world, can alone formulate the *cogito*. In this direction, Fichte radicalized the *cogito* as position, thus auto-position of Self (theme of the "transcendental agility" of the Self).

The act is an important stage within philosophy between Being as substance, in particular at its lowest degree as substantification (*hypokeimenon, substratum*, support, matter) and Being as *wesendes*, as activity of *Seiendheit*'s deployment or beingness of beings. The act is the most "idealist", "formal", and "active" form of substance, it is what subsists of substance when it is no longer "passive" and quasi-material. This is the "Fichtean" stage of thought, the auto-position of the Self being the act *par excellence* and a critique of the *substantia* as *res* (Fichtean and Husserlian critique of Descartes), though not his most radical critique which assumes seeking the meaning of being of the *esse* of *substantia*.

3) That of the *enunciation*, so of the language within which the *cogito* formulates itself and which is finally recognized as such or taken as viewpoint; the structure of language as signifier dividing or dispersing the Ego, which is differed, cut into, affected by a "hole" or "privation". This is the analytico-Lacanian stage which deconstruction radicalizes in leading the Ego to its extreme point of dissemination.

4) That of *language as force* in the hands of the will to power. Nietzsche, let us remember, denounces that metaphysics which claims to demonstrate the existence of the Ego (as elsewhere that of God's existence): the metaphysical "demonstrations", and above all those of existence, are no such thing. He makes a genealogy out of what is only a metaphysical belief in existence. 1) This argumentation must be inverted or reversed: existence is not demonstrated, it is a preliminary or a priori belief in existence. "It is thought: it thus follows that there is something thinking (*ein Denkendes*)". If this thing thinks, if there are effects of thought, we posit a priori something like the subject of thought, which it would rather be necessary to reduce to a network of multiple forces, every force being difference of two forces or a *relation* to another force. So there is no "subject" and still less a "substance", a hinter-world behind these forces. 2) This belief is a simple effect of language, a "habit of grammar" ("pragmatist" and "vital" genealogy through the reactive forces and the will to power which seize language and hide metaphysical beliefs in it). This critique proceeds by "intensification" of the "cogito" as belief in "a subject for every act", a critique that continues without reduction by language: not in the sense of the primacy of the

signifier, nor in the sense of the textual forces of deconstruction, but in the properly Nietzschean sense of forces and of the will to power within which language is one force among others, in relation to others. The act and the signifier are for Nietzsche still "metaphysical" terms. This critique, then, does not come under the "linguistic turn" of twentieth century philosophy. If Lacan submits desire to the signifier (as such, metaphysical desire too), Nietzsche submits the signifier to desire (as will to power).

5) An entirely other kind of critique, which is at once a critique of representation, of the reflexive auto-representation of the Ego within the *cogito* but this time no longer in the name of an instance of pulling apart auto-representation or differentiating it or its specularity (Nietzsche, Heidegger, Lacan, Derrida—and Kant before them: the "deconstructive" lineage), but to the contrary, of the lived's radical immanence to the self, the lived contra the signifier. The critique through the *cogitatio* or even through the *esse* cedes to a critique of the "cogito" through the Ego which then becomes the capital and first theme of thought. The Ego is a radical lived of the self, an immediate auto-affection. This is said of the Ego more than of that thought which would think itself thinking (auto-reflection of the *cogito me cogitare*). This is Michel Henry's interpretation of Descartes, and is his own philosophy. Here, there is a first attempt to finally distinguish the Ego and the subject, the immanence of the lived and thought, and to oppose itself to the ideal of dispersion and dissemination of the Ego that animates the other branch of the critique of the "cogito".

Nonetheless we will see later argumentation's ambiguous and limited character. That the Ego and subject, division and radical indivision, are dually distinguished is not certain: the Ego is still posited from philosophy and through abstraction, bracketed off from this abstraction which thus surreptitiously continues to determine it. A certain equivocation between immanence and the lived and thought exists, more or less intuitively, which gives it as a *quasi*-object: if the Ego is already somewhat a subject, it remains somewhat an object. There is one last amphibology here, no longer desired as such but by default persisting in the elucidation of thought adequate to the radicality of immanence. Auto affection, immediate as it is, is partially or, as we will say, "semi-" philosophical. Thought here is not still determined by the Ego but, following from the Aristotelian statement of auto-reflection, is simply reduced to an immediacy and an auto-affection, posited as identical to immanence through an operation of subtracting transcendence. The gain here is that the Ego becomes the viewpoint of a real critique of thought and being, their correlation as philosophical terms. But it is not certain that the irreflexive immanence of the Ego is already taken positively.

These most reflexive and most representational critiques of the *cogito* remain cases of the amphibology of the Ego and the subject, the Ego and thought (statement/enunciation/act/auto-affection or quasi-intuition), the latter being a "limit" interpretation and in any case very opposed, in its presuppositions, to the preceding ones. We will see a kind of antinomy in the systematic history of the "cogito", between a tendency where the subject overcomes the Ego and a tendency where the ego overcomes the subject, the immanence of the lived overcomes thought. The first four interpretations effect the statement of the "cogito" by reformulating it and critiquing the representations that are too immediate, too "representative" and not "abstract" enough, submitting it to a style of thought through axioms and hypotheses, deducing it for example from a belief, or even submitting it to quasi-scientific (linguistic) distinctions and to a style of operations which as it were treat its constituents objectively and in exteriority. They lead to a "theory" of the subject rather than of the Ego, without, though, abolishing their blend. On the other hand, the last interpretation operates in an inverse sense and seeks within the *cogito* more than an intuition, a true auto-given or auto-affection which tends toward a radical immediation. It leads to a philosophy of life and affectivity, but at the same time it tends to ignore the subject, undoubtedly because it too still thinks under the law of philosophical mixture.

One of the problems facing the unified theory of the subject is that of resolving this antinomy which affects the usage of the "cogito", for example an antinomy between theoretical access (to the subject) and affective access (to the Ego). How do we deal with the Ego (and therefore the subject) so that it is received no longer as auto-givenness but as a radical given? Undoubtedly through a theoretical but transcendental mode, not so much "theoretical" in the sense whereby philosophy can understand this as using mathematics (algebra, topology) or linguistics. It concerns substituting a new economy of the lived (Ego) and thought (subject) for the Ego/subject amphibology (Ego as subject and vice versa), but more profoundly still, a new economy of the Ego-without-subject and subject-in-Ego, grounding it on their identity, but an identity-without-blend.

# Real critique of philosophies of the Ego

After the philosophical critiques of the "cogito" which remain within the general transcendental appearance that affects philosophy, the real critique of these philosophies is crucial. The real critique intends to show that the Ego remains undetermined here, that its reality remains woven with irreality or possibility, and that its identity remains shot through with alterity and transcendence. What has not been elucidated is double: its reality, confused with a possible real as substance or transcendence in general; and its identity, confused with the auto-reflection of thinking thought. Altogether, its non-elucidation as *Ego as Ego*.

*Real critique of the philosophical "reality" of the Ego*. From this point of view the critique of the "cogito" is double: from the perspective of thought (*cogitatio*) or of knowledge and from the perspective of being (*esse*). Let us remember that the "cogito" pretends not only to be an aprioristic assertion (from this point of view the Ego only attains an essence or a structure, universal and necessary, the relation of two simple essentialities, being and thought; this is not yet a principle, it will not rise to become one as *substantia*); but an assertion that is more than aprioristic, something other than whatever valid knowledge: it is principle [*principielle*] and the Ego reaches it as *res cogitans*, thinking substance, and so assumes the role of *first principle* (according to being, according to time, according to knowledge or as knowledge, making other knowledges possible depending on the order). Hence a *principle* [principiel] *or substantial sum, the being (of the) substance*: a quasi-transcendental level in the sense that it reaches itself as real, as known and as determining the knowledge of other things. This claim was first the object of philosophical critiques that we will recount:

a) Kant (and Nietzsche following him) holds that the "I am" is a simple and not a demonstrated assertion, a conclusion without rigor; that a subject can even say *I think* ("must be able to accompany all my representations" and report them back to me), this *I think* is a simple *consciousness* or *function* without concept and so without an object, from which it is impossible to conclude anything about being or the reality of the subject in itself. In a general way Kant prohibits, as we know, any claim to knowledge of the real in itself and this goes for the "reality" of the subject too. The *I think* then is a simple "transcendental" assertion, a little like an Idea of reason, testifying to its role in knowledge but which proves nothing about my existence, which does not demonstrate my reality (critique of every ontological proof). Kant is the first philosopher to radically separate—without holding onto them elsewhere—being and thought, real and reason, existence and logic. Having arrived at this "ontological proof" of the Ego, Nietzsche shows that it is a web of simple beliefs. The reality of the Ego is therefore defective if we interrogate it from the point of view of knowledge in order to gain acceptance for a certain rigor, and distinctions of the scientific type (Kant's "Newtonianism", in terms of mathematical physics and experience).

b) Heidegger interrogates the reality of the Ego from the *sum* and no longer from the *cogitatio*. The ultimate metaphysical plane of the *substantia* is once again and otherwise questioned and 'superseded" with the entirety [*ensemble*] of metaphysics and its ontology: in terms of the *meaning of being* of Being and no longer of thought. And yet, the "cogito" remains silent on the question of its historical origin or its provenance, its sense of being, which is assumed to be regulated by the *res cogitans*. He promotes and mobilizes a particular historico-systematic conception of Being (as *res*, as *cogitans*, as *ego*, etc.) which is not elucidated further than itself, or which is assumed given. This questioning is undoubtedly too quick in its objection to Descartes because it directly connects the sedimented historical provenance of the *substantia*—this is not Descartes" problem as he gives substance as 'simple nature"—to the Cartesian affirmation of the substantiality of the Ego. In this way, it short-circuits a key step in Descartes" work which is, according to one interpretation "the egological deduction of the substance" (Marion): there is no substance or substantiality except through and by the Ego, which gives the sense of substance (exception made for God). This type of "deconstruction" carries metaphysics and maybe philosophy itself to their limits, but it ends up obscuring the possibility of another "essence of manifestation", more immanent, that the Cartesian Ego would be likely to reveal.

Effectively it seems that no question beyond those of Being and its meaning, or thought and its demonstrative rigor, will be possible any longer; that philosophy runs up against its edges here, those being the essence of Being as "real" and the real as possibilization of possibility; or even with thought as rigorous or quasi-scientific. Another thought, precisely "non-philosophical" or proceeding on another ground, would nevertheless be able to ask again if on the one hand the *real content* of "Being itself", the "meaning of the being of Being", and on the other hand the *rigorous content* demonstrative of thought have been examined and elucidated not only by the "cogito" itself but though its Kantian critique or through its Heideggerian hermeneutics, or even if, in all cases, they have not been equally and absolutely "forgotten" or "foreclosed" such that the "cogito" alone can declare itself and function within its nature as principle, the principle assumed to exhaust the Ego in its reality, and that this grouping gives place to these philosophical critiques. However, it is not clear that the Real, here, can still be an object for a question and a deconstruction: the Real is in some part necessarily unquestionable and undeconstructable. The Real must rather be already *given* even outside every operation of givenness, ontological or scientific, which would precisely possibilize it and would take it out of its "being-given". We are no longer within philosophical questioning here, not event at its margins, but rather in another mode of thought that thinks under the necessary and first condition of the Real as given without presupposition, and which is not itself a presupposed. In place of presupposing and questioning it in order to bring it to light or manifest it starting from the possible or the empirically effective, we treat it, in a hypothesis determined-in-the-last-instance by it, as integrally given or manifested: this is not a presupposition to clarify, demanding to be reflected and thought, it is a given *to make asserted and acted* at the heart of philosophy and, for example, of the "cogito".

If Heidegger affirms that the meaning of being remains unelucidated in Descartes" "radical beginning", then for us it is the radicality of that "radical beginning" that is in question, since by all accounts the "cogito" is a philosophical beginning [*commencement*] of the Ego, its resumption [*recommencement*] or repetition, rather than a *radical beginning for philosophy*; a philosophical beginning of the Ego from which philosophy excepts itself, rather than a beginning of philosophy within the Ego and "in-Ego". Heidegger refuses "radicality" and shows that the roots of the Cartesian tree penetrate a still deeper and more remote ground, but instead we challenge non-radicality, Descartes' all-too weak radicality, which understands radicality as primacy *and* priority of a principle, a principle as hierarchy, domination, power over…, and its realization as thinking substance. Nothing here is the Ego but all of it signals the Ego's subordination to the principle, to the transcendent "principleness" [*principialité*] of principles. It is as much a primacy as a priority, Descartes (as every philosopher) having confused the latter with the former subsumed the *Ego* under priority or under the order of the philosophy it had to initiate. It goes without saying that a unified theory of the subject assumes that we challenge together: 1) the philosophical construction of the Ego; 2) its interpretation by Being (*sum*) and thought (*cogitatio, ego cogitans*)—each time by one of the terms of the philosophical dyad reflecting itself in its essence; 3) its Heideggerian deconstruction by the "meaning of the being of Being"; 4) finally, the definition of the radical through the principle and its priority, which is *never* truly *the* radical or the Real. The problem is no longer metaphysically re-measuring the "cogito" nor of re-evaluating it once again by the yardstick of knowledge or being; nor by that of the "meaning of being" of the *sum* or the unthought of/within every *cogitatio*; or moreover—and we will say this incessantly—to that of an internal affectivity. "Radical" immanence is more demanding than all of these "measures". We do not bring ourselves to the philosophical limit of metaphysics here; nor moreover to the limit of auto-affection or the life of transcendence; nor still for example to that of the unconscious as signifying chain that dividing the subject and subtracting from it its substantial identity. We change the style of thought and adjust thought in the Real, with the goal of rendering it adequate to the Ego's being-given rather than taking up the philosophical style again and "forcing" the Ego into it once more.

*Real critique of the philosophical "identity" of the Ego.* In discussing the Ego, Descartes posited the *cogitatio* and then the *esse*, by assuming the Ego given, but posed the question of the Ego itself after this positing of essential attributes, or attributes which count as its essence. Who am I, what am I, me who is? We will call "the assumed Ego" this Ego philosophically divided by the philosophical dyad from the base of being and thought, which always divides the One or the instance in lieu of it. The response to that question came too late, to what is still the object of a question and a final doubt here and so is a presupposition rather than a given, this is evidently a response by the universal element, the *onto-cogitative* plane, which comes to settle for a simply assumed Ego that is subsequently determined by division and synthesis.

The philosophy of the Ego overwhelms it and divides it—these are the same thing. Despite certain appearances, it forbids all performativity of the Ego itself by attributing it to its (philosophical) formulation or thought rather than to its essence. This performativity is well maintained: I am as long as I will think (being something). But being grasped on the plane of either thought or language, it unceasingly escapes the Ego itself which as such never coincides with its own experience-(of)-itself, which is never purely phenomenon or identity of the Real and of the phenomenon-(of)-itself. Inversely we have noted the absence of thought within the formula of the *Meditations*: *ego sum, ego existo*. But we can form the more general hypothesis that in each of these formulas, and in the second in particular, something essential or constitutive, that being the philosophical operation (act of speaking, formulating, thinking), partially excepts itself (resultantly as a *deus ex machina*), or excepts itself from the form under which the Ego gives itself in the "cogito", does not fall under its law or in its form of Ego. In the formula of the *Meditations*, the act of thinking the statement fulfills itself outside of the statement, certainly in relation to it but by excluding it. But, in general, to think in the mode of reflection and even of auto-reflection is never to really fully accomplish a performative act, since the redoubling of (thought) thought by (thinking) thought is always at the same time an auto-exception of thought outside the thought and formulated Ego. In effect, philosophy—that which thinks, speaks, states, the subject of enunciation—distinguishes itself from the subject of the statement (the Ego) and establishes a relation of hierarchy with it that auto-presents itself as *identity* but which is only an aiming at identity or a claim.

The Ego is not formed through an absolutely autonomous "ontological" region by itself; it needs its representation, certainly not of thought thought but of thinking thought. The passage from objectified representation to the representation-act does not liberate it from representation. Its true liberation passes through the invalidation of the amphibology of the Ego and philosophy within the "cogito". The cogito is thus no longer an "empty" or "common" statement to be interpreted, an "easy" maxim, it is a simple material for a *dualysis* that will set the Ego and the onto-cogitative plane in a relation of unilateral duality.

To this divided and thus split Ego, Ego-of-Ego or Self-of-Self, at once under- and over-determined by the onto-cogitative plane, we therefore oppose the Ego absolutely *given* without reference, even of "immediate negation", to a universal horizon; we call it Ego-in-Ego, Self-in-Self, the *in* being charged with signifying its already reduced state or with annulling the philosophical splitting. It is no longer *restored* or *given again* with and in the *sum* at the risk of sinking into the anonymity and transcendence of Being. "I am a thing that thinks...": a simple repetition or tautology of what was presupposed. The problem here is no longer making the Ego protrude out of universal transcendence, through a supplementary gesture of abstraction and transcendence, an expulsion outside of onto-theo-logical transcendence itself, but "restoring" it in-Ego in a radical immanence. However, in order to be refilled, radical immanence demands that the Ego itself be subtracted *by first definition* in every form of transcendence: a completely positive subtraction derived from its essence as Given-without-givenness rather than from a final operation of unilateralization and negation of transcendence. It would be necessary to oppose to Sartre's title "the transcendence of the Ego" another title, "the immanence (understood as: (to) itself) of the Ego"; to the Ego's under- or over-determination by the World or indeed by being-in-the-World, or moreover by a more restrained attribute like thought or substance-being, it would be necessary to oppose its always-already intrinsically determined character. The Heideggerian type of question is more generally philosophical: where do we get the *sum from*, what is its sense of being, etc., must be replaced by a more precise question that its formulation causes to arise immediately: where do we get the Ego from? How does philosophy *assume* it as given, all the while refusing to let-it-be-given? If not from the Ego itself... The Ego cannot be recomposed from outside, with bits and pieces taken from philosophy, essences and attributes, transcendent faculties, from the empirical real and from the possible—it is not only *of* the real, it is *the* Real, a real instance through-and-through. Philosophy only gives itself the Ego through a filter which, since Descartes, annuls the radicality of its being-given, differs it, displaces it, submits it to a givenness and in general to an exterior operation. "*Ego aliquid sum...*": given as being, it is differed by Being-substance and more generally by the essence of Being, etc. In Descartes himself and not only in Nietzsche, Heidegger, Lacan and Derrida, the Ego is divided from the outset, differentiated from itself and (this being the same thing) its being-given (the Ego-in-Ego) is confused with that of a being or with being in general... Philosophy fails on the Ego by definition, it has innumerable techniques to ruin it (doubt, the signifier, differ(e/a)nce, the unthought, the Other, etc.) and to transform it into a simple Ego desire. Undoubtedly, Descartes, as opposed to Lacan and contemporary philosophers, has a strong sense of identity, but this remains metaphysical: the Ego is something (*aliquid*) in so much as it is thinking; the act of thinking is not a property of the Ego but indeed its essence, and this act of thinking defines it as a being. Thus its division and mediatization are now even more obvious: the Ego and existence are distinct but the former only reaches the latter through thought, being and thought mediatize it.

On the contrary, non-philosophy postulates that the Ego is already manifested before the manifestation of being and thought, and this is in its own mode. As for the identity of being and thought (identity that is real-in-the-last-instance or transcendental in as much as it claims to be the identity of essence and of thought), it will form a first order, though derived from the Ego—that of the subject. It will take place through the Ego, but outside of it. This will be something other than an already transcendent "immediate identity" (Schelling, Hegel) or the simple indissociability of my thought and my being, since it will concern a true identity (not dialecticizable, not "mediate" in this sense but "radical" as the Ego itself) and consequently will concern a unilateral duality of the two terms. They will no longer be given by/from philosophy in an empirical manner nor assumed to be simply abstract or as "pure abstractions" (pure substantiality and equality of thought with itself) in the sense whereby the formal objects of metaphysics are assumed "abstract" starting from experience. Non-philosophy will infer them as "abstract" through induction and deduction starting from the identity of the Ego, a radical and not semi-empirical abstraction. In a general manner, philosophy imposes its triad or posits the problem of the Ego as problem of the subject and from the subject: "to find a point at which the object (*Objekt*) and its concept, the thing (*Gegenstand*) and its representation, are originally (...) one" (Schelling). Non-philosophy, giving itself the Ego as already manifested or as the Real, does not seek it, does not seek a subject/object synthesis as subject; it proceeds by cloning the transcendental identity that is the subject of the real identity of the Ego on one hand and on the other hand of philosophical materials. But real or simply transcendental, identity is never a synthesis. So modernity along with post-modernity, which is nothing but the dissemination or differentiation of modernity, are invalidated by the new comprehension of the duality of the Ego and the subject as phenomenal content of the philosophical "subject".

# The phenomenal fulfilling of indicative formulas: "Thinking the Ego" or "Theory of the Subject"

## The invalidation of egology

*Position of the problem.* We have posited the following demand which we no longer know whether we can satisfy or not: to think the Real or the Ego as radically anterior to the subject of thought, determining it without being co-determined by it. Or moreover: to think the Ego such that it is neither thinkable nor unthinkable, from itself without relation to thought which is not without relation to the Ego. This demand has the effect of the very exclusion of the solution of Descartes or Henry, for whom thought remains *in spite of everything* co-determinant of the Ego, of its supposedly radical immanence. However it suffices to undertake "thinking the Ego" or radical immanence in order to be able to take the operation of thought into account, to record it and *to give itself* the duality of Ego and thought. But what does this "giving itself" mean? Philosophy assumes that to give = to think, so much so that thought is given or occurs twice; it presupposes that *to give oneself thought* is *to think thought*, skipping over a dyad. Descartes and his interpreter do not posit this reflection as overwritten or immediate, such that the Ego seems to be able to be given as auto-affection. In reality being issued from the Ego/thought duality, the Ego is thus at once identical and non-identical to thought, and so submits to thought which then, as thinking thought, reflexively re-envelops (or immediately in the case of Descartes according to Henry) the duality and reforms a triad (Ego/thought thought/thinking thought). If we must take account of thought, then in effect it must be about "thinking the Ego" and giving the Ego/thought duality; it is not necessary—if only philosophy demands it—that this *being-given* be once more a being-thought and that thought be redoubled or occur twice (as thought thought and thinking thought). It suffices that the being of the Ego be given-one-time and be sufficiently consistent and autonomous that it does not necessitate that thought re-occurs to give a supplementary reality of consistency and closure, of system, to this duality. *There is* thought—*in order* to eventually think the Ego—but thought is not necessary—and perhaps even foreign—to the Ego itself which can be *given* without thought (of the "givenness") regiving it. It suffices to posit the conditions which assure the radical autonomy of the being-given of the Ego in relation to thought, and consequently the being-given of thought itself. Why would the being-given of thought not be independent of thought, if not through will to all-power of thought or through philosophy? Philosophy could object that its modesty consists precisely in admitting that the only thing in its power is thought, and that consequently it can and must above all *think thought* and define the Real it can attain within the limits of this reflection. But nothing proves that thought has power over itself. This modesty is in actuality a sufficiency and a claim of mastery over self and of self. Nothing proves that thought is by essence master of itself, that auto-position, certainly effective and possible, is real… Thought can very well be thought and be radically irreflexive or immanent through its essence at least.

How is the being-given of the Ego "possible" without passing through the *cogitatio*, through the mediation of this, whether "immediatized" or immediately negated? This problem takes two forms: what type of experience and justification—fact? right? neither?—do we have of being-given-without-givenness (without thought) of the Ego? what experience do we have of thought *qua thought* but without reflection or without "thought of thought"? Before coming to the first problem, let us recall that the Ego-in-Ego is non-decisional, non-positional and non-giving-(of)-itself through-and-through, radical autonomy by definition, indifference to the *cogitatio* and *esse*, to thought and to being. The Real no longer confuses itself philosophically here with Being or the Other but with the One-in-One; its immanence is radical because it is immanence (to) itself and thus defines the Ego rather than being immanent to an Ego-form prior to and coming from philosophy.

*How to think Given-without-givenness as foreclosed to thought?* We can undoubtedly define it through a set of positive and negative traits: its radical immanence, the absence of a hinter-world, givenness or operation, etc. But this must be through using terms of a philosophical origin submitted to a certain axiomatic type of treatment—we have said this and will continue to say it. But there is seemingly an even more fundamental and prejudicial problem underlined by philosophy: does the radically immanent Ego… exist? How is it given in an "undoubtable" way?

Does this then concern an attempt to demonstrate the existence of the Real in the metaphysical manner of the demonstration of the existence of God and then the Ego in the *cogito* understood as demonstration or conclusion by most of Descartes" philosophical interpreters? Evidently not. These philosophical demonstrations must be suspended when it comes to the Ego if the Ego must be given before any thought, any concept or essence and if, as reflected-reflecting and as mediatized, they undermine or alter their object, give it and thus draw it out of reality, render it "doubtful" [*douteux*] in a new sense of the term implying the supersession of the Ego toward God or the system of philosophy. Thought in general is excluded, not only reflexive/auto-positional thought but also the unreflected or "overwritten" thought that we call 'semi-philosophical" of auto-affection (Descartes himself and Henry: "eyes closed", intuition suspended or reduced). This generally "cogitative" or 'semi-cogitative" process still ultimately alters the being-given of the Ego through an ultimate form of givenness. Moreover, the criteria of "fact" and "right", inadequate to the radical given, of the being-object, the given as objectification and of "intuition", however originary (Husserl), are suspended. If then there is no exterior criterion or givenness of the being-given, if not being-given itself, no thought or argument of the Real, can we and must we still prove that it exists? Does it need a proof? Is this simply about *recognizing* it from outside, a recognition of the Real? This philosophical question no longer has any meaning. Our minimal manner of defining the Real renders the demonstration of its "existence" useless since the Real does not *exist*, or *is* not... In effect though, since we think it, we must do so under the form through which thought manifests itself in relation to the proof but without being proof; we must posit it, and this is what we have implicitly done, as first term in axioms. The Ego, because it no longer comes under the "ontological" axioms of an ego-logy, comes under the axioms of an authentic axiomatic, not formal but transcendental. Not that it "exists", not that there are criteria (exterior, rational, cogitative) of the Real. Even in philosophy it imposes its "logic" and its own constraints which are not those of thought but those of the "given", such that it must accept it, or partially refuse it, but then it is always auto-contradictory like doubt in Descartes, and must finish by recognizing this given—philosophy is a recognition of the Ego (by the criterion of doubt, etc.). But here we are thinking a being given such that from it, thought does not put *itself* to, nor put *it* to the test, but *is* put to the test at the very point of being rendered useless and contingent: the "logic" of the given here is no longer part of thought or givenness. On the other hand, if this is a question of thinking this being-invalidated of thought by the Real, the problem is resolved through the positioning of the Real as first term of an axiomatic. As such this is undoubtedly the place for picking up again on a Spinozist motif and for radicalizing it: the immanence of the Real is *index sui*. Not that it demonstrates itself (through appeal to a hinter-world) but it *shows itself* (and thus other things) or manifests itself, it is a phenomenon-(of)-itself. Undoubtedly this generality can still have a meaning in the philosophical order. But this relentlessly seeks a proof of radical being-given, of Manifested-without-manifestation, a proof through something other than itself. We must stop posing the problem of the radical given in relation to any thought, but above all in relation to the philosophical form of thought. All of these hesitations, disjunctions and questions still assume the *power* of thought. *In reality we grasp the Ego "from" the Ego itself, the One "from" the One itself.* So much so that this real-Ego, is not to be admitted or refused, affirmed or negated—it is not demanded from us any more to rediscover it by closing our eyes—at least that the Real precedes this disjunction proper to thought, but to posit it simply as an authentic first term that we will define through a set of axioms. We will not form a (philosophical, cogitative or "exterior" and from recognition) hypothesis *on* the Real with this idea of a Given-without givenness, nor *in its name*, but rather alongside it we will give ourselves the means of positing hypotheses, which is to say the means of causing thought to function otherwise than philosophically. Radical immanence is an emergence or a discovery in relation to thought, but it is nothing without a thought appropriate to it. If we wish to pose the problem in terms of an argument, a proof as philosophy poses it, it suffices to exercise thought in a coherent or rigorous manner as an axiomatic demands, and conforming to its status as radical dependence on the Ego; to take as rule its determination-in-the-last-instance by the Ego and to undo its philosophical "stature"… and its "natural" or "sponta-neous" resistance to the Real. We can undoubtedly formulate this status of the being-given-without-givenness by saying that we *let-it-be-given* to us as first in relation to thought. But this formula must be understood as an axiomatic that demands the essence of index-(of)-itself of the Ego. There is thus no longer any reason to describe being-given in an exclusive manner through a philosophical choice rather than through another kind, or through a semi-choice of the *auto-affection* type and affectivity and through simple immediate opposition and negation of the *cogitatio*. The radical Ego has effects on thought that non-philosophy explores, the task being to draw out all of the consequences of the being-given for thought, philosophy included. But these effects are not what prove it, being rather *occasionally* deduced from it. It is essential to renounce natural or congenital objections from philosophy, its claims of givenness, the recog-nition and validation of the Ego, and instead to remodel "thought" or the cogitative in terms of the autonomy of the Real. If there is a relative "criterion" of the radical given, it is post-real, no longer of recognition but of invention and of discovery in and of thought. The thought "issued" from the Ego, when it is given through-and-through, cannot be a recognition but rather an emergence that is itself radical. All the objections of thought and its questions about the being-given express only the philosophical refusal of the Given, and moreover, of the foreclosure to what the Ego constrains in thought in its relation to it.

Thus the radical Ego is not one hypothesis among others—problematic in its title or in its genre as hypothesis. This is its reality, the only type of cause which makes thought into a hypothesis in a new way. Never the hypothesis of the hypothesis—the real-Ego is not this—but that which makes it possible that thought necessarily exercises itself under this form that is identically in-the-last-instance that of scientific hypothesis and philosophical thesis. This hypothesis is no longer itself reflected, sure of itself and problematic simultaneously: it is a "thesis", an un-reflected position or rather a "simple" one, not redoubled (neither certain of itself nor doubtful), which is "under" the Ego or de-duced from it and in its dependence. Non-philosophical thought is not comprehensible in an epistemological-experimental manner, the identity or essence of the hypothesis not themselves being hypothetical. In general, a hypothesis is a thought which submits itself to the real and to its proof: but here it is submitted to the proof of the foreclosed Real and not only to that of trans-cendent experience ("the limits of experience"). It is thus transcendental at the same time as experimental and it is this double relation to the given that determines it as hypo-thesis. Thus we will oppose the thesis or philo-sophical dogma, but not the philosophical materials: for the very reason that it is a transcendental hypothesis through its dependence on the Ego, it maintains to philosophy a relation of quasi-experimentation.

Finally, the given-without-givenness proves to be rather (of)-itself and *consequently* through the form of the thought it causes. It invalidates the objections of philosophical thought. There is no proof or argument here since it conditions all proofs and arguments, and in particular the most rigorous axiomatization. There is no admitting, nor any refusing. A "neutral" thought is required, without affirmation or negation, without any such position. This is already imposed, it is the "forced hand" that does not enter into the play of thought but determines it. That being-given-without-givenness is philosophically paradoxical or contradictory does not matter: it is no longer so for the thought it makes possible and which ceases to demand accounts and proofs from it…

*The non-egological status of thought.* A cogitation undoubtedly inter-venes to posit or give the Ego, more specifically as the position or givenness of its being-given itself without-givenness; *but in what sense does it exercise itself in the mode of reflection or of the doublet?* The being-given-without-thought of the Ego and thought-without-reflection (without redoubling, absolutely simple or un-reflected) come together with a certain non-reciprocal type of consistency, without reconstituting an auto-positional simultaneity (re-positioning by thought). It suffices, in order to be coherent and not to return surreptitiously to philosophy's habits, to think within the limits of this hypothesis, to take it as regulatory and not to contravene it. What does this simple thought, without reflection, entail as type of exercise or progress in order to remain precisely "simple"? It suffices to analyze the formulations which have been given until the present moment and to free up the rules, still implicit, of its exercise. They use philosophical terms (Ego, thought, reflection, givenness), but by submitting them to a certain operation of abstraction. Not of henological negation, mediate or immediate—it is not about taking terms from philosophy and negating them from the Ego as being by definition inadequate to it—but *of simplification or reduction of their nature as auto-positional doublet to a unique and simple usage—though positive—of each of its terms.* They are reduced to the state of *first terms* deducted from the philosophical field and deprived of their philosophical "signification". Not of their empirico-linguistic or representational content which, more often, serves rather to maintain the residual support of these quasi-symbols, but of their formal philosophical trait of auto-position, the "reflexive" or "semi-reflexive" redoubling: these are *simple terms*, designated identities. Non-philosophy begins as a quasi-symbolization or formalization proceeding by symbolic position of identities. We can say that a transcendental axiomatization, not mathematical, of philosophy, rather than an ultimately "negative" philosophy or a "scientific" axiomatization of philosophy. Of course this transcendental axiomatization of philosophy, which is an aspect of non-philosophy, is only possible due to and is only required by the being-given of the Ego as being without-givenness or "first" in relation to it.

The symbol "Ego" then designates the Real in the mode of a "first name" deducted from philosophy but philosophical indefinable and indemonstrable within a "cogito" or an egology; it is only implicitly defined by axioms that bear on its essence and its possible usage in relation to the *cogitatio* and the *esse*. This method of non logical *mathesis* applies to all the terms the theory of the subject uses. Outside of this treatment, "Ego" will designate a concept or a supplementary thesis, a hypothesis of the philosophical type concerning the Real assumed "in itself". For its part, the Ego "itself" will remain ambiguous from the point of view of its theoretical value. This will abandon it to the metaphysical state of the auto-reflexive mode, of the Aristotelian "thought of thought". This last philosophical concept is without rigorous theoretical value; the "thought of thought" is indeed an "axiom", but in the ontological sense of the term meaning a certain poorly defined intuitive obvious fact which oscillates, according to the philosophical context, between the psychological (the "internal", the "consciousness of self", or even "auto-affection" as internal transcendental experience) and metaphysics ("intellectual intuition", which is the object of the latter: thought or any corporeal act). These possible meanings constitute a system such that, within the philosophies of the Ego, no theoretical "decision" is any longer possible. They are never sure of being able to distinguish between the psychological and the metaphysical or the scientific and the theoretical. The distinctions of sensible intuition or intellectual intuition, and even that of auto-affection or intuition which is undoubtedly of a superior degree within the apprehension of radical immanence, are also too short because they are still situated within the philosophical horizon and do not pose the theoretical problem of the Real content of the real, the radical Immanence content of immanence, the Ego content of the ego etc., but infer through a philosophical operation of overwriting or identification in place of posing it as given-without-givenness. The philosophical axiom of the "thought of thought" can be realized under several undecidable forms; the act of reflection or thinking thought can bear on a thought already made or a corporeal act, so much so that auto-reflection, if it is immanent, is devoted in every way to the exteriority or transcendence that it claims to attribute to the Ego, and so the radicality of immanence is never realized. Even when auto-affection is substituted for the auto-reflection of thought, the latter continues to co-determine the former because *"global" philosophical auto-reflection remains the operative horizon of the assumed immanence of the Ego.*

In order to dissolve the amphibology of the Ego and philosophy and produce a non-Cartesian theory of the Ego and then the subject, it is necessary then to abandon the philosophical concept of the Ego and the philosophical *usage* of thought, the "concept", and to treat the "Ego" as a first name within a axiomatic determined by it in-the-last-instance. This axiomatic is in general transcendental because it is no longer logical or formal and bears on philosophical objects which completely maintain, by definition, a relation to the Real and so are not the symbols of "empty" pure logical forms. But it is transcendental first because inheres in the dependence of the Real—no longer the dependence of beings and/or Being, but precisely of the "anterior" Ego still in every ego-theo-logy. The Ego may be the "object" of axioms but it is the real cause of this "transcendental" usage of axioms and the reduction of thought to this form. It ceases to be an objectified object of philosophical axioms (divided, alienated by this "objective" status) and an objectifying subject. On the one hand it is cause, but in-the-last-instance, of a necessary (but not exclusively) axiomatic thought; and on the other hand it is a term or "symbol" of this thought, without circle. This aspect is that of a simple *mathesis transcendentalis*: not a mathematics but a *mathesis*; not a matheme but a mathesis of the Ego, of the *cogitatio* and the *esse*—this is the phenomenal content of the "theory of the subject". In this way the Ego abandons its relative-absolute autonomy, its principle [*principielle*] and amphibological auto-position of the "first" in order to only be a "first name" without primacy, name of the cause that that makes such a thought real and possible. The radical autonomy of the Real gives to thought its proper (relative) autonomy, which it comes to exercise as *axiomatic decision*. The transcendental axiomatic now thereby gives its phenomenal sense to the old idea of *philosophia prima*. This axiomatic aspect, it must be remarked, is no longer first in the metamathematical claim, philosophical in origin, which used the axiomatic as a foundational process. The axiomatic is no longer here a philosophy, but only an instrument "in the hands" of the Ego, or more precisely of thought given in the mode of the Ego and which therefore accepts the destitution of its auto-sufficient mastery.

# From the Ego to the Subject as "force-(of)-thought"

It remains to determine the essence of this "thought" which nonetheless neither reflects nor auto-affects itself. This can only concern the *identity of thought*. We must define the content this identity claims.

Non-philosophy "postulates" that the Ego is already revealed through-and-though in its proper mode before the manifestation of being and thought. But once the Ego is thus given without an operation of constitutive givenness, but only of givenness as first name, what happens beyond it for the dyad of thought and being, in which it no longer participates? The general economy of the philosophical triad is shattered as soon as the Ego "leaves" philosophy or, more exactly, possesses the precession of primacy. In philosophy, the Ego or the One is in general divided or composed of two heterogeneous, side-by-side functions: an undivided One, but *also* an inseparable division of the One, the One-(of-the)-division if we can put it that way. They are assumed to be the same One which is therefore a bifacial entity, real *and* transcendental with more or less mediation. But from now on, because the undivided One is itself radically autonomized and 'separated" as nothing but undivided or the Real, it takes leave from it, which is to say, without being still determined by it, the divided One or rather the One-(of-the)-division that also autonomizes itself though relative to the former. This One which "claims to be" of the division, and that the division reciprocally conditions within philosophy, is no longer real but only "transcendental". This is then no more the One of the philosophical triad which is real *and* transcendental, but it is what this becomes when it ceases to be *also* real in order to be reduced to the transcendental state and when the division no longer affects the real One nor even, as we see incessantly, the transcendental One; so that its intimate nature, the relation of this One and the division, must in turn be modified since the One in general ceases to be divided and split into two in order to be "simplified".

The new distinction of thought and being, which is the object of the transcendental One, can no longer be that of the duality at the base of the philosophical triad (for example in the *cogito*): it is no longer reflected within the terms that it links and that it opposes, nor are its terms reflected in it. This is a *simple* division, absolutely unreflected, a simple and formal void, a nothingness non-determined by its terms and limits; "abstract" and universal nothingness, without reflection or auto-position. We will also call this *nothingness that is non-positional-(of)-itself "non-phenomenological Distance"*.

The transcendental One for its part integrates with this nothingness or this universal irreal which serves, let us say, as its support but precisely maintains with this support an immediate relation such that the One and this division no longer are reflected one within the other: the transcendental identity is not affected itself by the support which it nonetheless needs.

If within philosophy the two usages of the One are drawn from the *same* One, the two states of the One elaborated here are not "the same" but are identical only through "cloning". The real One, when it claims to be of the universal division and when it is related by force to this division, or apprehended from its point of view, allows itself to extract what we will call a transcendental "clone". The transcendental function does not modify the One or the Real, but it is inconceivable without it: *they are thus identical in vision-in-One*; the transcendental clone of the Ego is identity in-Ego. The transcendental One is therefore situated "between" the Real itself and an "empirical" given, here the abstract and simple difference of thought and being, non-phenomenological Distance. Since in philosophy the difference between thought and being, which is neither one or the other, presents itself nonetheless as the work of thought itself, we will call the constituted structure of this transcendental identity a subject or *force-(of)-thought*, by its immediate relation to the "support" of universal and abstract Distance and of this vehicle itself. It is the identity not of thought and being, which would form a synthesis anew, but-(of)-their abstract difference.

The force-(of)-thought is beyond the Ego; more precisely it is the beyond itself, or the Other in person; the originary or first outside-Ego but in-Ego. Effectively it is necessary to distinguish transcendence from the unilaterality that affects it. This unilateralizing identity *for the* difference of being and thought forms the order of the first "after" the Ego but in-Ego, a transcendental order which is to say not of transcendence but of the essence *of* or *for* transcendence. The "subject" or the force-(of)-thought is the complex phenomenal content of what philosophy redoubles and hallucinates as "Other".

In order to avoid confusions it is necessary to distinguish between: 1) the Ego of philosophy, which is "the same" but divided between a first *presupposed* Ego or an Ego assumed as given, and an Ego concluded to be existent; between an Ego assumed-One and an Ego divided by being and thought; between the Real and existence: these are the amphibologies of the philosophical theory of the subject; 2) The Ego of "non-philosophy" which is indivisible Ego-in-Ego, but which gives place to a *duality* not obtained by division, that of the force-(of)-thought; or moreover which is accompanied by a *clone* or a transcendental function of unilateralizing identity, this too being radical. In place of the divided Ego itself, a unique undivided Ego, and an*other* identity which applies also to the difference between being and thought which serves as its support. This consists then in not confusing the (divisible) *philosophical division of the Ego* and (indivisible) *non-philosophical dualyzing of the Ego*. "German idealism", for example, conceives of the divided One made of two associated statuses, unthinkable since from one to the other identity is lost and since we then fall into contraries (philosophy confuses thinking and thinking-through-contraries, moving within contraries; it thereby confuses thinking and imagining…).

We can resume this real critique of Cartesianism and this non-Cartesian Ego through axioms opposed to those of egology and through a theorem which is the object of the following chapter:

**1** There is (the) Ego—but through the Ego itself.

**2** The Ego is not—but (is) in-Ego and thus foreclosed to Being.

**3** The Ego does not think—but gives itself as in-Ego and thus as foreclosed to thought.

Hence the theorem: *the Ego determines-in-the-last-instance, which is to say through transcendental cloning, the subject as force-(of)-thought.*

Finally: a) the Ego does not think and is not a substance; the amphibology of the Ego and thought, of the Ego and being, is invalidated (if not dissolved). On the other hand, it is the "cause" not of thought and being but of the essence of their difference, a cause called "in-the-last-instance". Auto-reflection but also the semi-(re)flection of "auto-affection" are excluded from the Ego as Real, by definition it is foreclosed to thought; b) Thought is no longer a *res*, a substance, and still less an object, an essence, an end that the Ego would strive to achieve; rather from the outset it is "force" because it confuses itself with this non-phenomenological distance that unilaterally emerges from its transcendental essence. "Force" is a unilateral duality that carries out determination-in-the-last-instance and transcendental cloning for the first time; c) The force-(of)-thought is the phenomenal content of the 'subject'. So much so that the Ego, purely immanent, neither objective nor subjective, can be accompanied but not necessarily by the subject of the force-(of)-thought. *The Ego and the subject cease to be confused and distinct at the heart of their sameness* [Mêmeté]: *the Ego enjoys a radical autonomy*, *the subject a relative autonomy*. The amphibology of the philosophical expression "theory of the subject" is dissolved within an immanence of the Ego and a transcendence (but transcendental through its essence) of the subject as clone of the Ego.

# How the Ego determines-in-the-last-instance the Subject or the force-(of)-thought: From auto-reflection to axiomatic thought

What does the duality of thought and being become when the Ego is radically immanent and thought in an axiomatic mode as such?

The *cogitatio* is in general, meaning within its philosophical usages, a relation to (representation, intention, etc.) Being. But this generality, as we know, is divided into two extreme cases. This relation can be unilaterally vectorized and related to already given or presupposed Being, as *ousia* (Aristotle) for example: a relation without correlation or reciprocity, thought is then relative to the known things that exist anterior to it. Or rather thought can relate itself to itself, it is thus auto-reflexive and, in this way, identical to the very Being it no longer aims for nor presupposes and with which it fulfills itself. Either thought is not substance and aims for substance, or it realizes itself as substance. But even in the first case a certain reflexivity belongs to it, even if this is only that thought of thought continuing to presuppose Being without being its equivalent in an idealist manner, as if auto-reflexivity failed to produce it. In both cases though, thought redoubles itself in two relations: a reflexive relation to itself and a relation relating itself moreover to Being, either essentially or inessentially, to Being with which it then confuses itself or which it even presupposes.

So on the relation of thought with itself, with Being, with the Ego, the traditional philosophical antinomies are always perceptible. Nevertheless these two cases are "the same" *in philosophy's interior*. Because (known) Being, to which thought asymmetrically relates itself, is in reality already posed in itself at least as knowable, either within an explicit statement or implicitly, through the most general philosophical argumentation which is (according to Parmenides' famous axiom) that Being never really subsists without knowledge or thought, so much so that philosophy's congenital idealism fulfills and reveals itself for what it is within the *cogito*, for example, where thought thinking-thought, auto-reflexivity, reaches Being with more or less mediation and closes its own loop. That thought swerves within its relation to itself toward being-*ousia* or toward some alterity that would come back to it, or that it appears directly to close in on itself and to reveal itself then as Being does not matter for a theory of the subject: *the relation always postulates, in its philosophical concept at least, its inversion or reversal, a co-relation*, a correlation that is less visible but more essential for the simple fact that it casts within the object the image of knowledge or within Being that of thought; finally it assumes the Real is knowable or thinkable and not—this will be the truly destructive asymmetry of the correlation, the most radical unilateralization—knowledge as determinant without reciprocity. On this point the Greco-modern conflict, for example, between Aristotle and Descartes, which Heidegger had believed himself able to recast through accentuation of the asymmetry of being and thought, through the (co)respondence of the latter to the former, then Deconstruction through the radicalized asymmetry of the Other and the Logos, is without relevance and leaves for the philosophical position the problem of its authority. The problem is instead of subtracting the relation… from the correlation, from the relation of disjunctive inclusion of reciprocity, of "community" or "system", which is its nourishing element and its essence, and of determining this essence by the Ego within the dependence in which it now inheres.

When the Ego is reduced to its immanence, it effectively subtracts the Real from being which is henceforth "irreal" but possesses a specific reality, that of transcendence; and the identity of thought from auto-reflection which is henceforth uni-(re)lational or uni-lateral. Thought loses its intentional nature, it is inessential or essential and auto-intentional, with regard to the now immanent Ego which can no longer be intentioned; and it only keeps it, transformed moreover, for the experience or the empirical given: not as inessential, indeed as essential, but in relation to what is given within the sole region of transcendence that is in-essential. If the constituted forms of thought, "sensation", "knowledge", "science" in the sense that philosophy is able to understand them, relate themselves to Being as to another term, or even to the Other, without constituting it, if their outline of auto-reflexivity is played out inessentially on the part of this term and if its principal term is instead the elucidation of the meaning of Being, the force-(of)-thought then from one perspective does not have for an end or intentionality the elucidation of the Ego that it can no longer "aim for" objectively and, from the other perspective, is in the first position but without primacy, determined by the Ego itself in this situation but not at all by its ontological or hierarchical inessentiality.

What then becomes of the aforementioned antinomy? With Aristotle, but under the now non-Aristotelian condition of the Ego's radical autonomy rather than under that the relative autonomy or intentionality of the *ousia*, we will posit the force-(of)-thought as a "unilateral" relation, not correlative or reciprocal; as "uni-lation" which, far from being a relation to… the Ego, takes root in-Ego and deploys itself unilaterally from the Ego without ever returning, either toward it and essentially so, or toward itself and inessentially so. The *cogitatio* reveals its phenomenal content within the force-(of)-thought as relation in-Ego rather than to-the-Ego from one perspective; and as relation-without-relation to experience (the philo-sophical given) from another perspective. Thought is certainly relative to… the Ego in the sense that it depends on it for its reality alone or its lived givenness (not for its specific constitution of relation). The *cogitatio* is lived in-Ego without maintaining the relation to the Ego but at the very most to the data of experience. This a-relational identity of "uni-lation" prevents it from dividing itself and from multiplying itself. With Descartes, but under the non-Cartesian condition of the truly radical immanence of the Ego, we will posit the identity of thought and Being, but a simple identity, not auto-reflexive and not even simply "unreflected", so much so that it is identity for abstract and simple difference (of Being and thought) which does not combine itself with its terms. We will call it "uniflected", thought only relating itself to itself because it is in-Ego or real in-the-last-instance: this is the internal constitution of the force-(of)-thought. With Aristotle we will affirm the subordination of thought to the Real, but to the Real as Ego rather than as Being or substance. With Descartes we will affirm the transcendental immanence of the force-(of)-thought and thus the priority of the a priori of knowledge over the object, but in a non substantialist and non idealist context. "Thought" is a force-(of)-thought, real through its cause, transcendental through its essence, woven with an abstract or non-phenomenological transcendence through its specific nature. The Ego-identity entails the priority of the Real over thought and thought over the object: this is the radical solution to the antinomy of Being and thought like to the antinomy of the "Greek" and the "Modern". The invalidation of the "first principle" consummates itself between the Ego with its primacy-without-priority and the subject or thought as first-without-reflection.

From the Ego to the subject as force-(of)-thought, from the Real to relation as unilation, a new type of causality is established, a non-ontological type, a causality called "*determination-in-the-last-instance*", meaning from the Real under the form of a radical transcendental identity, without synthesis, for identity and difference. This causality is the essence of the force-(of)-thought and condenses itself within it. It is this causality that destroys the spirit of hierarchy or the ontological *primacy and priority* that reigns in philosophy. It frees up here the real phenomenal content or order as irreversibility, i.e. the irreversible *radical priority* or the primacy of the Real over the force-(of)-thought and the priority of the latter over the abstractions that are "being" and "thought", and in general over the auto-reflexive circularity of philosophy. The order or unilaterality that results from the Ego no longer encompasses the Ego itself. The Real causes the order or the first to begin in thought or at least in its transcendental essence. This is less an order interior to thought, still transcendent, scientifico-metaphysical (order of reasons, of the anterior and posterior) than a transcendental order manifested within the exercise of the force-(of)-thought. That the Ego and the subject are identical, but in-the-last-instance alone. is the cause of order or the most originary order.

# Force-(of)-thought and auto-affection

If radical immanence understood as One-in-One or Ego-in-Ego would seem irreducible to an interpretation in terms of *auto-affection* (Descartes according to Michel Henry and above all Henry himself), the same does not necessarily apply for the subject rightly so-called or force-(of)-thought whose internal construction may at first appear identical to that of auto-affection. Does a difference exist or not between these essences such that in one case, the addition of the absolutely immanent Ego (deprived even of auto-affection) is more than a simple addition and implies, if we take it into consideration, an internal difference between them? Auto-affection is in one case assumed to be already the very content of the Ego, which is thereby reduced, while in the other the force-(of)-thought infers itself from the Ego which determines it. Not only must the Ego then have a more originary content but, if there is some equivalent of auto-affection in the force-(of)-thought, it had better amount to an instance that is no longer the Ego but the transcendental clone that follows from the Ego.

Complementarily—this is a consequence—an essential criterion of their real distinction which constitutes a symptom subsists in their possibility, or not, of thematizing thought adequate to the Ego and in general in their possibility of *thinking* radical immanence starting from philosophical discourse. The latter is in any case and in each case required, but it may be required rigorously in one case—its usage is thematized as part of the a complete gesture or is included within the "result"—or naively and so contradictorily in the other, philosophy imposing itself upon thought as a repressed entity, rendering the problematization of its status impossible. Auto-affection first assumes the philosophical horizon of the triad but as immediatized and consequently the essence of the Ego as still in fact co-determinant, so much so that the analysis cannot go beyond auto-affection and the usage of philosophy to be thematized and thematizable. The force-(of)-thought posits the problem of rendering philosophy immediately contingent or non-constituant otherwise, evidently for the Ego and relatively for itself which demands a certain usage and is capable of elaborating the proper status of this usage.

The inference of the force-(of)-thought from the real Ego alone (truly immanent in all its dimensions), but with the help of the philosophical triad as simple occasion, and additionally the production of auto-affection from a still transcendent immanence or from that triad conserved at once as presupposition or ultimate horizon of its constitution: these two gestures are unable to produce exactly the same effects. In one case the triad is a simple material from which the force-(of)-thought is extracted, admittedly through itself which presupposes it but already in-One or without auto-positing itself. In the other, it equally identifies itself with a "radical" immanence but one that still floats in transcendence and consequently *overwrites* it onto itself, producing the structure called "auto-affection". Let us assume that in each case the process is that of an "identification" of the philosophical triad. It then produces these two essences or at least the transcendental identity that is their decisive component (though not the only one); and the cause of this production is naturally an already given or real identity, characterized by its radical immanence. But this radical immanence is here, now, the object of a new distinction or a distribution not always made and which, unnoticed, leads straight to a new dogmatism: *the distinction between its thought and its usage as transcendent or as immanent.* The theme of radical immanence thus does not suffice to clearly decide on the situation and remains partially undetermined as long as the question of its usage in its specific mode within thought or its transcendent usage that it surreptitiously re-inscribes within the philosophical horizon is not posed. The immanent usage of radical immanence determines, beyond the Ego, a transcendental identity that undoubtedly relates itself by definition to the philosophical triad, but which is no longer itself co-determined by this triad which is effectively simple, non-positioning and non-giving-(of)-itself. Its transcendental usage on the other hand determines itself as a mixture and does so twice: as real *and* transcendental (hence the identification of auto-affection and the Ego); as transcendental *and* empirical or co-determined, at least negatively, by "phenomenological distance" simply repressed outside the Ego or overwritten in it. Auto-affection is thus an auto-reflection *overwritten* by (transcendent) identification (to a transcendent identity). This auto-overwriting only opposes itself very partially then to auto-position or auto-givenness. Its novelty resides in the introduction of radical immanence but it is a merely philosophical novelty since this transcendental identity remains transcendent in origin since it requires, still complementarily, not only the simple *support* of distance or abstract difference, but this support such that it co-determines it equally in its essence of auto-affection.

Strictly speaking, since this overwriting brings itself about through the means of a radical identity, we will have to describe it as a *semi-auto-overwriting* and symmetrically as a radical semi-immanence. Partially still or through one of its simply limited aspects, it remains a philosophical operation of the constitution of auto-affection. The emergence of transcendental identity, essence of auto-affection, has not found its most immanent cause, its cause *by immanence*, and remains ordered in the universal philosophical horizon, assumed as given and sufficient. Transcendent *and* transcendental, it always participates in the constitutive transcendental Appearance of philosophy.

The internal structure of auto-affection cannot at all be that of the force-(of)-thought. The philosophical triad allows itself to be recognized transparently; its simplicity is a forced or constrained simplicity, acquired through a partially *ex machina* operation, thus a life that is not radically and actually lived, performatively lived; it is only semi-non-giving-(of)-itself, being semi-giving or still semi-positioning-(of)-itself. Auto-affection is still a philosophical mechanism or semi-mechanism; still in one aspect a structure where the categorical relation (substance/accident) is not suppressed but truncated, radicalized within the element of transcendence alone. Identity, simplicity, unicity: these essences of auto-affection do not have the purity that they have within the force-(of)-thought. These are the residues of rational psychology or the science of the soul, which has only been repressed, the "immanent" critique of the Kantian critique of the paralogisms has not been carried to term.

"Radical immanence", no more than any unitary conception of the Real, is therefore, within its generality, not sufficient or reliable for the objectives that are assigned to it, if the "critical" question is posed concerning knowing how to think it, with what thought it is possible to vanquish philosophy's authority over its own terrain and to forbid it from surreptitiously returning. In any case, what can signify this appeal to "thought": is it some criterion of the Real? Philosophies of radical immanence (beyond that of Michael Henry), not having posited thought as determined through-and-through by the Real, are the victims of a "return of the repressed" and only can postulate one last time that thought is co-determinant of the Real, the first and last thesis of philosophical sufficiency. Of course, thought is not the only or principal criterion, how to think immanence is not the really decisive point. In reality, when "radical immanence" gives place to a return of philosophy it *has not been* put forward as sufficiently radical. It suffices then to think philosophy as absolutely immanent under any condition— except to think this radical adequately or by axioms—so that an immanent usage of thought can be made.

The modifier "semi-" signifies that the philosophical, the auto-reflexive or the mediated, phenomenological distance, too, has undergone the operation of an immediate negation, of an im-mediatization or an only transcendent "immanentization". From this point of view, the rock of non-philosophy inheres in this thesis, in this transcendental hypothesis: the Radical precedes and determines radicalization; Immanence precedes and determines immanentization or "immanates" it; the Real precedes and determines every operation (of negation, position, givenness, negation/affirmation, etc.). We will only put into relation the "non" of the (non-) One or "non-philosophy" and that of the "immediate negation" practiced by auto-affection in order to distinguish them by their origin, cloning within the vision-in-One, double or mixture within the auto-affection assuming the philosophical horizon co-constitutive; by their work. actual and performative in the first case, and partially differed and objectified in the second; by their effect, of positive and radical suspension or even repression and overwriting. By a paradoxical turn typical of philosophical reason, the deconstruction and philosophy of auto-affection respond, forming a new antinomy, the one aggravating the Dyad, the other the One or Identity, but each ultimately through means of transcendence, meaning through a still philosophical operation rather than one issued by the Real. So much so that auto-affection has certain effects of a deconstruction by radical immanence; and this deconstruction certain effects of an overwriting of the logos by the Other. The identity that Henry now adds to auto-affection and which overwrites philosophical structure is in fact assumed to be co-determined by thought and so already somewhat in the position of the Other rather than the One: hence it too severs or destroys within philosophy (it dismembers the mixtures or dissolves the amphibologies), such an ultimate auto-operation of philosophy upon itself; and it moves itself according to a circle, the structure *in itself*—auto-affection and thought reciprocally co-determinant—revealing itself to be *for itself* and "producing" the "immanent" Ego at the end of the process. This semi-hermeneutical sterility can only be overcome if thought is forced by the Ego to no longer proceed as a circle and to "produce" emergence: *the most immanent is also the most heteronomous to philosophy*, to the point of being unable to act on philosophy except by a subject that is a force, force-(of)-thought emerging ahead of rather than beyond philosophy. Auto-affection remains a ultimate amphibology that only the vision-in-One can invalidate, reserving the possibility of a relative autonomy of philosophy and the function that manifest it, those of simple "support" for the force-(of)-thought or of "fantasy" for the subject. From this point of view, the subject of non-philosophy is inseparable from a philosophical support that does not constitute it in its essence but only conditions the knowledge of that essence, and that testifies to philosophy's "consistency".

# The problem of "knowledge" of the Ego: Refutation of the idealism of auto-affection

Following this dualysis of the *cogito* do we already have a true knowledge or science of the Ego, at least such that philosophy demands it? Let us start with philosophy and its limit, auto-affection. In philosophy the Ego as immediate sensing or auto-affection is in an immediate relation, a non-relation to thoughts and ideas (*cogitationes* and *idea*e), but does this non-relation allow an authentic knowledge of the Ego itself? It is auto-affection from the point of view moreover of thought, of the *cogitatio*, and *for* it; this is why the problem of an *idea* of the Ego arises (Descartes), an idea of substance of which all that is sure is that, under these conditions, it is its knowledge. Effectively, there is a circle made up of substance and attribute in general: the Ego must be known, as substance, through its attribute, thus through the ideas; hence a certain reversibility or inversion of these relations: between Ego and *cogitatio*, between substance and attribute. Certainly the Ego can only be known through thought—by definition—but is this necessarily the same relation, a reversal aside, as that of the Ego to thought? Every thought *of* the Ego is in any case a thought *in-Ego*, this much is evident, but this is trivial and nothing will prove that thought *of* the Ego-substance is a true knowledge of it. The reasoning is effectively this: the substance-Ego would in principle not have to be perceived immediately as substance and it needs the mediation of the attribute; but it is that in which what we immediately perceive exists, the *cogitatio*, the *idea*, thus the attribute. So when the *cogitatio* relates itself to the Ego itself or is the *idea of the Ego*, the same immediate relation of the Ego to the Idea applies for the *idea* to the Ego. There is thus an immediate circle of the Ego-subject (of the *cogitationes*) and the Ego-object (of the *ideae*); it is the same type of relation: that of the cogitative immediacy of the Ego to the *cogitationes* and that of the *ideae* to the Ego, or the relation of substance and attribute. That the *cogitatio* is in-Ego thus replaces and applies to a knowledge *of* the Ego, so much so that the specific problem of a knowledge of the Ego does not arise; it is replaced by the omnipresent immediacy of the Ego to thought.

This signifies that thought—inverse, complementary, to what happened before—is as if absorbed by the Ego, it loses its specificity and its relative autonomy to the benefit of auto-affection, and so, reciprocally, the Ego confuses itself with thought or at least inseparably integrates with the second and so loses its radical autonomy. However, thought cannot come down to cogitative immediacy, at least if it disposes of a relative autonomy— this would be the index of a mixture of the Ego and the *cogitatio*, undoubtedly a "simplified" or "overwritten" mixture. Auto-affection sees its real sense reveal itself: *it confuses itself in reality with cogitative immediacy or immediacy from the Ego to thought*. So, the Ego is not elucidated for itself but it forms a cogitative Ego, a *co-ego-gitatio*… It is necessary to say rather that the *cogitationes* are given in the mode where the Ego is given, but that the Ego is not given in the mode of cogitative immediacy. The latter then complementarily frees itself in its own way, gains its proper autonomy, and a true usage of knowledge (if not knowledge itself) of the Ego—certainly not the philosophical type—becomes possible. The knowledge or the idea of the Ego is not itself "egoic" in its autonomy and its specific essence—only in its origin-of-the-last-instance—and does not reflect its object; this reflection is representation or immediate identity.

We are not contesting the following kind of circle, of identity rather: the thought *of* the Ego is itself in its turn in-Ego because the Ego is the ultimate "center" for all possible relations. But we refuse the confusion/ identification of the Ego and thought in the very definition of cogitative auto-affection and finally the disappearance of the Ego itself, of its own mode of manifestation, and the *cogitatio* which is only examined in terms of its immediate givenness. The *cogitatio* can turn itself toward the Ego, toward the "substance" in which it is, but it does not return to itself empty, without any effect other than indicating the Ego immediately because it would already be there, but with the specific effect of thought when it is not "blended" with the Ego and reduced to its immediate being-given... The idea admittedly does not weaken the cogitative immediacy but it does not simply "redouble" it, it precisely does not redouble it neither does it risk weakening it; it is other than it, or at least other than the immediacy of the Ego. Michel Henry seems to better elaborate radical immanence than Descartes, but in reality it is always *as the result of thought* that he elaborates it by depriving it of a possible autonomy of thought as knowledge and of a recognition of the relative autonomy of philosophy. The thinking "immediate knowledge of substance" is not a true knowledge any more than its "mediate knowledge" through the attribute: it evidently uses the mediation of the attribute but does so in order to immediately deny it; it frees neither the Ego nor the attribute—thought—from their respective autonomy. Certainly for Descartes and Henry, knowledge of the Ego-substance is not absolutely immediate but immediately contains (as substance) what it knows. Thus: 1) as Ego, it should have been radically "immediate", but then this would precisely not be a knowledge, a thought; these assume that the Ego is immediately object for a knowledge, a *cogitatio/idea*, and so they do not posit the problem of the specific immediation of the Ego or its essence of the vision-in-Ego; 2) that the substance-Ego immediately contains that which knows it does not signify that knowledge of the Ego is immediate as knowledge, but signifies that in its ultimate origin it is in-Ego—this is everything and there is nothing else. We cannot move from the real origin of knowledge to conclude its object, as if there would not be a distinction between the origin and the object of a knowledge. This is idealism. As a result there is a recovery (excepting a reversal or return that is not thematized) between the "epistemological relation (Ego→*cogitationes*) and the 'substantial" or ontological relation (the inverse). By its reality or its origin, the idea of substance is immediately given in substance but that cannot then be equivalent to a knowledge of substance. This knowledge does not reduce itself to the real (immediate) origin of thought, but it possesses an object. This is undoubtedly the philosophical type of transcendental reduction of thought to its cogitative immediacy which renders an objective theory of substance useless or impossible. But if the cogitative immediacy was thought for itself, axiomatically so, and not "with" thought, thought would gain an autonomy from objectivity and a consistency that it does not have here and the problem would arise of a mediate knowledge of the Ego ("immediate" in its origin but in its origin alone, and mediate by its axiomatic form).

What positive conclusions for non-philosophy can we make from these considerations?

1) It is necessary to abandon every *philosophy of the immediate* for a true theory or knowledge—in the axiomatic style—that assumes the scientific condition of a non-circle, of a real identity that frees thought and objectification, thought otherwise reduced to immediacy and without a possible theoretical or objectifying dimension. The condition of a *potential* theory of the Ego as first in-Ego is that the Ego be distinct from thought, absolutely autonomous, and consequently that thought be freed for its own work and not through-and-through repeated in immediation. Otherwise, the means of a theory are denied from the outset.

2) The paradox (cf. Kant: the conditions of a scientific psychology against Cartesian idealism and rational psychology) is that, for a non-philosophy or a theory, we need *a condition of objectivity that is not space/time here, but the "support" ("fantasy") or the substratum = subjectum constituted by the philosophical given itself.* Just as Descartes conserved an opaque *subjectum* as a substrate of "extended" substance and made this the object of a mediate knowledge, the same applies here in order to assure the subject a certain function of knowledge if not a knowledge of the Ego (One-in-One), a generalized subjectum is needed which is no longer space but this opaque support that is philosophy in its relative autonomy. The *Refutation of Idealism* must be extended and transferred to the idealism of auto-affection, of the all-affect. There is a return in Henry and those who use him to the paralogisms of a psychology that is no longer rational, but effective. This *affective or sensible idealism* is realist, that much is true, but in reality since the affect is inseparable from thought, it is still a realism-idealism, or a idealism-realism. So apparently three terms and not only two are necessary here in the theory of the subject but also in that of the Ego (and not the Ego-as-subject). But in a general way, when we say—in philosophy—that there are only two terms (Ego and *cogitatio*, substance and attribute) and not three terms, it is because there is a *semi-mixture*, an *inseparability of the two terms*, such that the two are exceeded and

accompanied by a semi-unity, semi-identity, or term of synthesis. To the contrary, within non-philosophy, there evidently must be three terms: 1) the Real; 2) philosophy; 3) non-philosophy; but the Real is not a term, so really there are only two terms, arranged according to the relations of determination-in-the-last-instance rather than those of the semi-mixture or of the alignment of terms within the overwritten dyad.

3) The unitary or philosophical relation of substance/attribute must not be deconstructed or overwhelmed; it must conserve its duality, Ego/ *cogitatio* duality, but that duality must be the effect of its duality in Ego and in subject (attribute-being/thought). The attribute will moreover no longer be a mediation in knowledge, and in knowledge of the Ego, because this knowledge signifies that the force-(of)-thought does not any longer aim for the Ego (which we can never aim for but which we can utilize as a first term), but aims for its transcendental image. It is necessary to dualyze the Ego/thought relation rather than to immediatize it as Descartes and Henry have. Overwriting it onto itself is not to abolish its amphibology; philosophy and its sufficiency conserve themselves in this im-mediate mixture of substance and attribute. Overwritten or not, this mixture does not allow a true *theoretical usage of the substance-Ego*, but only the spiraling hermeneutics of itself and its immediacy. In this way we can explore the immediate and first mixture of the Ego and language, and produce a semi-philosophy… where science is only an impression or an appearance created by the cut pruning mediation, the cut of immediation… Finally, it is always the mixture, the philosophical triad that functions here without knowing it as an opaque *subjectum*, distant and remote, a transcendent *hypokeimenon* or an occulted identity upon which auto-affection comes to run aground, or which it attempts to limit. The *Cartesian* or *modern cut* is not only "literal", it is also unreflected or auto-affective, it is the cut of radical immanence as auto-affection, but non-Cartesianism roots itself in the vision-in-One rather than in a cut.

4) From the constant failure of philosophy in its attempt at knowledge of the Ego, we will above all not conclude that it is necessary to abandon philosophy, to proceed by an anti-philosophy, to use the argument of this powerlessness of the *cogito* in order to take the opposing view of this history and wish finally to elaborate a knowledge of the Ego, then reaching the Real that philosophy has always lacked, etc. On the one hand non-philosophy does not draw its motivation from philosophy's failure but from the positive necessity of explaining it, of elaborating the reasons of this inability within the Real itself or the Ego that forces every thought to its foreclosure, philosophy on the other hand ignores this foreclosure and claims or wants to know the Real. On the other hand, the failure of the will

to knowledge prohibits if not every theory of the Ego, at least thinking it as first term of a *unified theory of the subject*. There will be nothing more here, even less than in philosophy, of the theorem of the Ego, of conclusions or inferences of the Real; but having recognized this impossibility, the possibility of a *theorem of the subject* as force-(of)-thought opens up. This is the object of the next chapter.

# 4 DETERMINATION-IN-THE-LAST-INSTANCE: TRANSCENDENTAL THEOREM OF THE FORCE-(OF)-THOUGHT

## The causality of the one as determination-in-the-last-instance: A general outline

Having enumerated the conditions of a unified theory from the point of view of materials, it still remains to do so with the conditions from the point of view of its "syntax", which explain the former conditions, particularly the so-called relation of "unilateral duality" which allows their intrinsic identity of science and philosophy, and the relation of their identity to their Difference. On the other hand, its conditions of reality, which involve the dissolution of the epistemo-logical mixture of the hypothesis-organon and experience, the organon finding its element within a transcendental indifference to the empirical, but susceptible to tolerating a last relation to it, and more profoundly again within a real indifference. The relations of the Real and effectivity are delicate and assume, in order to be understood, the elucidation of their "syntax".

After the One and before the force-(of)-thought in which it is condensed, its own causality, which it at least tolerates and which we call *determination-in-the-last-instance*, is the fundamental concept of non-philosophy.

All of these first terms designate the real or phenomenal states of things whose invariants they describe. In particular here, this is the phenomenal "bloc" of causality. The aim is to explain, from the essence of the One, why the One *precedes* Being and representation in general, and in what mode which gives it its sense of primacy to the thesis of "precession".[1]

In order that the One or the Real be called "cause-of-the-last-instance", we need conditions that we will describe in detail: 1) in its *absolute* autonomy, "radical" moreover, it does not alienate itself in its effects and even less in its object; 2) its object thus enjoys a relative autonomy; it first manifests or presents itself under a phenomenal form, distinct from that of the One, of transcendence's resistance (Principle of Sufficient Philosophy); 3) The One does not then act through itself on this object which is absolutely indifferent to it; but 4) it is moreover the One "in-the-last-instance" which acts in the "intermediary" instance or the organon it needs and which is being and thought insofar as they are in-One, the "force-(of)-thought", the concrete bearer of this causality. Determination-in-the-last-instance and force-(of)-thought appear after the One, but the former is the transcendental essence of the latter.

Since radical immanence remains by definition in itself, it cannot move out of itself or produce something like Being or moreover beings, and this will be a "negative" but universal condition. As cause, the One is first not the cause *of* (it does not produce anything of the ontic or the ontological "outside" of itself or from itself), but *for...* Being which must present itself to itself. This cause *for...* is inalienable in its "object" (*that which* it manifests) and in its effect (it *is* this, its effect is still (in the-last-instance) vision-in-One which remains in it). The One does not become (in) its effect, it is not circularly half-cause, half-effect.

Excluded, then, are metaphysical causalities through alienation and identification to self and to Other (expression, procession, emanation, action-reaction, projection, etc.). Determination-in-the-last-instance is the only causality that is not "immanent" but of radical immanence itself as being the Real. It is neither form nor matter, neither end nor agent, the quadruple transcendental form of causality. In this way, non-philosophy has a specific causality allowing it to eliminate formalism and idealism, materialism, teleology and technologism (an important characteristic of philosophy).

But if the One does not share this power of manifestation, it can only act if it presents itself with an occasional cause, a supplementary condition that furnishes it with the materials of its efficacy but does not limit it, itself being intrinsically limited by this efficacy of the One. The One is only cause (for thought or being) if these present themselves in turn: it is thus not a creation *ex nihilo* nor a production (a technological causality) but precisely a "determination-in-the-last-instance" *alone*. Hence the importance of philosophical resistance which only manifests itself as such through a transcendental suspension and which in this way enters into the description of non-philosophy's structures.

Moreover we distinguish the effect and the end result of the One itself, its power or causality—the organon of the force-(of)-thought—and its materials too: the instance of its "unified theory", determined as theoretical pragmatic, and its object: the "essence-(of)-X", if X designates some phenomenal region.

# Development of the concept of "determination-in-the-last-instance"

That the One only acts in-the-last-instance thus means: 1) that it does not exit itself, does not alienate itself in this act; 2) that it needs, not for its essence but *if* it must have an act-(of)-itself, another, transcendental instance, in order to act on an object which here is philosophy (and any regional phenomenon), but 3) that it is still, *despite everything, finally or really* what affects this object; 4) that the thought-manifestation of this object always occurs starting from the object regardless of the mode of manifestation proper to this object, or specific to its relative autonomy; 5) that the instance of (re)presentation of the object, the force-(of)-thought and what it produces, is ultimately seized in the mode of the One or in-One, not in the mode of an image or an auto-positional transcendence.

The expression "the One acts" or "the One has a causality" is thus ambiguous. The One must be cloned precisely because it does not act directly and because acting is not a necessary trait of its essence: *if* it must have a being or a thought = X in order to stir up the effect of manifestation. Consequently, to speak properly, the One does not act but is a necessary condition, however passive and "negative", of any acting of thought on its products.

1) The One "acts" without leaving itself, dividing/sharing itself, alienating itself through *identification-to…* a given other than itself, and to itself. It does not transform itself, does not become… with "its" efficacy over an object (this is only its efficacy in-the-last-instance). It does not enter into a becoming, it retains its undivided causality, does not split it "over" what it seems to act upon. The One is neither fundamental (in relation to an object = X) nor regional. It is absolutely un-localizable since it is only "localized" in

itself: it is the "last-instance" that breaks off or forbids any unitary thought or centrality more radically than an instance of alterity or differ(e/a)nce.

2) It resolves the problem of its impossible acting precisely through recourse to another instance which registers the occasional empirical cause but whose transcendental essence is a clone-(of)-the One. If it does not act on philosophy through itself directly and continuously, then even the suspension of philosophy already exceeds its real indifference which is without object. It can only act by means of another structure that it does not continuously produce, of which instead and in any case it is the "real" essence and which it can at least reveal in an immanent phenomenal mode. The general power of the specific manifestation of the One over the philosophical given needs this instance which expressly guarantees its causality: this is the force-(of)-thought, and moreover its transcendental identity.

3) Whatever the place or the object = X where the One acts, the object = X must also be manifested in-the-last-instance "in-One", in this most radical mode of the phenomenon. Taking the one as immanent guiding thread means never leaving its intrinsic finitude of the Given whatever the region of reality wherein it acts and whatever supplementary instance we add to it.

The manifestation "in-One" is then "in-the-last-instance" because, in spite of the intermediary causes, long as they may be, that of the One is inevitable; in spite of the causality of philosophy and in spite of that of non-philosophy, that of the one is the "last" in the sense of unique real causality. It ends up, in spite of everything, in spite of mediations or obstacles, not being the only thing which is "important" but the only thing which, as real, is not destroyed, annulled or created by intermediary causalities.

It is not, then, despite certain linguistic appearances, the cause that is differentiated in relation to the effect, but the effect which, from the perspective of its object, is differentiated or distanced in relation to the cause. But however far from the cause it may be, it is the effect of that cause which is always "present" in its transcendental mode. We could think to the contrary that, however distant the cause may be, it remains cause: but that would mean that it appeared to be distant, through the effect of and from the perspective of the transcendental mode, thus alienating the Real. Determination-in-the-last-instance entails that there is a supplementary or occasional causality that bears witness to the relative autonomy of a given = X. But that *this too ends up drawing its ultimate sense from the One insofar as it is by remaining in itself*: this is a "realism" of-the-last-instance, or rather a real-without-realism, not an absolute idealism.

4) Determination-in-the-last-instance signifies that the cause is not only cause through a certain vague effect or power in general, but more

precisely *cause of identity* for being (and) thought, and that thought will always go from the cause to the effect without watching over this process, without following a reversible path and sharing its efficacy over an assumed dyad of cause and effect. The real order and the order of knowledge are identical, not opposed or circular *but identical in-the-last-instance only*: knowledge does not determine the Real but the real order determines-in-the-last-instance the order of knowledge.

5) Determination-in-the-last-instance incarnates itself in a so-called structure of "unilaterality" (of identity and non-auto-decisional decision). In its aspect other than the clone of the One, it contains the proper essence of transcendence but insofar as it is in-One, or has this clone as transcendental essence. It is therefore not *in* One; this is not a *real* and abstract *part*—if it does not codetermine it. We will pay attention to language here: "to-see-every-thing-in-One" is not to find images or representations of these things in the One as though in a mirror. *The images-of-X, its "intentions", are grasped not "in" the One but in the only mode of the One and not in the mode of an image or a transcendence in general reflecting and redoubling itself here.* This "image" exists *once*, not a second time or redoubled in the One under the form of another image (philosophy = object + its image in the subject = *two* images or "re-presentation" etc.).

We can say that the One is determination-in-the-last-instance or acts through this new transcendental instance. As transcendental cause of the force-(of)-thought, it determines the very philosophy = X upon which it acts in this way. On the other hand if it is, as transcendental, "that-in-which" and thanks to which it is manifested, we cannot say that it is the essence of philosophy itself assumed "in itself" since it only displays indifference toward it. The One, being the Real, is the transcendental cause *of* non-philosophy (as science-thought or unified theory) but *for* philosophy itself. As such "determination-in-the-last-instance" is of the One with regard first to non-philosophy, its aprioristic remainders left by philosophy in their relation to the force-(of)-thought. The One as clone is their essence and, in this way alone, is the essence of philosophy not *as* philosophy but as *the identity of philosophy*. It determines philosophy to be non-philosophy, which is to say to enter as material into non-philosophy, which is the identity of philosophy.

# On causality as "unilateral duality"

Unilateral causality is not an *ex nihilo* invention of non-philosophy. Its usage in terms of radical immanence, rather, is a theoretical discovery which itself has a history, foundational for non-philosophy. Non-philosophy proceeds to its formulation as "syntax", as "uni-tactic" rather than "syntactic" order. Extreme philosophical decisions, for example those of late Platonism, insert this into the element of transcendence as the most transcendent forms (in other respects, immanent), of the One as Unspeakable. Non-philosophy discovers another regime—immanent only—of unilaterality and defini-tively snatches it from empiricism by manifesting its full anti-dialectical force. Transcendence on the other hand can only re-establish a grounding, an ideal, an accompaniment or of reciprocity of bilaterality which suffices to limit its power of emergence, as is still the case in so-called "radical" philosophies of immanence.

The classic axiom of the philosophical usage of unilaterality is as follows: *the effect distinguishes itself from the cause which does not distinguish itself from it.*

*The formula for the cause*: "which does not distinguish itself from it", is ambiguous or imprecise. Philosophy understands it as signifying: "which *identifies itself* with its effect". The cause (for example the unspeakable One) would thus be immanent to its effect, and the load of the distinction would reposition itself explicitly over this effect, and implicitly over the cause. But non-philosophy understands this otherwise and breaks the philosophical circle: if the cause does not distinguish itself from the effect, it does not necessarily follow that it identifies itself with the effect but that it remains simply in its identity as One-in-One, which allows it not to "distinguish/ identify" itself, so much that it is not immanent to Being, to Beings, to the Multiple as the transcendent One is, but rather immanent (to) itself. The load of the distinction of the effect also returns, but now under a form that no longer forms a circle with the effect.

*The formula for the effect*: "the effect distinguishes itself from its cause" is thus also understood by philosophy in an amphibological manner, as a *circular* distinction, *simultaneously the work of the effect and that of the cause* insofar as the cause is immanent or identical to it. Non-philosophy defines the distinction otherwise: unilaterality is certainly still double, but as empirical or occasional work of the effect (of its "subject") and as not the real, but only the transcendental, work of the cause, which is to say not of the One but of the One-as-"acting"-clone thus as transcendental identity next to the empirical. Unilaterality is first unilateralization or (non-)One exercised on the "opposite" term or resistance, a suspension through which it affects every transcendent given or non(-One). But it also possesses a transcendent origin, a core of spontaneous resistance which would also be transcendentally invalidated while being manifested as such. Transcendental unilateralization does not destroy the philosophical mixture precisely because it is only transcendental and not logico-transcendental like in philosophy where this mixture can only give the appearance of destroying, by reproducing nonetheless, the other mixtures (even the thoughts of radical immanence, which are still philosophical uses of the real-One, not do not get out of this appearance).

Insofar as it is determined by the One, the effect is *in-One* without ever being able to be a real part of the One, its constituent part or its ingredient: therefore it is of an only transcendental nature. Insofar as it is autonomous in its "subject" through relation to the One, the effect is in-One only in-the-last-instance alone. Being in-One does not signify that the One reciprocally identifies itself with the effect like the Neo-Platonic solution would like to have it. Rather, it is the effect that identifies itself with the One (it is in-the-last-instance-manifested-in-One) while maintaining its autonomy though under a merely relative form. "In-the-last-instance" therefore *identically* signifies that the cause does not alienate itself in the subject of its effect or in its effect itself and that the effect for its part retains a relative autonomy.

We call *relative autonomy*, as opposed to *radical autonomy* of the One (cause), this form of unilaterality with a double origin but without circle: an empirical origin, a transcendental other. It opposes itself to the fully philosophical and idealist appearance of a dissolution of reality proper to the mixtures and of the miraculous annulment of resistance. Unilaterality thus must be specified and repositioned in the more general question of the order or the "syntax" determined by the immanence of the One-in-One. The *unilateral duality* is the syntax that excludes the philosophical simultaneity of the terms, their circle interior to auto-position, and which instead would merit the name "unitax", this word signifying not that there is only one term in play but *only* "two", a duality that is precisely unilateral (or without synthesis). It is no longer bilateral like the philosophical "Two", nor unilateral like the immanent One is in certain philosophies which strive to reappropriate it by confronting it too directly with this bilaterality. The unilateral duality, thanks to transcendental cloning, thus combines the "causality" of the One which limits it to remain in-One, and the relative autonomy of Being and/or of philosophy which has resistance as the empirical origin. This apparent contradiction is resolved by the double origin, without mediation, of relative autonomy.

But this syntax could evoke that of "Difference". This is reversibility of cause and effect, of immanence and transcendence, of the One and Being, *fold* of the Two. So much so that the One, if it is about this, does not remain in-itself but alienates itself in its effect and in transcendence, whereas its effect does not distance itself from it or does not divide it without identifying itself in turn with another effect. The minimal machine of Difference is the immediate identity of identity and duality, their coextension, the becoming or passage of the cause-effect, which is cause in relation to another effect, effect in relation to another cause. Non-philosophy breaks with this last circularity even if we can say not that the One identifies itself with Being or its effect over Being, but that Being simulates it or captures it in an originary transcendental clone but without "responding", or without a simulation-without-simulated. The reversibility of the One and Being is thus only a derived objective appearance, that from which philosophy forms its element.

As for "philosophies of radical immanence", they give themselves this explicitly but give themselves resistance in a solely implicit manner, just long enough to believe it annulled or dissolved without remainder. Thus they simply ignore resistance and thematically only give themselves immanence which, as identity assumed as already unilateralizing by itself, is an "auto-contradictory" mixture or a last form of philosophical mixture. This is to say that they necessarily confuse, moreover in various modes, the Real of immanence and thought, and refuse any idea of a force-(of)-thought as *purely* transcendental. They assume that the Real is just as transcendental and cannot somewhat avoid still objectifying immanence or projecting in it, as a real implicit part, some transcendence. In fact, in their effective practice, they place themselves at the level of the force-(of)-thought and confuse it with the Real itself, attributing to it at once the absolute indifference of the Real to philosophy. The first axiom of non-philosophy on the other hand is that the One only has the One itself as content, not any other experience drawn from transcendence that would join it with more or less immediacy. If for example the One is *also* cleft, loss, crisis, or if it is quasi objectified, quasi intentioned, the object of a simply blind and not eradicated intuition, the rigorous concept of radical immanence is lacking and, on the basis of this release, itself issued from philosophical resistance as not theoretically thematized, then it is all of thought which initiates anew a philosophical movement throughout the mixtures. The distinction of the One-in-One and the force-(of)-thought as a priori transcendental is the angle of opening which allows these philosophical normalizations of the Real to be "placed" and classified.

The force-(of)-thought responds to the properties of this unitax at the point of creating them. As transcendental in its essence in effect: 1) it is determined by its identity or is uni-dentified; 2) it is unilateralized or its philosophical auto-position is suspended, which is to say the "real" claims of the philosophical mixture, which ceases to be spontaneous in order to be "fixed" as simple a priori giver of materials. This given is not annulled but fixed as a priori of material, receiving a relative autonomy and a "right". Under the form of a duality and not a solitary identity, the unilaterality no longer signifies the dissolution of the transcendent given and its resistance before of the radicality of immanence, the pure and simple annulment of being: there will always be a remainder of the mixture and of resistance "before" [devant] the force. But this duality, no longer being bilateral and through division of terms, puts into play *identities* rather than a varied pre-identity (or "pre-individual"). Even if these identities have a variety of content, they are not unifying *forms* for this variety which in turn is transcendentally constituted of identities.

# Problems of a transcendental syntax: Critique of transcendental arithmetic

We have *discovered* the form of thought adequate to the absolute autonomy of the Real, to its primacy over thought, the form of thought which registers the first character, *thus* subordinate, of thought, its only relative autonomy. Precisely if the philosophical matrix is in fractional or semi-real 2/3 terms, then non-philosophy is a simpler matrix, in two real "terms" + one transcendental term—which thus are simple identities. But how can we form a unity with only two terms, without a third term of synthesis or of development, or a fourth and a fifth, etc.? This is possible on the condition of changing our manner of thinking and no longer reducing it to philosophy alone.

Let us assume, then, the given-without-givenness of the One, the instance of the Real. The One is seen-in-One and reduces itself to this essence; no other structure belongs to it or is *de jure* included in it. But this essence is no more an exclusion than an inclusion of transcendental givens, it is *really* indifferent. Correctly understood, real indifference signifies that *if* such a given presents itself, it will be indirectly received through the means of the force-(of)-thought and also seen in-One but transcendentally, without determining it or belonging to it in a structural manner. If the term "empirical" which presents itself belonged *de jure* to the essence of the Real, the Real would dissolve reality. The absolute radical immanence of the Real, without the slightest morsel of transcendence, is thus the "condition" of an autonomy of reality subject to the transformation of this empirical term from which it is seized "in-One" ("relative autonomy").

One may object that we are in fact first given two terms face to face, relative to one another, then a third term which is only one of the two raised to a superior power. We have precisely not done this. We must seemingly, which is to say philosophically, give ourselves "two" terms but in reality not in the manner of a closed two, which is to say a face-to-face or a finite *set* that we contemplate or oversee and that is already inscribed in a third term, for example space or the spirit—this is philosophy. No: we must give ourselves two terms such that the first is sufficient, absolutely independent of the second; such that it is not reduced to it or does not even join "terms" with it, such that it does not form a set with it. But have we not already stated and demanded "two terms"? Of course, but the "set of two terms" *qua* two only exists from the perspective of the second isolating it, not for the "first". We call "unilateral duality" or "dual" the *identity without-synthesis of a duality* where identity is assumed by the first term or more precisely its clone, not by the second, and duality by the second alone and not by the first. This matrix is read then from the perspective of clone as identity and from the perspective of the second or unilaterally as duality. The "first", now the clone, does not enter into relation with the second or into duality except from the perspective of the latter, not from its own perspective wherein it remains unsplit. The clone-identity, grasped-in-One, is not a term counted in a Two, an overseen term. But it is a term as *transcendental* clone in a *unilateral duality* with the assistance of the occasion-term, a duality which is not arithmetical or homogenous. As for unilateral duality, it *carries* the a priori extracted from the empirical term, for example from transcendence, but devoid of its reduced mixed-form as support of the a priori. On the one hand, it is a relation without re-lation [*un rapport sans re-lation*], a simple unilation or provision/ "lation" [*apport*], of the "identity" of the term in its contingency as not "relatable" or masterable. On the other hand, it does not provide one term *rather* than another (by negation or hierarchy, even), but every possible term and, as we will see, the mix itself as a priori. This added second term is not however complementary nor supplementary, nor supernumerary, but meta-unary (whereas the One is ante-numerary), and this is where the transcendental possibility of counting begins.

Necessarily and sufficiently then, the *identity* "of" the "relation" of the two terms must not be a third distinct and "fractional" term, and must not be shared between these two existing terms, but further it must not be one of the two only by its clone. It must be then, although this is implied in what was just said, that this term be itself such that it is self-sufficient or has no need to participate in a third term superior to it; that it no longer be determined in return through this relation that the other has with it. It is this "term" that we call the One-in-One or moreover real Identity. We must finally add a clone to the One which will not be a Two, the clone not being able to be counted and re-included with the One in a *set* [*ensemble*]. The adding of the empirical term (its relative autonomy) transcendentally outlines a duality which is not a Two but which must be called unilateral, not being qualified as duality from the viewpoints of the term and the One (having still less than "two sides") or as forming a set.

Just as the One is not a mixed idealization of the arithmetical one that it would interiorize, unilateral duality is not one form of two and does not interiorize it in a concept: in the two cases the face to face of the first and second are excluded along with that of the overseeing assumed by this face to face in order to constitute a set. So the Real as vision-in-One destroys at its root the "transcendental arithmetic" which aspires to supersede it under the form for example of the equation mathematics = ontology. This thought is here radically depreciated, expropriated of its auto-position by the One-in-One which, unlike an arithmetic or even a metaphysical or transcendental One, does not form a number or a synthesis and derails the number and the "set" beyond the Real.

So evidently this One, if it is not at all the one of arithmetic or its philosophical interiorization, is the Real itself and not at all the transcendental One. We must stop confusing the Real and the transcendental if this, *excepting one distinction*, is a philosophical distinction that is always too weak to respect the radical autonomy of the Real. Identity is precisely the Real, and respectively its direct transcendental "image", and the duality posed by the second term is the transcendental dimension, respectively aprioristic. This is unilateral rather than reciprocal, combinatory or reversible. But if the Real('s)-Identity by definition does not need duality, then duality, being only an aprioristico-transcendental identity, needs the real and takes root through cloning in it, without consequently constituting, determining or differentiating it.

# The ingredients of syntax: Unidentity and unilaterality

Duality is a uni-lation of the empirical or transcendent term and the real-One such that it can "produce" a term function or clone function. But this "relation", necessarily lived-in-One, which is to say on the model of the One, has no reality "for" the One, is not a real structure and does not determine its essence which is in its constitution indifferent to any relation. Consequently the relation of duality on the one hand does find its (real) essence in the One but only from its point of view; on the other hand and by virtue of its relative autonomy, the relation of duality cannot think and receive its own identity except as transcendental identity—sometimes we say "unidentity". The empirical core of duality "extracts"—in order to be what it is—an identity from the Real that claims to be of it, for it and by it, but which does not bring any real new property to the One, which thus does not entail any transcendental *becoming* of the Real. The One-in-One does not alienate itself in transcendental identity, does not convert itself into this.

So the relative autonomy of transcendence, its real non-dissolution, is guaranteed by the real indifference of the One, which would be surreptitiously understood as being transcendental indifference if it dissolved it in a nothingness or if it only suspended its pertinence. But it and it alone demands a transcendental identity which cannot arise out of a procession of the One and still less from its "version" or "conversion". The real One and transcendental identity are not the 'same" in the philosophical manner, nor are they simultaneously given as the two faces of an "auto-affection" in the manner of "philosophies of radical immanence". The One remains in-One through-and-through until "within" the operation through which the element of transcendence of the force-(of)-thought relates to it in a transcendental mode or through a process of cloning.

Regardless, the transcendental acting of the One does not only manifest itself through an identity. We must recall that the One only "gives" the One— this is the vision-in-One—; it does not give of itself or does not "carry" any other reality any more than it negates any. We can say then—though the status of this operation is transcendental and not real—that it also undifferentiates the mixture, that it annuls its validity without annihilating it. Moreover this transcendental operation is only a unilateralization: no more a negation than identity is an affirmation, all operations which come under Being and non-Being rather than the One and the (non-)One. The real-One cannot affirm and negate, not being *also* a transcendental relation. So the One can receive the empirical term but this is no longer grasped in its auto-positional sufficiency but as non-positional identity. It can, only as a necessary but absolutely insufficient condition, receive-transcendence-in-One, live-in-One its identity-(of)-transcendence and unilateralize—rather than negating—that by which it claims to negate or affirm it.

Let us return to the problem of duality. If duality is called unilateral because it is only thinkable from the (second) term—the non(-One), it is also and more profoundly unilateralized through an effect of the (non-)One which comes under the same transcendental status as unidentity. Just as the relation or transcendence is affected by a transcendental identity, it is affected by a transcendental unilaterality, from a real though conditional origin that is consequently dependent on a "subject" which is affected by it. We do not immediately confuse unilateral duality in the first sense and the unilateralization or the (non-)One which affects it as clone of the One and which precisely finds a subject or a support in the first. Transcendental unilateralization can equally be said to form a unilateral duality or more precisely a *duality of unilateralization* between transcendental unidentity and the empirical term which, in this instance, is a relation or transcendence itself. In reality these two unilateral dualities come back to themselves by forming one structure, first glimpsed from the transcendental term and secondly from its empirical cause. If for example transcendence presents itself, it must in any case be lived-in-One and, consequently, identified/reduced by the Real but specifically in a transcendental manner. Unilateralization is thus a radical form of transcendental reduction but it does not occur without transcendental identity.

The two dimensions of syntax, identity (without syntax, immanent) and duality (without division or synthesis) are thus discernible in an originary manner at the level of the Real but only as the transcendental clone of the One. This distinction entails two others. The first is that of transcendence or Distance, a component of the force-(of)-thought, and the unilateralization, real in origin, which affects it. Consequently we will not confuse this unilateralization with the effect of opening or of distance which can be that of transcendence, nor the transcendental identity of transcendence and the identity or forms of a priori identity that this can bring with it. Neither unilaterality nor identity redouble, divide and refold the transcendence that is thus from the very start unilateralized or "emplaced" by the Real rather than by and inside itself as philosophy would have it. Transcendental unilaterality only distances transcendence (philosophical or reduced) from the Real or distinguishes it from the Real by imprinting it with the transcendental hallmark of the (non-)One. Tearing transcendence from the Real, it renders it irreal or deprives it of its claim to reach the Real through that auto-position which is always its own: this is the effect which prolongs its unilateralization through the Real. But unidentity also gives it a simplicity or a transcendental identity which substitutes it positively for its auto-position (the unilateralization of this is not sufficient) and gives it—and first to its essence of transcendence—the form of a non-autopositional Distance. This is thus the term received-in-One and put together with the clone (determination-in-the-last-instance) which receives it from that experience which is philosophy but which gives it or manifests it in an original mode. Unidentity and unilaterality thus form the essence or the "syntax" which articulates radical immanence and radical transcendence in the force-(of)-thought, they form a syntax *for* transcendence but are irreducible to the phenomenon thereof; in particular, unilateralized duality is not a mode of transcendence (or of relation) but apply to it. Finally, in terms drawn from philosophy but rectified under non-philosophical traditions, the force-(of)-thought is a transcendental a priori: transcendental by its cause or its real origin (it is thus identity *and* unilateral duality, or duality determined-in-the-last-instance), but a priori insofar as its component is transcendence, and pure or abstract transcendence, the *identity-(of)-distance*. The transcendental is thus not here a redoubled a priori like in philosophy; it has another origin altogether (the Real) than the a priori, but evidently claims to be from it.

The second distinction, less fundamental, is that of identity or unilaterality insofar as they constitute transcendental syntax *for* the force-(of)-thought and of what they become when, carried or recast by it (which is to say by transcendence) they have repercussions for the content of the reduced or "material" mixture. We will examine these effects later.

What is the relation of the unilateral duality and identity which "clone" the Real and substitute themselves for it? The One makes possible a unilateral duality by giving it a transcendental form which is evidently not itself unilateral in its essence, no more than the One itself, but which claims to be from duality.

Identity and duality, the originary constituents of the transcendental or non-philosophical order, have a real common stem which contains nothing mysterious or transcendent to human consciousness, being only the vision-in-One which is cause through immanence, thus heteronomous with human consciousness but heteronomous rather than transcendent. As components of this syntax, they themselves are identical by their (negative) cause in "uni-" but do not return to themselves in a "sameness" [*mêmeté*]; these are two qualitatively primitive and heterogeneous functions of the in-One itself or of the clone. With them is the primitive form of the order which appears such that the Real imposes it (negatively) by relation to the World or to philosophy (to thought). They do not form any bifacial structure, any structure of *simultaneity*, only being identical as real, nor a disjunctive and alternating structure, not being mediatized or separated by a difference. We call *determination-in-the-last-instance* this duality of structures that are however identical without forming a synthesis, without consequently having been obtained through a division. Unilateral duality is identical in-One to identity without dividing it, without alienating it, but without closing itself up into a synthesis. The entire sphere of what we have called the transcendental clone *is* the in-One but diversifies itself into identity and unilaterality precisely through the occasion of transcendence or adds an empirical term, such that the syntax of determination-in-the-last-instance begins with the added empirical term, duality, but does not reduce itself to this or derive from it, deriving rather, but not in a positive or direct manner, from the One. The syntax is precisely only a clone and not the Real. More rigorously, it constitutes the very order of "syntax" in its transcendental reality. Determination-in-the-last-instance is this transcendental order, which appears in a primitive manner, or for the first time.

But because they are identical in-One, identity and unilaterality are not simultaneous in the philosophical sense as bifacial, nor do they form a "set" to engender a philosophical syntax, but form a properly transcendental "uni-tax". Identity remains in itself but exists as duality without existing "in" duality and alienating itself, it exists dually or exists-duality without primacy over duality, since it is *not* the One but a clone. Like duality or unilaterality, it assumes an empirical given and thus cannot, as assumed real, be opposed to that duality assumed itself and itself alone to be transcendental.

# The essence of the transcendental as originary cloning of the real One: Cloning and speculation

The causality of the Real is distinct from the Real, it is not transcendental. It is the element of pure syntax (of uni-tax) that articulates the force-(of)-thought and the One-in-One through cloning. The phenomenal status of the transcendental—and thus the "real" essence of the force-(of)-thought—must be elucidated through the introduction of the thematic, transformed here, of the "mirror" and the "reflection".

Let us recall that philosophy, as undecidable decision, structure of division and repetition, contains a specular mirror moment, sometimes developed under a speculative form: any term inscribed in the system of the Philosophical Decision is the double of another and so of itself—with some nuances including differ(e/a)nce—it is a mirror-reflection mix, every reflection representing a mirror for another reflection and vice versa. The reflection is divided here into two reflections which comprise the real content of representation which is on the one hand reflection of the Real and on the other hand reflects itself in the infinite. The duality of the thing and its representation entails that the representation is mirror and reflection and that the reflection is divided. The mirror is the *common form* or the *common sense* mediator of the thing and its representation; it relates the former to the latter. For example the *ego* as *perception* which Leibniz gave canonical form is one such common internal form, at once the mirror of the thing and so the thing itself (mirror-thing) and reflection-representation of the thing. The *ego cogito* belongs to this circular structure of the mix at least insofar as it is interpreted as *cogito me cogitare* and more profoundly insofar as the Ego is defined as *cogitans*.

At least two types of philosophy have started the critique of this conception and have denounced the idealist flaking of metaphysical doubles of the Real. 1) Materialism and its concept of knowledge as "reflection without mirror". On the one hand, the autonomization of the process of knowledge is affirmed here and signifies that, in referring itself to the Real, it is "reflection" without being the image in the mirror, which is to say a thought without proper consistency or whose consistency is only that of the mirror/reflection mix, the common form that strives to deliver the relation of knowledge and the Real to interpretation rather than to the possibility of theory. On the other hand, the process of knowledge here is relative to the Real and consequently, philosophical idealism, which wants to produce the Real with the speculative auto-position of knowledges is eradicated. But if materialism begins to correctly pose the problem of knowledge, without specular idealism, it always poses it within the element of transcendence, that of "matter" or of being in relation to "consciousness", as such still surreptitiously measuring the Real by the yardstick of consciousness and reducing it to the state of reflection of a thing, of a transcendence-thing. It thus conserves the structure of mirror/reflection but as truncated and repressed in the name of a "bad" identity, a transcendent identity of matter which determines knowledge without being determined by it. In fact materialism recognizes the existence of the reflection but believes itself able to negate that of the mirror when it only denies and represses that existence, such that materialism then falls into the cynicism of the Real toward which any primacy of transcendence drives, and precisely a primacy of transcendence which is nothing but the dismembering and inversion of the old philosophical hierarchy and its inegalitarian spirit. 2) The philosophy of radical immanence as Ego or "transcendental life", as sensing-(of)-thought or auto-affection—an interpretation which moves from Descartes to Henry through a short-circuiting of auto-reflection or of auto-position used by its critics and users (Kant, Fichte, Hegel, Nietzsche). Immanence excludes representation; there is no longer any mixed mirror/reflection structure between the one and the other. Nonetheless what this type of philosophy excludes is representation as a reflected form of distance, as auto-reflection of thought, but it continues to surreptitiously associate the immanence of the Real with pure abstract distance, unreflected, or the *cogitatio* abstracted from any reflection of its terms. This type of philosophy proceeds to overwrite onto itself the triad or the philosophical hierarchy through identification with a strict identity, which is to say a radical immanence, but immanence still thought in a transcendent and quasi-objectified manner. It thus overwrites, one onto the other, the mirror and the reflection and thus believes them to be eliminated. In reality the intraphilosophical critique of the mirror and the reflection is almost universal (Fichte, Husserl, Wittgenstein, Heidegger, Levinas, etc.), but it remains precisely inscribed in philosophical auto-position.

The One-in-One of non-philosophy is defined through the identity of a radical immanence but itself thought in an immanent manner, which is to say that thought does not join with it and consequently project it into transcendence. It at once eliminates transcendent matter and transcendental life, the mixtures of the Real and the transcendental. Hence a simplification—rather than a decision—of the mirror/reflection structure which becomes non-autopositional and which consequently can no longer be assumed to be eliminated by illusion in totality. The Real does not allow that it be seized or captured as a thing by a mirror which alienates it in an image or an intention *of* it. The Real is not an object of representation and consequently auto-representation; the One cannot be reflected as it is. To assume that there would be reflection and mirror, concerns a *reflection-without-a-reflected*. In effect Being, thought and transcendence are received and lived in-One on the mode of the One and not on their specific modes, but from their perspective, in terms of their relative autonomy, they function as "mirror" in relation to the Real. Undoubtedly, they have nothing, no thing, beings or beingness, to reflect, but their relative autonomy explains that they behave like a mirror and produce a Real('s)-reflection of themselves, which bears on them and which they convey. On the one hand, the One cannot reflect *itself*, be its own mirror or a reflection in another mirror, but the mirror exists elsewhere, solicits the Real and reflects it as its only power. We will say that the One is the necessary but negative condition of the reflection and that the reflection is drawn out of or borrowed from it. The indifference of the Real is such that it neither participates in nor "actively" refuses this operation, but such that it is the indispensable negative condition thereof, or *sine qua non*. We will thus call *transcendental* the sphere or instance of this absolute reflection, this clone which has only an effective cause. The transcendental is the Real become cause, reflection which is not reflected but which is indeed Real-reflection. The order of the transcendental as essence of non-philosophical givenness is thus a radical reflection which is formed between two givens, as a between-two which is an identity: Given-without-givenness, which itself does not participate in the reflection and is not the "subject" of this operation, and the given-by-givenness or the mix of effectivity, which is the—occasional—subject. It "articulates", if you will—this expression is too transcendent—the two types of given and constitutes the transcendental essence which will unceasingly be that of the force-(of)-thought.

If the One is absolutely necessary but absolutely insufficient for "producing" a transcendental identity which can be said to be of transcendence, then with this identity we are speaking of a true *transcendental clone* of the One or, more rigorously, of a *transcendental clone of the Real*: a unique and originary clone, clone('s)-essence of the clone. This originary cloning of the One is the surest destruction of metaphysical doubling or philosophical doublets, it is even, if we can say this, *double('s)-identity as such* [*l'identité telle quelle (du) double*]. This is a reflection of the Real, a reflection in the mirror not of Duality itself but rather of its empirical term. But a reflection "without mirror" at least in the sense whereby philosophy instead puts the Real face to face with the mirror and produces the third term, a mixture of the reflection as transcendental *and* real, simultaneously. Philosophy consists in the transcendence of the dyad or the Two of the thing and mirror as a new set, and draws from them a mixed or itself divided reflection, a double reflection in which the real and the mirror alienate themselves. With the radically immanent Real which does not reflect itself and does not thus alienate itself in this reflection, it is more precisely the mirror-term itself—which is not however the mirror as separate organon, face to face with the Real—which draws from the Real a simple clone, an undivided reflection, the same identity of reflection that is not split between the real One and the opposing term. This is not exactly a "reflection without mirror", a concept that is still philosophical and the difference between mirror and reflection, but *the identity of the mirror/reflection pair, which is to say precisely of their unilateral duality*—as if it had a reflection without-a-reflected. The belief in the absolute elimination of the specular is a philosophical one, as we have said, and leads to a failure and a simple repression. What is possible and positive is the *radical* (and not "absolute") invalidation of the structure of the mix or the double which affects the mirror/reflection duality, and the manifestation of its transcendental identity.

With these principles it becomes possible not to repress or deny philosophical specularity but to *dualyze* it, to put into a relation of unilateral duality its philosophical form and its non-philosophical a priori, which is to say the *identity of specularity*. The triadic specular structure of philosophy (thing/mirror/reflection) is not dismembered to the gain of one of its aspects; it always carries "three" terms (but outside of any transcendental arithmetic, so three terms that are not fractional) and cannot be, other than by an anti-metaphysical abstraction, defined as reflection-without-mirror (in the sense of an absence of any mirror) or even as simple unilateral mirror/reflection identity. The Real does more than drawing specularity out of itself; it gives place to a new organization that we will call *non-speculative*, without which it would be opposed to specularity and its speculative development since it is rather the *identity of speculation*. Whereas the speculative structure of any philosophy is divided in two in each one of its dimensions, the vision-in-One, without suppressing the mirror and the reflection, extracts simplicity from them or manifests it in them a priori. The speculative triad is removed from its division and its duplication, from its reflection. It acquires the status of the non-autopositional and comprises three identities, or their first names: 1) the non-reflected-Real; 2) the reflection-mirror (philosophy); 3) the reflection-without-a-reflected (the transcendental and the entire non-philosophical sphere), undivided or unique reflection, refusing to divide itself in other reflections. These three instances do not form a transcendent-transcendental number or set in the manner of a philosophical system. Non-philosophy is no more "anti-speculative" than it is "anti-philosophical", it presents itself as the very identity of speculation insofar as it has renounced the sufficiency of auto-position and is thought as commanded by the Real.

It is this transcendental element of determination-in-the-last-instance that is the transcendental essence of Being, and which forms with Being the unilateral duality of the force-(of)-thought. We will thus pass from determination-in-the-last-instance to its first a priori correlate, the force-(of)-thought, and position this in a transcendental theorem.

# Theorem of the force-(of)-thought, first axiom: The one-in-one or the real, the transcendental and logic

The One itself, being only in-One, without any content other than its own inherence or immanence-(to)-itself, for all its riches only possesses the solitude and uselessness of the Real, its being-given-without-givenness. But it is not the only given: *there is* a given, not radical but absolute, or requiring givenness. What is the relation of these two givens, of the One-in-One and "experience" to such multiple figures which go from Being to Other, and to regions of being? From the perspective of the One itself, there is no such relation. It can only have one if this other given, the relative-absolute given, demands it on the mode of the refusal of the One. As things stand: philosophy is the universal medium, the a priori form through which any experience whatsoever thinks the foreclosure of the One-in-One or participates in resistance. We will not ask ourselves—we will see later why we do not hypothesize in this way—if this resistance is that of experience and precedes that philosophy which would only be a simple means or "language", or even if experience is *in itself* indifferent to the One and if resistance is the domain of philosophy alone. Rather, we will conclude that experience and philosophy are not dissociable and that it is this "totality" that spontaneously expresses itself as avoidance of radical immanence. *There still is* resistance, and it is through this that a relation to the real-One is postulated for the first time and it is necessary to right it; to detect here a certain thought in action "of" the One and to elaborate it within the limits of this contingency. Being itself absolutely indifferent to this resistance, the One-in-One can neither "analyze" it nor "avoid" it—its indifference to the Real precludes this. To the contrary, it suffices to admit resistance in order to posit a relation of thought to the One and to elucidate, critique and transform this relation, the theoretical object of a new discipline.

In order to present this point of departure, we will examine it through two axioms and a theorem, comparing them schematically though to three principles of Fichte's *Wissenschaftslehre of 1794*, which is to say to one of the most lucid positions, one of the most beautiful solutions to the problem of philosophy. Here, non-philosophy will only be better elucidated in its "objects" as in its manner of thinking, without being reduced to a neo-Fichteanism.

Axiom 1: The One is the One-in-One; or moreover: The One is not but is-in-one or "vision-in-one". In other words: the I is I-in-I.

*Wissenschaftslehre* 1st principle: I = I.

What distinguishes the I-in-I and the I = I, two forms of the identity of the I? In spite of the variation of its significations or usages in Fichte, I = I remains an intellectual intuition in the most general sense of the term whereas the I-in-I is a non-intuitive identity, and real rather than logical or maintaining a last relation to logic.

An intuition… that is to say, the *givenness of identity (as sameness) of a singular object*, so through a phenomenological distance or in the element of transcendence. Fichte refuses intellectual intuition as "immediate consciousness" of a non sensible being, a thing in itself or an absolute I Am. He makes it the immediate consciousness of an act, an activity of the I, such that it is invested in a simple corporeal gesture or in the practice of needing-to-be. Nonetheless this philosophical distinction has no *phenomenal* worth; it is too short and still remains, like Husserl's "Principle of principles", within the limits of consciousness or objectifi-cation—of *intuition*—and does not achieve radical immanence. The act is undoubtedly neither a fact nor an object of representation though it bears the indelible mark of objectification. Fichte opposes the object and representation as immediate consciousness of the act, but the act is objectification and thus auto-objectification. If not the transcendent, at least transcendence suffices to leave it enclosed in the determining primacy of this auto-objectification which philosophy makes. On the other hand, the vision-in-One is not an intuition or the givenness of an object. Not a givenness, but a given-without-givenness such that the I = I, at its limit, signifies a givenness-without-given or a position-without-posed. Nor an object, which is to say a given through phenomenological distance; it excludes any transcendence from itself. It is neither a substance nor an act, but an identity whose entire consistency is inherence or immanence (to) itself. In order to understand the vision-in-One, we must admit that the Real('s)-identity is as "positive" and "real" as the object and moreover as the Real. For Friends of the earth and Friends of Ideas, the duality of Is which know themselves to be free and those Is which take themselves as things or substances, we substitute the duality of One(s) that think themselves "objectively" as absolutely-not-objects, as radical immanence, and One(s) that perceive themselves in a philosophical-all-too-philosophical manner as transcendence and distance.

I = I is then an intellectual intuition, givenness either of a *res* = substance (metaphysical and substantialist interpretation) or of a pure *act*. This act remains nonetheless, from a phenomenal point of view, in the order of an object which, even if it is no longer an object but an act of position, is in turn the object of an originary or intuitive givenness. On the other hand, the vision-in-One is not an intellectual experience, a givenness of the *mens* or of the *nous*, or even a pure image or an Idea which are the transcendent faculties and entities of a transcendental psychology, but the already-given of immanence in person or of identity as such, which it must admit has just as much or even more "reality" than transcendence and the fetishes that populate its void—that it is the being-given (of the) Given or the Real.

I = I is moreover a synthesis of intuition and object, so an *auto*-intuition, the circle of an absolute I which is resolved in the circle of a transcendental imagination that condenses and concentrates all philosophical activity, which is to say the auto-position of phenomenological distance. On the other hand, the vision-in-One is not the circle of an auto-given; it is the circle of an auto-position-without-given. As given-without-givenness, it excludes any circle, overseeing, or auto-position. We distinguish: the "devoid" irreal identity, of logic; the semi-real, semi-irreal identity of "transcendental logic" or of the circle of philosophy; and the real and respectively transcendental or "uni-ideal" (and not "semi-irreal") identity, without form and without circle of the vision-in-One. Consequently: if the vision-in-One is not a circle, it does not enclose all of non-philosophy and its objects within it, but determines it only "in-the-last-instance", which is to say that it determines, as real One, the transcendental identity of non-philosophy. For this circle of "transcendental logic", be it cut into or differentiated, non-philosophy substitutes a pure-transcendental thought of identities-in-the-last-instance or clones.

Fichte would undoubtedly refuse this importance logically and would denounce this interpretation of his principle. But we know through the philosophers themselves, in an undoubtedly still limited manner, that they do not say what they are doing, and do not do what they are saying. In particular, they neither exclude nor destroy metaphysics as they say they do, nor do they access the Real when they claim to. For example, Kant defines metaphysics and its transcendental illusion by using "general logic" in philosophical or ontological reasoning. He thus opens a path different from the Anglo-Saxon one, or the non-analytic path of a pure or purely transcendental thought, depending only on the Real, excluding regional or general scientific models from itself: the exclusion of mathematics must be followed by that of logic. Nonetheless, as the example of Fichte only demonstrates too well and in spite of the critique of "empty" and purely logical thought he will address here, Kant too settles for an *Aufhebung*—an interiorization/exclusion—of logic by the Real (this is *real possibility*), which is to say a transcendental which interiorizes the base or logical soil in lieu of docking it to the real-One alone. Hence neo-Kantianism explicitly gives transcendental power to logical form.

As for Fichte, if he is careful to distinguish the originary action of auto-position of the I and his factual and contrived initial model, the principle of identity, he nonetheless only interiorizes or takes in the A = A in the I = I, whatever the interpretation of this might be, even as a simple form of transcendental imagination. The Fichtean thesis that wants formal logic to be obtained through formalization and abstraction of transcendental principles like I = I and would not be constitutive *de jure* of these principles is already partly invalidated by all contemporary philosophy which in the final calculation tallies all of the operations and demonstrates that the simple transcendental interiorization, and no longer metaphysics of logic in a "transcendental logic", still equates to a claim of constitution of the Real, and that obtaining it is merely a retrieval. Furthermore the One-in-One, the Real which is *de jure* without logical facticity, causes the appearance of the indissoluble alliance of the philosophical and also the logical and restrained comprehension, the definitive enclosing of the transcendental in "transcendental logic". Non-philosophy neither justifies nor grounds collective consciousness and its assumed facts, even if this only negatively or dialectically assists logic. It does not settle for destroying the conceit of general logic in favor of a merely transcendental logic or a dialectical critique thereof. Rather, it transforms philosophy by managing to subtract it from logic and from all scientific models of thought insofar as they are gathered by philosophy in their facticity then auto-posed, which is to say fetishized. Undoubtedly in Fichte logic does not determine thought in a more or less unilateral manner, like in transcendent metaphysics, or no longer determines itself *without remainder* reciprocally with the Real. But transcendental logic, even as decomposition of metaphysics, remains a simple formation of compromise with metaphysics where logic and the Real determine themselves reciprocally in an *Aufhebung* or an *abstraction* (abstraction of the fact of logical consciousness starting from the transcendental I = I). No operation whatsoever, dialectic or not, is any longer sufficient to absolutely "separate", the Real and logic from the point of view of the Real and *to recognize the absolute indifference of the former for the latter*. Moreover in accepting the pertinence of the logical *fact*; by treating logic as fact (*quid facti?*), Fichte arrives at the Hegelian critique which rightly exploits all possibilities of logic, including contradiction and thus the destruction of logic. But with Hegel, this concerns an anti-logical generalization of logic, a complication of Reason, never of the discovery of the conditions of the pure transcendentality of thought.

Forewarned of these difficulties and desiring to deliver thought from logic, Heidegger shows that abandoning logic leaves the primacy of the *logos* untouched and undertakes to *differentiate*, from the real of the essence of Being, this primacy. Wittgenstein, too, attempts to free logic by *breaking*, through language games, this "mirror". But like Wittgenstein, Heidegger fails in the radicality of this project; they ultimately remain "naive" philosophers because they begin by admitting the pertinence of philosophy and thus of its logical substrate and ask themselves after the fact (even if it is not only after the fact) how to limit logic in thought and the claims of thought over the Real. This is the flippancy—and the lie—of the famous explication through the necessary ladder or scaffolding we abandon, passing them through loss and profits; or moreover of the cynicism Nietzsche gave the formula: "I will avert my gaze…"

Philosophy is defined and delimited by two "confusions" which form a system: of the real-One with Being, and of thought with logic. It is inevitable that so-called "continental" philosophy be in a position of weakness when faced with analytic positions or when it consents to unstable mixtures that are violent and hardly rigorous. This is because it has not freed up thought as transcendental-pure organon and has delivered it to the logical organon.

Still, this task is not possible if, first, the Real is *given* as the Given-without-philosophy, Given-without-thought, and if any "real distinction" precedes its being-foreclosed or its solitude, a distinction which is in reality only logico-real. It does not suffice then to dissimulate logic "in" an assumed real, such that it remains fetishized, first, and in a state of auto-position. An organon always contains the universal and consequently transcendence; but it suffices to posit the latter as first and determinant such that it must identify itself with the vehicle of logic and logic in general. And it suffices, on the contrary, to submit it to the real-One such that it can free itself from here and only finds the universal and transcendence through materials. The weakness of philosophy is its congenital empiricism and its complement of logicism, its spirit of compromise, its powerlessness to define a simply transcendental thought (and not a transcendental imagination) and consequently to transform experience.

Non-philosophy is not then a logic, either dialectical or transcendental, of acts of philosophizing or indeed a logical elucidation of its statements, but rather a theory and a usage through the force-(of)-thought—so in-Real rather than logical—of the Philosophical Decision as undivided totality of its operations or acts, forms, ends and matters. From this point of view, we no longer make the value-distinction between logical analysis and transcendental logic, between Russell or even Wittgenstein and Kant or Fichte or Husserl.

# Theorem of the force-(of)-thought, second axiom: The non(-one) or resistance to the one

Axiom 2: There is a non(-One) or a resistance to the One.

*Wissenschaftslehre* 2nd principle: a non-I is opposed to I.

As reaction to the foreclosure of the One, but which the One opposes to thought, there is resistance that is philosophical in origin (in the sense whereby philosophy is its place and its body) and which manifests itself empirically first of all. Resistance or the non(-One) is by definition a "more" real thing than logical opposition, which is not real, and even more purely real "in-the-last-instance" than the semi-real semi-logical opposition of the I and the non-I. Nonetheless "more real in-the-last-instance" signifies that it is transcendental-pure and no longer logico-transcendental. Because the One is absolutely indifferent to the non(-One)—this is what we call its foreclosure through the thought it constrains—it itself is without repulsion, negation, nihilation, etc., which now are operations of transcendence. This is what explains that the resistance or the "opposition" of the non(-One)— resistance to recognizing and assuming this foreclosure—is "unilateral" or not constitutive, of the type that is a solely "secondary" repression of the One (but which would articulate with this foreclosure and would be its repression). There is an absolute and irreducible contingency of this given of philosophy in relation to the One, more than a contingency: a radical or real in-existence which is not the result of the negation of philosophy by the One. But if we position ourselves in the point of view of this resistance, it ceases to be absolutely contingent, it is no more than relatively contingent or acquires a first sense in relation not to the One but to a thought *according to* the One, a sense which does not make it belong to the Real but which qualifies it as transcendental and which already demands that, without really leaving the One, a *thought*—since this is what it now concerns—be possible which takes resistance into account and can determine it. Hence a relative autonomy not as much of philosophy assumed "in itself" as of philosophical resistance, where the One will be indirectly engaged rather than engaging itself. An autonomy assured and consequently validated as proving not to be determined by the One itself. In taking on a transcendental signification, resistance will be more "real" than the semi-real, semi-logical mix of the opposition of the non-I to the I.

How then to understand this "thought" whose existence is necessary in order to regulate the relation of the One and the non(-One)? This resistance is sufficient such that the One necessarily determines it in turn but not directly, consequently partially inside of itself, but without being obligated to renounce its real difference and to enter into a process of negation, nihilation, etc., where it would alienate itself. It must be the case then, probably, in order to resolve this problem, that an organon is added to it, a thought-organon drawn from determination of resistance or of the non(-One): not directly by the One itself but, as we have said, by the One-in-the-last-instance or by this organon. The theorem of the force-(of)-thought will resolve this problem.

The aporia of Hegelian interpretation or Fichte's classical interpretation— how, if the I = I is all of reality (subjective idealism), do we still admit a non-I or a variety of effective consciousness?—is resolved, as we know, through the revolutionary interpretation that turns the I = I first into a purely philosophical construction simulating the logico-metaphysical illusion in order to deconstruct it, then into a simple intuition of the act of position, which thus passes from the I = substance to the I = act. But this distinction continues to interiorize the logical contradiction in the not-I. It only overcomes the transcendental illusion under the metaphysical and dogmatic form in order to conserve it under its most modern form of a transcendental logic. This is a new "decision" between dogmatism and transcendental philosophy, it is incapable of positing and thematizing the indissoluble identity of logic and philosophy in general, and in particular that of the contradiction or of the non-I, under the form of a radical identity, without *Aufhebung*, which would here be resistance, a concept belonging to a purely transcendental and not logico-transcendental thought. Non-philosophy, precisely in reducing the Real to its solitude of One-in-One, without logical determination or even an interiorized transcendental, opens up the possibility of the manifestation of a non(-One), of an empirical *there is* which is now that of philosophy itself, of the World, Being, Logic, etc. In effect, *if the One is absolutely indifferent, it no longer negates and can leave thought (as organon rather than ready-made or fetishized thought) to validate this resistance within certain limits or give it its "true" object*, a new object that is less the One (from the perspective of the One which is now ours through this organon) than thought in as much as it needs this resistance in order to constitute the order of non-philosophy and its statements. The non-philosophical conception of the real-One (which is not the Whole) and the resultant pure transcendental style, pure or without logical blend, leaves a certain place and a relative autonomy to the empirical or to the enigmatic appearance [*factice*]. It is unilateral duality that permits the "conciliation" of empirical givenness or the relative autonomy of philosophy and the necessary determination of this non(-One) by the One (even if this is not enough), and to begin an effective process of determination. There is a facticity of the non(-One) which is assumed transcendentally in and by the organon of thought (as in-One).

We could have imagined an immanence said to be equally "radical" but which would unilaterally determine the factical given without recognizing its positivity or its own reality of resistance, which would dissolve it purely and simply, reconstituting an idealism of radical immanence on the ruins of this non(-One). There would indeed be a second instance, a purely transcendental non(-One), without origin or at least without factical dependence, a second instance just as autonomous as the Real in a way, or which at least possessed its necessity of the One alone, its factical origin being effaced or annulled. This would be a new philosophy, a philosophy of *unilateralizing identity*. The second axiom of non-philosophy signifies to the contrary the supposedly absolute autonomy of resistance or of the factical non(-One); a viewpoint that is neither excluded, affirmed nor positioned by the One-as-real which is nonetheless the ultimate and universal viewpoint. Next, it signifies the problem of its determination despite everything by the One (cloning) and of its only relative autonomy; the delimitation and validation of resistance, which alone render possible a theoretico-pragmatic process including this non(-One). This is probably still a philosophical conception, intuitive or semi-intuitive, of radical immanence, a certain objectification of the One which thus, in the remembered conception, causes the One to function directly as unilateralizing identity and immediate but total negation of the philosophical mixture, giving the illusion that knowledge of transcendence is reached or indeed, an objectification of the One, itself carrying out the transcendental reduction: confusing the Real and thought, the Manifestation and knowledge. But on the one hand the One is too real to reduce itself transcendentally, or it is converted from Real into transcendental in another way. On the other hand, how then can we explain, if the real-One dissolves all factical or mixed reality, that it is nonetheless simultaneously accompanied by a new structure, that of transcendence, if not because transcendence has been factically presupposed in spite of everything and immediately negated in favor of its pure remainder assumed to be known without being the object of a knowledge? Indeed, this philosophy does not only let radical immanence be given but equally gives, as already known and not only manifest-in-One, radical transcendence under the form of a completed and fixed structure. Hence a dualist structure double in region and opposed to monism, a new dyad for immanence and transcendence. In reality, it does not destroy auto-position, the immanence-transcendence doublet, but simply levels it from inside through identity, at once giving itself this as manifested-in-one and known by transcendence, always associating the Real and thought, refusing to renounce its claim to think the real-One directly. We will come back to this philosophical "normalization" of non-philosophy.

# Theorem of the force-(of)-thought as transcendental organon

Theorem: The One-in-One is the identity-in-the-last-instance of the unilateral duality of the indivisible One and the divisible *and* indivisible non(-One); this identity is the organon of thought or force-(of)-thought, as solution to the problem of the determination of the non(-One) by the One.

*Wissenschaftslehre*, 3rd principle: I oppose in the I, to the divisible I, a divisible non-I.

The implications of the two axioms each thought in-One rather than in a "system" show the necessity of "superseding" them: they posit and delimit a problem which arrives under the form of a quasi-contradiction, a contradiction of determination (conditional: if there is resistance) by the One and of some unilateral resistance to the One. Not being a logical or logico-real contradiction, it demands a solution that is not, in spite of philosophical appearances, a philosophical kind of supersession (principally a synthesis or an analysis, a dialectic, a differentiation, etc.). There is only one appearance of contradiction between the One and the non(-One) but an appearance which excludes the contradiction rather than being its "philosophical" solution. The solution to this problem cannot be a synthetic supersession but a simple deduction—as a theorem implies— because it occurs in respect to an absolute rule which is immanent *identity*, the non-synthesis of the One-in-One—absolute respect of the intrinsic being-foreclosed of the vision-in-One that forbids overseeing the problem and interminably re-asking it as philosophy does, but which is the indestructible "property" transmitting premises to consequences. There will be a definitive solution to this problem and it will have the same degree of "truth" or immanence as the axiom of the One-in-One itself, precisely because being "in-the-last-instance", this immanence only transmits itself and itself alone—this is cloning.

1) Fichte distinguishes in the same problematic position, like all philosophy, its object and the philosopher, the *Me* [Moi] and the *I* [Je] (as what he does and what he says). They are only the Same, at once different and identical: this is the philosophical dyad, the structure in 2/3 or 3/4 terms. This structure repeats itself and is proved in the solution, the resolution of the contradiction occurring through the division and limitation of opposites. Non-philosophy by contrast only knows a single radically indivisible One which is thus never a Same. On the other hand, it knows several states (as Real then as clone or cause) of the One *identical (to) itself*. The indivisible Me of knowledge, to the contrary, must finally resolve itself in the synthetic solution evoked in a divisible Me, since it is only indivisible according to the qualitative criterion of its own logico-real element, never from the perspective of the general structure of the Philosophical Decision which is proved in its solution: from this perspective it is in reality divisible and is thus only indivisible inside of this decision. The One-in-One on the other hand remains indivisible from premises to consequences, from the problem to its solution. As such it determines a "logic" of real-transcendental identities, whereas philosophy lays out logico-transcendental and ultimately divisible identities.

2) Having posed the problem in terms of opposition, Fichte can only find a solution in the quantitative, that is, as the philosophical dialectic

always demands, a qualitative quantitative like the "divisible". And indeed it is the philosophical decision itself that impregnates the framework of the *Wissenschaftslehre* with its bilateral or reciprocal distinctions. The solution of non-philosophy, though, resides in determination-in-the-last-instance rather than in the synthetic resolution of the logico-real contradiction. It already entails, as we have seen, the ultimately radical exclusion, without remainder or counterpart of interiorization, of general logic (Kant) from the Real—and undoubtedly of logical deduction—rather than its effacement or its final Fichtean interiorization in the Real, its *Aufhebung*. More positively: whereas the (logico-real) contradiction names synthesis through division and circular identity—this is logic "in" philosophy and the philosophical logic of the dyad in 2/3 terms—resistance (from an empirical though transcendental origin without mediation by logic) names, being given the preceding axioms, the transcendental and not logical inference of an identity thus called real "in-the-last-instance": determination-in-the-last-instance, such that it produces the organon of the force-(of)-thought. This is not between the One and the non(-One) but proceeds, in line with the intrinsic being-foreclosed of the vision-in-One, from the One (which it does not leave nor alienate in a division) to the non(-One) according to a vector of unilaterality.

3) The force-(of)-thought is the "key" to the possibility of non-philosophy. We can also understand it, for example, as the pure transcendental remainder of the famous "transcendental imagination" (in reality semi-logical; semi-transcendental) when the One is substituted for the Me [*Moi*], the vision-in-One for the agility of auto-position. The force-(of)-thought is force because, as transcendental imagination but through duality and more simply than this, it holds the "contraries" of the One and Being "together" but unilaterally. Nonetheless this last formula is ambiguous; several distinctions are necessary to nuance the status and internal composition of the force-(of)-thought.

a) These are no longer "overseen" [*survolés*] contraries in the sense of philosophy and logic reunited, but a relation of indifference (on one side) and resistance of the other, both "unilateral". However, characterizing the radical indifference of the One through its unilaterality does not make sense if that unilaterality has it as transcendental clone. Resistance is unilateral, the One-in-One is not, and the force-(of)-thought in its relation to philosophical *data* will in turn contain a form of unilaterality: consequently a circle is only sketched out at this level, but a *simplified* circle, without auto-position and without the claims of the philosophical circle. The organon "combines" the One and Being: in reality without synthesis, without division of the One and consequently then of transcendence. The force-(of)-thought is the phenomenal core of what philosophy has named convertibility, or even reversibility, of the One and Being, convertibility prevailing to the benefit of philosophy alone. Ceasing to divide and redouble them one by the other, it associates them in an intrinsic, unique, simple, unilateral manner, not letting them intervene more than once each time, the One once as One, Being once as Being. The syntax of the dyad or of bilateral duality is excluded: the force-(of)-thought really has "two heads" but precisely only has two and not 2/3; no common *interior milieu* remains between the One and Being, or accompanies them. This is a unilateral duality in which the dyad ceases to reflect itself so as not to continue to be the a priori materials (the mix-form) of a determinant identity.

b) These are evidently not the One and Being assumed to be separately "in themselves" within metaphysics, which would then be united in a unilateral manner. In effect the One cannot undergo this synthesis: we have distinguished the identity of the One and the transcendental identity that undoubtedly is that of the One, but when it affects transcendence. This clone is inseparable from the Being at the heart of the force-(of)-thought: not the One, but the One('s)-"image" over Being, whose effect is "non-autopositionality". Thus the dyads or philosophical antinomies will be explained and reduced through an identity that cannot directly be the One itself, but an *identity* which gives its transcendental essence to the force-(of)-thought. It is with this first transcendental identity that the force will impregnate its objects, the dyads. Identity cannot in fact "pass" from the One to the philosophical mix unless a mediating instance (but not self-mediating), an "absolute" and simple organon, transmits it, thus allowing the One not to alienate itself. If this transcendental identity (joined to unilaterality) is said to be the transcendental essence of the force-(of)-thought, what is the other component, aprioristic rather than transcendental, constituting the force-(of)-thought?

c) The force-(of)-thought is received in the mode of the vision-in-One but is not itself, on pain of philosophical idealism, the One-in-One or a part of the Real. If it receives its real essence from its immanent cause, it must receive its a priori component, its specific nature, from transcendence or Being. But thus all it receives from transcendence is *essence* and the form of this essence that the one tolerates or extracts from Being. We call non-phenomenological or non-autopositional Distance that specific essence of transcendence: an "infinite" and indivisible distance, a simple exteriority, without redoubling or return, without circle or loop, precisely identity retrieved from transcendence, which the force-(of)-thought will transmit to the philosophical mixture. The force is thus this distance as lived in-One but as transcendental; in-the-last-instance only, consequently in so much as it does not confuse itself with the One itself. The specific essence of Being is its universal a priori, but this essence as received in-One or having become organon is the transcendental a priori.

In its composition, the force-(of)-thought is that which can act on the *data* of transcendence, sharing the essence of transcendence with them. With this difference that they repress as essence, they repress the One itself all the more, whereas the force-(of)-thought manifestly contains this essence.

d) The force-(of)-thought consequently does not form a common *substrate* of contraries, when this would only be an "interior milieu", a "plane of immanence" or even a fluid substance formed of an extreme speed—an infinite becoming. There is no third term in this duality, the first is the purest. There is no longer the "I" or the "We" of the philosophers as correlate of such a substrate, the One does not divide itself into One-object and One-subject, between One subject-object and One object-subject. The *force* resides perhaps even more profoundly in this last poverty, irreducible, which is not survival [*survie*] but the life [*vie*] itself of thought far from any fetishization or factualization. The substitution of the act, agility and movement for substance = *res* constituted "progress". That of the becoming-unlimited and of infinite speed for agility was another… But these are only "forms of progress"… The extreme, or even infinite mobilization of movement in the future and moving, mobilization of logic having become coextensive with originary time, is no longer the destruction of substance and its logical infrastructure, rather it is its infinite interiorization, not impoverishment. But the contemporary pauperization of philosophy is not the true poverty of the Real beneath any substance, act or becoming.

Unlike the Real, the transcendental is always a relation, a relation to experience. The force-(of)-thought is a double relation since there is a double given: from one side, a special relation, a relation of cloning identified (with the) real-One; from the other it is a relation relating to transcendent experience in general. Such fork-tongued or two-faced [*bifides ou bifrons*] Beings already exist in philosophy but never have the simple identity nor the minimality of structure of the force-(of)-thought and are regularly doubled if not by an external synthesis, then at least by an interior milieu or a plane of overseeing and transcendence through which philosophy continues to assure its authority. For example "desiring machines" (Deleuze) as structure of flux/cut, flux/partial object, or the reversible correlation of forces, their difference or indivisible difference (Nietzsche), or the continuity-indiscernible system (Leibniz) do not contain only two terms, but 2/3, since the cut cannot by definition equate to the identity of a radical immanence and assumes in turn another flux;

and since ideal and relational flux does not content itself to root itself in the cut but conditions it in turn in a becoming-unlimited. Immanence and transcendence are only coextensive and in a state of reciprocal overseeing, not unilaterally ordered. Unilateral duality is ceaselessly exceeded and complicated for philosophical reasons; Indiscernibles are not singular enough by immanence or real intrinsic identity, and Continuity is too powerful, and determines Indiscernibles in return, etc.

e) Two axioms thus conclude the theorem positing the existence of the force-(of)-thought. This is not the synthetic concept of the real and the ideal, but the transcendental identity which articulates the Real and the ideal without synthesis but by cloning. The force-(of)-thought is not only a "concept" in the philosophical sense, it is also identically a true knowledge; not a synthesis but the identity-in-the-last-instance of the One and Being. This is more than an "indubitable fact" since it is not an ontico-ontological fact but a force or a transcendental drive [*pulsion*] rooted in the immanence of the Real ("uno-ontological" perhaps); more than the synthesis of realism and idealism since it is the identity of the Real-without-realism and the ideal-without-idealism. This is the ultimate phenomenal core of the "transcendental imagination" (Fichte), of "intentionality" (Husserl) or of absolutely transcending the essence of Being (Heidegger). With the manifestation of the force-(of)-thought, it is philosophy that appears as transcendental illusion and sees its function change, being reduced to the status of simple a priori of experience.

With the two initial axioms of non-philosophy, the question is not of a metaphysical or speculative construction, of an absolute I and absolute totality, but not either of its simulation by philosophy in terms of its deconstruction: in both cases general logic is required, whereas non-philosophy excludes it from the first axiom and does not conserve it in the object of the second other than as datum. It is in fact a question of "composing" them, or according them and, to this end, of carrying out an analysis—or more precisely, a "dualysis"—of the resistance posed by the second axiom. Without being able to speak of a dialectical decomposition of this dualysis, in the Fichtean manner of the classic transcendental illusion, it is necessary to deliver philosophical resistance from its dogmatic and naive aspects and to arrive at giving it a rigorous sense in terms of its effective role or phenomenal validity in non-philosophy. Resistance, too, is a transcendental illusion that will not be legitimated except by relation not directly to the Real but to the thought adequate to the Real.

Finally, for the first principle of the *Wissenschaftslehre* factically resolved by recourse to the identity Principle, non-philosophy substitutes real identity, the One-in-One or (radical) immanence, neither a principle nor an an-archy but the "object" of first names and those axioms called transcendental (that the One determines in-the-last-instance). For the second principle, the contradiction, non-philosophy substitutes resistance and relative autonomy, transcendence under its philosophical given. And for the third principle, the synthesis, it substitutes the pure transcendental, without logic but as clone of the real-One, essence of the force-(of)-thought which articulates the One and Being in this way and which is thus not a third term, not even the internal *fold* of the One and Being (a fold both running through and glancing over itself despite the charge of unilaterality that it can sometimes contain), but their identity-in-the-last-instance.

The force-(of)-thought expresses the primacy-without-priority of the Real over thought, the Real over the transcendental (not transcendental realism, not "realism" but the Real) and the detachment of the transcendental through relation to its logical substrate. The famous "transcendence in immanence" is not a solution but rather the formulation of a problem whose solution is: transcendence does not form a mixture with immanence; it is in-immanence but in-the-last-instance only. This is the solution to a problem: the possibility of intentionality or even that of being-in-the-world.

# Problems of the manifestation of the force-(of)-thought

Touching on the aprioristico-universal dimension of transcendence or of Being in general and such as it is present in the force-(of)-thought, several problems appear which allow us to understand that the force-(of)-thought is the object of a transcendental theorem:

1) The manifestation of Being through the One or in-One, a manifestation that is thus non-"ontological".

2) Its necessary presupposition through itself, a presupposition of its specific or proper essence. Not being produced or created by the One, it is *in its own way*, which is not that of the One, an absolute given (before being relative "to" the One); it thus also possesses a properly ontological mode of representation, however conditioned by the One-in-the-last-instance.

3) Unlike the "manifest" mode of the One, that of Being assumes in general the givenness or the empirical indication of transcendence, or of the philosophy which, there, is thought.

4) Its complete, achieved knowledge, its manifestation *as Being*, beyond its manifestation insofar as it belongs only to the force-(of)-thought or enters into its constitution. The manifestation of its complete nature or

connaissance properly so called assumes in effect, in every case, a necessary reference to facticity: but this itself is not homogenous and contains distinct forms of necessity, precisely between the supposition of Being or its specific essence and its presupposition only by a philosophy which does not exist without it but which specifies and envelops it.

5) The theoretical distinction, within knowledge of Being, of knowledge of the force-(of)-thought itself (the inaugural theorem) and that of Being in its complete concept and as instance.

The first point is evident: if an X manifests itself in its own way, which comes under transcendence, it will *just as necessarily* be manifest in-One (but in-the-last-instance and in its a priori).

The second point, Being as presupposition or a priori, signifies that "knowledge", regarding Being in general or the organon, does not designate a simple formal garment thrown over it, or simply juxtaposed with the One, but equally its properly ontological manifestation, distinct from that of the One and which the One tolerates in-the-last-instance. Non-philosophy, unilaterally distinguishing the One and Being, refuses to conflate the phenomenal manifestation of the One (and of Being-in-One) and knowledge of Being by itself (the philosophy of unilateral Identity conflates them in a transcendental idealism of immanence). How do we conceive this manifestation? As that of a not-yet-manifested (that which cannot claim to be of the One). But if Being precedes its manifestation, if it presupposes itself, is this by means of a circle of auto-position? This is no longer possible here since it is presupposed by its knowledge; it is also necessarily already lived in-One, in the finitude of the One. From this point of view it is a circle concentrated on itself, identified from within, by that aspect where it is in-One, as if the circle, its diameter, its span were not unified and synthesized in the form of a superior, all-encompassing circle ("circle of circles") but rather fixed in an internal manner by a radical identity. We will call "uni-flection" this relation (to) itself or this manifestation that is Being when reduced in its philosophical auto-position—become non-autopositional—without being suppressed, by its insertion in-One. It concerns the identity without synthesis of a miscellany, an identity which comes from the One but where the One does not alienate itself.

The third point signifies that with the organon of the force-(of)-thought, non-philosophy is in any case already constrained to associate a radical transcendence with the One (but outside of it), but it signifies too that it does not do so immediately or in a first manner. It does not presuppose this connection to the One *at the same time* as it leaves the One itself as being given, but only presupposes it within thought, within the project of thinking the One, so under a condition which necessarily has an autonomous empirical origin (since the One itself does not provide it) or which derives from the non(-One). The organon is in effect given and known through the theorem that posits it and it partially holds the givenness and knowledge of its aspect of transcendence of a factical transcendence, of that which the transcendental "extracts" when it manifests itself by manifesting in its mode. What transcendence or non(-One)? That of which philosophy is the symptom or indication: not only the forms it gives in the uses it makes, but the very element or "region" of transcendence that these forms presuppose and which (cf. second point) auto-presuppose themselves, so relatively autonomous and discernible from philosophy itself. Without experience and philosophy informing it, we would not know that *there is* transcendence: but knowing that there is some does not make it so in an absolute sense for metaphysics: if it is given, it is given phenomenally with the One, manifested necessarily in and by it and, moreover, manifested in its proper mode of knowledge for which it is needed this time by a giving experience.

The fourth point signifies that if the facticity of the non(-One) is unnecessary for the manifestation of Being in-One, then it is unnecessary for the two forms under which Being is concretely given, but under distinct relations: 1) for the manifestation-in-One of its specific essence (that of Being which belongs to the force-(of)-thought), an essence indicated by the relative autonomy of "transcendence" as determinant for philosophy; 2) for the complete and larger manifestation of Being *qua* Being which assumes the active intervention of its properly ontological manifestation (and not only in-One) and the taking into account of the facticity of philosophy itself in its essential structure. The manifestation of the organon by the inaugural theorem registers the general conditions of knowledge but also registers the relative autonomy or distinction of Being or transcendence as essence of philosophy in terms of knowledge. The force-(of)-thought is known not independently of any facticity but independently of the forms that the Philosophical Decision gives to transcendence, which presupposes itself, and independently of the properly ontological manifestation of Being which is already present in the constitution of the force but which is in some sense inactive. It is this mechanism of the constitution of the force-(of)-thought that we must specify.

The structure of the force-(of)-thought (rather than its relation to material) responds to a quasi-syntax we have called "unilateral duality". It "activates" [*agence*] the transcendental clone and the proper essence of Being, non-autopositional Distance reduced to its identity in this way, in a uni-tactic manner (without simultaneity or synthesis). In each of the two cases examined the relation to experience remains necessary. However, the manifestation of the force-(of)-thought precedes that of Being *qua Being*. There are two reasons for this distinction. One reason already examined holds that the proper essence of Being as component of the force is sufficiently manifested when it is empirically indicated and transcendentally received or lived in-One without still being manifested in its proper ontological mode. This is not necessary for the force which can thus appear before the manifestation itself of Being qua Being. In the force-(of)-thought, Being is only manifest in-One, no longer in its proper mode of Being as it must be in the specific theory of Being. The force will evidently be required for this properly ontological manifestation since it contains the essence of Being as organon. And the ontological manifestation of this will be understood within that of Being qua Being.

A second reason evidently comes from the occasional cause, philosophy, in which transcendence itself presents with a certain autonomy, more or less accentuated, in terms of being placed in the concrete philosophical oeuvre. How does this autonomy mark itself? In the force-(of)-thought, Being is real by its insertion "in-One" but it conserves an autonomy, only relative since it is transcendentally unilateralized not by the One which does no such thing, but "by" its clone as essence of the force. This in effect can in general, as transcendental a priori, only presuppose itself in relation to experience and moreover it cannot be, from the aspect of its "Being", anything but a given as absolute as the One itself, at least for thought and under its conditions. The radical indifference of the One itself does not only apply to the philosophical mixture but also to its element, transcendence; but this makes the difference and resists (from its own point of view) the force-(of)-thought even more than the concrete mixture. Not a "radical" resistance to the One from the point of view of the One itself, but an essential and first resistance, absolute in its order of transcendence. Necessarily presupposing itself, it resists, from its own perspective, that of thought, the One. This resistance thus first opposes its determination by the One under the only form that it tolerates, that of a solely transcendental identity that seizes this essence from Being. The One is indifferent to the form and content of thought, its essence too, but it is solicited by it. It "demands" a minimal support in order to determine the resistance under which thought presents itself. The One does not determine it directly and from itself but, *if* it presents it, then it presents it as essence *then*, being necessarily received-in-One, it is fixed in a transcendental identity that only demands this essence and reduces it. What is necessary and sufficient, beyond the One, is the givenness of a relative autonomy of the *essence* of transcendence in order that the force-(of)-thought constitutes or manifests itself.

The force-(of)-thought, which includes Being through its essence, is thus more autonomous than what it produces, Being qua Being, because the core of resistance or relative autonomy of the essence of Being is stronger in its order and phenomenally more autonomous than the philosophical mixture grounded on it. It has a primitive core of resistance which "occasionally" explains the appearance of the force-(of)-thought presupposing itself as Being or a priori (at once "transcendental" as soon as in-One); and a more superficial resistance, more "modal", which manifests itself as philosophical mixture and which resists… the force itself. In its proper constitution, the force-(of)-thought preserves, from its double origin, the relative autonomy of the only essence of Being (the mixture being suspended or useless beyond its indicative role), whereas in its exercise or rather in its materials, the mixture in its concretization as Philosophical Decision finds a necessary function. This situation suffices to autonomize the force-(of)-thought through relation to experience itself, to the materials of the mixture from which it is nonetheless inseparable as from its transcendent "indication", because it includes nothing but the essence of Being and never its more specific dimensions.

The fifth point signifies that Being, when it is not only manifested in-One but already known as organon, is necessary to its own knowledge, Being qua Being: there is thus apparently a circle between the organon *for knowledge* and the organon *object known* or posed by the first theorem of non-philosophy. It is the transcendental identity invested in the organon itself which resolves this problem: as first knowledge of non-philosophy and transcendental a priori, the organon is at once the object known as such and the means of knowledge in a specific theorem, with the necessary aid of a philosophical facticity which allows the "solitude" of the One to occur.

In non-philosophy, thought in act is not distinct, in its essence at least, from its effects or its speech because, if it is relatively free regarding its cause, this is its cause as imprinted with a radical performativity, unlike philosophy which only reaches this under the form of a circle, or more or less a circle, or in another case some sort of unconscious which destroys it. Non-philosophy is constrained—materials aside—from doing what it says and from saying what it does. The object of reasoning and reasoning itself are identical not circularly but in-the-last-instance only. On the one hand the force-(of)-thought is thus not a thesis or a dogma but the object of a transcendental theorem. There are two axioms it has been possible to effectively infer under the condition of the radical immanence of the One: a theorem called "transcendental" because it is produced—excepting a facticity not programmed into its content—by an induction-deduction that itself is transcendental, which is to say consistent in-the-last-instance in the vision-in-One as Real. On the other hand, the force-(of)-thought itself is a structure or a transcendental a priori in the sense we understand this term at least: as that which induces-deduces itself not through metaphysics or directly from the real-One (procession, emanation, etc.) but under or conforming to the rule of real immanence, starting from a facticity, without itself being the Real or a part of the One (thus "in-the-last-instance" only); as transcendence insofar as it is finally received and lived in-One in the mode of the One rather than its own. As the transcendental nature of non-philosophy demands, the reasoning that produces the first theorem of the force-(of)-thought as solution to the problem defined by the axioms is, identically but in-the-last-instance, without circle, without distinction of what it says and what it does, the solution itself: the force-(of)-thought which concretizes determination-in-the-last-instance itself is at once the solution to philosophical resistance and transcendental reasoning necessary to produce this first knowledge of non-philosophy.

The theorem, then, does not posit the force-(of)-thought as transcendental without putting it into necessary relation with spontaneous philosophical resistance, at once as the empirical indication of its existence (the pure transcendental force of such an empirical occasion), and as material, once it has reduced this, where it draws out its own a priori and the a priori which specify the essence of Being. It thus validates the claim made by the second axiom or registers resistance, giving it an acceptable sense coherent with the first. The operation of force "over" resistance makes non-philosophy, rather than a "pragmatic history of the human spirit" (Fichte), a *pragmatic theory of philosophy in terms of man as last-instance.* Non-philosophy or whatever unified theory it renders possible is a theory rather than a history, a theory infinitely opened by the contingency of the given and by the unilateralization carried out by the force-(of)-thought rather than a history circularly accomplishing itself in the synthesis or "philosophical" reconciliation of the contraries of the I and the non-I, of philosophy and collective consciousness, albeit in a non substantial manner and in an infinite effort of realization of self. Non-philosophy thus re-opens history by liberating it from its philosophical enclosure.

# Reminders and remarks

The concretized causality of the One, the force-(of)-thought, is the specific power of the already-Manifested to undertake *manifestation*, which is the means by which it can affect any thing = X, by which it can "recognize" this or be the immanent lived without however destroying it. This transcendental efficacy of the One-in-One is in reality a double, more than identical, without however reforming a reversible coupling of operations:

1) On the one hand the "positive" side of the force-(of)-thought. Being immanent, without necessary object, the One, the already-Manifested "remains there". But if we give it the occasion of an object which presents itself, then it is its revelation "in-the-last-instance", when all is said and done or finally, by the force-(of)-thought in the very mode of the One. We call this power *Unidentification*: the transcendental power which adds nothing to the One, which is the One itself "acting" through the proper essence of transcendence to even the concretion or effectivity of this transcendence. What is to be manifested does not modify its essence. The One itself already has its specific "oeuvre" distinct from that of Being or transcendence: this is the Manifested-without-manifestation. But it also has as force-(of)-thought that of manifesting any X or Y under the sole conditions of itself rather than under those of what presents itself to it (it does not contain the image of the X as a real part of itself), but on the condition of modifying the originary auto-positional structure of the mixture where X is given, in the sense of its identity or simplification, its non-division. This is the Unidentification of transcendence, its being non-autopositional and non-autogiving, an effect of the transcendental identity that the force-(of)-thought transmits.

2) On the other hand, radical, non-transcendental indifference of the One—not even an immediate negation of… —to anything that is not itself is here still concretely cloned in transcendental indifference which affects Being, indifference to what does not have the structure of the One, so to philosophical resistance. We call *Unilateralization* this quasi-negative aspect, (non-)One rather than non-Being, of vision-in-One. This is how science-thought is in general a *cut* or *unilateralizing indifference* rather than auto-positional difference, an operation of depriving itself not of transcendence but of the illusion attached to its auto-position. The finitude of thought-in-One, that too of radical immanence when it becomes "point of view" or force-(of)-thought, signifies in one sense that the One believes in itself when it manifests X or Y as it does or communicates a transcendental identity to them; and in another sense it signifies that the One refuses to cede to philosophical prestiges: the intrinsic finitude of thought operates then as non-philosophical "cut".

Unidentification and Unilateralization are the most general components of unitax which is determination-in-the-last-instance and they affect (as their transcendental essence) Being or transcendence insofar as these are in-One, depriving them of their suspended auto-positionality. The relation between the two "operations" of the One has a special nature. Their grouping, as we have said, does not form the third synthetic term of a philosophical reduction always hanging over the I and the World and always more or less menaced by reversibility. The notion of suspense for example is not a real division in the object, a decision of this type: it is the indifference where all that is not transcendental unidentity is struck. Hence the conservation—the "residue"—of unidentity (in-One) of X or of Y. The One or even unidentity do not then manifest themselves "outside" of themselves through a *division-over* the object X. On the contrary: they do so through a "non-autopositional" simplification which is accompanied by a unilateralization of the suspended side. Thus we can say that manifesting "in-One" and suspending that which resists unidentity are exactly the same thing from the point of view of the One, this real identity conditioning the transcendental unitax. This causality proper to the One alone (with its two aspects) is constant, precisely inalienable. The description must take this into account regardless of the material described.

An empirical condition is assumed by this unitax of transcendental nature, since what we come to describe has not been unitax from the point of view of the One alone, for which the object = X does not even exist, nor does identity or the unilateralizing suspension of its representation. Because X (Being, for example) presents itself, it *occasions* identity and undifferentiating suspension. The force of the One is thus a more complex structure than the One itself and one which adds to it once we assume an "empirical" occasional cause. Acting "on" X in this double manner assumes a relative autonomy of X but signifies its manifestation or vision-in-One. The Unidentification and Unilateralization of the given are not contradictory, this is not the monstrous synthesis of a center and a margin. It is neither that one is a center nor that the other is sent-to-the-margins.

A distinction must be made, but it is not philosophical. Strictly speaking we will no longer say that the One unidentifies and unilateralizes X—this X is absolutely indifferent to it. We will say that it neither affects nor acts on it other than through a new structure that it frees up under its form of non-positional a priori of X. The relatively autonomous structure of the force-(of)-thought, it is, along with material, the first correlate, presupposing itself without autopositing itself, of the unitax which is its essence. We will call it *Unilaterality itself*, as thought of X which takes X into consideration or registers its existence as "occasion". This structure is thus only necessary for the One('s)-representation (not the One itself) and as function of the causality of the occasion. Moreover here there is a structure that is at once noetic (non-phenomenological Distance) and "noematic" (*that which* is manifested from X). We can see that we surpass the noetic description of the force-(of)-thought toward the noematic moments of it (the materials) when we introduce the occasional cause, the philosophical representation of the One which, on this basis, operates the genesis of more specific noematic moments.

The force-(of)-thought, in virtue of its transcendental essence, resolves the paradox of a cause which is the sole real cause—at least from its viewpoint which is the unique guiding thread of thought—but which cannot act directly on its object: precisely because being the sole (undivided) cause, it cannot itself sustain any relation to an object. It is thus it and it alone who acts, but using a transcendental organon wherein it consequently does not alienate itself. This is the only non-technological causality or, more exactly, non-(techno-)philosophical, since it does not alienate itself in its instrument. There are thus two absolutely hetero-geneous *orders* of causality, identical in-the-last-instance, which break unitary philosophical continuity.

Uni-laterality is this structure of the most general duality "between" the One and philosophy. It is the figure or form within thought insofar as it opposes itself to reciprocal Determination or to bilaterality, to philosophy's mixture. Uni-laterality is the form of non-philosophy as the Mix is that of philosophy. Non-philosophy is an enterprise of *determination* of the given, not its *objectification*, but a uni-lateral determination of the given. The One does not play a role except, absolutely and in every case necessary, as the *mode* of the lived or the manifestation of the image of X, but it does not contain this image. The "last-instance" that is the One is only a last-instance because it does not contain any part of the World and of knowledge: it is simple, without fold or inclusion.

Some terminological points now on determination-in-the-last-instance and the occasion: the first, in the strict sense, designates the double aspect of the causality of the One, and in the wider sense designates all the relations in play: the occasion is thus a phenomenon included in the fully developed concept of determination-in-the-last-instance. We can make the same type of distinction for Uni-laterality…

We equally distinguish, according to the same distribution, determi-nation and overdetermination. The former only conceives itself in the mode of "in-the-last-instance". The latter designates the whole efficacy of the occasional cause, of philosophy as transcendent condition of the existence of non-philosophy.

# 5 THE METHOD OF DUALYSIS: (PERFORMATION, CLONING, A PRIORI)

## The identity of thought rather than its totality: Its unified theory rather than its encyclopedia

Philosophy evidently does not exhaust thought. Certain philosophers admit that regional ontologies (science, art, politics, love, to take up this quartet again) produce thought and even truth. Nonetheless they demand that philosophy define their essence and itself be their excellent form and their ultimate type, whether the thought of thought, or what totalizes or simply gathers thought, picks it up as a last resort, etc. Non-Philosophy's problem is different: can we discover a new form of thought, purely transcendental in origin, unknown to its regional forms, to science, politics, art, etc., but also to its fundamental form, philosophy? And a form that would be a certain theoretical usage, and so explicative of philosophy and the regional forms? This does not concern reshuffling what already exists or what has already *taken place*, of "making something new out of the old", but of discovering the new itself, the statements and forms of thought that are not already given other than through their data but which we ignore because we have not realized them or manifested them and which thus, in a sense, have not yet taken place in thought itself. From this point of view, the One as philosophy understands it is the very type of discovery and installs thought in the dimension of philosophy. The One is absolutely given and thought cannot add anything to it, but it is still absolutely invisible to thought, and not only foreclosed, insofar as up to the present it has essentially been philosophy. If non-philosophy has some sort of objective, it is to constitute itself *in the place of tests and of unique manifestation* of what there is of the *data* of thought under the divided and opposed forms in the sciences and philosophy (and art, politics, etc.). Neither "totalization" nor "encyclopedia", neither "reflection" nor "compossibilization" of the philosophical type: all of these conceptions of thought proceed by division, subtraction, addition, supplementation, multiplication of its heterogeneous species, by operations which for the most part reproduce the philosophical gesture and its practice of blends and which, all things considered, simultaneously repress in another sense the emergent possibility of thought constituted identically from science, art, politics *and* philosophy. We will no longer say, then, contra philosophy: "science (or art, etc.) thinks too"—this is to return to the terrain of philosophy and to do battle with it. Still less: positive science thinks better than philosophy and defines the essence of thought—this is to lapse into positivism as return to philosophical hierarchy. But:

a) *There are* regional forms of thought which present themselves as such—we do not have to decide *de jure* on this claim, nor decide on their nature, we do not forge a hypothesis on their essence "in itself" that we would have to think, rather we simply take their auto-presentation and claim into account.

b) *There is* evidently thought in philosophy but we no longer assign it primacy or a teleological and encyclopedic function, this being simply to "reassemble", "gather", "compossibilize" the other forms assumed to be unthought, and thus to think; it is nothing more than an "equal" "experience" among others. It undoubtedly raises this claim to think these, but we no longer recognize this claim. We are obligated to take it into account as symptom, under the title of our *data*. Within these conditions it is artificial to wish to distinguish epistemological reflection *on* the sciences from the overlapping of philosophy and some science, for example the immediate position of a transcendent identity of mathematics and ontology. In this instance it is still despite everything an intra-philosophical distinction which perhaps exceeds such or such an epistemology, but certainly not the *epistemo-logos* philosophy lives on. The overlap, the mixture, the amphibology, etc., whether implicit or explicit, reflected or dogmatically posited, what difference is there in terms of philosophical sufficiency and primacy? What difference when philosophy is said now to ground not truth but rather a *place for* these truths, as if elsewhere it never had wanted to be such a place... for what has already taken place? An auto-topology, an-auto-position?

c) From the open set of these *data* which are already *data* of knowing, can we invent and discover the thought of a transcendental origin capable at once of explaining them and rendering them intelligible, critiquing their immediate representations and complementarily of procuring a usage of them in terms of thinking and identically having knowledge of the essence of this new thought itself (and not the essence of science or even philosophy, as philosophy claims)? Can we discover and manifest this more "powerful" thought since, being the identity of science and philosophy, an unknown identity of them, determined by the One, it is more universal than the functional correlations of the sciences and the generalities/totalities of philosophies (precisely because it definitively abandons the *telos* of totality, its avatars or partial forms? There are heterogeneous regimes of thought outside of and within philosophy, but non-philosophy's goal is no longer to describe, inventory or assemble these in an encyclopedic or simply reflexive-categorical manner. It is to *discover* a new specific regime or a new continent of thought, which is consequently more heterogeneous than these former regimes (which are always still philosophizable) *and which identifies them from within, in an absolutely immanent manner*, without recourse to the philosophical fetishes of the "Whole", "Being", the "Same", "Collection", "Compossibilization", etc.

# The determination of thought rather than its subtraction

Through more or less voluntary decisions, undecidable in various proportions, philosophy has always distinguished its own activity from the regional ontologies it has reflected in extremely varied ways. This decisional economy is that of the auto-decoupage of the philosophical body—metaphysics itself. A non-philosophy proceeds entirely otherwise.

It still autonomizes thought—which it both exercises and elucidates—by giving it a form and a material that are identically theoretical-(and)-pragmatic, as well as a cause that is no longer "metaphysical" or supposedly real, but really transcendental; the range of an ontology immanent to the hypothesis-form or axiom, but irreal. Leaving thought to be determined-in-the-last-instance by the very immanence of the Real, it purges all finality, giving it its autonomy in relation to regional *and* fundamental knowings which respond to determined ends which cannot be their own. In these knowings it now only finds simple *data* to constitute its statements and manifest a prioris in them. It also abandons the teleology of the fundamental claims of philosophy, which are reduced and amputated as simple "collection", "compossibilization", "categorical reflection", etc.

But far from annulling the sphere of so-called "empirical" proce-dures or reducing these to an irreal or an absolute (non-)One, it grants them a relative autonomy while also, treating them as *data* or occasional cause of this science-thought, recognizing their reality, something philos-ophies of radical immanence—which are in a way normalizations of non-philosophy—have generally had trouble admitting. These regional and fundamental knowings, these "empiricities", possess a consistency that is correlative not to their absolute contingency regarding the One, but to their contingent necessity with regard to thought (in-One). Multifaceted "empirical" knowing must have been produced in order to render non-philosophy not possible and even less real but effective insofar as it is, additionally and in-the-last-instance thought-in-One.

Philosophy itself, in its totality and simultaneously in each of its positions or decisions that parlay it each time, is thus now one of these empiricities and no longer distinguishes itself from the others except in the depth of its claims, which we no longer admit except as symptom. Furthermore, non-philosophy does not extend empirical knowings in the mode of their reflection, categorical or not (still a philosophical operation of auto-position); it treats them as materials but as consistent and necessary. In a general manner, if philosophy totalizes, collects or more modestly compossibilizes knowings produced elsewhere—put together from systems and mixtures—it definitively abandons this gesture to test itself and know itself as immanent identity of thought and science, of *philosophy* and art, ethics, etc. We call *unidentity* this identification without remainder—but not without work to produce knowledge—that is determined-in-the-last-instance-in-One. It has no sense except the abandonment of philosophy's encyclopedic claims which are always, even when truncated under the form of a "compossibilization", auto-positions of knowings in the service of the obscure and transcendent ends of philosophy. It maintains a necessary relation to the knowings and even the ends of "our time", but it does not turn this quibble into the reason for its exercise and does not reconstitute an ultimate teleological horizon. It assures empiricities, including philosophy, their relative autonomy or contingence of givens and it prohibits any pretence of intervening here. But it does not prohibit their usage, their transcendental pragmatic. It is rather that *unilateral duality, guardian of autonomies, duality irreducible at once to the One and to the reciprocity of the philosophical Dyad*, is the transcendental "syntax", the order rather than the causality of the Real.

Can we say that vision-in-One and its correlate of thought, non-philosophy, manage to subtract their objects, ends, mastery, from philosophy? It is finally sterile enough to substitute for "complement", "supplement", "supersession", within which philosophy still recently grasped its own movement, the "subtraction" through which it now radicalizes the Heideggerian "sobering", for example auto-subtraction of the "void" or the "multiple" from the old transcendent One of ontology; or moreover subtracting the immanent One specified as "transcendental Ego" or "Life" from philosophy's amphibological mixtures. In philosophy's favorite operations, the famous Nietzschean "reversal" of Platonism and the even older "critique" have ceded their place to the deconstructive Ideal and then to the subtractive Ideal: but these operations continue to assume the philosophical sufficiency they inhibit, or from which content themselves to tear their principal, Multiple object, to be valid. Immanent Other or One, whichever. The traditional auto-position of transcendence already expressed a thinly disguised ascetic ideal. What can we say of this tearing away, this subtraction, this backwards transcendence which does not even have the Jewish edge, which only expresses a Platonico-Christian ascetism and often a practice of purification and a posteriori defense, which sometimes exceeds even the purism of pure reason? Subtraction in particular—whether by science: that of transcendence (of the pure Multiple, the Event) or by mysticism: that of immanence (the transcendental Ego)—finds its ultimate cause in the Principle of Sufficient Philosophy along with its element and lets that which it liberates subsist faintly. All of philosophy is still assumed to be pertinent for the Real—which is to say that philosophy is still interpreted philosophically—and from philosophy we subtract: whatever affectivity, whatever essence of Being, whatever Language Games, whatever inconsistent Multiple. If non-philosophy subtracts or rather suspends something, then it is, from the very beginning, the assumed sufficiency or pertinence of this sufficiency for the Real. This subtraction is second and not first: it is only an effect of the positivity of the vision-in-One, the correlate of its transcendental or determining action. Rather than "subtraction", it rather speaks of "unilateralization" which sufficiently indicates that the One is the *cause* of the operation rather than its passive *object*—subtraction *always* implies the distinction of the philosophical and its object, a distinction that non-philosophy definitively annuls.

Thoughts of radical immanence, when they in turn practice subtraction, evidently have not *discovered* the original and positive mode of thought which must accompany vision-in-One. This is why they devote themselves to a formal activity of tautological repetition which is the counterpart of subtraction by transcendence, of philosophy as simple reflexive and categorical collection, whose field is increasingly reduced. The subtractive ideal is the new mask of philosophy's death-without-death: far from being contrary to it, as it claims, it only "manifests for philosophy" in this mode of progressive restriction, of extenuation and the cut. This is how philosophical sufficiency lives on: either by *auto*-affirmation or by *auto*-dislocation, etc. But this style of surgical amputation and prosthesis can decidedly occupy only the philosophers while a new problem would rather be of discovering what has not already taken place in thought precisely because the Real is only *given*, given-without-givenness and thus *de jure* invisible or foreclosed: the type of positive thought adequate to this Real('s)-invisibility, or capable of thinking in terms of this foreclosure.

Contemporary thought feigns modesty and reduces philosophy to a minimal program: the smallest program possible (but because the philosophical is an over-program exceeding any fixed program); the smallest encyclopedia and totalization possible (but because the philosophical is an over-encyclopedia conserving the systematic and argumentative link through relation to which the encyclopedia is in reality a restriction). The ruse is evident: philosophy can no longer assure its power or satisfy its sufficiency except by renouncing its immediate and dogmatic claims, reducing its definition in order to continue to assure itself a universal pertinence and to survive disaster. It feigns weakness—it "plays dead". Only redoubtably naive spirits can fall for these traps and commit all of their science to proving themselves wrong. If there is a higher genius than philosophy in thought, it must renounce these teleologies and this tired repetition and attach itself to the spirit of discovery that exceeds acquired knowings rather than reflecting or reappropriating them.

# The performativity of thought rather than its deconstruction: From the judaic turn to non-philosophical performation

In many ways, when this would be only through the "non", non-philosophy could recall the dominant currents of contemporary continental philosophy. It is sometimes interpreted by its adversaries as a new species of "deconstruction" and by deconstruction itself as a form thereof but an ungrateful one, devoid of its spirit of appreciation. At best it would bear witness to a supplementary gap imprinted in the already injured course of philosophy, but this gap would evidently be anticipated, undertaken already by existing deconstruction, it thus would be useless for the most part for renewing experience, etc. For another thinker, a thinker of a concept other than difference, it would take place in the Spinozist tradition of the One-All. For others still, it would take place in the tradition of Parmenides or Plotinus, not to mention those who readily identify it with an occidental return of the *Zen* experience... Is this about a simple conceptual or systematic indetermination, an obscurity through excess or through lack of an elaboration of its concept? Or rather a philosophical indetermination *de jure* of this concept? About the sign sure enough that it no longer situates itself on the terrain of philosophy, having precisely posited a *de jure* equivalence of all philosophical systems in terms of the Real? It would then be about the *resistance* that philosophy globally opposes, projecting its fantasies or imaginary onto it. In order to grasp the historical signification of non-philosophy—insofar as it is susceptible to having one—we will schematically characterize what we call the "historico-systematic formation of deconstructions" and the "Judaic turn of philosophy".

All of the "continental" history of thought after Nietzsche and with Freud, Wittgenstein, Lacan, Derrida, etc., can be condensed into the history of a fight between Being and the Other (more simply: these terms suffice to show what is involved here), a fight between Greek ontology and Judaism through psychoanalysis and "deconstructions" which will have given a new seat to the old conflict of philosophy and the Human Sciences. On the other hand, a thought of the One signifies that this struggle is no longer our business. We are no longer interested, even if analysts would like us each to carry our "Torah" in lieu and in place of Greek destiny. The appeal to the joint authorities of Parmenides and the Bible, Plato and the Talmud, cannot convince a spirit which places itself under the law of "phenomena" alone.

The solicitation of philosophy by psychoanalysis animates and traverses their recent history. It is impossible to give a table of the avatars of twentieth century continental philosophy without taking this struggle as guiding thread. A secret struggle first of all—where the adversaries seek each other out (until Lacan); then a struggle that is manifest and demanded as such— where the adversaries are recognized and in turn play the role of forcing peace (Lacan). From this point of view, the proportion would seem more and more equal. Between philosophy and psychoanalysis, the issue is not a banal combat of positive mastery nor even of a unilaterally philosophical attempt at appropriation alone (and only reflexive and hermeneutic, even if this case is produced and represents a spontaneous solution), but of a tense conflict sometimes stronger than the adversaries themselves, of a "différance" which relates them to one another in the greatest distance through a strategy of reciprocal appropriation and disappropriation variously balanced according to the authors. This would be a unilateral interpretation, already too philosophical to see philosophy alone undertake an enterprise of defense without nuances, and it is not always inversely psychoanalysis which brings with it the charge of alterity, of critique, of possibly the strongest deconstruction. That this combat is superior to the parties involved: this is what determines these crossed becomings and orders offensive and not only defensive actions of philosophy. Its most recent history, even though not hermeneutic, is that of the hardest blows that philosophy had tried to land on psychoanalysis: Foucault's *History of Sexuality*, Deleuze and Guattari's *Anti-Oedipus*, Derrida's *Post Card* and finally Henry's *Genealogy of Psychoanalysis* all display an offensive will where philosophy too lets itself be determined, as in all grand combats, by the adversary. In reality this style of Difference, which is to say of its struggle against the angel of analysis, a struggle recognized infinitely and drawing its nobility from its inability to end, had begun at least with Wittgenstein.

It is useless to say that nothing lets us foresee the treaty of a real peace, even if from Lacan's perspective and from what followed, the question of philosophy *in* analysis and no longer only opposite analysis is ceaselessly reopened. Of course, it is on the basis of this combat (that supersedes them and claims itself to involve thought) that the particular history of contemporary philosophy must be re-examined and re-evaluated beyond any problematic of cultural "influences". Perhaps even, to go deeper, it is with Freud rather than with Wittgenstein that the *Judaic turn* begins, a turn which profoundly determines twentieth century philosophy and which is even vaster, even more dissimulated than this combat with analysis which is in some sense its surroundings or its foreground representation. We will hypothesize that this *Judaic turn* is the point of inexhaustible fecundity of philosophy after Nietzsche, from this drop in the Heraclitean river which would remain Rosenzweig's protestation for so long: beginning with Heidegger through his reactivation of the "thing in itself" and of a Kantian *summa* impregnated with ethics; then through Wittgenstein, then Derrida; to move on again through infinite provocation, interminable echoes (Levinas); to punctuate the actions of a more or less "hard" resistance of Kojève, Ricoeur, Deleuze, Henry.

Whatever there may be in each of these avatars that no longer interest us in their diversity, thought is definitively installed in the milieu of this Judaic turn; a new economy of relations of the Philosophical Decision and the Other is fixed bit by bit in order to form *the new common sense of philosophers.* In spite of the heterogeneity of possible interpretations of this Judaic provocation that philosophy has not been able to internalize first and in general except under the form of a *turn*—the style of the turn already being an interpretation inside of philosophy and a manner of *turning* the Judaic affect in general—in spite of this Greek pre-emption over the Jewish, it is indeed from the point of view of this now infinite struggle that it is possible to move to the essence of the "philosophical" such as it is actually and globally practiced: as a *problem* which confesses to be more and more *impossible.* What do we mean by this?

If the bulk of contemporary philosophy, what at once counts beyond any calculation and begins to form a tradition, then comes together in "the" deconstructions, which is to say the philosophies which have posited the equation Real = Other or more rigorously Real = Unconscious and have substituted it for the equation Real = Being = Same or Unity-of-Contraries, we recognize a principal axis *now in terms of this circumstance and from this perspective*: Wittgenstein, Heidegger, Derrida; and secondary axes which recoup this or accompany it in parallel: Nietzsche then Deleuze on the one hand, Lacan then Badiou on the other—all other differences aside (and these are innumerable).

The philosophical, under the form of what we call the structural invariant of the "Philosophical Decision", is the circular combination of the One and the Dyad (whatever the empirical worth of these variables), the reciprocal determination of the One and a Dyad of immanence and transcendence. This is to say that it contains in a sort of hollow, through this transcendence or decision, the possibility of a reception and an insertion of the affect of an unrepresentable alterity. A complicated insertion, not without damage for the Greco-Philosophical and the Judaic, but a combination which *can* form, which forms more and more through a thousand conflicts and ruses, and which forms on the strength of *an amphibological appearance, the appearance of an identity or sameness of the "Other".* Between the *Other who is* (that of the Greco-metaphysical decision) and the *Other who "is" not* (that of Judaism), for example between the signified signifier as such and the unsignifiable signifier, *there is an appearance of identity reduced to its forms or its most empirical givens.* This objective appearance suffices to explain the reciprocal fascination that constitutes this Judaic turn wherein philosophy has been engaged by force, this negotiation with the non-negotiable to which it is driven, this will to devote its clearest forces to this conflict now.

The unnoticed result of this struggle, now comprising a symptom, is that philosophy crudely exhibits its destination of auto/hetero-dislocation. This forced will of dislocation of the Philosophical Decision is the most discussed theoretical symptom of this Greco-Judaic combat which is evidently not a becoming-Jewish of the philosopher, nor his mass invasion by a culture which would be stranger to its origin, but rather a resistance to the destruction of the Decision by an Other('s)-affect which would risk being stronger than it. Philosophy has shown enough cunning and enough force to turn this unprecedented meeting into a good trial, a surmountable trial. So much so that it from here never ceases to mime its destruction, its pure and simple dislocation, or to maintain this dissolution of the Decision within boundaries that are still those of the *logos*. A logos eaten into until the rope has slackened, but which will finally have resisted the infinite tractions exerted upon it. What is contemporary philosophy if not, *on the occasion of* its wranglings with psychoanalysis, the always recurring demonstration that it is stronger than any attack; that the One, at least as philosophy perceives it, resists in spite of all attempts to slacken the Dyad or augment its charge of alterity? Philosophy does not cede: that it be susceptible to proofs (by the unconscious and not only be language, logic or power) proves it sufficiently. Hence this impression that it has never been anything but this claim and this demonstration of force, this auto-deconstruction, that the One, as always and as already in metaphysics, has only ever served to maintain and save the Dyad, and that if psychoanalysis has raised the bar of proof and rendered the task nearly impossible (nearly: since it has made the very content of the task impossible), philosophy is still capable, in an infinite turning, of lifting these weights which would have had to be the heaviest.

Without a doubt the specificity of twentieth century philosophy, the interference of the metaphysical tradition and the Judaic affect of the Other *qua* Other, has allowed this tradition not to die of sterility and ennui. By fixing its new object, which goes from the Unconscious to the Other by passing through Language Games or the various forms of Differ(e/a)nce, etc., it has modified the image of thought, invented a new relation of thought to its "object". For the most part, this invention is as follows: thought is no longer what describes an already given object or one that is present before it—ideal of certitude or of the ontological type of performativity—but what discovers it or manifests it in the aftermath of its exercise, "project" or "decision". To think is to exceed or transcend, but absolutely, beyond the objective given toward the "in itself", and so reveals the *de jure* opaque or unconscious, unthinkable face, of this: it conditioned thought and thought espoused it without knowing it. This is to undo the old metaphysical performativity which concentrated itself in the ideal and the practice of auto-position of concepts, of the auto-grounding or the auto-legitimization of philosophy, and finally its auto-nomination.

It is not necessary here to oppose the variants of this grand historico-systematic formation: the ecstatic-horizontal project, the excess of the force of decision, the after-the-fact of writing, the backwards transcendence, etc., even if it is evident that important nuances subsist in the radicality, opacity and alterity of this instance in relation to "consciousness" or the "logos", the "same" or "presence", the "hermeneutic interpretation" or "reflection", etc. On the other hand it is essential to grasp that thought is nonetheless assumed from here as partial and dehiscent, more than divided: unsealed or cut off from itself, without ever being able to regroup in a totality or in a performativity; devoted to a supplement, a surplus or an excess which, from its other perspective, forms a space, lack or subtraction. Variations on this theme abound in the twentieth century and from this point of view the harmonies of metaphysics or of this ontology which goes from the Ancients to the Moderns have barely resisted this fracturing and extra-territorial intervention. Contemporary philosophy is globally—this characterization suffices here—the invention of thinking the unthinkable (Unconscious, Other, Unthought, etc.) and the end of ontological performativity. The ideal of this would be given by the statement of Parmenides: "Thought and Being are the Same"; it tries to conserve itself in Spinoza, Leibniz and Nietzsche, then Deleuze—in spite of the blows it suffers—and moreover in Hegel who, in order to do this, redoubles—as all philosophers do in reality—identity and difference through identity. But under the Judaic affect of what we would gladly call the "Most-High-Other" [*Très-Hautre*], deconstructions run a double game: they renounce the auto-position and the auto-legitimization of transcendence, its performativity, but accentuate the priority that philosophy has always reserved for transcendence. They aggravate transcendence to the point of calling on the most active and most opaque transcendence against the fixed empirical, factical forms of the transcendent and against their element, auto-position. Hence the "excess", the "decision", the 'surplus" as subtraction, or even "backwards transcendence" or any other operation, decisional or not (semi-decisional), which reveals its object like the order of a past that is more or less absolute or irreducible to the present.

Nonetheless if "deconstructions" have fortunately delivered us from a certain latent mythology of metaphysics—the old One of philosophy—it is only to do this inside of philosophy's invariants. They have used the ontological One, they have deconstructed the One of Presence, to the point of saying here and there that "the One is not" although "there is the One", but they have not said this in a new and positive manner, renewing its experience, but in a reactive, anti-metaphysical manner, beginning by ratifying its sufficiency and that of philosophy, its claim regarding the Real:

they have cut into, displaced the auto-positional kind of performativity, not suppressed it by and in the Real itself. They have only re-accentuated or reactivated the Dyad; recharged the alterity of dehiscence of the Two become "process" irreducible to the One and against the assumed power of unification of the One. They have only "streamlined" the Greek One to the point of this meager film or limit, or else this derisory "one-of-the-count" that it has become after them. Through this Judaic aggravation of the Dyad, they have conserved the Dyad, "cutting" the Greek with the Jewish and diluting the Jewish in the Greek. Philosophical thought has undoubtedly gained and produced new affects in this way, a new mode of survival, but it is spared, through this miscegenation it has overseen and ultimately ruled, from having to change "basis" or "terrain".

Apart from the new philosophical effects, there is thus no really new thought to await in this combat philosophy wages against itself, and which now continues through interposed psychoanalysis. No new thought, that is to say, and this conclusion is inevitable, no *real* peace and no *really* new affect or no affect *other than the affect of the philosophical*. The Judaic would have had to be—and is, perhaps, more than the philosophical—this Real('s)-affect, this Real as affect. But that it spontaneously joins up with philosophy is proof or symptom that it is only the affect of the Other, of the Real as impossible, not of a nothing-but-Real which would no longer let itself be pitted against the possible, if at least the Real is not the Other but the One that determines the Other itself in-the-last-instance. What can we gain from moving out of the Greek amphibology of the Real and the possible, the One and Being, if this is to throw ourselves into another amphibology which would now be all the rage, that of the Real and the impossible, the One and the Other? Since the problem of problems is this: amphibology (philosophical, analytic, philosophico-analytic, etc.), is perhaps not the only measure of the vastest and most democratic thought, the conflict or Greco-Judaic difference is perhaps not the only measure of man; the philosophico-analytic war is perhaps not the only measure of the most precious stake…

The "historical" signification of non-philosophy is established thus: it is neither Greek nor Judaic, nor the crossbreeding of the two, but *the ante-Greek and ante-Judaic identity of thought, the experience of thought "before" its Greco-Judaic disjunction*. It substitutes for the terrain of Being, that of ontological difference—the philosophical tradition up to and including Nietzsche—and for the terrain of the Other—that of the Greco-Judaic inter-ferences of the twentieth century since Freud and Wittgenstein—the new terrain of the One not "*qua* one" but as it is or One-in-One. This substi-tution does not commence any historical or philosophical rivalry but rather a new relation of explication intelligible to the identity of Philosophy and its history. It explains that non-philosophy is not a classical philosophical ontology nor one of its contemporary deconstructions—nor the will to destroy these in order to substitute itself for them on the philosophical scene—but a *theoretical usage*, a new practice if you will, a peaceful one, of these two grand historico-systematic formations of thought. It concerns, beyond Being and the Other, coming to the principle of *a performativity that is now immanent or radical, absolutely non-autopositional but of-the-last-instance*. Vision-in-One can understand itself as one such performativity of real essence and of transcendental rather than linguistic efficacy and which thus does not suffer the faults of its ontological and linguistic concept which can at any moment be subjected to an inevitable deconstruction by the Other and its avatars. Rather than a performativity, we speak then of the One, in the axiomatic style familiar to us, as of a "Performed-without-performation", which is to say as identical-(to)-itself through-and-through, regardless of the local property or attribute under which we purport to seize it, which only serves as material for the statements which are deduced from it or reflect it adequately without however still claiming to aim at it or objectify it as a being, or "approach" it and "co-respond" to it as they do to Being.

# On the performed-without-performation

Vision-in-One or the Real can thus be understood starting from "performativity". This term is at least a datum given by ordinary language philosophy; it must be transposed and generalized here outside of the linguistic sphere under certain conditions of work proper to non-philosophy in order to characterize the radical kind of immanence, compared to the efficacy of language or to the action of Being in a regime of logos.

In the sphere of linguistics, that is to say still partially that of philosophy, "performative" purports to concern certain statements in which the signifying value and the action value, as well as the sense and the operation, the signified and the practice, are identified—without this identification being examined in its intrinsic possibility. They say what they do and do what they say, with the exception of a philosophical decision which nonetheless remains implicit the rest of the time and is the internal limit of this transcendent concept of performativity.

If we now assume a radical transcendental identity of saying and doing (to-do-in-saying, to-say-in-doing), the only instance whose usage speaks itself through this identity without fault, but which at the same time retains nothing of "doing" and 'speaking" as opposed to philosophical concepts for itself as first terms, is evidently the One itself, which is to say the Real such as it is defined by an immanence of phenomenon or a "lived" inherence (to) itself. The Real is named starting from the performative because it is not the Real without (being-)given in an absolutely unreflected manner in an experience which no longer opposes itself to a transcendent object and still no longer forms the couple of a "same" with it. Non-philosophy thus frees up, by manifesting it on its behalf, the phenomenal core of performativity which was always despite everything somewhat divisible in the usage philosophy made of language. It particularly subtracts it from its verbal and active dimension and leaves it to-be-given as Real('s)-passivity, prior to the noun of beings and the verb of Being (we can still speak philosophically of "passive performativity" whose Husserlian "passive synthesis" would only be one instance). We will carefully distinguish the phenomenal given concerns, to which we designate the first axiomatic abstract name of Performed-Without-Performation (the past participle not indicating here the result of an action but the phenomenal state of things immanent (to) itself) from the set of axioms and statements of knowledge we form about it; a knowledge that is adequate, though rectifiable, to the phenomenon it indicates.

"Understood" in this way as the essence of the Real, radical performativity no longer enters at all, even less than into certain linguistics, into a *coupling* with the constative function of language: little by little it introduces an identity (said to be of-the-last-instance) in the linguistic couples that it "unilateralizes" outside of the Real. It prohibits the auto-reflexive then philosophical usage of language and shows that, in first science, language is required without still speaking by redoubling its own ground, or of a *hinter-language*, since it speaks only from the Real and submits to the transcendental law of its identity and of unilaterality, of non-autopositionality.

If deconstructions and almost all philosophy since Freud (up to Badiou's work) are a "hetero-critique" of the proper identity of Being (of the *ontological* One, or the One attached to Ontological Difference) as performativity, they have only destroyed the ontological and transcendent forms of performativity, never the core of the Performed that necessarily precedes every operation of performation and from which they themselves draw a treaty they cannot honor. The practices of the decision or of the Other-thought that reveal the Real after the fact as irreducible past are thus themselves downgraded or suspended in favor of a thought which, far from regressing toward the old ontology of the One and/or the Multiple, instead radicalizes what they themselves have brought anew into the experience of thought—a heritage it honors with recognition. The past revealed by operation of decision after the fact is undoubtedly in effect an absolute past which has never been present, but which remains associated or contiguous with a present it still assumes and with which it maintains an ultimate constitutive relation in spite of everything. On the contrary, if we use this problematic as provisional material, the One as Performed is a radical past or a given, a past without transcendence. An identity revealed "in" itself rather than following or in the shadow of a decision. This is the *phenomenon* in its identity, *the phenomenon as real past* "within" and "from" which we can think. The past of deconstructions remains in the order of an unconscious ultimately integrating itself with a consciousness, and this only unveils it in order to disappear with it in a blackout or a new veiling (flash, eclipse, retreat, decision of the undecidable, etc., all very different notions but all of which modify an invariant characteristic of "post-modern" thought). The absolute past (of) the One, on the other hand, is the already-Manifested which determines the decision in-the-last-instance and, if it recognizes in the decision a relative autonomy, then this is only the autonomy of an operation that is non-constitutive of the Real and strictly limited to the sphere of thought. The decision is thus the simple non-specular clone of the real-One. It thinks from the real-One but does not reveal it as it is—it is a transcendental (re)flection-(of)-the One that does not reflect the One itself.

The radical Performed signifies the definitive destruction of hinter-worlds: there is no longer even any performation reconstituting a world sketched out behind the One, and moreover none of these ultimate hinter-worlds such as Phenomenological Givenness, Desiring Production or the Will to Power, Writing and general Textuality, or even Language Games. It is this Performed, stripped of its fetishes of "performativity" and in general of activity and the *causa sui*, that transmits thought itself as identity (in its relatively autonomous order of thought) of science and philosophy, more generally of the "theoretical" and the "pragmatic". We will not say too hastily—confusing the Real and thought once again—that this is directly performed "in-One", but that *it is in-One in-the-last-instance only through the One as the Performed itself*. We will thus deduce the essence and specific structures of thought—or of non-philosophy—starting from the radical Performed and its effects on the transcendent relations of science and philosophy.

# The force-(of)-thought as transcendental performation: The identity of practice

We call performation—rather than performativity, which indicates a general property—the operation of the force-(of)-thought, its activity of immanent organon. Transcendental performation, rather than trans-cendent or linguistico-philosophical. The force-(of)-thought is such that the intention, end or effect of the act are immediately realized with the act itself, without any division or transcendent distinction being able to slide between them and differentiate what emerges in one piece. The act is its work and the work or the value of action confuses itself with the act itself. Nonetheless certain precisions are decisive here. Performational immanence can only be in-the-last-instance, which is to say never given in the already constituted milieu of transcendence, even if this immanence is the essence of a simple or non-autopositional transcending. Philosophy will object that the identity it uses is given with and by the performational act; that it does not remain in the background "behind" this act and conse-quently that it already presents the authentic concept of performation. This is a string of illusions. On the one hand the most performational identity that philosophy can present is that of Autoposition, either explicit when it concerns the Philosophical Decision itself or implicit when it concerns the linguistic "performative". But Autoposition is precisely never really performational; the act of autoposition is *always* differentiated/different, always somewhat late and early for itself. Deconstruction and Greco-Judaic types of thought content themselves with accentuating or aggravating this difference but evidently do not reabsorb it. Contrary to what we had thought, Autoposition precisely forbids any Real performation and produces at best an *objective performational* appearance that a certain linguistics feeds upon. Complementarily, the *constative* act does not really exist; it is an objective appearance since the auto-positional element or philosophy of linguistics excludes the possibility of a true description that does not modify its object. What exists is in reality the mix of performative and constative, sometimes remarked in one sense; sometimes in the other, and this is the form of performation that Judaically inspired thoughts critique and differ from.

On the other hand, if the identity or immanence said to be of-the-last-instance, because of what we say about "performation", is not *given* transcendence through the performational act, then it does not it contain anything of it "in the background": determination-in-the-last-instance is not a "background" [*retrait*], retraction or even subtraction, which is to say a transcendence. It is rather radical immanence which *gives itself* the act of transcendence *as without-givenness* and communicates its performational character but precisely without alienating itself there or driving performation to its disappearance. The performation of the force-(of)-thought is thus not an auto-positing act, auto-executing—a form of *causa sui*. It alone, on the contrary, puts performation to work against the cause of itself, and can put it to work because the radical immanence that gives performational Givenness without-givenness is itself what we call a *Performed-without-performation*. Performation is thus not auto-performation either.

Complementarily, the force-(of)-thought, being only the *essence* of manifestation or knowledge, is only performational as organon itself manifesting all the other aspects of knowledge. But moreover these have a double aspect or are affected by a duality-without-division: they are undoubtedly the work of the force-(of)-thought but they relate themselves to this essence, a second time and in a mode where they can be said to be descriptive or constative, "constational" to be precise. But the a prioris freed up by the force-(of)-thought are *constational-(of)-themselves*. They describe themselves as phenomenal states of things and the description thus has performation for its essence. They are thus not auto-constational but constational-(of)-themselves in-the-last-instance. The duality of performation and "constation" or description is a unilateral duality; it is their identity in the force-(of)-thought but only in-the-last-instance.

More rigorously, we will thus sometimes but not always distinguish the *Performed* or the *already-Performed* (the real-One itself) and *Performation* as the One('s)-activity or work of the force-(of)-thought on its materials: it is performational without being the Performed itself. So Performation, if it designates the immanence of-the-last-instance of a thought that only authorizes itself (that is to say strictly speaking its real cause), when subject to this radicalization equates to the Marxist criterion of *practice* which still very externally designates a certain real immanence contra the transcendence of ideology, or even of philosophy. To the practice philosophically understood as the scission of identity (Hegel), we oppose practice as performativity, eventually by calling it "passive" too ("passive practice", c.f. "praxis"). If "practice" has been understood, in a rather Marxist manner, as immanence and criterion of transcendence, non-philosophy achieves what Marxism only ever began: the liberation of practice outside of every operation or transcendence assumed as first. Its real core, through which it indicates itself as sufficient outside of any philosophical decision, even any scientific objectification (for example the history of sciences or of society) is precisely the immanent phenomenon of the Performed, which gives norms of validity their reality-of-the-last-instance. The *identity of practice*, the force-(of)-thought, has nothing to do with the "methods" fetishized in the artifact "methodology". This identity of practice is the unobjectifiable cause of science-thought. And we cannot decide on the cause of this, *it can only assume itself as an immanent posture, the force-(of)-thought.*

The distribution of the theory/practice couplet thus must be modified from top to bottom in terms of the real essence of practice as determining-cause-in-the-last-instance of theory. Practice roots itself in the phenomenal real or in Given-without-Givenness and in nothing else, but without confusing itself with it. The last forms of their Hegelian blend in Marxism can be abandoned, practice passing transcendence or Being on the terrain of radical immanence.

First science is a theory and at once a doctrine (*Lehre*), under the form of a unified theory of science and philosophy, precisely because it is in-the-last-instance a practice or a force-(of)-thought. This means that if it recognizes that a science must be able to teach itself, it is careful not to turn this property into its criterion of recognition as Plato, Aristotle and others did, and it finds the cause of this science-thought in practical performation rather than in the ability to communicate itself or to teach itself which, overvalued and fetishized in this way, is at the origin of actual "communicational" and "technologizing" drifts of knowing after having been at the origin of Platonic redoubling, of its epistemo-logical doublet.

This immanent performation is the heart of non-philosophical thought. Grounded on the radical autonomy of the Real, it allows a usage of science and philosophy to be liberated outside of their auto-position. It is the only theory that is "all execution", to parody a famous formulation, whereas philosophy left to its spontaneity is not execution without also being tradition and memory. It holds everything in the immanence of its exercise—even the a priori rules of this exercise, which there are, have a principal immanent usage—and does not meet the external limits, but only the internal limit with which its real existence of process confuses itself: the intrinsic being-foreclosed of its cause joins up with a *de jure* limitlessness of the application of these rules to another material defined by them.

Vision-in-One liberates thought from its authoritative philosophical fantasies; it obligates it to "change the terrain" in order to assume science and philosophy in their identity-in-the-last-instance rather than in their conflict. It liberates philosophy by giving it another content like immanent performation which only obeys its own rules. The theoretico-pragmatic performation proper to unified theory distinguishes itself as much from technical "operativity" as from philosophical "meditation", "reflection" or "creation". It will need to exercise this, produce statements on this identity of science and philosophy, in order precisely to describe this performance which absolutely excludes auto-position and which is thus no more the famous positivist or idealist "operativity" than the "affirmation" of differences and hierarchies, no more the "analysis" of propositions or of ordinary language than their "deconstruction".

# From the repetition of difference to the performance of identity: Possibilization and performance

Whatever its gap, generally between scientific motivation and metaphysics, *philosophy remains structured as a metaphysics or as a triad.* a) Metaphysics is assumed as *given* as anthropological and/or historical fact, it is in every case the level of the empirical; b) it is then "possibilized", brought to its essence or its "intrinsic possibility", to Ontological Difference for example—this is the level of the universal or the a priori (itself still "metaphysical"); c) this possibility or essence is finally related to the "grounding" of essence, which is to say to its real condition: the grounding is positive and the object of a re-positioning, a re-grounding (Kant: *Grundlegung*), or marked with de-grounding and object of an originary non-grounding (Heidegger, "fundamental ontology"), and this is always the invariant level of the "transcendental" convertible with the Real. It prepares the inverse and complementary movement of the transcendental deduction and respectively of Ontological Difference or the metaphysical a priori which succeeds, from this circle, in closing philosophy into a system (affirmed or repressed and simply prohibited).

Thus metaphysics is a "fact" either of history or of human reason, a superior interest of the latter (Kant) and this facticity is simply reprised or repeated by philosophy which interiorizes it under several forms and in several possibilities. Given as tradition, naively assumed without examination, pertinent for the Real, philosophy only examines metaphysics under the ultimate authority of metaphysics, taking it up again without really critiquing it from the perspective of the Real. Hence the philosophical effort, always problematic and always repeated to clarify itself rather than the essence of the real or of man. Metaphysics is already repetition, philosophy is the vigilance of this repetition, here, where "human efforts turn in a perpetual circle" (Kant), there is philosophy. To this circle belongs not only metaphysics but every return to metaphysics, or even its most originary grounding. At best, philosophy reformulates this intrinsic essence of metaphysics with the assistance of the criterion of science; it problematizes it, but by "forgetting" altogether the problem of the essence of the Real.

The task of non-philosophy is different. The condition of repetition is in effect a non-essence co-belonging to essence, for example obscurity or the retreat into light of the logos. But the condition of a performation of identity is that essence manifests itself through-and-through before any blend of essence and non-essence; that identity is without remainder or excess. Of course, the task of clarification of the concept of "philosophy", its repetition, precedes de facto—the "fact" itself—its "non-philosophical" identification; the clarification of differences is the *occasion* of the perfor- mation of identities, more profoundly because more superficially hidden than differences. The struggle for the overinterpretation of the World, the philosophical replenishment of this aim that is the World: this first degree activity that is philosophy thus can and must be accompanied by a pragmatic performation.

Let us elucidate the mechanism of metaphysics and its corresponding performation more concretely. Philosophy presupposes, conforming to the triplicity of the ontico-ontological question, to the triad, a triple affinity of metaphysics with:

1) The rational man as its agent and addressee, that which decides on it, in preference to any other being and any other interest. Metaphysics redoubles rational man in his own rational style (Kant), it is the relation of man to himself and still another relation to man or "conforming" to the nature of man (Kant), and which together divide Reason (doublet of the spontaneous, natural or innocent rational, and metaphysical rationality). Metaphysics is only "real" as "natural disposition" in all men and conse- quently it is empirico-real. Hence the real of metaphysics and the real of man reciprocally determine each other and divide the Real together.

Non-philosophy ratifies this doublet of the metaphysical subject as *datum* but suspends its validity for thought. It elaborates a subject *of* non-philosophy and *for* philosophy or metaphysics. This is the force-(of)- thought as "subject" that roots itself in the One (or the Ego) but without confusing itself with this or with the philosophical *datum*.

2) The physical being and physics itself: metaphysics has the same object (beings) as science (physics, mathematical or not) and still another relation to this object, the relation of interrogation that is the *whole* of beings to beings, or the Being of beings; it is empirical science and so is another thing: metaphysical or suprasensible science.

Non-philosophy ratifies this doublet of the object as *datum* but suspends its validity for thought. It elaborates a simple object, not divided, of the essence-(of)-science and -(of)-philosophy, the essence-(of)-thought of thought, and object to which it relates the *data* of the relations of philosophy and science.

3) The type of thought or the method of mathematics: it has the same method as mathematics (knowledge through pure reason) and still another relation to this method, knowledge through concept (Kant) or rational and a priori knowledge; this is a "mathematics" of the concept, a mixture of concept and mathematics without matheme.

Non-philosophy ratifies this doublet of method as *datum* and elaborates a simple, non-auto-positional concept of thought as "force-(of)-thought". For the amphibological mixture of concept and mathematics in *mathesis universalis*, it substitutes a pure, transcendental usage, without blends, in the spirit of the "unified theory" of procedures of induction and deduction, of experimentation and axiomatization.

Each of these affinities gives place to a division into two [*dédoublement*] and to the position of an identity = X of metaphysics and the subject, being, method—an identity unknown to or unelucidated by philosophy.

If there is an essential obscurity in metaphysics, an uncertain and ambiguous state of it, it is the unillustratable of an identity without cause and a specular division into two without fecundity. They situate themselves at the crossroads of experience and the whole of experience not given in it, and it is from here that they reproduce themselves, until the attempts to deconstruct them or to think them more philosophically. More generally the minimal—or *meta*—operator of metaphysics is that of the partial (of the particular, "ontic" being) and of the whole (of the Being of the being and its regions as modes of this suprasensible whole, the whole affecting the two branches of metaphysics). This operator itself contains this assumed identity and this specular division into two. How can metaphysics have the same object as physics (the partial, the particular being) and nonetheless overtake it toward totality? How is the assumed identity of the partial and the whole possible? Metaphysics is the uncontrolled form of an amphibology discernible in its most elementary constitution (partial/whole) and the most vast (the Being of being as such *and* beings in totality), or more generally a chain of doublets through identification to a difference, and not dualities through a true identity. The most critical contemporary philosophies repeat the most profound metaphysical habits, give or take some appeals. Perhaps this amphibology cannot be effectively dissolved, being the very tissue of effectivity, but it can at least be thought as invalidated under the conditions of the force-(of)-thought. Non-philosophy does not have the metaphysical power to claim to dissolve the metaphysical schema, or more generally to affirm it or refuse it philosophically, to *accuse* it of incoherence and sterility beyond the recognition of these, to receive it as the failure or deception whose invariance Kant showed—and only showed; to think the being without the whole and its regions equally without the whole. But it can affect it with a radical suspension, without metaphysical motivation, so without any cause other than real cause, and draw from it as simple object, rather than a boom of "rational" knowledges all equally illusory, non-philosophical knowledges explaining it or issued from the force-(of)-thought.

Metaphysics and consequently philosophy remains an *ontic* science (of beings as whole or suprasensible); even when philosophy wants to be "ontological", it thinks in the difference of Being and beings and remains simply supra-ontic, contenting itself at best with repressing or forbidding the presence of beings in Being. Non-philosophy thinks the equality of Being and beings, no longer of their mixture or difference but their equation Being = beings as identical-in-the-last-instance. Hence a definitively non-metaphysical problematic. The internal impossibility of a metaphysical realization holds to this aporia of an amphibological identity, quasi mythical in origin and of a magical essence, forbidden to radical elucidation and which makes, for example, its rational or a priori concepts too empirical (codetermined by the empirical or beings) and not empirical enough (not able to maintain a quasi-experimental relation to beings). It is no longer about posing the problem of the intrinsic possibility of such a rational knowledge, but simply of taking this in turn as object of a thought-through-identity and substituting the problem of the *reality* of the knowing of metaphysics for the problem of its *possibilization*. Below possibility but not higher than it, there is still the problem of the content of metaphysics in reality, of its performation rather than its possibilization and thus of a "unified" transcendental science, our criterion not being experimental science and our problem no longer being only that of the ineffecitivity or the sterility of metaphysics but that of reality. If it is still a question of a certain transgression of metaphysics itself by non-philosophy, this transgression is now *simple*, the identity of the *meta*-itself, not a double translation like metaphysics itself is. And finally it is not the practical or even quasi poetic realization that we substitute for its old theoretical ambition but its performation without qualities which alone can transform it (really and not effectively) by making this happen in another order.

The force-(of)-thought neither grounds nor un-grounds nor razes-to-the-ground [*éf-fondre*]; it is never a mode of philosophical grounding, but is grounding itself in its identity and its ante-autopositional or ante-autofoundational simplicity, such that the One holds it in the lived reality of immanence. Axiomatic rigor demands saying that this concerns a grounding-without-autogrounding thus without-regrounding, a *uni-grounding of the identity of science and philosophy outside of their metaphysical relations.* We take all the complex modes of philosophical grounding or those which assume auto-grounding in lieu of simplifying it together and in an equal manner in *data.* The distinctions between the pre-ontological comprehension of beings and the regional objectification of Being, the fundamental ontology or the question of Being itself lose all their pertinence for the Real (but not all operativity) and contribute to the constitution of the absolutely universal field of non-philosophy under the name of materials. The force-(of)-thought aprioristically constitutes from philosophy and science—we will examine this in the following chapter—*a regio similitudinis*, something entirely other than a flattening or leveling of the differences of philosophical decisions: their transcendental equalizing, rather than an empirical or philosophical equalizing. The essential effect of this change of terrain is that instead of accusing it of being a den of difficulties and historically determined obscurities, assuming it globally valid in principle (for example in Heidegger, but all philosophy proceeds in this way), we cease to assume it to be pertinent and simultaneously to accuse it, in order to take it with all of its claims but without giving its credence to them: it no longer concerns philosophically changing metaphysics but changing our view or our "vision" of it.

# On transcendental cloning as dualysis of mixtures

Now that we know the origin and structure of properly transcendental causality, upon what "within" and "of" philosophy can it operate? What is its effect if we no longer confuse it with a last effect of transcendence or alterity—its simple support or intermediary—as is the case in all philosophies ("critiques", "deconstruction", etc.) and perhaps still in the philosophy of the "radical" immanence of Life? Transcendence as constitutive process of the force-(of)-thought only serves here to transport and revert this causality to all the levels of the Philosophical Decision. No structure, however constituting, of the Philosophical Decision can come to blend with transcendental causality, but can only offer itself for its purposes and consequently serve as "support" or "occasion", one of these supports—pure transcendence—being first and more fundamental than the others. We must thus distinguish its transcendental universal effect (relayed by the force) and the specific effect of the only transcendence or Non-Phenomenological Distance, moreover the empirical or occasional causality of the terms and the aspects of the Decision in relation to the preceding in the constitution of the non-philosophical order.

Furthermore, if the organon is conceived as unilateral identity or even as Unilateral Duality, it seems in a sense to correspond through-and-through to the mixed-form of philosophy and simply to negate or replace it. But the Duality, being transcendental through-and-through, cannot simply negate the mixed-form and only suspends it insofar as it presupposes the mixed-form in its relative autonomy in the name of occasional cause, relating to it as its object and finally—but only by way of the force-(of)-thought which requires it under this form—conserving it at least in the name of support. The real indifference of the One, being without (transcendental) relation to the mix, does not signify the dissolution of the reality of the mix and its sufficiency, which is to say a thesis on its nothingness: neither its philosophical negation or destruction but only its insignificance or its radical non-pertinence. The problem of the mix, its causality and the limitation thereof poses itself only when it is taken into account and when it draws a transcendental clone of identity and indifference from the Real. This is why the operation of the force-(of)-thought does not have—as is the case with a unilateral identity—the form or effect of a tearing away or a continued breaking. It does not retain a term of the mix in the mode of choice or unilateral decision (Henry), nor does it suspend the adverse term in the mode of the immediate, constant negation of the decision. It conserves the richness of the given, each of the two terms, but in a relation of unilateral duality and consequently a relation of transcendental identity which conditions this duality: not a real identity which would bear on a sole term and dissolve the mix itself, but an identity which declares itself to be that of duality, whose new, "unilateral" form excludes the mix on its behalf or invalidates it. Consequently, non-philosophy is very exactly, through the force-(of)-thought, a *transcendental cloning and a dualysis* of the philosophical materials.

This method, grasped from the side of duality, can be said in effect to be a dualysis as it is said to be a cloning when it is seized from the side of identity. Being only transcendental and not equally real, it cannot broach the mixed-form but suspends its validity and thus distinguishes, as we have said, the a priori residue of the mix and the mix itself as support having abandoned its auto-positional claim. The "sidelining" of the mix is "total" but its conservation as materials is equally so. This "totality" that affects an object without breaking it is in reality radicality, the source of dualysis.

*Dualysis does not divide its object; it proceeds by cloning it in the mode of unilateral duality.* What is excluded from the One because it does not have structure is not excluded in the mode of transcendence since the (non-) One affects transcendence itself, which only serves as an occasion for it in spite of the spontaneous or philosophical idea that if the One or the Real excludes a term, this exclusion is necessarily a form of transcendence, specified and determined by transcendence. It is rather a question of the originary place, of the emergence of the first possible *transcendental topos*, a place which has not already taken place but which is offered without counterpart. Unilateralization is thus only the *identity-(of)-place* of the place; the (non-)One('s)-identity—this is an absolute or rather a "radical" determination which contents itself with situating the mix-form and distinguishing the mix('s)-identity, but never with attacking the structure of the mix, intervening in it and dismembering it in favor of one of its two terms or moreover a "matter" deprived of "form".

The method of dualysis, adequately expressing the grounding of the Real as identity or One, not only does not separate form and matter or any other transcendent dyad but also does not separate the "terms" which apparently give themselves as individuals as much as "relations" and even the most concrete "mixed-form", more complex than terms and relations. Each of them is in any case treated as an a priori possessing an identity, in all possible philosophical dimensions. The "put-into-duality" [*mise-en-dualité*], with its identity, can bear on a sole empirical term (here comprising the variety of its conceptual composition) or indeed on a relation, or even on the mixed-form itself: it always treats this as a "term". As for the duality, it is what affects the given X term, between the transcendental identity of its a priori, or the a priori itself, and the materials from which this a priori is extracted and which serves as its support, now—and only now—reduced.

For example ontological difference becomes unilateral duality of Being and beings; that which demands a new syntax and new contents filling out these terms. We will say for example that Being determines beings in-the-last-instance outside of any relation of difference, but this statement only has validity under the set of conditions of syntax, reality and materials that have been posited. Non-philosophy is a thought not *of the* term—the *real* term does not think and it thus is equivalent to a quasi-materialism of the internal or of interiority—but *according to* the term (as determining-in-the-last-instance). The Real or the One give the type and order of the terms—identities or transcendental clones—which form the heart of the dualities at each level. Being determinant, it prohibits the relation or duality as determinant, and so prohibits the unilateral choice of one term rather than the other and the rejection or exclusion of this other—the ultimate avatar of philosophical hierarchy. It demands the conservation of dualities of terms which are at the base of philosophy, but it demands this as unilateral and simply determined. In other words, ceasing to make transcendent hypotheses on the true essence of the Real and of philosophy, and ceasing to decide for example between terms and relations, internal *or* external (it takes the philosophical as it presents itself), non-philosophy is a theory and a pragmatic of *clones* which assume the identity of terms, relations or mixtures. The transcendent philosophical choice must cede its place to the transcendental duality of identities and mixtures, clones and doublets. Transcendental cloning rather than repetition.

# Non-philosophy and a philosophy of immanence

A decisive difference between non-philosophy and "philosophies of immanence" (of life, of auto-affection, of the internal, etc., which is to say Michel Henry and beyond him, thinkers who invoke "radical immanence") manifests, then. Indeed there is an apparently bifacial order in non-philosophy, at once of identity and of unilateral duality, but this is only transcendental: it is the order of the force-(of)-thought. It assumes the Real only as negative but absolutely necessary cause rather than positive cause. A double confusion affects philosophies of immanence, from this perspective. The first is that of the One and the transcendental, the Real and the thought that conditions it anew in a bifacial entity assumed as first or the Real itself. As real, this One can then negate the reality of the mix; as transcendental, it can relate to it. The One is assumed unilateral by itself, which is to say associated *de jure* with a transcendental relation to experience. "Unilaterality" in this context signifies the choice, in a mixture, of a supposedly identical term, retained in this way, and the immediate negation or exclusion of the second term. The principle of this procedure is evidently the *unilateral identity* directly opposed in this way to the mixture. The One itself is not in all rigor the One-in-One but it is already relation and implies the transcendental retention of a term assumed to be bearer of identity and the exclusion of the term bearing duality. How can this unilateralizing One, still very close to the philosophical mixtures, and which assumes the Real to have a force of negation not itself be affected by its work, and unilateralized in return? *Unilateral identity is the philosophical simulation of non-philosophy, a still semi-transcendent practice of radical immanence*. This adjoining of the Real and the transcendental, the Real and the operatory, blends the three orders (real, transcendental, empirical) two by two and drives them to interprevention and to losing their specific *identity*. Even if this blend is less vicious than that of the philosophy of Being, it still substitutes identification for identity. This is why non-philosophy, in conceiving the One in a truly radical manner as One-in-One rather than as One-in-Being or even as One = Being (an equation in fact assumed by Henry), obligates the transcendental to relatively autonomize itself, but also obligates the empirical order of philosophy and science to more liberally play without the obsession of synthesis whose last form is this "overwriting" of the philosophical decision that is "auto-affection of life". This overwriting undoubtedly opposes itself to the deconstructive quartering of the Dyad but like this it still comes under the decidedly unshakeable authority of philosophy.

Non-philosophy is the thought adequate to real Identity or according to this Identity and it can only operate under the form of Unilateral Duality and so under the form of Determination-in-the-Last-Instance. It retains the duality of mixtures; suspends their simple relation of "superior" blend or of synthesis. They do not begin by entirely dismembering constitutively philosophical dualities (the Dyads) as a Unilateral Identity would do, but also retain the "matter" of the Philosophical Decision. Why, if not because it is transcendental only, can the force-(of)-thought not affect the core of the *given* or of the reality which contains the mix? Force precisely already acts as such a unilateral duality and not as an identity, which it only is in-the-last-instance rather than immediately. Beyond the Real (itself deprived of any relation to experience) there is always first an "empirical" given, an irreducible autonomy of the Real, a "matter" which "makes" duality beyond the One (but in-One). This relative autonomy has repercussions from the "empirical" given to the force-(of)-thought. Only the force-(of)-thought, by the One, is unilateralizing in the dual mode: it alone, and not the One, can act "on" the mix that is empirical in origin.

A second confusion affects philosophies of immanence: that of unilaterality and transcendence. Unilaterality or the (non-)One assumes transcendence but only as its a priori support. If it becomes an effect or the principal effect of transcendence, it takes the form of an immediate and supposedly real negation of one term of the mix or its matter, thus of the very reality of philosophy. The dissolution of the true syntax adequate to the Real as immanent, of its determination-in-the-last-instance, is consummated in its confusion with a syntax adequate to transcendence and of a newly philosophical type. The same problems then reappear. The negation surreptitiously spreads throughout the heart of the Real which, freeing itself from the mixture, unilateralizes itself in turn by unilateralizing the term given. Unilaterality however is only an effect of the One occasionally, never its positive effect, and depends partly on the relative autonomy of transcendence. This is why it is of the transcendental order or affects transcendence, a necessary co-occurring "matter" or an occasional cause.

In these still philosophical or semi-philosophical, mixed or semi-mixed systems, the One is lost in immanence, the Real in radical autonomy, the transcendental in relative autonomy, thought in positivity. The relative autonomy of the transcendental order, which is to say the force-(of)-thought, is a "gentler" or "weaker" solution than that of Unilateral Identity, but it is also less metaphysical, less violent and World-negating. The philosophy of immanence appears less dependent on the empirical than non-philosophy but depends on it nonetheless in the negative philosophical mode of the blend, whereas non-philosophy seems to link itself to the relative autonomy of the empirical but liberates itself from it by going to the trouble of analyzing philosophical resistance, of dualyzing the blend by no longer assuming it as anything but simple "support" and material of the force-(of)-thought. The philosophy of immanence prolongs that philosophical ideal of a direct intervention in the World and even an intervention for the World itself, whereas non-philosophy, suspended as a purely phenomenal Real and without proper action, is "condemned" to treat the mixture of the World or of philosophy as a simple phenomenon without claiming to negate it in its reality or destroy it, in an "immediate" manner, and to offer it simply a usage in terms of another autonomous thought. A radical modification not of the World but of our vision(-in-One) of the World, non-philosophy cannot appear weak or inefficient unless measured by the still metaphysical and violent ends of philosophy. Radicality, which is to say thought from the vision-in-One, is always less violent than philosophical "radicalism". The Radical or the Real does not imply "radicalism", which is a philosophical position.

# The givenness of non-philosophy

## The being-performed of the phenomenon: Transcendental foreclosure of the Real and philosophical resistance

Non-philosophical practice distinguishes between two correlated problems but without confusing them: between its real essence or its mode of being phenomenal given in-the-last-instance, and its effective practice or its operations which assume a philosophical and other material. What does it mean then to *follow a rule* when it concerns non-philosophical operativity? Philosophy blends these two viewpoints, rendering them convertible in evidently diverse degrees: all putting to work of rules is assumed to engage and transform the Real in the more or less long term. In non-philosophy reality renders real its possibility, without action in return of this possibility over reality, but there is such an action, however relative, of its effectivity over its possibility. Hence a double description: that of its real essence such as it conserves the One in the force-(of)-thought (and in the knowledges that participate therein); and of its operations and its knowledges insofar as they assume materials.

Let us begin by its being-given or its reality. The question is of elucidating this paradox: non-philosophy is concealed or denied by philosophy, without a doubt, but through its real cause it is necessarily given through-and-through. These two traits form a system: philosophy which in its manner of action necessarily ignores everything of the Given in the immanent, non-decisional and non-giving sense-(of)-itself, but which necessarily uses it—no thought can surpass the Real-One—cannot support this foreclosure that is imposed on it by the Real except by denying the Real not only when it is explicitly proposed to it, but when it is given or imposed implicitly and always. It is precisely this trait of radical actuality or Performed-without-Performation, of being-given identically without excess or reserve, which renders the real-One absolutely invisible for philosophy in its spontaneous state of sufficiency, and which makes this into an object of denegation for it when it is explicitly (or in thought) confronted. Still more difficult to seize than the slippery logic-mirror—this is not a mirror; the internal structure of the One excludes all specularity—it is impossible to represent it, to make it into an "uneven ground" [*sol raboteux*] to try to seize it through its relief, it has no relief or multiplicity-by-division. Nonetheless it is indeed what philosophy tries to do in refusing it any existence: to think it by differentiating it. Inversely it suffices here to think it or to represent it in order to repress it. Only non-philosophy can end this repression, by grounding itself on foreclosed of the Real for any thought.

In effect, the *phenomenon*, given par excellence with the One-in-One, is what only appears (to) itself without backdrop of non manifestation. It radicalizes the old phenomenological equation appearing = being, and resolves it through identity rather than through the "same" of appearing and being. No distinction runs through this, sharing it between appearance and disappearance, or even between what appears, the appearing, and its apparition, at the risk of reestablishing the non-manifestation in manifestation. The One is thus no longer, unlike Being, that which is *prima facie* hidden: it is rather foreclosed *de jure* for all possible thought because it is *prima facie* manifest, on the condition of understanding this "*prima facie*" as primacy in relation to the play of philosophical veiling and unveiling, without possible play with its contrary, and as "actually" and "definitively" Manifested-before-all-Manifestation. If it is impossible to instate the slightest phenomeno-logical distance in the identity-(of-the)-phenomenon as phenomenon-(of)-Identity (a demand which is not really fulfilled by the most radical philosophies of immanence), non-philosophy has for its task no longer recalling the manifestation of the real-One, recalling the finally visible of the invisible, or thought of the unthought (thought specifically of the unthought) but rather adding it—this is its contingency—to it as Manifestation of the already-Manifested (and not to the not-still-Manifested), and of elaborating itself as clone adequate to the phenomenon, as *the* Manifestation in its identity-in-the-last-instance, autonomous in its relative order of Manifestation rather than of the Manifested. Since the One does not manifest anything other than itself, it is not immanent to its proper "form" of One, does not precede itself and does not precede the Manifested (without-manifestation) that it is through-and-through. On the other hand, thought manifests itself in its own way and manifests the Manifested in a certain sense—but in a unique mode each time, without redoubling. It gives the Given-without-Givenness which moreover is foreclosed, thus giving it on the basis of its foreclosure "recognized" as such. The Real expects nothing from thought but it liberates it all the more in its specific work of givenness and of position. Between Real and philosophy, thought reduced as force-(of)-thought conserves or finds its identity and its specificity. It has its ultimate place in the real-One in which, as transcendental, it really roots itself, "participates" if you will or "shares" its essence, but without sharing in this operation, itself preceding the philosophical sharing, never to desert it. Through the radical performativity it holds as its cause, it will neither demand preparation nor listening—no decision or injunction, question or response—but will suffice to exercise itself.

As for philosophical resistance, one of the effects of the force-(of)-thought is to manifest it as an effect of foreclosure, or as transcendental in-the-last-instance. We could speak of a "secondary" rather than a "primary" suppression, but here that would mean: constitutive not of the phenomenon of the Real but of thought alone. The phenomenon of the One, defined by its being-foreclosed for thought, implies that philosophical resistance does not give place to primary repression and that the One in any case cannot entirely be—like Heidegger's "Being"—a quasi-unconscious produced through an originary or constitutive operation of repression. Resistance is thus indeed real in its transcendental origin. It results from the foreclosure of the Real for all thought but it is effective and belongs to the relation that comes from philosophy to the force-(of)-thought and more originally to the Real, which suffices nonetheless to represent it in order to repress it, which is to say in order to refuse to recognize foreclosure. Neither the One nor the force-(of)-thought are thus supplementary refinements belonging to the actual thoughts of the Other, psychoanalysis included: philosophy is an *indication* of non-philosophical practice, specifying and overdetermining it, but it is not constitutive of the real or phenomenal order, which is to say of the phenomenal ingredient of effective knowledge.

It especially falls to non-philosophy and to non-philosophy alone to describe the phenomenon of foreclosure and resistance through which philosophy confronts non-philosophy; to describe its invincible appearance of ethical, political transcendence, and more generally the metaphysics which seems to need to never affect thought, to forbid it vision-in-One and re-inscribe it in Being and its attributes (Society, History, Power, etc.). The idea of unified theory implies that the sciences most especially attached to the regional properties of beings do not have for their object the explicit phenomenalization of philosophical resistance and its effects which they nonetheless confront regularly. Delivered from themselves, they are condemned to exclude philosophical resistance practically and to identify with it anew when they make the slightest gap in their practice. On the other hand, non-philosophy manifests as such this effect of non-autopositional transcendence which affects its essential operations. It does not destroy it totally in this manner but limits its range; *positions* or unilateralizes it as being a condition of existence of its practice, though *inessential*: as *Objective Philosophical Appearance* which accompanies the thought-in-One in the manner in which light accompanies the blackest thought and believes itself necessary to it.

## The triple being-given of rules

Non-philosophy does not exist "in itself" to become "for itself", nor must it realize itself or exist in the manner of the idea of phenomenology. It exists under the already actualized form or the form already performed as phenomenon-in-the-last-instance or as transcendental, and it must become possible and realize itself as effective knowledge. We cannot judge the reality of non-philosophical thought by its effectivity; by its manner of being-given by local realizations. From this perspective, it cannot continue to advance many realizations or works, if this is not its problematic under its first "principle" [*principielles*] forms, but in any case it first takes responsibility for itself performatively or phenomenally *before* manifesting itself in the World. As for its "possibility", a question philosophy poses as its holder, the force-(of)-thought is rather first real, not being possible except as transcendence, non-positional (of) itself, the very identity of the possible. These two traits in dual relation distinguish non-philosophy from philosophy which is first empirico-ideal or rather possible-real or virtual-actual. As possibilization of effective thought, it first results from the Real-given-before-all-givenness or assumed-before-all-assumption—as its performativity wants, demanding only, unlike an injunction or a decision, that the consequences be deduced correctly from its being-already-assumed and induced from its *data*.

It constitutes itself effectively as such by obeying the rules of an immanent practice, those of the force-(of)-thought, but these are not thematically elaborated in the order of the possible and the effective. With these rules and philosophical materials, it produces the knowledge of a certain number of a priori structures which in turn can be converted thematically into these rules; the same goes for their knowledge. Moreover, their specific being-given must be elucidated if they are not already assumed as the real-One is or are no longer of the order of the Performed but given too as transcendence (even "simple" and deprived of the folding of its re-presentation as it is here). This work allows us to clarify the manner in which non-philosophy, which works with philosophy and "simultaneously" with science for example, forms and exercises the hypotheses or axioms it formulates and the general rules of induction and deduction it puts to work. With these, it is in effect a question not only of the first appearance of transcendence, such as it is seen-in-One as force-(of)-thought, but of its being put to work as materials.

Through their cause, which leaves them their relative autonomy, these general rules of non-philosophical operativity give themselves in an immanent manner: but in-the-last-instance only because they *are* transcendence itself, or the concrete manner in which it exists. But they do not give themselves inside of transcendence assumed as already-there a first time: nothing in the effectivity or necessity of the World prescribes or gives reality or the type of necessity of non-philosophy. Non-philosophy does not respond to any mundane or philosophical motivation in general. This radically unreflected necessity gives it a certain allure of *transcendental automatism*. Not that this is about a lack of reflection and decision, but rather the necessity or the order such as it appears the first time, under its minimal and phenomenal form. This necessity of a priori rules does not return to other older or more profound rules, to these hinter-worlds that are Substance, Being, Spirit or Signification, Language, Will to Power, etc. The operatory rule has at least one face through which it is given without operation of givenness behind it—without "mythology"—but in the-last-instance in the mode of the One: only the most immanent Real can determine these rules in heteronomy. We are tempted to say that it suffices to "apply" them in an automatic manner in order to take up a non-philosophical posture, of discovery as much as invention, deduction as much as induction. The non-philosopher reflects as much as whoever else does but under a first "reason", anterior by immanence. This application or this "calculation" is not exterior or dogmatic; non-philosophy in fact gives us the experience of a quasi-automatic or immanent yet still thinking thought, whose internal necessity is no longer reigned over by any Tradition, Logic, Grand Necessity or Destiny of Being—by any philosophy. This autonomy of rules in relation to these fetishes, mixtures of thought and the Real, is liberated from itself by the Real which is not a new form of thought but which determines it in-the-last-instance only. These rules are not susceptible to non-respect but constitute the interior minimal form of all possible transcendental pure thought, without which philosophical disorder would reign, along with its unitary pathos.

Nonetheless the concept of non-philosophy as effective practice is at the intersection of two causalities. If in effect it does not have any sense for the real-One alone, it has one for the World or for philosophy. This last cause, only "occasional", thus explains that vision-in-One is "overtaken" and cloned by the order of a non-philosophical representation. The rules thus form a region of transcendence, but a simple or radical one, not reflected in itself. This is the same thing as to say: they are performational without being auto-performational; they act but without intervening, like philosophy does, twice; without reporting back to themselves or redoubling themselves infinitely. They are not the application of constitutive principles already given in a transcendent form and a dogmatic content that would need to be reversed, displaced, intensified, deconstructed, etc.: they are their own usage, *only-once-each-time*, *immanent* to some material which, has precisely previously been reduced to the state of material and discharged of its old status as dogmatic "rule" or meta-physical "principle". Non-philosophy is the only thought which acts according to rules absolutely deprived of a hinter-world because their usage is phenomenal or performational but not auto-performational. Not only, of course, deprived of signification and of textuality, of mundane or ontological referent, of logical norms, of transcendent or meta-physical redoubling, but equally of *system*. They do not draw their necessity from their systematic order or from their logico-transcendental auto-grounding. Thought-in-One obligates us to distinguish between the systematic necessity of a body of rules, a still "transcendent" necessity which works to the benefit of philosophies or entities (transcendental subject, reason, language games as forms-of-life, etc.) which represent the forms of auto-position more or less overwritten in immanence, which is to say of possible meta-physics, and a necessity and universality without fold that we will say forms a *Uni*-verse [*Uni-vers*] (uni-versal, unilateral, etc.). They undoubtedly still derive from philosophy but "under" cause-of-the-last-instance, and no longer ground themselves in their transcendent reversibility and systematicity, in their principle [*principielle*] auto-position, so eradicated. If philosophy thinks "system", non-philosophy thinks "uni-verse" (this evidently concerns transcendental concepts belonging to the theory of thought, not empirico-regional concepts) and the Universe perhaps "opposed" in particular to the auto-positional "World" and to the cosmo-political essence of philosophy. So the phenomenal cause of thought is not affected in its essence by its effective practice: both are liberated from one another (but not *by* one another). Moreover its practice is not affected or decided by philosophical finalities. Non-philosophy only knows immanent impossibilities (pragmatic and theoretical) but not prohibitions; axioms and hypotheses that are real-in-the-last-instance but not imperatives. The necessity of these operations is neither technical (if…then) nor ethical (you must), but inductive and deductive, albeit in a transcendental mode. If there is an "imperative", it is to *give as true* such "first" statements formulated by axiomatic abstraction starting from philosophy, and thus to treat them simply as axioms, as the emergent given, and to make a transcendental and scientific usage of them.

Furthermore it is important, in the complete concept of non-philosophy, to reintroduce philosophy at least as simple materials of the force-(of)-thought. Non-philosophy marks, in a limited way, a certain taking stock of the philosophical type of relation to experience (philosophical type: this can be common sense, perception, scientific ideologies, religions, etc.). So much so that the force-(of)-thought gives itself, on this grounding of experience not still reduced and always reborn as transcendence doubled/divided into two [*(dé)doublée*], a certain mixed form of prescription and interdiction which is never completely eliminated to the periphery of work. Not only is a new confusion always possible between the force-(of)-thought and scientific or philosophically fetishized knowing, but the problem becomes ever more insistent—under the pressure of philosophical resistance, insistent though already limited—on knowing what "following a rule" means. So simple is transcendence, without auto-position in its essence, that it necessarily announces itself, though, with a certain exteriority (its redoubling) even if it is only from the effective point of view or from the material that this problem is posed. But given that, in any case, the essence of non-philosophical presentation excludes the fold or the doublet which affects spontaneous transcendence, the rules that capitalize on it no longer give themselves in their essence as an infinite debt, either becoming-philosophy unlimited by the World, or imperative or inexhaustible injunction. "Following a rule" is a problem resolved straight away by phenomenal performativity and ceases to be a question that is unsolvable by definition, a question of the possibility of thought, of its *fact* and its *right*, of its mode of existence and its necessity that an injunction announces, etc.

These points define a transcendence-without-metaphysics, overdetermined only by metaphysics driven by the material and its 'sufficiency'. Finally, nothing of the World hides itself or refuses manifestation if almost all manifestation, the bulk of it at least, remains concealed to philosophy, which denies this manifestation. Non-philosophy is not "the highest" exercise of thought; this no longer means anything for a non-philosophy which does not know the 'superior form'' of thought: it contents itself to respond to the conditions of rigor and reality. No absolute obstacle—it knows and demonstrates that there is non-philosophy rather than only philosophy and science; that, for example, the only "epistemological obstacle" is "epistemology" itself or even philosophical aesthetics, etc. And with this obstacle undoubtedly comes normativity, apprenticeship, injunction, the control of thought too—rarity—but all this is phenomenalizable in-the-last-instance.

Moreover there is no continuous passage from philosophy to non-philosophy unless we can speak of the abyss between them, which would still be to philosophize. There is a foreclosure of the Real for all thought—this explains cloning—and a resistance of philosophy to non-philosophy. There is no passage if not precisely through the exterior, through philosophical Appearance. How do we become "non-philosophers"? Not for any reason drawn from philosophy, if not occasional, or *according to* it and if not, *moreover*, at least from the Real itself already-assumed. We do not do non-philosophy with philosophy alone as our contemporaries believe and hope.

## *The axiom and the injunction*

Philosophy is an affair of movements and becomings, of lines and vectors, of reversals and displacements—it mostly uses transcendence, which comes (in a circular although broken manner) from experience toward the ground, from being toward Being, from Being toward the Affair of thought. This is why it functions as the injunction or the motto, the more-than-categorical imperative, destined to fix the movement, to accelerate it, to "repeat" it. Every decision—by the fact that it is "first", arbitrary in its more or less undecidable aspects—needs a supplement of transcendence, alterity, an injunction not programmed by the old state of philosophy and which causes it to pass to effectivity against common sense, against the state of fact, against an anterior philosophy, etc., and helps it to reverse them. It is the thought which divides itself in two and redoubles itself in a motto, doubletalk, a thought at once already-thought and not-yet-thought, etc. The injunction can only bear on the necessity of the philosopher's act, which is always relative and absolute. It says that it must absolutely philosophize for two reasons at once, for their unity and for the supersession of relative and empirical reason toward absolute reason, a supersession which is a reason more absolute than reason, a necessary overcategory. It thus must *absolutely* philosophize without any reason that is not philosophical, it would be if not local, then infra-philosophical and too strict: not in terms of the form of law for example, but indeed in terms of the very form of philosophy, and finally of philosophy itself as superior form of law.

There is no injunction—if this is not through philosophical overdetermination—to enter into non-philosophy as we enter into philosophy; no injunction interior or exterior to it. But there are freely formed axioms respecting, as immanent cause in-the-last-instance of thought, the real primacy of the vision-in-One over thought, a primacy which precisely renders possible the positing of axioms and in general the style of hypothesis and the usage of the organon. Non-philosophy is thus not grounded on itself or auto-applied, auto-posed by an idealist *coup de force*: there is no axiom of axioms, no idea of the idea, no "principle of principles" as is the case in phenomenology, no semi-exterior and dogmatic injunction, for example ontology of evidence or even of intuition, to use "axioms". Any axiom correctly formed according to the first rule of the force-(of)-thought and its demand for symbolization and formalization (cf. below) on the basis of naive knowledges (regional and fundamental) already itself has a transcendental content in the Real-in-the-last-instance (rather than an internal logical type of necessity) and which suffices to "validate" it internally, even if it is not still confronted with empirical effectivity and has not given place to operations. This is an immanent practice without mottos or finalities: if there are any, and there are (politics, etc.), then they belong to its *data* or to its phenomena, not to its real essence. There is then no imperative fixing a transcendent, ontotheo-logical necessity to "do non-philosophy": this is a "posture" or a "force-(of)-thought" which has only the criterion of immanence as its real cause—which takes itself performatively as force-(of)-thought—and the occasion of its *data*; which contents itself to posit axioms or hypotheses in the transcendental mode and to deduce or induce starting from them. No necessity or finality of the metaphysical or ontological type can "ground" non-philosophy and fix its installation in the Real. This is why no supplement of a superior knowledge to actual knowledges, no experience of a more or less absolute "call" is necessary in order to begin its process.

# Thinking once-each-time: Generalization of the transcendental dialectic

The philosophical style procures imaginary satisfactions or benefits linked to its repetition and to tautology, to the play of circulation and redistribution, to the mythological activity of doubling or dubbing [*doublage ou de doublure*]—"thought thinks" "speech speaks"…—but not any longer. For example, as Heidegger showed without drawing all of the consequences out of it, thought proposes to explicitly come, excepting a small gap, to the state of *presence*… that which is already given as *present*. As if thought were to stroll from one amphibology to the other, in particular from that of the-being-which-is to that of the-Being-of-beings. The only real operation appears to be an ontological, not simply empiricist, generalization; a discontinued passage from the beings to their universal or a priori horizon. But in reality this is the passage from an implicit or unapparent state to a more explicit or apparent state of this horizon. This modest generalization can be considered—though this demands that it liberate itself from philosophical tutelage—to be a sterile redoubling, hermeneutical in nature. Hermeneutics and infinite doubling comprise the bulk of philosophical "practice" and remain such, albeit more hidden, when this practice reverses and displaces, differentiates and disseminates… To philosophize is thus to circulate, or to circulate-in-half: "to turn". What is sought is already given, but given in a different state, or is sought-and-found—this is the system of presupposition and auto-position. Always the same mechanism: first the dyad or decision that divides/doubles—with more or less undivided distance and positivity in distance—then its reprise and reposition in a synthetic and systematic unity, and finally the "transcendental" return to the empirical dyad. Hence a more or less impeded or more or less rapid circulation up to the apparently "immobile" or eternal reversibility—the appearance of the *Same*...

It is doubtful that this is a question of the only thought possible and especially of the most "real". But philosophical faith's power of bewitchment is such that the scientists themselves, the artists, etc., always cede to it anew with relief, assured of a fresh "thinking" at last through this "return"—a philosophical return, moreover... The dimension of non-philosophy is of the type of a universality that cannot appear, or is incommensurable with this internal specular structure proper to the ontological horizon, to Ontological Difference itself. That by which it distinguishes itself from philosophy to the point of rendering itself intelligible to it is a "*unilateral gap*" more than a *logical gap* (Einstein) between its essence and the contingent *data* of philosophy and regional objects. Since this heterogeneity has its source in the Real itself, in the cause of thought which gives thought its autonomy of essence, but without forbidding it—to the contrary—every relation to the *data* of "experience" thus no longer has nature of a general dis-ference, of a transcendence divided and re-folded into itself. The result of this transcendental unilateralization (through transcendence itself in its "simple" identity, such that it belongs to the force-(of)-thought) is a universalization of that which would no longer be sufficiently universal for it, the old "empirical" knowledges whose content it relativizes a priori in theory, along with their type of universality, at the same time as it suspends—which is the same thing—their philosophical claim, always reborn. It excludes all of the mixed, empirico-transcendental processes of philosophy: it begins by invalidating the claims of the old knowing (philosophy included) that philosophy begins by ratifying; it reduces amphibologies, circles and doublets a priori to their identity and unilateral duality. From here it induces and deduces and "simplifies" the knowledges from their claim to posit themselves absolutely and to cut themselves away from the Real (which does not at all destroy their chaotic complexity and heterogeneity...); it ceases to repeat them one by the other in some reversible gap or other. The new discovery does not redouble the old knowledge, it implicates it transformation and integration into a new theoretical space of a purely transcendental origin.

Non-philosophy's perspective thus allows us to problematize philosophy in thought. It defines the philosophical style as expanded dialectic, through the exclusive primacy of the blend, of the mixed form grounded on hierarchy, on the reciprocity or reversibility of terms, more or less inhibited or imperfect, but whose always conserved presence is the invariant criterion of the philosophical. Philosophy is not only that which proposes itself under this name in history and in the World; it is every thought which represses the non-decisional identity of the Real as One and posits itself precisely as decision-of-itself. Non-philosophy distinguishes a thought where the decision is essential and determinant and claims to affect the Real itself—this is philosophical ambition; and another for which the Real('s)-Identity alone is determinant (but in-the-last-instance) and the non-decisional decision-(of)-itself. When the decision is essential or determinant, so submitted in its exercise to invariant rules which derive from it and whose range it also limits, it engenders a transcendental appearance, a supposed knowledge of the Real, more powerful than the Kantian appearance of Reason.

Contemporary philosophical solutions to the malaise constitutive of philosophy (unity-of-contraries, aporia, antinomy, etc.), we will say, are more subtle or less authoritarian. But they are equally of this restrained type, and consist to extend or to intensify, prolong and vary the aporetic structure without excluding it from the essence of thought. The history of philosophy is that of variations of the prime matrix, already dialectical—the unity-of-contraries or contrasts—whose generality housed the possibility of several types of disjunction: exclusive, mediatized, inclusive, differed, etc. There is a softening of antinomies, a dialectical gentleness, in contemporary philosophy, above all that of Differ(e/a)nce. The types of solution are numerous and draw invariant lines. For example: an infinite becoming-immanent of the dialectic and of antinomies as "differences" or even their becoming-transcendent, their reversal-displacement for a more universal and transcendent antinomy, that of Logos and the Other. But these considerations remain intra-philosophical like every decision. Contemporary deconstructions of "metaphysics", of "logocentrism", of "mythology", are only supplementary forms of the old philosophical faith. They content themselves to vary, breach, break, displace, disseminate, differentiate, etc, the old knowing always assumed as real and valid; to observe or aggravate the ruinous character of the edifice without daring to really put it at the base in order to construct other things elsewhere—this ground remains "promised" without anything more in Kant himself and in deconstructions which have "resolved" its heritage. We take up the Kantian idea of antinomy and the Heideggerian idea of the onto-theological doublet in order to decry philosophy, but by *generalizing* them in an invariant under conditions that are no longer intra-but rather non-philosophical. We understand the transcendental dialectic thus expanded to every Philosophical Decision—Kant and Heidegger included—even when the decision is limited or deconstructed, including the modern forms of decision (difference, différance, differend, etc.). Generalizing the transcendental dialectic in this way is evidently not possible unless we dispose of a viewpoint—the vision-in-One—which formally excludes any dialectic from itself and defines all thought as non(-One). Distinguishing itself without the nuance of deconstructions, *it begins by creating a tabula rasa not of philosophy but of philosophical faith* that it eradicates from the roots, or which it begins by suspending before any supplementary operation. The "grand genres" which have succeeded the primacy of Being among the contemporaries—the Other, Difference, Différance, the Game when it is not Judgment reflecting in the weakest case—have in common that they still assume this primacy in order to limit it, move it, etc. Only the One-in-One, not convertible with Being, can from the offset suspend ontological faith. Renouncing these half-solutions of which the philosophers are just afraid enough to persist all the more in their being, which is to say in Being, is not to renounce "all" philosophy—only its spontaneous belief.

# On philosophy as "transcendental mythology"

Philosophy is no more the manner of thinking ruled and structured by the transcendental mixture of an *undecidable decision* than it is the set of objects upon which this decision bears and feeds. But it must necessarily be associated on the one hand to a regional sphere of objects over which it legislates in a 'superior" manner, and on the other hand and above all to a sphere of already constituted and universal objects of knowing upon which it relies now, taking them in general from science and identifying them partially with those it then makes usage of as a prioris for experience and of which it is precisely, to come back to a Kantian expression and generalize it, the "superior" or "transcendental" form in the wider sense of this word. This utensile relation, of the exploitation of science, tends to efface itself in deconstructions or scientisms, but never completely disappears. In the first, it subsists under the form of a necessary reference to the history of metaphysics ("overcome", Heidegger), to logic ("broken", Wittgenstein), to linguistics ("deconstructed", Derrida), etc. Philosophy is thus the "superior form" of a regional knowing that it takes from elsewhere, and which remains partly contingent. It can be called, in terms of these already constituted objects of knowing, "transcendental geometry", "transcendental topology", "transcendental linguistics", "transcendental aesthetics", "transcendental sophistry", etc: it is susceptible to multiple possibilities where the transcendental is always blended with the empirical and never attains the "purity" to which it is susceptible when it results from the Real-One.

Subject to the limits of this type of definition, limits which come from the diversity and contingency of objects of knowing with which they identify themselves, we can equally define philosophy as "transcendental mythology", a "superior" form of mythological knowing—or of supposed knowing, mythology functioning *as* knowing. Two cases among others show the fact that philosophy *can* (this is one of its possibilities) be defined as such, through definitions which bear on invariants:

- Heidegger interiorizes-and-overcomes (*verwinden*), in particular thanks to Höderlin, the residue of mythology which at the time of its original break still necessarily bordered Greek philosophy. Mythology is deconstructed here, as moreover is the rationalist form opposed to the transcendental, but this deconstruction itself as operation always joins up with these mythological groundings that is postulates without simply confusing itself with them, of course, no more than with this rationalist experience of the transcendental. Heidegger only deconstructs *Mytho-logical Difference* on the condition of "interiorizing" it and conserving it as one of the necessary halves of 'sobered" thought. This is precisely a deconstruction, not a true "unified theory", and a deconstruction finally does not lose anything of the *past* of philosophy, which is to say of the authority of philosophy itself.

- Wittgenstein can only denounce or "put into play" the "mythologies" secreted by and as philosophy on the condition of interiorizing and generalizing the principle in them, even if on another mode than that of Heidegger. Interiorizing the mythological: this is the "breaking" in the manner in which the "Great Mirror" of logic is "broken" by language games. Mythological Difference is dispersed in language games but it conserves itself traced out as such in their debris and explains precisely that thought reduces itself to produce and inventory debris, just as positive as "games". Nothing of philosophy, of its authority, is really and definitively lost by this thought which aims to intricate the mythological a little more with the linguistic.

But the true mythological force of philosophy, its fetishizing force, is perhaps still elsewhere and in its essence. What is its principal operation in terms of the knowing produced by science—the "objects-of-knowledge"—or any other regional datum [*donné*]? It is well known but not often denounced enough as sterile: *auto-position*. Not in the Fichtean sense of the word, which is too strict and only applies to the I or absolute Subjectivity, but in the sense where the operation of the "Philosophical Decision" consists in redoubling-unifying by dividing, folding and distancing, etc. This is a fundamental invariant, applying to any doctrine whatsoever. Auto-Position is the concrete form, the mode of existence of *reciprocal determination* or grounded on transcendence as determinant, which is the principal drive of all philosophy. Instead of defining philosophical mythology through the conservation of entities that are not still rationalized, it is more interesting to define a superior mythology through the formal philosophical trait of auto-position of a knowing which is first abstracted from the process of knowledge, absolutized next as transcendent entity, related finally to itself rather than to the Real.

More precisely, the mythological destination of philosophy consists in thinking, as we have already said, by the unity-of-contraries or indeed contrasts—by dialectic or indeed by difference—in general by a blend or reciprocal determination of difference and identity; by "superior" equality or Same; by identification (global or partial). Its activity resumes in the exacerbation and intensification of ready-made dyads that thought spontaneously finds in abundance in these two purveyors, language and perception. It relates them to themselves, re-cuts and over-cuts them by potentializing them through one another. On the one hand it is thus the manner of thinking that installs itself in the spontaneous mythology of language and perception and which will no longer leave; for which the dyad will remain determinant and given primarily. On the other hand it can only combine these dualities or contrasts according to a principle of unity itself affected by division, which is to say according to a "One" from which no thought can escape. Philosophy is thus simply an appearance of science for example, which utilizes effective science, a premature or precipitous science which thinks the Real from the linguistic and perceptive milieu instead of thinking this from the Real. Non-philosophy treats this philosophy precisely as a transcendental appearance and a material, without denouncing it in a positivist manner as a "false science", entirely irreal.

From this point of view, philosophy is *our* myth, our second and superior "occidental" mythology, a mythology without myths. Even if it is still "superior" topology or linguistics ("superior" and consequently "reversible" but always superior through their reversal, etc.), it is definitively compromised by this possibility—as its type of generality wants. The old fight against mythos is complicated, nuanced, differentiated, but mythos is only even more involved and installed here at the more and more rational heart of the logos.

Given this situation, if we must have a thought that we could really call "modern", we must also break with *the philosophical tradition of modernity* (Plato, Descartes, Husserl, etc.) and its rationalism, which is to say its usage of science in terms of Mythological Difference. The "non-modernity" of thought is not the modernity of philosophy which uses science in an inegalitarian manner to its own profit. It delivers itself not only from constituted mythology, but also from mytho-logical Difference itself, which is to say the authority of philosophy. Ceasing to prolong the overly restrained fight of rationalism and the Enlightenment (dogmatic or already deconstructed, either way) against mythology, it widens this fight to be against all forms of authority linked to transcendence in a state of auto-position and redoubling. It proceeds by a change of "terrain"—of the objective illusion of the Real—by the constitution of a unified theory of science and philosophy. Rather than by a new philosophical or first decision, it proceeds by a cut, non-decisional-(of)-itself, irreversible, in terms of all mythology, transcendental or common. This is thus something other than a reversal of the old groundings of common sense and its philosophical form. The latter is already one such conservational reversal, one such "turning on its head" of common sense and mythology which nonetheless conserves most of these transcendent presuppositions. Non-philosophy does not reverse perception and ordinary language; does not conserve them in the mythological state, does not transcend them in general; it unilateralizes them or dualyzes them starting from the sole immanent-force-(of)-thought. There is no common form, no possible bond between non-philosophy and philosophy: the former treats the latter as simple datum with a view to knowledge, without thinking to dominate or appropriate it—this is a problem of organon and usage. It delivers us from the mythological impulse and its metaphysical avatars because from the outset it no longer grounds itself on innumerable dyads which haunt the World, which reproduce through auto-division and auto-potentialization, which overcome themselves or transcend one over the other, which thus constitute the Authorities and the most part of the process through which they affirm themselves. Changing the terrain or passing from the non-terrain of transcendental appearance to the Real is not to repeat, it is to assume the non-philosophical posture toward this new object—philosophy and its regional dependencies. The assumed "superior form" of the sciences is thus examined and now required from thought-science. For the philosophical demythization or demythologization of thought we substitute the demythologization of philosophy itself, and better still: a "non-mythology".

# Theoretical universality: Generality, totality, identity of universality

The concept of theory must be related to its cause and defined by the transcendental force-(of)-thought which explains its autonomy and usage and above all its universality. As aprioristico-transcendental it undoubtedly presents, without re-presenting, this cause. It is the non-specular clone of it, as we have said; simple and absolute reflection, present once and not twice ( = divided or speculative reflection). If thought is a Real('s)-simple non-autopositional presentation, it does not claim, like philosophy to be auto-presentation of its cause, nor does it intervene as aiding in the manifestation of the Real itself. The Real is the already-Manifested before any manifestation; it does not come to manifestation in non-philosophy, in the sense whereby this manifestation would succeed in making arrive at its essence. It is rather existent thought that is transformed—according to the a priori rules which explain the structures of the non-philosophical field— in order to enter into the order where it becomes adequate to this cause. This thought is only "adequate" to the Real in the sense whereby being first or unilateralized allows it to be. We distinguish adequacy as purported equality or "conformity" of the Real to thought supposed to be valid (ontological idealism) from the adequacy-clone, equality of thought to its *de jure* inequality to its real cause. This inequality, determination-in-the-last-instance, does not prevent—much the opposite—thought from being the originary reflection, the only possible reflection, (of the) real-One, and *thus the vastest universality*. A reflection that is relatively autonomous thanks to cloning and which ceases to dissolve itself in the mirror, to vanish in another equally inconsistent reflection, which is to say into itself.

The supposed "universality" of philosophy gives place to the worst misunderstandings. It is not its universality that is dubious, it is its restrained character of "abstract" generality (metaphysics as "abstraction" of its objects), thus of partially empirical "generality" which appears too strict or too limited when it is measured by what the vision-in-One tolerates. Philosophical universality, as we know, is double or divided: at once *generality* and *totality*. Divided from itself through the type of relation it maintains with the empirical, a relation always irreducible to the type of "difference" and reversible, so much so that this reference claims to co-determine its essence. It is thus cut from what it can be and from its theoretical form, that which the force-(of)-thought exercises. And far from reinforcing it, its redoubling by totality only better signals its weakness through the potentialization of its claim. It is in the internal constitution of its universality that it is thus shared between two forms of existence, weakened then redoubled or "auto-posited". Totality—finite or infinite, becoming-entirely-infinite—is the surest sign of the empirical conditioning and servitude of philosophy. Philosophy is not too "abstract": it is still not abstract enough, or is only "abstracted" from experience and has not known how to liberate itself sufficiently enough to maintain with experience freer relations of a pure transcendental thought finding in the empirical nothing but a simple occasion and some support.

Compared to philosophy, non-philosophy appears without a doubt to be "abstract" too, which is to say, now, poor in "concrete" totality. In reality it enjoys a qualitatively distinct universality stronger because emergent, adequate now to the Real: this is the theoretical dimension of the hypothesis or of the thought-organon which is not a mode derived or stripped from totality or even the logico-formal, but which is the "logical('s)-identity". A more rigorous concept of "theory" like the scientific one has nothing in common with the fetishizing usage of metaphor philosophy makes. What then does the qualitative specificity of non-philosophical theory, which is to say the noetico-noematic a priori, define *for* philosophy? Its *identity;* its non-division into generality and totality. Universality here is of one type alone because it finds its cause precisely in the force-(of)-thought. The non-philosophical opening is without horizon, as we know; it is describable neither as extatic-horizontal generality nor as unitary totality. It is the affect of the identity—not of the totality—of theory and utterly abandons the passably reactive idea of the "parceling" of the sciences for example, and the complementary and fantasmic idea of the "encyclopedia". It is not a question of parceling, unlinking or differentiation, nor moreover of a re-totalization, if not on the surface and on the mirror of philosophy, but of a unification-in-the-last-instance of knowings through their subordination to the Real of the force-(of)-thought. In this way, the theoretical representation liberates itself from any constitutive claim. As for philosophy, the role of simple occasional cause (which returns to it in the heart of the noetico-noematic a priori that is the product of the force-(of)-thought) does more than just desubstantialize it in order to functionalize it—here it plays a positive role of specification and overdetermination in the constitution of noetico-noematic identity, which does not though modify the transcendental-pure being of the theoretical. This is such that it depends only on its cause, the force-(of)-thought.

To give theory a reality-in-the-last-instance is to recover the power and in a sense the *discovery* of its precession over philosophical forms and sharings. This is why non-philosophy announces itself from the outset as a universalization, *of the "non-Euclidean" type* if you will, of the philosophical generality/totality. It delivers itself from the axioms which defined the structure of the Philosophical Decision and which were not absolutely necessary to any thought but which coagulated, condensed, and refolded the philosophical space in on itself, encumbering it and separating it from its force. And if it presents itself as the universalization, through their unification, of philosophy and regional knowings, this is because it is not meta-philosophy or philosophy-of-philosophy, auto-reflection or supplementary auto-position. Theory is plainly and actually theoretical once-each-time, liberated from the internal limitations that always impede philosophy in excess/fault over itself. If philosophy is the superior form *of* common sense, non-philosophy is the "universal" form, pragmatic and theoretical par excellence, *for* philosophy itself rather than *of* it and in continuity with it.

# Dissolution of the amphibology of the real and knowledge: Their unilateral duality

To philosophize is to move from a given *assumed as real…* toward its grounding, horizon, condition, etc. We say *assumed* because it is taken at random from the experience of circumstances and especially from experience conceived as transcendent or inscribed in the form of auto-position. Taken as such a departure point, the given receives a supplementary value or pertinence: as constituent of essential thought, even if it must be "critiqued", "reduced", "analyzed", etc., by this in the act of moving past it toward its a priori horizon. There is a constitutive empirical contingency at the base of every Philosophical Decision, which drives it to internal limitation and to 'supersession" by motivating its critique by another system. A philosophy only attacks another because this—and indeed the next—is intrinsically fragile and dependent on a transcendent experience, auto-positional by philosophical delegation and *at once* chosen from among others without essential reason. The cause and the complement of this internal weakness is evidently "philosophical faith".

If non-philosophy too starts from a given—as every thought does—it is not from an assumed given, from transcendent *data* elevated to the state of *fakta* (amphibology of experience and the Real) but from a radical given—from the real-One—the only given that is given without givenness accompanying and conditioning it, and which demands another thought in the axiom-form. A given not divided and redoubled by a givenness cannot any longer be "metaphysical" like a mixture of transcendence and immanence (*fakta*) and names another experience of thought. There will be no ontological principle of axioms, no more ontological than logico-formal, but from the outset axioms without superior legislation, without ontological closure. They are "posited" in-the-last-instance from their cause without a doubt—these are the modes of the force-(of)-thought—but this is identity and by definition takes from them any aspect of mixture (for example of hypothesis that is simultaneously anhypothetical—philosophy). Instead of transcending from the already virtually transcendent given of "experience" or of "beings" toward Reason, Being, Grounding, etc., and proceeding thus by specular dividing into two/redoubling, First Science gives itself or rather remains "in" the real-One, and so in the transcendental dimension of the force-(of)-thought. The unified theory, as we have seen, is transcendental induction and deduction, an order defined by a set of a priori structures which are equally rules for these operations. Through its cause and theoretical nature, First Science is of a necessity and a radicality without equivalent in ontology. In order to understand the type of "existence" or usage of sciences and philosophy in terms of the Real, we must eliminate both their ontological grounding and their scientistic and positivist images. From this point of view, the hypothesis and the axiom are operators that are real-in-the-last-instance or transcendental; neither "substances" nor "functions", nor even the difference between the two.

The force-(of)-thought, as organon of theoretical usage, evidently makes use of experience or of *data* which have been, at the origin of their scientific usage, more or less elaborated as criteria (with the effects of verification and falsification) of theory. However, it does not recognize them for all their ontological or constitutive value. Furthermore it has nothing empiricist in its usage obligated to experience: induction and deduction, hypotheses and axioms put it into play without giving it a role of decision in the essence of theory; in any case, and locally, through relation to such a regional and limited "theory" which finds itself rerouted to the status of *datum* of knowledge and which will serve principally to specify the a priori theoretical dimension. Epistemology confuses, in an amphibology that is barely differentiated and which appears "natural" in the principle, properly scientific relations and ontological or assimilated relations between theory and experience. The first undoubtedly include the effects of falsification and verification, but they do not introduce them to non-philosophy except in the general limits of their identity with philosophy, and thus of the specification and individualization supplied by philosophical givens.

Like any mythology, philosophy believes it can decide the Real or even know it. It intervenes in it practically (or believes it can do so) and takes this operation for that of knowledge. In particular it gives a decisional and auto-positional image of scientific knowledge which then permits it in all circularity to proclaim the affinity "in itself", and even sometimes the underlying identity of science and philosophy. But a science and a fortiori a non-philosophy do not decide the Real. Properly speaking they redistribute objective givens, "phenomena", according to their proper theoretical demands: it does not confuse empirical or transcendent divisions of *data* or knowledges with a purported decision over the Real itself. Experimenting and deducing perhaps do not essentially consist in analyzing and synthesizing but in establishing a simple or identical *order* of priorities and secondarities, irreversible each time. Non-philosophy, rather than a lesser or anti-philosophy, is a transcendental *mathesis* (identically formal and material) which proceeds through a certain type of order: unilateralizing or determining-in-the-last-instance; excluding the philosophical processes of overseeing, domination by analysis, synthesis, dialectic, etc. In fact, it exceeds the internal play of a dyad, the simple redistribution of decisions and simultaneities, of contrasts and folds, etc. To the contrary, it transforms the existing dyads of knowing into a function of the force-(of)-thought which is of another type, theoretically emergent and which precedes, rather than anticipating, these *data*. This irreversible precession is the condition *sine qua non* such that the new knowledge is produced and that this science-thought is not confused, through mythological epistemologies, with the hermeneutic turnstile [*tourniquet*].

# Inducing-deducing as much as transcending

Is this a question of *superseding* philosophy once again, or indeed of making a usage of it whether of knowledge, art, ethics, etc., within non-philosophy? Is non-philosophy superseded here by thought, toward what it puts into movement, thought which questions it and inversely, is it superseded as continued? It is rather, as we will explain, "materialized" by the force-(of)-thought, as a priori of objective experience. Philosophy is the thought which exceeds thought, which assumes it as given in order to supersede it, which takes it as constitutive of the Real, precisely of the given. Non-philosophy is the thought which only exceeds itself secondarily, which rather assumes the Real-without-thought and philosophy as givens first of all, philosophy which transcendentally induces and deduces the forms of thought thanks to the force-(of)-thought. It does not start by assuming itself valid, nor the existent forms of thought: it is practically anti-idealist and defetishizing. From the cause as "affair" to the cause as "last-instance": this is the change of terrain requiring a positive non-philosophy. The style of this questioning increase [*remontée*]—of the *remounting* more or less reversible as turning—of transcendental *in-duction* and *de-duction* which proceeds "in a unique sense" or one-time-only-each-time rather than twice or once divided (once-for-*all*).

Philosophy, as we have already said, is "auto-vectorial" since it is topological, non-philosophy is only so in a very secondary way. Auto-vectorial, because it grounds itself first and foremost on transcendence. A necessarily mixed vectorality, empirico-transcendental, which assumes the possibility of a double vector and a change of direction, "turning", "reversal", "point of transmutation", etc.—thus a quasi-circularity. On the other hand if non-philosophy does not ignore transcendence, at least as organon, not as metaphysical entity, it no longer grounds itself on it; it is deprived on its behalf of auto-position or of absolute pretension. So much so that its transcendence, retaining something of simplicity or the identity of the One, cannot be in a double sense, refolded in a circle, with an angle, perspective and turn—this is a "linked" vector.

The order that forms the force-(of)-thought is thus of a more "rectional" or uni-rectional nature rather than di-rectional. A transcender, undoubtedly, but without the back-and-forth of "ontological" transcendence. It is precisely not a becoming, a field of lines and vectors like the "transcendental field" of certain philosophies. Thinking is no longer opening and traversing a space, deploying a horizon. If philosophy Platonizes, directly or in reverse, if it raises its eyes toward the *eidos* and lowers them again toward experience in the same gesture, if it always questions more in the background, non-philosophy positions knowledges in terms of a static order of later-alization which extracts concrete a prioris from this material. If then any "direction" is di-rection, rection already divided and doubled, induction and deduction—understood in their plain phenomenal sense—are unirection or unilateralization: insertion of *data* in a *uni-versal* "space-time" which proceeds each-time-in-one-time, without the more or less dialecticizable fold or turn of philosophy. If there is no longer a possible circle between the Real and thought, thought being reduced to the state of non constitutive materials, they cease to form a dyad or difference. Rigorous, non-amphibological thought is not in *difference*, dis-ferring, but in induction and deduction as operations in the wholly transcendental sense.

Here then is another "image" of thought. It no longer transcends toward Nature then toward the World, or even toward the *object* supposedly co-constitutive of the Real: but unilaterally and non-positionally from the Real toward knowledge, rather than the inverse, and from knowledge toward the empirical. The heterogeneity of origin, thus of a reality-type, of the thought-in-One and the *data* (which themselves contain thought, a distinction of qualitative spheres, not "epistemological" ingredients), prohibits thought from overtaking itself toward the Real (if not reduced to "Being", "Nature", "Objectivity" which are philosophical artifacts) and dissolves their amphibology (for example, theoretico-experimental), establishing instead the positive absence of circularity and the relative autonomy of the terms in presence. We can no longer say for example like philosophy *tends* to do that a theory represents experience for another theory, and vice versa. Even if the new theory enters in turn into *data*, the theoretical-unified order of non-philosophy, including the reference to experience, does not confuse itself with the experimental or "transcendent" empirical order.

# The force-(of)-thought as non-rational identity of reason: Real critique of pure reason

According to non-philosophical "logic", we say that the force-(of)-thought is the *non-rational* identity of Reason, and consequently that it unifies-it-without-totalizing-it. The non-rational is not the opposite or the margin of philosophy. The non-rational is the *theoretical usage* or identity of Reason, itself always impure or empirico-rational, under the cause-of-the-last-instance that is the vision-in-One. The "non" limits Reason to its identity-of-the-last-instance and tears it from philosophy, universalizing it beyond its philosophical forms which all *share it* between generality and totality. We will analyze these different aspects starting with Kantian materials.

In their Kantian definitions, Understanding is the power of concepts as rules, rules being the power of determination thinking the singular cases through a general representation which is the concept; Reason is the power of principles or of grounding rules, the power which furnishes the principles with a priori knowledge. The structure of the Philosophical Decision evidently reigns in these definitions: in the hierarchized dyad of powers, the superior assuring the unity of the two; in the conception of thought as power and authority, and of power as psycho-political mixture ("faculty" or "power to do" but also to "rule" and to "ground"); in the division of the organon of thought (as rule and as principle); and finally in the operation of determination understood as hierarchization, either as subsuming or as grounding. Moreover the force-(of)-thought can be obtained from such a metaphysical material through an operation of immanent "simplification" and of unilateral dualyzation which determines it as non-rational identity of Reason or, more precisely, given that Reason is the power of auto-position *par excellence*, as non-rational identity-(of)-itself.

Through an immanent cloning, vision-in-One extracts the transcendent forms ("faculties") and the auto-positional forms of power, simple identity, without fold, from the force (of thinking)—and not of "thought". The force (of)… is the simplified transcender through its insertion in-One-in-the-last-instance. It is the plain phenomenal core of any subject constituted by the "faculties", their hierarchy and their conflict without the authority of Reason. The "subject" ceases to be intrinsically divided (by the faculties but also *as* subject by the Other or the signifier, etc.) and recovers a radical identity it no longer holds. Rule and principle are replaced by the simple and unique organon of non-autopositional transcendence, pure non-phenomenological distance, whose radical exteriority is no longer limited and closed off *by* and above all *as* concept and idea, as rule and principle. The philosophical organon is always auto-organon or technology of thought, the non-philosophical organon is *Logic*—the transcendental identity-(of)-logic—insofar as it orders the Real.

The operation of determination (of rules by principles and of principles by themselves) ceases to be transcendent and hierarchical. It progresses through identity-of-the-last-instance: this introduces an equality (not arithmetic or abstract), through the identity of a unilateral duality, between Understanding and Reason. The force-(of)-thought establishes democracy where antidemocracy begins: in the very essence of thought, torn away from its reified forms.

The force-(of)-thought is a concrete, a formal-without-form and a material-without-matter. It is no longer codetermined in a mixed manner like the forms of the concept and the idea, the rule and the principle, by the empirical, which is to say the philosophical given. It is form and matter *for* (and not "of"…) philosophy, but form and matter of identity and duality which organize materials. This is an infinite dimension (because it is finite *intrinsically* or in-the-last-instance) which applies for every possible dyad that comes under philosophy. More generally, if the philosophical form itself as mixture of form and matter such as it condenses itself in the rule, in the principle and in their hierarchy, is folded and closed over itself like an infinite loop and thus simultaneously finite, the force-(of)-thought is a radical opening, delivered from any spatiotemporal topology because it is "un"-folded in its intrinsic identity. This is no longer a *general representation* (concept or idea): universality has destroyed re-presentation or auto-presentation in it and has liberated the element of pure presentation. With this aprioristico-transcendental instance, the question is not so much of an in-formal or an a-formal as of the non-formal identity of form, a formal-without-form—this logic applies to matter respectively.

Non-philosophy involves the identity-of-the-last-instance and the unilateral duality *for* form and *for* matter. Formality without logical form, but transcendental, cannot act on the singular cases or even on the philosophical concept treated as case, by informing or re-forming them, but by freeing up their a priori identity which is that through which reason-in-One reaches experience. In reality, it cannot directly encounter the infra-philosophical and even philosophical empirical, modify it, or represent it, but "see" it or present it otherwise than it has been represented throughout philosophy. On their part the singular case and the concept, most generally the Other and the Same but also the rule-concept and the principle-idea, cease to form a mixture in a superior degree and are each subjected to unidentification and unilateralization which brings them to the true or real equality.

The set of these determinations represents the determinant, transcendental and a priori side of the force-(of)-thought. But there is also a determined side, given as relatively autonomous. Just as the force-(of)-thought presupposes itself, beyond the One, as phenomenal transcendence in its essence without however being able to auto-pose itself starting from philosophy, transcendence too as a priori presupposes itself, under the form of a support with which it unilaterally identities itself, a support constituted through the level of the philosophical type of a priori. The force-(of)-thought, unlike Reason which simply represses this condition, explicitly calls this an empirical support—instead of negating it—with which nonetheless—in reality for the same reason—it no longer reciprocally determines itself: this is the *fantasy* of the force-(of)-thought, relatively autonomous given with which, *as subject* (not as vision-in-One but as non-autopositional transcendence) it must identify itself, though unilaterally, in order to be what it is.

The idea of Reason being thus reduced to its phenomenal or non-rational identity is entirely the aporetic aspect of Reason, empirically and ontically determined but refusing this determination, which receives a coherent solution in the concept of force-(of)-thought. More radically than *Dasein* which cannot establish a real unilaterality in its relation to the World and which interiorizes certain existential and psychological determinations thus making them the essence of its indetermination, the force-(of)-thought ceases to be a *com*-portment; it is indeed a relation-without-relation but which is only "without-relation" for the positive reason of its identity, never by a certain indetermination that would join up in some way with the metaphysical auto-position of the relation. We have formed the first name of *uni-lation* to speak of this unilateral relation, infinitely open because intrinsically finite-in-the-last-instance. The force-(of)-thought is the phenomenal and transcendental power (of) itself but without being an auto-power like Reason is—a power (of) the non-positional a priori (of) itself but which needs the philosophical or rational a priori. The aprior-istico-rational serves as materials for the identity of the a priori, a new type of a priori. We remember the manner in which cant outlined the a priori: as that which allows us to "see what reason produces completely and only from itself". This specularity of the rational a priori, which is seen in the object or experience and for which experience serves as a mirror, is eradi-cated by the force-(of)-thought as real critique, not simply philosophical, of the power of Pure Reason, as organon of a "non-Kantianism".

# The non-philosophical usage of language: Conceptual symbolism, first names, and words-without-language

The end of the "grand narrative" (metaphysical and rationalist) has been announced prematurely by the post-moderns. Not having the means to really suspend its validity and to reduce it to the *identity* of the narrative, they conserve it sketched out in the background, as repressed horizon, as hinter-world of debris, remainders and partial objects they make do with. If it is impossible other than by metaphysical abstraction and illusion to abandon any aspect of conceptual and discursive exposition, any aspect of book, treaty and systematic principles, it is at least necessary to radically suspend their validity and that of the narrative-form in thought and reasoning, and particularly to introduce an axiomatic or first *aspect*, with the operations of induction and deduction which result from it. And to introduce this right up to the usage of language and not only in the general question of thought or in the problematic. These "Principles" combine in the manner of non-philosophy which they introduce, but undoubtedly in a still insufficiently decided manner, an axiomatization of the language of thought, of "discourse", and an overdetermination of this axiomatization through the materials of the most traditional philosophical narrative. The philosophical proposition under its forms, rational or not, predicative, analytic, judiciary-synthetic, speculative, aphoristic, topologico-transcendental, etc., remains the element from where the force-(of)-thought emits and manifests its axioms and its theorems. But this element of narrative continues to envelop—without determining it, this is not a question of eliminating but of unilaterally suspending—the essence of thought.

Philosophical speech, philosophical language has become impossible for us. A unilateral rather than a global aphasia, it bears on the innumerable doublets, redundancies, circles with which this language is charged and which devote it to an idealist usage where it redoubles the Real of its narrative [*récit*]. The philosophical usage of language gives place in effect to metaphysics as *recital* in the simple sense of re-citation [*ré-citation*], doubling itself, engendering the infinite rolling [*moutonnement*] of philosophical entities and mythologies. This usage is *de jure* absolutely inadequate to the Real—this is a transcendental illusion which refuses the foreclosure of the Real—and unilaterally inadequate to the force-(of)-thought. The force-(of)-thought does not take into account its performance force and its descriptive force, which linguistic metaphysics attributes to them, other than to suspend them under this form and make a usage of them that is adequate to its proper formation, more exactly here still to identity-of-the-last-instance of its powers of performation and description. When it is thus returned not to its cause directly, by a new metaphysics as "transcendental linguistics", but to the cause of its pure transcendental usage, language undergoes a reduction to what we are going to call *words-without-language* or to *symbols*, not literal but verbal and conceptual.

That philosophical language be natural and/or formal-symbolic, the force-(of)-thought in effect deprives it of its proper reflexivity or indeed reflexivity philosophically re-grasped as logos, and the avatars of this, without though negating it, nihilating it, differentiating it, deconstructing it, or dialecticizing it. Devoid *at least in its essence* of opening or ontological touch [*frappe*], required by non-philosophy which makes a usage of it that is unilaterally non-signifying-(of)-itself, in terms of its identity-of-the-last-instance, it ceases to be divided, redoubled, at once rare and redundant, more or less directly or in priority in all its dimensions, signifying or semantic. It thus acquires an identity of symbol, which permits it to fulfill the functions of linguistic support of the force-(of)-thought and the a priori structures it frees. "speech" no longer "speaks", without a doubt, when it is non-philosophy which speaks, but precisely the tautology of "speech speaks" is only the sobered form of doublets at work in the philosophical conception of language and which has not broken any links with the old auto-position, the mythological auto-speech of the logos. Non-philosophy opposes to this the unique usage, *once-each-time*, of language. To the certainly unique (*Ereignis*) but still transcendent event of speech, it opposes its immanent identity, rather than last-instance identity, more precisely language('s)-identity, under the form of words-without-speech or first names with which they think. Why these terms? The transcendental axiom-atization of conceptual language or philosophical discourse equalizes, but in the mode of the "last instance", the *first term* (necessary for axiomati-zation) and the *proper name* (every language must be reduced to "speak" the Real('s)-identity or to receive a transcendental function) under the form of *first name*. One such symbol supports the usage of thought in its identity and itself is only conceivable as non-formal, non-literal identity of the symbolic. If the philosophical redoubling of "speaking speech" signifies the last and least capture of language by philosophy (without doubt aided by language), the first name, axiomatico-transcendental, does not signify that the non-philosophical does not speak, but instead of speaking from language itself as from its hinter-world (an auto-hinter-world…), it speaks "from" the Real, in-the-last-instance from the vision-in-One, but with the entirely occasional aid of the philosophical logos. This is the end of philosophical "ventriloquism"; language speaks from the immanent phenomenon to which it is reduced through-and-through.

Just as non-philosophy claims to be a Real adequate thought/adequate to the Real under the most radical form as One, through a new conception of adequacy as determination-in-the-last-instance, it claims to be a (Real adequate) usage of language (adequate to the Real). The paradox is even more violent here, philosophy refusing—beyond its classical style—the idea of an adequacy of the Real-One and of language to the point of declaring, in psychoanalysis, the Real as impossible or non-symbolizable. As always, the *conditions* through which they pose the problem exclude any solution other than eternalizing it in an aporia: it places the transcendent real-One face to face with a language given in an equally transcendent manner in its auto-reflexivity. The aporetic "solution" to this antinomy is philosophical idealism: language is only "of" the Real on the condition of determining it in return, transforming it in signifying it, constraining it to renounce its identity (moreover assumed arbitrarily, which is to say by tradition and forgetting phenomena), dividing and "extending" this transcendent entity to the point of the "loose" irreality of Being with which language has more affinity. It is no longer a question of registering this position of the problem which returns to saying that the ingredient of identity in the Real and its modes (the One, Life, Being, etc.) escapes the concept, discursivity, and remains undetermined. The conceptual and discursive indetermination of the Real as radical immanence is evident but the problem is precisely elsewhere in philosophy now and on another terrain: indetermination is not a crippling handicap to thought nor to discourse, if not to philosophical decisions which can only want to *posit* and *objectify* the Real, taking the One "in-view" and falsifying it as object or even as mode of being or horizon of objectivity. If philosophy is the thought adequate to the object, even when it supersedes this toward its conditions of possibility or of genesis, a scientific model of thought exists, no longer for the object given intuitively but for philosophy itself. An axiomatic—transcendental now—is possible for philosophical thought which makes abstraction of every object of philosophy, of objectivity itself; which certainly are the objects taken from philosophy but not definable or demonstrable in the naïve philosophical element, but through the system of axioms formed to "describe" them. The discursive or philosophical indetermination of objects of non-philosophy thus can receive a positive *theoretical* status on the condition of elaborating this as having an *aspect* of the axiomatic that is not formal but "real" or more precisely "transcendental". For this it is necessary that the Real('s) non-philosophical language be taken from philosophy—under penalty of transcendent abstraction or auto-positional idealism—but that it be treated through the means of an abstraction that would be of a new theoretical type, scientific or axiomatic (first terms, axioms, etc.) but of the transcendental nature and ultimately pure or not blended with the Real. Hence the symbols and not the concepts of "One", of "Real", of "vision-in-One", etc., and their theoretical function.

The transcendental symbol, even that of the Real, is not the Real itself or a part of the Real (contrary to the most general philosophical presupposition, even if *repressed*), more radically still than the idea of the circle is not circular, but it only is in-the-last-instance, which is to say it is transcendental. And if it is not, this is precisely *because* of the Real: the Real determines-it-in-the-last-instance in its identity as symbol and tears it from its linguistico-formal state as from its claim to ontologically constitutive object. It is thus possible to take up again, in a new way, all the terms and statements of whatever philosophy and to treat them such that their metaphysical abstraction is suspended, which is to say the circularity-of-grounding which makes the Real and language codetermine each other. Non-philosophical language reaches an apriority whose transcendental purity is a guarantee against the illusory claims of metaphysics and speculation. The operators of this informal axiomatization of concepts are equally drawn from the words of philosophy and are highly variable: "without", "outside...", "in-", "(of)", etc. These are no longer those of a subtraction, reduction, privation, at least insofar as *metaphysical abstraction* is what structures and determines, by its repressing, all these philosophical and sometimes "anti-metaphysical" operations. The axiomatic abstraction is here a mode of the (non-) One in its relation—the force-(of)-thought—to the non (-One) given in a relatively autonomous manner, and does not let it determine itself through this which only serves as occasion and support for it.

Non-philosophy thus has its usage or its own conditions of symbolization and formalization and does not let these impose on it as they are, without transformation through logic. They are no longer logico-formal, which is to say from reduction of signifying supports to given identities in an idealizing geometric intuition. Unlike for example the *eidos* of the perceived (Husserl) and its intuition, which combines the multiplicity of 'sketches" and the unity of the thing, coextensive to one another, the formal axiomatic assumes a radical idealization, to know that the thing gives itself as the same in a radical identity, without diversity of *Abschattungen*, and consequently in an intrinsically simple identity. The formal symbol is thus already a *one-without-unity* but which remains in the element of transcendence, obtained through passage from idealization to the limit. If we assume now that this *one-without-unity* is not produced through an idealization proscribed by a cause through immanence or of-the-last-instance, we obtain the pure transcendental symbol. Philosophy assumes a transcendent process of production of scientific ideas, half-linguistic and half-operatory, starting from the "world of life", etc. But how do we produce an ideality, an ideal identity-one if we do not already have, a priori, the transcendental "model", which is to say already *given* or real? The idealizing or identificational assumes materials to be idealized and it is this relation to materials that philosophy thematizes. But the repetition itself, in its real or phenomenal content, if it is not itself specular or viciously transferred from the transcendent ideality whose genesis it carries out, only being an activity of transcendental cloning (non-specular reflection (of) itself of the real-One or of an entirely immanent identity). If there is a logic of identities, and moreover an identity-(of)-logic or of the symbols of thought, it is transcendental in the "pure" or rigorous sense where we have understood it. It is the clone of the Real and, as transcendental, it conditions the a priori identity of the symbol on the basis or support of the logico-philosophical.

The transcendental possibility of the symbol being acquired, non-philosophy can now be—beyond its phenomenal content—a form of thought proceeding with such symbols, a sort of calculation although a purely immanent one in these last reasons. Just as the formal axiomatic is only possible through a material and formal (signifying) identity of symbols which assures it a possession and mastery without remainder of its objects, non-philosophy too—but this is not its only aspect, it equally possesses an aspect of transcendental induction—calculates its theorems by means of a deduction operating on first names. Nonetheless these theorems remain *transcendental* or put to work rather than the transcendent logical system, the force-(of)-thought (determination-in-the-last-instance) over this type of symbols on the one hand, and in relation to the experience furnished by philosophical discourse on the other. Transcendental by their origin, these theorems take the form of equations putting old contraries into operation, terms of philosophical couplings and antinomies. These equations are resolved; the equality of their terms assured, through their transcendental *identity*, the only identity capable of assuring their unilateral duality. This identity functions on two planes which articulate themselves in effective knowledge: the plane of phenomena or of "phenomenal liveds [*vécus*]"; the plane of symbols or of "language" which serve as support for these phenomenal liveds of the force-(of)-thought and the a prioris it frees from philosophy.

# The measure in which the real is not symbolizable: The non-linguistic identity of language. A non-philosophical translation of philosophies

The transcendental determination of the being of the symbol in general by the Real allows us to define to what extent the Real itself is or is not symbolizable, and what sense this problem could still have formulated in this antinomic manner and consequently, beyond the vision-in-One which is its essence, to define in what sense it is the object of knowing. The symbols now being real-in-the-last-instance identities on a base or a support that are themselves material and formal (signifiers), it seems to be inevitable to conclude here that not only philosophical material but also the Real itself is knowable or thinkable and to believe that whatever first term "designating" the real-One is one such knowledge of it. The danger of this appearance is the greatest for this class of symbols which refer explicitly to the real-One or which enter into the axioms charged with describing it. It is in this manner that non-philosophy can lose its rigor and turn to a new philosophy: to the metaphysical thesis of the determination of the Real through thought. Hence the hope of its direct definition through the first names of Life, Affect, Internal, Impressional, or any other term which appears to have, or which has had within the metaphysical tradition, a special affinity with radical immanence and power—a divine surprise of naming—managing to finally touch the finger of the true Real ignored by other philosophies. This is a transformation of the first term into philosophical concept. Kant would have spoken of the confusion of the phenomenon with the noumenon: we will generalize all philosophy here through the idea of a confusion of radical or real phenomenon with the transcendent noumena of thought. The real-One allows us to understand that Life, Affect, the Originary Impression or the Internal, etc., are real in-the-last-instance and that, precisely because of this, they are not the Real but only—given their constitution as symbols—the first terms which describe it without determining it.

The mechanism of this transcendental appearance can be outlined in the following manner. Let us assume that the Real is named in the register of "life", the "lived", in the phenomenological manner. The first term which corresponds to it must thus simultaneously detach it from life in its psycho-metaphysical senses. We thus form the first name of the *lived-without-life*, a manner of radicalizing the phenomenological *Erlebnis*. But this is insufficient: this name only has a transcendental status. The Real itself has nothing to do with life or even the lived, it is only immanent-(to)-itself (therefore nothing to do with a metaphysical or phenomenological immanence, etc.), without particular ontico-ontological determination. The lived, even "without-life", remains a simple symbol that does not *approach* the real-One at all in an asymptotic manner: adequacy excludes approximation. Simply put it is possible to speak the Real (this term itself is a first name) with the means of "life". But this does not permit us to conclude from the name to the thing. Why then proceed as such? Because it is necessary to think life in the ontico-ontological sense, which is to say philosophy-of-life, of thinking not from the undetermined Real but from the Real *as* "life" and of forming the operatory first name of the lived-without-life. The problem of thought as force-(of)-thought—precisely the sense of this substitution—is of thinking rigorously and in reality the sphere of ontico-ontological givens of philosophy under the conditions of the vision-in-One, rather than of thinking the vision-in-One under the conditions of philosophy. The Real does not think itself—the vision-in-One suffices—and is not directly thinkable as object but through its specific effect, here through the determination-in-the-last-instance it exercises or through the intrinsic finitude it imposes on any theoretical usage of fundamental and regional knowings and consequently as simple first name. The symbols which *appear to intentionally aim at* the real-One in the manner of an object, the World, Being, in reality they do not transcend toward it but "from" it "toward" philosophical objects, without however being a question of an auto-positional transcendence, divided and refolded. The symbols as "lived-without-life", "given-without-givenness", etc., are symbols *for* philosophy but not symbols *of* philosophy and still less knowledge *of the* Real. They find their cause in the Real; their operatory destination, their intention or what remains of it, in philosophy. In the Real *qua* life, qua impression, etc., the "*qua*" is discharged of its apophantic function and subsists as witness of the causality of the Real, which is thus never the *object* or the referent of the symbol. The non-metaphysical sobering is here: that the Real is neither the possible nor the impossible; neither the symbolizable nor the non-symbolizable posited as first, but that it is the cause by immanence which explains the possibility of the symbol without necessarily being symmetrically to assume the Real knowable (since it is already vision-in-One). The philosophical antinomy of the Real and the symbol is thus invalidated, outside of any reversal or synthesis possible, by their unilateral duality. To be extremely rigorous, we can say that the Real, being cause-of-the-last-instance of the symbol, *appears* as designated/targeted by the symbol—but this is an objective appearance. The Real is more like Kant's "thing-in-itself": unknowable and even unthinkable, but with the difference that it is not so from transcendence but from immanence (the One and not the Other) foreclosed and that it consists in an experience or a knowing of the third type, the vision-in-One.

In these conditions, can we say at least that the Real is precisely symbolized like the philosophical *data* and equally that they or inversely philosophy is no more known by its symbolization than the Real? This nihilistic indifferentiation is in admissible and would end in a linguistic idealism. There is a difference between the symbolization of the Real and that of the force-(of)-thought or any other knowledge acquired partly or totally from experience (from philosophy): the force-(of)-thought, moreover. The a priori structures of non-philosophy must be actualized in a process of knowledge and this requires a symbolization of philosophical *data*, whereas the real-One, which is of the given, in its essence has no need to be known and *thus is not* (if not through its philosophical appearance) and this means in any mode whatsoever; consequently it does not find in its symbols the same benefit of knowledge as experience does. We can thus say that the "symbols" *of the* Real are what permit us to know and think experience which, without (this type of) symbols, cannot be the object of a rigorous theory. Of course the source of philosophical appearance upon which non-philosophy still feeds, and where it only motivates itself conditionally, and which it limits ("thinking the Real itself", "*if* we wish to think the One…"), implies that the Real too be "symbolized" like experience, but this is still an appearance: precisely the Real, when it is the issue at hand, entails the dissociation of the logico-philosophical usage of language and its usage of "non-philosophical" symbols *for* a theory of philosophical knowing into which it enters only as first name, as "unknown" but given. Finally there are no symbols in this sense, purely transcendental, other than *through* the Real and, in an apparently inevitable sense, "of" the Real, but symbols *through* the Real or *in*-One are symbols *for* philosophical experience and in this sense, they permit the production of a non-philosophical knowledge. But even in this function, it is not the existence of the symbols which determines knowledge but the procedures thereof which delimit the power and function of the symbols; this is not an axiomatic idealism. If the first names of the One particularly do not allow us to say that the Real is known through them, then it is the essence of the Real which "decides".

Renouncing what is ordinarily and philosophically called "*Language*", which is to say its usage as *narrative of the real*, non-philosophy has neither private nor proper language. Each philosopher claims to possess the universal language of thought and of the Real but only carves out a sphere of private usage over a vaster domain that escapes him and that he believes himself to exhaust here where he renders it adequate to *his* real. The non-philosopher proceeds otherwise and draws from all possible languages, philosophical or not, and, in this case, finally philosophizable. He is forced to return here and to find materials here. First, to form a language-without-speech, a language-without-discourse, words-without-language, which is to say the primitive language, or language given-without-givenness of the transcendental axiomatic, a language *according to* the Real and in-One. Next to manifest the non-linguistic [*non-langagière*] identity of language (and not only the non-Linguistic [*non-linguistique*] essence of language) which is that of non-philosophy, an identity which must be said to be the essence of language when language is related pragmatically to its real cause rather than decided by a philosophical position. This non-philosophical language is in fact the identity of-the-last-instance of language and speech or of any other antinomy "*Language*" covers. From this perspective it is thus the only intrinsically performational language, which only exists insofar as it is practiced, being already practiced when it only exists in the phenomenal state or *as it is* (the phenomenon of the force-(of)-thought is performational) and being already practiced, moreover, when it is actualized *as such* in the production of non-philosophical statements. In other words, it only exists in these two modes belonging to it insofar as it is *lived*, neither dead nor living, but lived-in-the-last-instance-without-life.

Philosophy always attributes a generality to language such that it reduces it to its essence according to various modes, as well as a totality which shares it according to Onto-theo-logical Difference, specified here in Linguistico-theo-logical Difference. But neither generality nor totality, taken separately or together, are the universality that non-philosophy exposes, which is moreover not the theoretical universality of the sciences. It is the aprioristico-transcendental universality such as it is determined-in-the-last-instance by the vision-in-One. Also, Language-without-language [*langue-sans-langage*], or non-linguistics, is *universal* language, the identically philosophical and scientific idiom, the resolution of their equation through the identity of their unilateral duality. This language is neither a "universal characteristic" if it is not the case that it is identically theoretical, axiomatic or first, nor a language of the Real as Being, if it is not the case that it is identically pure transcendental.

It is thus in this *theoretical usage*, in this transcendental theory of private philosophical languages (at once general and total), from this non-linguistic identity of language, that the problem arises of a translation of philosophies "into" one another, which is to say in-One-in-the-last-instance, rather than an inter-philosophical translation under the ultimate authority of philosophy. Non-philosophy *is* this translation of Kant "into" Descartes, of Descartes "into" Marx, of Marx "into" Husserl", etc. That is to say under the condition of the vision-in-One as un-translatable Real. To put it more rigorously, no more than it is im-possible or un-symbolizable, the Real is not un-translatable, but is rather that which renders the possibility of translation real-in-the-last-instance, the Real itself being foreclosed, without negation, to any translation and not becoming the untranslatable other than as force-(of)-thought or, in this instance, *force-(of)-translation*. It is in this manner, through a translation of philosophical decisions or through solely transcendental equivalents of their respective identity, that a democracy that is not a simple transcendental appearance can be introduced into philosophy and between philosophies in place of their conflictual and hierarchical multiplicity.

# Transcendental theorems on the idiom of the One

## *Definitions and axioms*

I call "language of the One" the formalism adequate to the thought of the One-in-One.

I call "idiom of the One" or "language" in the wider sense of non-philosophy the type of statements formed from this language.

I call "formalism of the One":

- the conceptual symbols: One, Being, Multiple, Other, Identity, Same, World, Philosophy;
- the "non-philosophical" functions or operators: non-, (of), outside, post-;
- the initial or derived formulas: One-in-One, One-in-the-last-instance, One-outside-of-Being, One-qua-One, Being-in-One-in-the-last-instance, Being-qua-Being, One-to-Being, One-to-the-Other, One-to-Unity, etc.;
- the operations: transcendental induction and deduction insofar as they are permitted by the One.

I call "immanence" or "identity-of-the-last-instance" the non-philosophical or unified-theoretical type of closure of a system.

## *Theorems*

**1**  The theorems said to be of the idiom of the One bear not on the linguistico-philosophical properties of this idiom but on their transcendental identity, always said to be real "in-the-last-instance", insofar as it transforms these properties into simple aspects, occasions, or supports of this idiom.

**2**  This is a private language of the Greco-Occidental epoch: by its aspect of philosophical materials.

**3**  This is a universal or non-private language: by its aspect of non-philosophical generalization of philosophical language.

**4**  This is a philosophical language: by its aspect of materials, symbols and rules of syntax, drawn from Philosophical Decision.

**5**  This is a scientific language: by its aspect of materials, symbols and operations drawn from the sciences.

**6**  This is a poetic language: by its aspect of a priori identity of contraries, for example of the philosopheme and the matheme.

**7**  This is a mystical language: by its aspect of identity (of the philosophical and the scientific) drawn from the radical immanence of the One.

**8**    This is a theoretical language: by its aspect of theory of language which contains every non-philosophical performation of the language of the One.

**9**    This is an experimental language: by its aspect of induction starting from philosophy and science as from its experience.

**10**   This is an aprioristic language: by its aspect of universal and necessary structure which regulates its exercise and which applies *for* the private languages of philosophy and science.

**11**   This is a pragmatic language: by its aspect of transcendental usage of philosophical and scientific languages.

**12**   This is a transcendental language: by the immanence of the force-(of)-symbolization it receives from the One and to which it neither adds nor deducts the One-in-One.

**13**   This is a fractal language: speaking of fractality, it is itself performatively fractal.

**14**   This is an identically constational and performational language: it acts or describes (in) speaking; it speaks (in) doing or (in) describing.

**15**   This is identically a language-object—but not a regional object: by its aspect of the language of non-philosophy; and a universal language—but not a metalanguage: it applies to philosophy, science and their relation.

**16**   This is a language of identity rather than of tautology: by its aspect of identity-of-the-last-instance through which it reduces philosophical tautologies to the state of unilateral dualities.

**17**   This is a language-which-does-not-speak(-itself) but which is enjoyed-in-the-last-instance: because it speaks from the real-One rather than from itself or Being.

**18**   This is a non-Platonic language (except for Platonism): because it signifies or speaks in the relation of the One-of-the-last-instance which is on the side of essence, to the essence or Being which is beyond the One.

**19**   This is a non-Aristotelian language (except for Aristotelianism): because it only speaks of Being on the occasion of experience or by helping experience now generalized as philosophy.

**20**   This is a non-Cartesian language (except for Cartesianism): by the force-(of)-language which, with the materials of philosophical statements, produces an infinity open to new statements that are not enclosed in rational closure.

**21**   This is a non-Leibnizian language (except for Leibnizianism) or universal: by its content, identically philosophical (or natural) and mathematical, as being solely determined and no longer determining.

**22**   This is a non-Kantian language (except for Kantianism): by its aprioristic, transcendental and real structures which contain more than the simple "real possibility" of language—the manifestation of the identity-(of)-language of language.

**23**   This is a non-Fichtean language (except for Fichteanism): by the subordination of its continuously realized practice of the speculation and illusions of the philosophical autolanguage to the ordinary man and "non-philosophy".

**24**   This is a non-Marxist language (except for Marxism): by the real or in-the-last-instance determination of philosophical language through the force-(of)-symbolization.

**25**   This is a non-Heideggerian language (except for Heideggerianism): because it only manifests Being or gives it in being-given by the One without determining it in return; a language struck by an opening rather than re-striking an already-open in the opening.

**26**   This is a non-Wittgensteinian I language (except for Wittgenstein I): because it speaks what we cannot say, or speaks the identity-in-the-last-instance of saying and silence; or said-without-saying for example "whereof one cannot speak, thereof one must be silent" instead of simply remaining silent or speaking it.

**27**   This is a non-Wittgensteinian II language (except for Wittgenstein II): because it liberates the language games from the ultimate closure of the amphibology-of-the-One-and-the-Other and manifests the radical transcendental multitude of language.

**28**   This is a non-Gödelian language (except for Gödelianism): because it assists the relations of philosophy *and* science as the (non-constitutive) metalanguage of the essence-(of)-philosophy of philosophy and the essence-(of)-science of science, and produces philosophical and scientifically unintelligible and indemonstrable, though pertinent, statements on these.

**29**   This is a language neither living nor dead but lived-in-the-last-instance.

**30**   This is an immanent language: because the theorems on the idiom of the One belong to this idiom or constitute its statements.

# An intelligible kingdom of thought

Philosophy is always possible: it suffices, as is always the rule, to give a philosophical definition. Like the famous "argument", it concludes its existence from its essence. Whether in the passage of its death, under the sign of the end, threatened by completion or substitution, it is never false: this is a triviality in all eras, all philosophies; a statement which is congenital here. As such it is useless to protest otherwise or to brandish a banner in support: it suffices to philosophize afresh. But if we always philosophize in order to take up the challenge of the declared ruin or death of philosophy, "inflating" the play and the combat, then it is thus in the secret hope of dying a little later, after oneself and for posterity. The philosopher consumes the past, complains about the present, hates the future and refuses birth. He does not cease to inherit, all the while refusing to give birth to new thinkers: instead he cedes his own philosophy and wishes to create and form disciples to receive it. He thinks in terms of heritage—for himself and sometimes for others—not of birth; he cedes his taste for death, not for life—his terrible pathos of survival and combat…

A non-philosophy postulates that there will always be philosophy, not because philosophy has not died or has survived, but because what is essential for it is *that it is*—by definition of its own posture or by internal postulation. The death of philosophy is as small a problem for non-philosophy as the death of physical phenomena or mathematical beings is as the problem of physics or mathematics. *There are* such phenomena, *there is* philosophy—it postulates this to be able to exercise itself. It thus no longer *forges* hypotheses on its essence, history, future, ends, genesis, "epochs" any more than it would declare inauguration or closure, manifesting here its authoritative character more than its real authority. These questions are insoluble, either because they give place to vicious or antinomic (philosophical) solutions, or because they register the attempt to destroy philosophy by the existing sciences ("human" sciences but not only human) which claim to clash with it. But that they are insoluble in this double manner is not a sufficient and motivating reason for non-philosophy. The positive reason is that it makes philosophy into a *phenomenon* in the double sense of this word. In one sense, it treats it in a radically pragmatic spirit – philosophy having no sense for it other than when it falls into a usage ruled like a simple phenomenon having no sense in itself or through its essence. On the other hand it is treated in an equally radically theoretical spirit, philosophy needing to be only manifested or phenomenalized under the conditions of the *phenomenon as such*, which is to say the phenomenon in its identity: the radical immanence that forms the One-in-One or the vision-in-One.

It thus does not have to define itself through its situation on the philosophical scene, its site, its neighborhoods and bearings; to ensure its markings, define its allies or adversaries in the supposed combat it must take up against its neighbors and for its survival as "authentic" or even "modern" philosophy, or even "post-modern" or even "scientific", etc. Rather it is obligated, in a certain sense, to take notice of a resistance that is not "philosophical" but *of* philosophy, rather than of neighboring adversaries; to defend itself against the falsifications regulated by that which this resistance responds to and which are, it must be noted, *philosophical re-normalizations rather than deviations.* Actual proper names have been suggested, philosophies evoked, which are such poles of resistance and which only sometimes appeal to immanence in order to finally refuse it. These normalizations are philosophical masks of non-philosophy. We must, against all this confusion, proceed to the recognition of their identity or their status as philosophies even when they bring themselves to the limits of philosophy and when they do not speak a word about their secret desire to kill it and to cede the tragi-comedy of this death to posterity.

Let us assume that poetry must be relieved of its overly grand tasks sometimes assigned to it by contemporary philosophy and, as always, let us generalize in the "non-Euclidean" style: why would philosophy itself not be relieved, undoubtedly against its will, of the overly new tasks that thought discovers, and discovers more than it makes do with sensing them? "Relieved", yes, but rather than a philosophical relief of poetry or such and such other system, an explication of philosophy and its mechanisms linked to the emergence of metaphysics. The experience of thought is only the most emergent when it stops intervening —so naively in fact that we hesitate to remark on it—in empiricisms. What would philosophy be for if not *forcing the decision* while thought would be more fecund if it ordered the Real, in-the-last-instance at least?

It is not the role of the most minimal and most real experience of thought to fix objectives and to fulfill ends, the health of the soul, the therapy of philosophy, the contemplation of truth, the revolutionary idea, all ends with which philosophy is occupied. The attempts to eliminate finality—Spinoza, Nietzsche, Heidegger—have repeated philosophy as their cause, still constitutive and sufficient. Only a thought of vision immanent "in" One rather than simply of "what is" can purge thought of philosophy's ends. Philosophy has so much demanded its own dignity that we will say without reservation, considering its ends and its masks, its opportunism, its pathos of the "inactual" or to the contrary its being-in-terms-of-the-tradition, that all this comprises a certain indignity.

With the vision-in-One, non-philosophy is the experience of the passage from philosophical teleology to a science-thought. Discovered, rather than becoming, in a kingdom of *Intelligence*, a *continent of thought* which is nothing without the most profound order of the vision-in-One as immanent "mystique". What is finally implied in the vision-in-One or what can be deduced from it? The discovery of the new dimension of a *language intelligible because it is seen-in-One-in-the-last-instance*, and in which all empiricisms can "translate themselves" into one another without philosophically and sterilely dividing each other in two. A universal dictionary of knowings, a dictionary "without-encyclopedia", if you will, rather than a still exterior compossibility.

The discovery of the "Intelligence"-continent is not in contradiction with the vision-in-One. Vision-in-One is not an intuition—precisely not an intuition—and the problem of its ineffability or not only arises through insufficient analysis. Vision-in-One is philosophically ineffable because it is thinkable, or rather utilizable, axiomatically. It conditions the order of thought but only in its reality and its rigor, though affording it a relative autonomy. It demands that science and philosophy participate now in an equal manner, inside a dual unity, in this constitution. It is simply that the cause of this identity cannot be confused with the ingredients and the form of thought, as would be the case if, for example, instead of submitting mathematical discoveries to this identity with philosophy, transcendental identity or identity coming from elsewhere, we instituted them as this cause: a supplementary idealism. Vision-in-One without a doubt forbids an absolute autonomy of the thinkable on pain of idealism and philosophical sufficiency, but it also protects the thinkable from an abusive impingement of the empirical, and the Real from a vicious reduction to the thinkable. Non-philosophy has no identifiable effect outside of its immanent exercise, which is to use philosophy and science to render thought adequate to the *jouissance* of an eternal or immanent "life".

# 6 THE CONSTITUTION OF THE NON-PHILOSOPHICAL ORDER

## SECTION I: ANALYTIC OF PHILOSOPHICAL DECISION

## Structure, layers, or levels of Philosophical Decision

If the preceding chapters have dealt with the theoretical hypothesis of non-philosophy, this one deals with the preparation of non-philosophy's object or domain with a view to being able to *test out* that hypothesis—insofar as it can be tested. Non-philosophy resolves the paradox of being identically pure-transcendental and experimental, and of producing explicative knowledges *of* and *for* philosophy.

Given the technical nature [*technicité*] of this chapter, which presents some aspects in a combinatorial construction, we will progressively introduce the following abbreviations (which are also, as we have just said, the letters or symbols of first names or of a conceptual symbolism from which they are used in a non-philosophical regime).

PhD: Philosophical Decision.
G: Givenness.
P: Position.
DT: Distance (the essence of transcendence).

AP: Auto-Position (auto-positioning).
AG: Auto-Givenness (auto-giving).
NAG/P: Non-auto-giving/positioning
FT: Force-(of)-thought
DLI: Determination-in-the-last-instance

More local symbols or those designating specific a prioris will be introduced in due course: for example T (transcendence); P (position in the strict sense of a plane); U (unity); etc.

With the force-(of)-thought, we have cleared the (aprioristic) transcendental sphere between Real and effectivity. What remains is to describe the aprioristic sphere between force-(of)-thought and effectivity, to manifest the non-philosophical identity of philosophy, for example the identity of "Ontological Difference". This work excludes the possibility of a simple dissolution of philosophy and its amphibologies, whose consistency non-philosophy postulates, in contrast to philosophies of "radical immanence". The identity-(of)-mixture of mixture will thus be the first form of material, the material form itself, given "facing" the force-(of)-thought. But, in order to arrive at this point, it is necessary to pass through philosophy. The force-(of)-thought is the theoretical instrument of philosophy's non-philosophical transformation. It is only an organon, the force of decision-making, itself determined in-the-last-instance by the Real. This force does bring with it any material and less still any differences within any material. If philosophy is this material, it must be analyzed within all of the *de jure* dimensions of its structure, as "Philosophical Decision", independently of any particular realization but oriented *de jure* toward one such realization. One such description, formal but not empty, must bring the distinct and significant layers of determinations to light, in order to give them to the force-(of)-thought: significant insofar as, without one of them, Philosophical Decision no longer exists; qualitatively distinct in terms of their degree of autonomy or dependency, as if they concerned "independent" or concrete and "dependent" or abstract parts. With the reservation that this autonomy or dependency cannot be rigorously unilateral or absolute, but relative in any case in relation to the "whole" of Decision as alone being concrete and independent. We will say that Philosophical Decision is the Idea of *a relative-absolute whole*. Its most encompassing and least detailed mechanism can in effect be described—and we have done so here and there—as a structure in 2/3 terms, as a Dyad + One, as an empirico-transcendental mixture, a quasi-circular and topological doublet, etc.

Here we have some invariants that are diversely exemplified or initiated, respected or truncated, deconstructed or simply repressed, etc. It is evident that most philosophies *appear* not to present this form expressly; that some appear more "pure" than "blended", more "topographical" than "topological", more 'structural" than "transcendental", more dualist than monist, etc. But on one the hand, Philosophical Decision is already a particularly manifest description of philosophical structure, claimed by philosophy itself when it strives to show itself in its purity or to affirm itself *as such* independently of ends, objects and models taken from the regional spheres of experience (sketches or fragments of this description exist in Plato, Leibniz, Kant, Fichte, Hegel, Nietzsche, Heidegger and their contemporary disciples). More generally it only takes a *de jure supplementary interpretation* in terms of this structure for whatever doctrine to manifest these invariants and their structural-transcendental mechanisms in turn. One such meta-philosophical interpretation is in fact possible, necessary *de jure*, having overcome the narcissism of such a system that assumes itself to be absolute and to be alone in possession of the thought of the "true" Real, a narcissism that nothing obligates a posture of the scientific type to follow. In effect no philosophical system exists and in fact none is thinkable outside of a supplementary interpretation (the "philosophical critique" of philosophy) and this is *de jure* made once as the only point of view of the supposedly irreducible multiplicity and continuity of systems, which is to say the philosophical *tradition*, outside of which they have neither existence nor essence, neither death nor life. Two philosophical decisions are distinct from one another, but are inseparable and mutually give each other meaning, in a manner that is certainly more or less global and pertinent, but never without reciprocal reduction. The law of continuity and equally the principle of indiscernibles are reconciled when they are invested in the philosophical tradition as such, and consequently in the structure of Philosophical Decision. This concept, only admissible if this "traditional" multiplicity of the philosophies is taken into account, is a first universalization of philosophy beyond the forced givenness [*donation factice*] of such a system and its narcissistic pretensions: the first form of *Philosophy*, undoubtedly not yet its most radical identity. It is an a priori: it remains ambiguous depending on whether it is philosophy or non-philosophy describing and using it.

In the architecture of Decision taken as an invariant, we will distinguish five layers of determinations, which are themselves complex and will come to play for us, within non-philosophy, the role of guiding principle, played by the table of judgments in Kant's *Critique*, for example.

*The essence, considered in its form, of the PhD, i.e. its real core* (or claimed by philosophy as real). Insofar as philosophy exploits "transcendence" and even "Being" in an prioritizing and dominant manner, this will also be the essence of transcendence or Being in their philosophical experience: this essence is the *Auto*, that is to say the idea of an absolute autonomy of *Philosophy* under the form of a circle, of a return to itself, such that it appeared within the dimensions of Auto-Givenness and Auto-Position which we will see are fundamental for Philosophical Decision.

*The essence, considered in its contents, of PhD, i.e. its transcendental core* (or claimed as such). These contents shelter a dyad of determinations combined according to varied but always mixed relations of *identity and difference*, that is to say the predicables or reflexive concepts that may serve to describe Decision. Other essential traits derive from these two and explain: a) Decision's divided and so doubled, redoubled nature, its nature as doublet (a double, a stand-in, etc.), specularity and speculations; b) its hierarchical nature, with its attached operations: inversion, reversal, return, about-turn, turning, etc. So we will consider that these traits (absolute autonomy, identity, difference, doublet, hierarchy) share in the *essence* of decision, even if its essence and existence are not separable and form the circle of a system or reciprocally determine each other excepting some "gaps".

*The two dimensions of PhD or the possible conditions of existence of its essence.* Here again is a dyad of determinations: the givenness of Decision determined by itself as a result or Auto-Givenness; its position determined by itself or Auto-Position. Givenness and position are as though two dimensions of PhD; they are not dissociable or exclusive except by means of abstraction. Separately they are "unilateral" intra-philosophical interpretations, either idealist ("Fichtean") or phenomenological. Decision cannot be reduced only to the activity of auto-position or only to auto-givenness. Hence the demand of the dyadic style of philosophy by philosophy's dyadic style and so the demonstration of the necessary existence of a pre-philosophical presupposition, semi-empirical and semi-philosophical ("pre-comprehension", "general concepts", "ontological plane"), which is destined to be or to become philosophical; which is "implicitly" given, "in-itself", "as limit", but which must be "posited", etc.

*The specific a priori*s *that arise from these two dimensions, a priori*s *deemed "dimensional".* From its side of "Auto-Givenness", philosophy is thus given (in to itself) a first time under the form of a relatively contingent and exterior *extra-philosophical*, then a second time given *itself* under a semi-empirical form (and not purely empirical), and re-given a third time, but this time by and for itself. As such, Auto-Givenness signifies that philosophy is, in a way to be determined each time, its own presentation, its own offer and givenness; that, for example, sketched out as a "need" in experience or within the World, it alone would be able to bring itself to manifestation and expression. It entails a difference and contains the duality: 1) of a givenness of any empirico-regional given whatsoever or a *real* transcendence, with which it implicitly identifies; and 2) of a the givenness of the philosophical itself, in its specificity in relation to every other type of existence or as an Idea not given in experience, but as an Idea itself given in a still exterior and transcendent way. 3) This divided givenness itself occurs throughout the unity of philosophy alone (conforming to the essence of Philosophical Decision). Thus as one-Auto-Givenness (3) of extra-philosophical or regional givenness (1) and of pre-philosophical givenness (2). The a priori of givenness (1) may be called "Affection"; that of givenness (2) may be called "Reception"; that of givenness (3) may be called "Intuition". In any case, we will say that regardless of these categories, philosophy is *de jure* inseparable from an *auto-givenal* [auto-donationnelle] dimension and that this includes three a prioris.

As for Auto-Position—once isolated from the layer of the *Auto* or essence, and without confusing it with this layer as is still the case when it is generally spoken of as "Auto-Position"—it more properly designates the dimension of ideal transcendence, of objectifying activity over itself, of auto-formation, auto-production, *of* Philosophical Decision (at once an objective and a subjective "of"). Position, in this sense, like givenness elsewhere, is *form*, not devoid of a real object like logical form, but a priori form, endowed with a transcendental claim (distinct from "transcendental givenness") and with a value "for" experience, meaning for itself too, for philosophy given in the contingent state of presupposition. The "position" in this broad sense is the objectification of philosophy itself, Decision's auto-objectification, and consequently involves those a prioris which are always by and for philosophy. In effect, it in turn contains three a priori moments: the position of transcendence in the sense of exteriority (1); the position in the sense of a philosophical plane, of the philosophical base (2); the one-Auto-position (3) of these two positions in a dyad. The concept of position is no longer limited, then, to designating position (1) or (2) but takes on a more rigorous generality as (3) or as Autoposition and a concretion that is less empty or formal, like position (1) and (2). Position (1) could still be called "Transcendence"; position (2) "Plane", a position properly so-called or in the strict sense; position (3) "Unity".

Each of the sides or dimensions of Decision's existence is thus in turn structured by Decision as Dyad + One and acquires concretion. It is tempting, if we follow Kant on this without pursuing the analysis, to posit a triplicity of position opposing a unicity of givenness, but the auto-reflexive structure of Decision complicates this analysis. Strictly speaking, it involves distinguishing three a priori structures of Autoposition and three of Autogivenness. It is thus by an abstraction or an idealist decision, a premature end to analysis, that philosophy's essence is reduced in general to a single triplicity (dialectic or differential), to the side of position or to that of givenness.

*The terms (regional, categorical, transcendental) that effectively individuate essence and the* a priori*s within which they exist.* These are representational invariants, quasi-"symbols" that function throughout a system or tradition. These terms are also linguistic generalities that assume prior individuation of Philosophical Decision by its essence and forms. They are in turn always philosophizable; the machine of Decision is always able *de jure* to be recast in their name, and to produce in and with them a new specifically philosophical *sense* intended to "fulfill" them more or less intuitively.

Essence traverses, encompasses, and conditions the two dimensions, along with their a prioris, even if these are given to it in some manner or another and bring to philosophy the supplement of existence which is not confused at all with essence and its components of identity and difference (doublet, hierarchy, etc.). The essence of transcendence in a philosophical regime possesses a primacy, priority *and* hierarchy over the dimensions and over the a priori, but essence is concretely co-determined by them from the point of view of its existence. Witness and surety of the absolute autonomy of Decision, it is itself more autonomous than the dimensions that depend on it, than their a prioris and the terms that depend on the two preceding layers at least for their sense or philosophical usage, but which are necessary and without which essence and a priori would be abstractions outside of any condition of empirical and linguistic existence. These relations of unilateral dependence are thus partially reversible, Decision being globally (excepting some gaps) a circular system (in the transcendental and not empirical mode), a relative-absolute machine. That there is always, for example, a given base and an activity over itself in whatever philosophy signifies that they for the most part determine each other reciprocally, with more or less displacement by one another.

This sketch remains schematic but will suffice to create very complex problems during the passage to non-philosophy.

# Mechanism of Philosophical Decision in terms of givenness of the extra-philosophical

We have made extra-philosophical's givenness an a priori of PhD. Not only because this is the manner in which philosophy treats the inevitable problem of the non philosophical, so much so that it is on this point that what distinguishes "non-philosophy" from the philosophical concept of the "non philosophical" will show most clearly. But also because if PhD must be the most universal structure of philosophy, it must be able to account for themes like intentionality and the noetico-noematic relation. If the historical combinations of philosophy and regional knowings are innumerable, they will nonetheless need to respond to an invariant within Philosophical Decision itself, to the relations applicable *de jure* for the multitude of philosophers.

1) Philosophy does not know the absolute singularity that falls under "life" or certain sciences, but the ideality of *Singularity* (*Day*, *Night*, *Impression*, *Sensation*). The problem of the extra-philosophical is in reality that of idealizations destined to be philosophically seized again. Even the most radical alterity, which does not let itself be reduced to any impression, appears through a certain idealization of "this" (of the "particular being"), from which it hides, or of which it is a symptom.

2) There is a hierarchy—precisely already philosophical or circular—of the types of extra-philosophical idealizations, a hierarchy within universality and within concretion. Decision anticipates or tends a structural place for these "empirical" idealizations. In order of decreasing universality:

a) Linguistic idealization that is universal. We can no longer say this and above all we cannot say that it is *total*, a thesis which already assumes a philosophical reinterpretation of the function of language. The co-belonging of any layer whatsoever of language and Philosophical Decision is solely concrete and undivided, so much so that this universality of the "language" element is instead one of the conditions that make the project of philosophy's "totality" possible. Moreover, linguistic idealization is insufficient and only plays a role through the medium of another idealization, that of science, but not of just any science: of logic (even when the "logical mirror" is "broken" or logic is 'swallowed up in the whirlpool of anguish"), formal and/or transcendental logic. Linguistic idealization is most often a universal and necessary but negative condition of philosophy, sometimes a more positive condition, in particular when logical *telos* is replaced by a poetic or ludic *telos* ("language games").

b) Empirico-perceptual idealizations that are made between the universal of language and a usage that treats them as implicitly scientific or pre-scientific before being pre-philosophical. "Day-Night" is already a system of idealities sustained by a whole cosmological knowing destined to take scientific form.

c) Idealizations empirically or deductively validated as universal, whether local or regional: those of science, still otherwise universal than that of language since they are regional and relatively closed or enclosed while the idealization of science is more open and tends "naturally" toward the fundamental. The introduction of science forms a system with the logical organon.

d) Equally regional idealizations that are received within philosophy itself as more concrete than the sciences: art, technics, ethics, etc.

All these types of idealizations enter *de jure* into Decision and contribute to determining and reactivating it and not only to "incarnating" it, to "realizing" it, etc. They enter into it as anticipated in necessary functions and as variable contents according to variously proportioned blends which seem to obey a certain invariance. It seems that the relationship to science, to the sciences of everyday [*mondains*] or "empirical" objects, is the most fundamental: science is at the same time universal like language and concrete like art, perception, etc.; it touches language through logic and touches the concrete of the World through perception. So much so that philosophy itself thematizes its relation to science as more funda-mental than its relation to art or ethics, except in "deconstructing" it by "drawing" linguistic idealization toward poetry (Heidegger) or toward ethics (Wittgenstein, Derrida) rather than toward science (even though the horizon of the logical organon will only be pushed back or repressed). Decision is that playground, that *de jure* oscillation between these limits: it does not confuse itself with the spontaneous use of language, perception, science, but with their mid-place, mi-lieu, or their between-two, and it is often a certain blend of science and Philosophical Decision that, as a center of gravity, fulfills and determines that between-two by ensuring the possi-bility of knowledge or rigorous use of these extremes.

3) The extra-philosophical is a necessary reference for Decision; the latter needs the former but not vice versa, at least in principle and except in furtively surreptitiously anticipating philosophy in the extra-philosophical. In what measure does it determine Decision itself? This is the essential problem of a *philosophical intentionality of... the extra-philosophical and pre-philosophical*, a complex problem that must be broken down. a) The philosophical universal (the "general", not yet the "total") is the Dyad's unity or plane, the fact that two terms are given, and so a universal. The

latter does not confuse itself with extra-philosophical idealizations with which it nonetheless maintains a necessary relation. We call a priori the philosophical universal in order to distinguish it from generalities or empirical "legalities". The a priori is the object of an *acquistito orginaria*; it is acquired "over", "from" the empirical universal or "begins with" it but does not at all "derive" from it. The a priori therefore assumes a cause that is not only *meta*-empirical or *meta*-physical but *transcendental*, that assures it its irreducibility to these idealizations that remains ontic generalities. b) Initially the a priori as Dyad-form is given as confused with empirical generalities, in particular scientific ones; it is still only implicitly philosophical when philosophy takes a regional datum and uses it as a factum, as a "rational fact". The rational fact is ambiguous and designates the state of prime confusion of the a priori and its incarnation in the contrived [*factices*] idealizations which philosophy needs but is unable to produce. So it is only the a priori's form in itself that does not exist any longer for itself; the philosophical universal is presupposed but it is still a form whose content is borrowed; a form that will only receive proper content, the a priori *as such*, when it is "extracted" from this dross. This will be *a metaphysical or specifically philosophical* a priori; it separates itself from its borrowed incarnation and manifests itself within a field proper to philosophy. c) What is the mechanism of the two universals' relations, the empirical and the aprioristic; what is the organon of the a priori passing from one state to the other? The a priori can only be freed up as such or as philosophical because there is a hierarchy where the two universals are taken together, identified and distinct at the same time, and because this hierarchy is overturned. The empirical universal does not remain only "empirical"; it is anticipated and captured by the structure of Decision, by the Dyad as hierarchy, so much so that retroactively or afterwards it gives itself *as empirical* for aprioristic reasons or for insertion into this structure (so that it constitutes an autonomous order, for example that of science which affirms its autonomy by subsisting and by producing other knowledges), but as a dominant empirical, as the first given. This primacy of the empirical assumes a hierarchy, but this is a philosophical or aprioristic hierarchy that itself is about to reverse its dominant side: in reality it is only structured as such implicitly by the Dyad. This is thus the dyad-state of the two universals' relations: (dominant) empirical Universal / (dominated) aprioristic Universal.

   In order that the a priori, at first concealed within the depths of experience, be manifested as such, it is necessary and it suffices to overturn this hierarchy, but to overturn it philosophically, so to displace it as much as overturn it. An *organon* is necessary for this specifically philosophical operation which must go past a simple sterile inversion of agents in their places. This organon thus must contain or bring *a supplement of alterity* to the alterity already contained in the Dyad that remains limited and stabilized under this form, incapable of overturning domination by the empirical. So this is to overturn the dyad-state in the name of the dyad, of its ability [*puissance*] as alterity, but by consequently remaining within the universal, meaning within the aprioristic universal that is the essence proper to the Dyad, a dominated essence but which now takes the dominant place or is manifested as such. Nevertheless this force of alterity or reversal is not sufficient to constitute a true philosophical organon itself alone. Left to itself, it is a pure violence and a terror which could only want itself and destroy the hierarchy in the end by using it for its own advantage. This supplement of alterity—the Other itself as essence proper to the a priori—must then be carried, localized, emplaced by the Real, either by the One or ultimate Unity which Philosophical Decision adds to the Dyad and which, with the Other, forms its transcendental "motor". This *Other-as-One* is none other than the essence of the *transcendental* a priori, at once the most pure universal and the universal most irreducible to empirical generalities. It is the organon that ensures the onward march of Decision and the passage from domination by one universal to that of the other. We will thus reformulate the complete state of Dyad and no longer its dyad-state or given state in order to understand its becoming, meaning its overturning: a Dyad (empirically given but in itself a priori) here comprises the One/Dyad or a priori (including the supplement of alterity + One). This new hierarchy is automatically inverted, thanks to the transcendental a priori, in favor of the Dyad as such, which is to say the a priori as such or *metaphysical.*

4) What usage does philosophy then make of regional idealizations or of the extra-philosophical? Through which state does the extra-philosophical move? This consists in describing, correlatively to philosophical noesis whose mechanism we have just seen, the noema, insofar as it is what becomes the extra-philosophical in this operation. Philosophy does not so much predetermine the types of idealization as their precisely "philosophical" usage and status. Philosophy "decides", within certain limits, to inscribe itself within the undecidable universality of language and science, within the variously proportioned limits of their idealities, which it assumes and receives as "in themselves" or real-objective, but ends by determining as "only empirical" or "only ontic" and by arranging them for its usage and service. Philosophy chooses science rather than art, etc., or this science rather than that one, for semi-empirical, semi-transcendental reasons but in itself determining their pre-philosophical meaning after the fact. What does the extra-philosophical become in this process?

Take the case of science: philosophy relates itself to what it calls *Science* through a determined empirical theory that, for philosophy, is assumed to be the essence of *Science*. It anticipates and retrospects its material and raises it to the status of the essential model of thought; it generalizes from *a* theory to science's essence, and sometimes to every science therefore confined in a forced encyclopedia. Through what mechanism does one pass from *a* science to *Science*? By passing from the empirical universal to the philosophical or a priori universal: the former was the incarnation of the latter but the latter is the soul or essence of the former; undoubtedly it no longer simply confuses itself with the empirical, but, freed from it and having become essence, it intentionally aims toward it, carries it with itself and communicates to it the potentiality of the essence that it is. So much so that in this passage, empirical theory loses domination but, by delegation, receives the a priori in whose service it is now the seal of essence, counterpart to its being-dominated.

This is a fragile acquisition: only the a priori itself rather than a theory is science's *essence*; but the a priori is finally only the essence of *science* in a contingent way. A particular theory is "of" science but is not essence; an a priori is essence but is not "of" science. This is the real content of what Kant called "a priori knowledges" and the synthetic: it is the perpetual motor of philosophy or its "black box": postulating an impossible identification, assumed but not given, of opposites, consequently being only a "technologically" sprung amphibology rather than a real identity. This critique is evidently already underway in non-philosophy. Whatever it may be, an extra-philosophical given is never essence or a priori but "becomes" such in serving as a support or vehicle of the a priori with which it looks to confuse itself, whereas the a priori cannot not manifest itself as such except on the condition of residing in the depths of experience and emerging theatrically. It is distinct and inseparable from this theory and from any empirical legality; this is why the empirical legality continues to co-determine the a priori essence of science. A theory, a particular sequence of knowledge, is posited as a priori essence when taken as incarnation thereof, and when this a priori essence recasts or internalizes it—two complementary operations that are strictly speaking each impossible, but whose impossibility gives philosophy its movement.

Whatever it may be, the metamorphosis of regional and local theory by Decision's noema is not yet finished. In the "metaphysical" passage to the a priori as such, this theory is subjected to a first philosophical generalization; it becomes essence only as *universal*. But the motor of Decision, the transcendental a priori or the Other-as-One, has yet to complete its work. It in turn claims to be the essence of Philosophical Decision's auto-position, essence of the a prioris themselves, or of essentialities. So much so that such a theory is first posited as essence within the movement of the metaphysical a priori and reposed or put forth a second time as essence within the movement of the transcendental a priori. Neither is it any longer only the universal of *Science* but the totality of science for the sciences, at least the virtual project of this totality that only empirical limitations prevent from self-realizing as such under the form of an encyclopedia or a circle of sciences assumed to be complete *de jure*. The equation: a theory = Science = the sciences, is mediated by the magical apparatus of Decision. So much so that every philosophy from its perspective requires *de facto* a determined science, or even an isolated empirical knowledge, but thinks in return *for* all the sciences or appears as "absolute science".

There are nevertheless at least two divergent kinds of solutions. The primary or raw given, in each case autonomous within its order, is only accepted by Decision on the condition of also being also anticipated by it and being raised to the state of a "given", or an "empirical condition", etc. Strictly speaking it can itself serve as a symptom rather than a given when it shelters an otherness still more withdrawn or more irreducible to the philosophical than itself. It thus insists as limit and even as beyond limit. Philosophical anticipation must then always raise itself higher and further up over the given; it internalizes or rationalizes exteriority more and more, but this is a *non philosophical* that delimits the philosophical from the exterior but that we do not see, or whose effects we no longer see other than inside Decision's circle. Decision traces the limits through or from the interior from where they can see, without reaching, the beyond-limit [*outre-limite*]. From its perspective this non philosophical feeds on new "reals" that are extra- or pre-philosophical and which Decision reappropriates for itself by remodeling itself and by expressing a new philosophy each time through transcendental scissiparity. It belongs to the logic of philosophical mixture either to be a certain auto-position of itself and without remainder, or to tolerate a remainder and to still be an auto-position but repressed as peripheral, undermined, solicited, etc., by this non philosophical residue in a state of permanent flight.

5) What is the essence of the philosophical and the extra-philosophical, noetico-noematic correlation in a wider, ultra-phenomenological sense of these words? Philosophical mixture includes the non philosophical, even the extra-philosophical. In its most "empiricist" state Decision identifies itself with one such given which from its perspective unilaterally distinguishes itself from Decision: it is absolutely indifferent to it by origin, relatively indifferent by function. This is the general structure of the noetic-noematic correlation, asymmetrical and bipolar. *The identification of the*

*noesis with the noema that it aims for, as we have seen, is assumed given without being elucidated because it is* de jure *hidden or only functions within dissimulation or opacity.* Philosophy pursues one essential end, realizing itself, affirming itself, but does not pursue the task of rigorously elucidating itself. It is essential for philosophy that it make itself touch itself within a limit or the length of a limit and a becoming rather than *within* or *by* the radical immanence of an identity, the philosophical and the "non philosophical" at best, the philosophical and the "pre-philosophical" at worst.

Philosophy's essence is this *opaque identity*, this *black immanence* of a technological box or of "difference". An identity that houses a difference and so a relative indifference between contents of empirical and philosophically designated idealizations. This relative indifference or semi-indifference is then reflected in the operation of the a priori that distinguishes itself as such from its confusion with the empirical; Decision exceeds the empirical to make what it calls an "object". It is then reflected in the transcendental organon, in the Other-as-One, which in turn supports this relationship of indifferent identity with the a priori. The system of black identity reproduces at every stage and causes the amphibology with which it confuses itself to migrate from one layer of Decision to the other. This identity with included and divided indifference (bilateral, from the extra-philosophical to the philosophical and vice versa) forms the real content of what here and there we have described as a philosophical hierarchy. Philosophy *needs* the indifference of science (for example), and reciprocally only philosophy's indifference to science allows this to be posited as essence. There is "dialectic" internal to identity, internal to difference, internal to their combination. This dialectic is born from transcendental identity's non elucidation for itself, and from the indifference for itself, which is to say in terms of identity. Philosophical identification does not reach real identity but remains paralyzed in indifference; indifference does not reach its own identity but remains paralyzed in reservation and identification. The black box only offers an indifference through opacity and technological secrecy, a mystery through a lack of identity's manifestation *such as it is.* Philosophical Decision only knows identity by blocking it; it only thematizes it on the condition that philosophical speech represses it. And it only knows indifference as a formal indifference or universal, that of form to content, not yet that of the Real in the mixture of form and content, in the mixture of philosophy and science. Even in the most universal and most "transcendental" structures of Decision, empiricism continues to form a system with formalism. The ultimate form of these relations is precisely *the noetico-noematic relation as mixture*, as a circle or even as a simple parallelism resulting from a circle that is truncated or broken in the middle. Internalizing noesis "of" noema and vice versa; the aim is twice objective, auto-positional, in lieu of only being objective once; the noema is twice object (empirical and ideal) in lieu of only being object once. It is this useless complexity that will be reduced or "simplified" under the form of the noetico-noematic relation's new "non-philosophical" state: as "simple", without reciprocal determination of noesis and noema, as non-autogivenal/positional. The new noetico-noematic relations will take the form of determination-in-the-last-instance; noesis and noema will be "identical" only under this form.

# On philosophy as non-philosophy's guiding thread

## In terms of the internal relations of Philosophical Decision

In order to resolve the problem concerning the order of presentation of non-philosophy's objects (an order that replaces that of general metaphysics and special metaphysics), we must have first elaborated the philosophical given, under the most universal and most invariant form in which it can present itself—"Philosophical Decision", a structure combining a Dyad and an immanent *and* transcendent unity in the Dyad. This is the concrete structure of the categories of "mixture", "amphibology", and of "antinomy", of "auto-position" which we use here and there, but always understood on the model of Philosophical Decision. How does this function now?

The philosophical triad is not dismembered when it is offered to the vision-in-One and to the force-(of)-thought. But it does not offer itself in its functioning in an indifferent way from just any perspective. There are three principal aspects within a decision: 1) the auto-positional circle and its modes or the existence of Decision's essence; 2) transcendence or Decision's ultimate essence; 3) the abstract moments or the a prioris specific to Decision. Does philosophy present itself primarily through transcendence, its essence, or through the mixed-form, its existence? This cannot concern choice or exclusion. The mixture-form is not a form... formal, without relation to Decision's particular moments. This is a transcendental form blended together in these moments and conditioning them. It does not present itself, then, as first without giving itself as insepa-rable from Decision, for a moment at least, undoubtedly a moment that is also abstract from the point of view of Decision's existence, but which is the essence or determining force of Decision: transcendence. Under whatever form we take it, transcendence is the heart of Decision and what conditions it as auto-position, and the mixture or auto-position is existence under which transcendence gives itself as Decision's essence. So we cannot choose between them; we must take them in their auto-presentation which is that of their correlation, and not imagine a general "naked" transcendence that would not be given by the experience of philosophy. Whomsoever thinks the presupposition of transcendence, for example perception, has already philosophized; whomsoever philosophizes has already presupposed transcendence. As soon as there is a project of thinking the Real, so a philosophy, philosophy presents itself as a correlation of essence and existence, which is not to say that there is not a certain asymmetry or hierarchy in this correlation. But, at first, this correlation of essence and existence within Philosophical Decision has as a consequence that non-philosophy will simultaneously produce itself as force-(of)-thought and as a priori of philosophical mixture itself or of the materials as such. From this point of view, the mix-form is not dismembered, annulled by a *real* negation, dissolved as a cloud without reality. It is only dualyzed, which is to say its sufficiency or its auto-position (what is it already is in itself) is suspended but it itself is conserved as an internal mechanism of Philosophical Decision. The mixture is sterilized once and for all without for all that being effectively destroyed. Its residue is the identity-(of)-mixture of the mixture: an identity that philosophical sufficiency cannot itself see since it is always at work within the mixture and under its own law, whereas non-philosophy isolates the mixture: no longer relatively under itself, but absolutely or "radically" under its a priori identity.

And yet this dualyzation of "mixed" form as pretension, sufficiency and resistance, cannot already be the work of the force-(of)-thought itself or in its form of transcendence but that of the transcendental element or (non-)One that acts within the force-(of)-thought. As transcendental, this element determines this residue that presupposes itself, and corresponds to the aspect of essence or determination in philosophy, and determines this other that is the a priori identity-(of)-mixture or -(of)-material that corresponds to philosophy's auto-presentation, existence or being-given. From this transcendental point of view, the force-(of)-thought and the reduced material are contemporaneous and the second, through their "common" transcendental stem, may find in the first its correlate and object. They are transcendentally destined—at least—one to the other.

But this identity is accompanied by their unilateral duality. In effect, a distinction is equally implied by the (non-)One or transcendental essence.

This distinction rests on the material of differences that structure philosophy's auto-presentation: on the one hand difference between essence and existence, as firsts alternatively and thus circularly, and on the other hand between those two and the most abstract and dependent moments of Philosophical Decision. What will become of them in non-philosophy, or rather what will they give place to under the impact of the (non-)One or the transcendental causality of the Real?

1) *The difference between essence and existence.* On the one hand the (non-)One takes back and transforms the *specific priority of essence* over existence, a priority put forth by philosophy, in a unilateral priority of the force-(of)-thought over material, the second aiming at the first as its simple correlate: in some sense its noetic dimension. On the other hand it takes back and transforms the *specific and complementary priority of existence* over essence, a priority put forth by philosophy, under the form of material as necessary correlate to which force-(of)-thought is bound: in some sense its noematic dimension. This explains, on the basis of their reciprocal philosophical relation, now exhausted in its two aspects, the destining of the force-(of)-thought to the material of mixture freed from its auto-position and its philosophical authority. Maybe we cannot say that the force-(of)-thought precedes the material-form in non-philosophy: this ambiguous formula may give rise to philosophical reinterpretation. Force-(of)-thought's priority over the material is of a real origin and has the form of a unilateral duality: it does not signify any idealist return to the primacy of activity over material as nature. If the force-(of)-thought, without first freeing itself (in the temporal and ontological or philosophical sense), possess the kind of priority of noesis or essence over the correlative form of material or noema, it must possess it in its transcendental insertion—not in it alone since this is also the case for the identity of material, but in what this transcendental essence transforms of philosophical priority respective to essence and existence, the one over the other.

2) *The difference between these and the most abstract or specific properties of Philosophical Decision.* It is on the double base of the force-(of)-thought and the material's a priori that non-philosophy chases after the manifestation of the a prioris specifically corresponding to the particular and dependent moments of Decision. These a prioris will also have a relation said to be of the specification of dimensions of force-(of)-thought, but they too will be structured, as modes of force-(of)-thought, by the noetico-noematic relation (transformed, such as the force-(of)-thought constitutes them in the non-phenomenological matrix).

# In terms of the layers of Philosophical Decision

The recourse to Philosophical Decision cannot content itself with the notion, although essential, of Auto-Position necessarily completed by that of Auto-Givenness. The analytic has brought to light a certain interlocking of layers of determinations that make the internal mechanism of Decision. We will inventory them by putting in parallel each time, as an announcement or even a reminder, that which the force-(of)-thought extracts from them as non-philosophy's constituents, which we will develop in more detail in the third section of this chapter.

*The transcendental* a priori. The "Auto (G/P)" essence of PhD is constituted by the One and Dyad of identity and difference. The One includes, under an abstract component or part, this Dyad, which is to say the Other in its given or incarnated state, not isolatable as such. The FT then extracts from this essence or its transcendental side (the real One being given and no longer the object of a non-philosophical operation) a transcendental residue (in the new sense of this word) that we know is first the FT itself. FT therefore presupposes itself but only from the point of view of its component of transcendence or distance (DT). DT is henceforth absolutely reduced as indivisible or NAP/G. It lets itself be determined by the One, without being able to auto-posit/give itself, as being this NAP/G distance. FT is the *transcendental* a priori of non-philosophy: but insofar as it is thought primarily through the perspective of its determination by the Real, thus as transcendental rather than as a priori.

Everything that the FT subsequently extracts from PhD comes under an operation at once (we will say this incessantly) of transcendental deduction and induction. What is extracted? Two kinds of determination: 1) first, the universal a priori of non-philosophy that it acquires from the corresponding universal a priori of philosophy; 2) the variety of aprioristic dimensions of non-philosophy that it acquires from the corresponding dimensions of philosophy. So we finally distinguish: a) the transcendental a priori (respective of PhD and non-philosophy) that has just been in question; b) the universal a priori (respective of PhD and non-philosophy); c) the dimensional a prioris (respective of PhD and non-philosophy).

*The universal* a priori. What is it that, from PhD, can give place primarily to a non-philosophical a priori which is no longer FT? It is the Dyad-form not as simply given but as universal a priori of philosophy. Once it is acquired (as it has just been) the FT that, under this angle, is rather the side of position, takes for an object the Dyad side of PhD. Non-philosophy thus develops in its turn, but never exclusively, the side of givenness. The principal interest, the privilege of givenness, is to contain the reference binding philosophy to experience, the fundamental to the regional, or even philosophy to itself as extra- or pre-philosophical. And yet this reference is the same thing as the dimension of the Dyad as universal a priori structure of PhD. In effect, isolated as such from the concrete of the transcendental a priori, the Dyad formed of identity and difference in general is a necessary internal relation in every philosophy, as it were, the ultra-phenomeno-logical form of the noetico-noematic relation. FT extracts in this way a new noetico-noematic relation of the NAP/G type, which is a mode of FT itself but equally, on its other side, of unilateral duality: the duality of the NAP/G Distance and the transcendental corresponds to the Dyad, and the NAP/G-distance corresponds, in the non-philosophical order, to the essence of the Dyad as Distance (AP) or Alterity.

*The dimensional* a priori. With FT developed as such in its identity and its universal noetico-noematic duality that implies reference to the material, we possess the essential structures of non-philosophy. The one and the other together form the complete structure of the identity-(of)-unilateral duality or of completed actualized determination-in-the-last-instance. We can go further in this description. PhD was already a first formalization of philosophy and comprised the reciprocally determining dimen-sions of givenness and position. Non-philosophy connects altogether otherwise givenness and position, without mimetically transferring their relations onto those of PhD. Every knowledge subsequently established under non-philosophy will be a mode of this aprioristico-transcendental structure. FT as duality is the essence of NAG a prioris, which is to say of knowledges established not on the philosophical Dyad in general but on its privileged function of given, and that derive from its aspect of duality. And the NAP a prioris will be every knowledge established not on the Other-as-One in general but on its privileged function of position which is that of the transcendental a priori, and which come under PT in its identity. This concerns describing, as modes of this double dimension, a variety of determinations that correspond to equivalent layers within philoso-phy's structure. We therefore distinguish the material or quasi intuitive dimension of givenness (with its a priori), and the formal or quasi logical dimension of position (with its a priori), to extract the philosophy-form that no more maintains this relation to the latter (to "experience") than to their material.

a) The dimensional a prioris: AG and NAG. These are the specific a prioris within which givenness functions as an affection of the extra-philosophical, as reception and as intuition. Givenness of the extra-philosophical is essential here, as we have seen, and codetermines philosophical auto-givenness and then, respectively, the NAG-givenness proper to non-philosophy. This requires moving from philosophy's "non philosophical" to the non-philosophical usage of philosophy, a usage of a *Generalized Transcendental Aesthetic*. The NAG a prioris are directly modes of the universal a priori and indirectly still modes of the transcendental a priori, and in both cases modes of FT according to the side from which each is convened.

b) The dimensional a prioris: AP and NAP. If givenness returns rather to the Dyad, position emerges rather from the side of the Other-as-One. Within PhD, the One does not occur alone and in an autonomous way, unless as an ontological entity assumed abstractly thematizable by this or that philosophy. It intervenes, precisely as "positing" under the form of three unequally autonomous functions that together constitute the "position" side where it is each time engaged in a campaign together with another "transcendental" (or with itself). These are the Other-as-One or the Other properly and specifically so-called, the Plane-as-One or position in the strict sense, finally Unity-as-One—in the sense of those formulae where the final One, which must be placed between parentheses, is only the transcendental impulse hidden in the a priori —not elucidated—without being itself a priori. These three functions are each modes of a circle of auto-position, which is their essence. We will distinguish in particular, always in philosophy's interior, the aprioristico-transcendental dimension of the Other-as-One that is the instrument of philosophical clearing of the a priori. From these a priori, FT in its turn extracts NAP a prioris: Other, Position, NAP-Unity, which are direct modes of FT as identity, and indirectly from its side of duality or universal a priori. From this angle, non-philosophy uses philosophy like a *generalized transcendental Logic*.

Of course any object or philosophical category, being structured in its philosophical sense by the whole of Philosophical Decision, may serve as a guiding *theme* for non-philosophy which will extract from it the corresponding a prioris. It is possible to treat philosophy on any of its levels, on those of Decision itself as we have done or on those of its most singular statements, what is essential is that their philosophical amplitude is first posited and identified.

# SECTION II: MECHANISMS OF PASSAGE TO NON-PHILOSOPHY

## Transcendental induction and deduction of the noetic aspect of the a priori

Non-philosophy is produced by the FT but as we have just seen, from the point of view of its material and its usage of the former, needs a guiding thread constituted by the preceding analytic of PhD. The "passage" of philosophy to non-philosophy is identically, but-in-the-last-instance, a transcendental deduction of the second carried out by the FT, from the perspective of its identity, and a transcendental induction from the PhD and always carried out by the FT but from the perspective of its duality. In each case it is not a passage of the philosophical kind, meaning by continued or topological transformation.

The general principle is the following: between the One and philosophy— Philosophical Decision, in particular philosophy assumed "in itself" i.e. posed in and by its own sufficiency—there is no process of knowledge, only a foreclosure of the One sanctioned by a philosophical repression of the latter falsified from the outset as "philosophically unthinkable/thinkable". Their most general relation, that which establishes itself on the basis of this resistance such that the One can tolerate it, is determination-in-the-last-instance (DLI). This is *transcendental identity* (in-One and so from the point of view of the One) *of the unilateral duality* of philosophy and of this identity (so from the point of view of philosophy, of its relative autonomy or duality). Identity and duality no longer reform a philosophical synthesis. The identity or clone is in-One and is not properly speaking unilateral but unilateralizing. Duality is unilateral duality, at once through relative autonomy and through unilateralization, and yet it too is in-One or transcendental; it is no more synthetically reabsorbed by identity than identity is undermined by duality. Each is autonomous in its own way, one absolutely, the other relatively, and the latter thus being unilateralized by the former. This matrix is susceptible to two realizations or being put to work twice according to the aspect from which it is exercised. These aspects or "points of view" do not contradict or synthesize themselves. The relation of the two terms has its unity (in-the-last-instance) not in a third term but in the identity that is one of them. Not synthesis; the One does not form a number or a set with the Two. Undoubtedly identity as real, that of the One, is apparently distributed by duality, shared "between" it and the second term, but it is only "shared" from the point of view of duality—this is its clone—not at all in itself or in its reality. Identity is transcendental because of its real origin; duality is only transcendental and aprioristic.

The first concrete realization of this matrix happens from the point of view of transcendental identity, which takes from the dyad only its essence or its a priori that it extracts as simple or precisely as duality within the form of identity "NAG/P". This is of course the FT, which is also a duality but a duality grasped "in" its identity or from the point of view of the in-One. It assumes philosophy or transcendence as given, but it is not itself received or lived *as* a duality, but as "in-One" and as sufficiently manifested in this way. The FT is the transcendental a priori such as non-philosophy conceives it. Nevertheless, identity (of duality) does not exhaust the complete reality of FT, which has its own power of manifestation that it would be necessary to identify on the plane of concrete determinations of PhD.

The second realization of this matrix effectively happens from the point of view of the duality itself, of philosophy given at first through a dyad "opposite" [*en face*] the One and that *claims* to form a number or a set "with" the One because of the very fact that it has a certain reality that the One itself cannot intend to dissolve, that it ignores rather through a radical indifference but which it can limit through transcendental indifference, that of the FT. The point of view of the duality must then be considered as such, within its relative autonomy, by the fact of the existence of a resistance rather than through what philosophical resistance explicitly "thinks" and 'says' about the One. However, from this point of view, DLI manifests itself as a dual relation as such that, in order to establish itself, requires the level of the given other than the One or the level of the material. FT and the material as such, as we have said, both manifest as concrete modes of DLI, they are articulated within a duality and are both dualities, but one of them is manifested-in-One or its very transcendental essence and its duality not yet manifested in its specific mode, while the other—that of the material to the identity of FT—is manifested also as a duality in the mode proper to manifestation such that the material and what is extracted presents itself with the structure of a dual relation, for which we will pick up the phenomenological formula "noetico-noematic" or "double thematic". If in its identity the FT is the transcendental a priori of non-philosophy, this dual "relation" is the *universal* a priori and its role must be elucidated as soon as it concerns superseding the simple essence of PhD and respectively of FT, in order to pose the problem of the a priori in relation to experience.

What relation is there now between the two dimensions? If FT "represents" identity (transcendental and real respectively), and the noetico-noematic relation represents duality, as the two possible aspects of DLI, these two aspects cannot be contradictory or synthesizable, etc., but FT is precisely what determines-in-the-last-instance the materials under the form of a noetico-noematic duality. Undoubtedly this formulation expresses the point of view of identity, not at all that of duality or relative autonomy of the *material* that succeeds, in the structure of PhD, to the presentation of its essence or to transcendence. Yet, from this final point of view, transcendental identity, elicited in and drawn out of the One by transcendence as empirical occasion, is succeeded by a new cloning when the "inferior" or "particular" forms of the material, which follow transcendence, are taken explicitly as point of view. Cloning is identically the general mechanism of induction and deduction of progress in non-philosophy, and assumes philosophical materials and their relative autonomy. Here it is specified and modulated as a priori cloning—the a priori as clone—under the form of an a priori identity that is now essence as noesis of duality, or what gives form to this aspect of the duality and the bearing of a noesis (for example, "noesis" in the phenomenological sense, or philosophy in relation to science as extra-philosophical given, etc.).

We will therefore not say, without expanding and without passing through the FT, that in the universal a priori, noetico-noematic properly so-called, noesis determines-in-the-last-instance the noema. The level we actually speak of is only a dependant level of the FT, the FT alone being the concrete element of DLI. It is necessary then to "pass" through the FT in order to take in the universal non-philosophical a priori that structures all the particular determinations beyond simple transcendence. Noesis is a mode of the FT, the mode under which it announces the FT itself from the point of view of the most particular and most "concrete" material, insofar as it apparently enters into the duality posed with philosophy. It is the FT such that it does not manifest itself any longer only "in-One", but extracts itself from the PhD beyond simple transcendence and manifests from the latter. FT therefore determines the philosophical materials through the noetic mode it assumes or determines and noesis does not have another reality or essence in-the-last-instance than the FT, even if it still has another manifestation that comes under what is proper to duality. FT and noetico-noematic relation are identical in-the-last-instance or from the point of the view of the FT and are not separated, they are only such from the point of view of the datum of the mixture which demands that the FT presents itself as noesis that it is, if we can put it this way, "correlative".

If the FT enters then into a relation of the datum of a mixture, i.e. within duality, then it finally exercises itself under the form of the NAG/P a prioris of this mixture and it is modalized or specified not only by the universal a priori in general but by all of the dimensional a prioris extracted from the mixture and which still have the form, by definition, of the universal a priori. Concerning the FT-essence, in particular as DT-NAG/P, we can say that it is specified in a necessary although unilateral manner (if…) as noesis from an empirical origin and exercises itself through the dimensional a prioris that are themselves extracted from the mixture.

Strictly speaking—though the complexity of the task is considerable—if the blend "philosophy-of-X" (science, etc.) is the material from which the noesis is drawn or extracted, given that it is a mode of FT but that it appears more as reducible to or at least forming a duality with the undismembered mixture itself, noesis cannot appear as much in its content of support (not in its function) as under the forms composing the mixture, of the philosophy-of-X and not the only philosophy facing the X. But if noesis and noema are extracted not from philosophy alone but from the philosophy-of-X, then they are no longer taken from X such as it gives itself "in itself" but "in philosophy". The noetico-noematic relation thus associates and distinguishes not philosophy and X, not even philosophy and the philosophy-of-X, but the non-philosophical extracts, noetic and noematic, of philosophy-of-X.

# Transcendental induction and deduction of the noematic aspect of the a priori

Unified theory is the form or genre of thought adequate to the One or determined-in-the-last-instance by the Real. Why "unified"? It assumes on the one hand a material condition: the philosophical and the extra-philosophical rather than philosophy *and* itself a second time, even though we can in fact describe a unified theory of the *philosophical* and *a* particular philosophy that would play the role—the general role—of the extra-philo-sophical, the essential thing being the necessary reference to the latter. And on the other hand an aprioristico-transcendental condition, the FT, that determines this correlation of the philosophical and extra-philosophical in a unilateral duality. Of course this is the essential condition: that the intentional (spontaneous) philosophical correlation, "alleged" correlation, redoubled and contingent on philosophy and the X object or itself, be transformed by an aprioristic, necessary and objective identity, but from a pure-transcendental origin, that frees itself from the philosophy-form in order to take the form of a determination-in-the-last-instance.

Why do the content and the cause of non-philosophy take shape as a unified theory? The One demands, in the relation to experience and if it must be thought, an organon, a FT; this is transcendental and thus such that it must take an empirical object or assumes an occasional cause that can only be the undivided total of philosophy, i.e. the mixture rather than the impossible empirical totality of philosophy. This philosophy-form is such that it is always impregnated with an extra-philosophical given, variously regional on the one hand (science, art, etc.), universal element on the other hand (language). The One as cause is more able, if we can put it that way, than philosophy and now obligates it a priori to radically open itself, by an NAG/P identity and no longer through hierarchy, to the regional data of experience with which it was already, but only by its philosophical pretension, blended.

What is the internal mechanism of non-philosophy as unified theory? If, as transcendental, FT maintains a *de jure* relation of blends of philosophy and regional experience, blends that are at once contingent from the regional point of view and necessary from the point of view of philosophy, this relation is not itself of this mixed kind, it is a transcendental duality and thus 'simple'. But it can only maintain such a relation to this complex experience by extracting from it or manifesting an a priori-*(of)-experience*, to which it reduces auto-positional transcendence and the sufficiency of a philosophical origin. The internal object or the correlate of FT is neither PhD nor science (art, etc.) assumed as separated, "pure" or "in themselves"—in reality this still concerns philosophical hypotheses on the essence or the in-itself of things conceived as auto-position. This is their relation of identity and difference, but insofar as it is no longer paralyzed by its redoubling but takes a "simple" form or a form of NAG/P identity, that it inherited from FT.

In effect FT, not being a logico-transcendental synthesis of contradictions, but a pure transcendental identity (and) a duality, begins by reducing and "fixing" the spontaneous mixture (philosophical-and-extra-philosophical) as simple a priori form of every experience; by internally "identifying" a residue or a "mixture-form", residue of a relation that is indissoluble from now on and intrinsically indivisible and that, consequently, no longer itself falls under philosophical authority and division but for which it needs explication nonetheless. It frees from the relation-of-mixture that philosophy maintains for itself and within experience a stratification of dual a priori identities, neither synthetic nor analytic (etc.) but "dualytic". It does not destroy the mixture but only destroys its claim to constitute the essence of the most real and most rigorous thought. The mixtures, the hierarchies of philosophies-of… are indissoluble in a relative and contingent manner alone, "affirmed" meaning *alleged* but not legitimated. Non-philosophy can only substitute for them a necessary and objective connection on the condition of suspending this form of mixture, not absolutely but in its pertinence and as simple "support", and by extracting a simple a priori correlation, transcendentally grounded, from philosophy and experience, which of course implies the transformation of both the former and the latter, and which functions as an explicative hypothesis. The intra-philosophical logic of the mixture is suspended at the same moment when philosophy and the region are required in an a priori relation of another kind, which falls under the FT and no longer philosophical auto-position where it previously had inscribed itself. With this manifestation of the "relation" [*rapport*] as such or of duality, it is the (noetico-)noematic aspect that is manifested; it is the noema that is brought, and necessarily so, to the noesis.

The FT also explains how non-philosophy is constituted by a double *provision* [apport]—philosophy and each time a determined region.[1] These provisions are no longer already simply empirical and contingent as they are in the "philosophical" state. But FT ties them otherwise still, in an a priori duality pure-transcendental in origin. If FT itself is sufficiently determined with the provision only of philosophy, non-philosophy is more complex still; including the level of the a priori, it assumes the relation to extra-philosophical experience beyond philosophical experience. Hence the objects in two heterogeneous dimensions (both serving to support, we will see, from a philosophical origin and a regional origin) that are precisely the modes of this a priori duality that is the matrix of every finished product of the unified theory. As a result, non-philosophy is constituted of dualities, noetico-noematic and doubly constituted by their empirical origin within philosophy and within a region; and transcendental through their origin within FT. It is evident that the philosophical and regional correlation is not identical to that of the noesis and noema. Each of these two functions is empirically of a mixed origin and refers to a philosophical and extra-philosophical support. Nevertheless if it is not the existence of an extra-philosophical that deduces itself by positing experience as materials for non-philosophy, these are the two relations that "correspond" and non-philosophy manifests the a priori of noetico-noematic duality from this datum of a generally necessary extra-philosophical.

Thus the form of philosophy's mixture is resolved within its greatest generality, raised in its sufficiency and treated as a theoretical problem, and consequently so is the more or less alleviated antinomy that it has sheltered. Its phenomenal core is an intentional "relation" of a new kind (we avoid speaking of relation and even more so of correlation) that on its part excludes the economy of the mixture and its varieties (phenomenological, analytic, synthetic, dialectical, differential, structural, etc.). In particular their topological, frontier or limit undertakings (connecting and separating, joining and differentiating the philosophical and the extra- or pre-philosophical) are now abandoned and replaced by an identity-in-the-last-instance that each time puts the two aspects into relation. These are all the old hierarchical and authoritarian clefts of philosophy, following the distinction of fundamental ontology and regional ontology (variously empirical and "logicized") or the distinction of general and special metaphysics that are excluded or displaced by that pure-transcendental ontology but "unified", under which non-philosophy appears.

Once philosophy posed as new or simple a priori necessary *for* the phenomena, limited in its claims and prohibited from forming any hypothesis on the in itself or the real of them, a second step can be made. If philosophy is forbidden any hypothesis on the allegedly "authentic" in itself, this limitation forms itself through the idea of a totally other in itself, which now claims to be the mixture itself of phenomena and philosophy, in itself from their identity and no longer a philosophical hypothesis of an in itself of phenomena. Outside of this philosophical givenness of regional phenomena (and not of "sensation"), or of philosophy as simple condition, there is indeed an "in itself" of the real, but as vision-in-One distinct from the philosophical type of in itself. It is given and for that precisely unthought or unconditioned, but in relation to philosophy alone, "negatively" posited as delimitation of the latter and its sufficiency, integrating with the reduction and universalization of the latter as a priori condition. This new unconditioned "in itself", which limits the validity of philosophy, must and can nevertheless also be not thought/known but posed as first term of a knowledge-thought. Non-philosophy no longer opposes thinking and knowing but thinking/knowing according to philosophy— which makes dogmatic (in a wider sense) hypotheses on the Real in order either to know it or to think it—and according to non-philosophy which makes its own hypotheses not "on" but rather on the basis of a relevant "in itself" of a new theoretical status. If there is a non-philosophical "in itself", it cannot be a "thing" (corresponding to the "cause" of sensation) or even an Idea (Reason). We have left the ground of empiricism, intra-philosophical ground, in order to think globally the problem of philosophy itself, of its a priori identity and we have transformed philosophy into materials. Consequently, the question cannot any longer be of raising the "thing in itself" into a "noumenon". It is the FT that takes the (displaced) place, now purely transcendental, of the "thing in itself" marked by empiricism; the place no longer of the unconditioned limiting the phenomena but rather of the unconditional phenomenal itself determining and limiting thought. This "in itself" is not thinkable and knowable objectively, but it is this "in" which and through which we are able to think philosophy-as-a priori: Kantianism is more than inverted and gives place to a non-Kantianism: this is the in itself as phenomenon or given-without-givenness that limits every philosophical givenness and position. It cannot then concern either an ontic or empirical in itself, a simple (philosophical) object projected beyond philosophy; nor an in itself posed expressly by philosophy under the form of an essence of things or a metaphysical entity. But instead of an in itself that manifests itself as a mode of FT itself and which, without being a philosophical operation, can reduce philosophy to the state of a simple a priori. This in itself that delimits philosophy is the *identity* of phenomena = X and philosophy. It has the following general concrete form: the *essence-(of)-X* or *thought-X* (essence-(of)-science, essence-(of)-art, thought-science, thought-art, etc.).

# Production of the non-philosophical a priori as such: The noetico-noematic duality

As an example of non-philosophical labor, we precisely take the problem of the a priori, treating as simple material the 'synthetic a priori judgment' within which Kant simply revealed the essence and algorithm of philosophy as a mixture of metaphysics and science.

The law of the dyad and sprit of the PhD are immediately shown in the way Kant poses the more general problem: "On what grounding does the relation of what is known to us a representation in the object rest?" The dyad "representation ↔ object" refers to a synthetic grounding and forms a structure in 2/3 terms. As a priori synthetic judgment, the a priori knows a classically philosophical structure: the dyad of beings and Being (a priori, essence)—we will say: the "onto-logical" difference—is accompanied in its synthesis by a term that is only a unity because it itself is a priori in turn, but transcendental a priori. The reason or the ground of liaison is a term at once taken from the dyad and exterior to it, and a priori but qua One or transcendental, at once exceeding the representation of the subject and that of the object. It is this schema, critical or not, always philosophical, that we are concerned not with subverting but explaining by a non-philosophical a priori. The problem is no longer that of a representation or an intentional consciousness of an object, but rather the problem concerns a simple a priori representation *for* philosophy and through the force-(of)-thought.

What becomes of the dyad under the impact of FT? FT is neither analytic nor synthetic (nor their combinations) but dual-unilateral, so much so that the a priori is now no longer contained in beings, nor does it add itself to them, nor does it dialecticize itself with them or take any figure of ontological difference. No synthesis or liaison still inhabits or oversees their duality become unilateral: the a priori is no longer determined by being which, however, wants duality. Strictly speaking this duality is a pure synthesis without a liaison to drown it in a generality and soon a totality. No prior representation, given a first time, of the subject or object, of synthetic generality, no duality already there, anticipating a philosophical labor of redoubling. The a priori or Being, first term of duality, conserves its inalienable identity. It does not divide itself in two in an other; is not *also* a transcendent unity and ceases to be blended with beings. Their relation [*rapport*], no longer being that of a mixture, ceases to be that of a horizon (Being) and an object (beings). In the synthetic a priori judgment, the provision [*apport*] of the a priori is that of the horizon and the direction in the manner of a relating to beings. But from now on the ecstatico-horizontal mixtures is invalidated, the a priori (or Being or what is extracted from it) relates itself to beings outside of every horizontal structure, as a radically ecstatic intentionality, an opening always outside-itself and without folding [*repli*] (noesis in the new, universal, sense of this word). And beings, from their perspective, or what is extracted from them, abandon their status as ob-ject or the re-folding [*ré-pli*] of transcendence in order to no longer be only the noema of this ecstasy, a being-without-object, that which does not want to speak without-Being (dismemberment of the mixture), but without-being-doublet (simplification of the mixture). As for the starting ontological difference, it passes into the state of a simple support of the new relation.

What becomes of the unity of the synthesis under the impact of FT? The a priori is no longer only a *simple* a priori in every sense of the word, really pure or without blend (not redoubled as and with the One or the transcendental) and applies all the more to the blends. From its perspective, beings or the object are on the one hand simply beings-noemata having recovered their identity and, in addition, "simple" support. From the One-synthesis, FT extracts itself and so extracts the identity that is applicable for the a priori and for beings, which now form a duality-without-dyad. The FT is the transcendental or in-the-last-instance identity (and unilaterality) of the a priori and the object, of Being and beings, of the noesis and noema. DLI is the simple transcendental syntax, or the syntax without folding/doublet, that substitutes itself for philosophical unity-of-liaison or synthesis.

Two clarifications: 1) The suspension of the mixture's structures is only transcendental and does not annul the mixture itself but rejects it as outside-pertinence for the support functions. 2) The invalidation of hierarchy does not leave the residue of a multiplicity of flattened terms, but a new noetico-noematic articulation of the a priori and experience. The equality that we "oppose" to philosophical hierarchy is neither a quantitative or arithmetic reduction nor a simple dismemberment of the mixture, the anarchy of an atomism or a two which would faintly assume 2/3 terms. What remains after transcendental reduction is always a unilateral duality, characteristic of the a priori in general.

# Constitution of the a priori: Occasion, support, materials, overdetermination

In order to comprehend the non-philosophical meaning of these notions which clarify that of the a priori, it is necessary to go back to the philosophical relation of philosophy to the empirical and to completely dualyze it. The empirical plays two blended roles: as content included residually in the most "abstract" and yet impure concepts of metaphysics, and as empirical departure for abstraction, somehow "activating" the operations of PhD. These two functions are transformed by FT. On the one hand, the reciprocal conditioning of the a priori and the empirical, for example the intentional direction and the noema-object, is resolved in order to take the general form of DLI: when the noesis becomes a mode of infinite ecstasy of DT-NAG/P, the two functions of the object separate: its object function as such becomes the a priori of a noematic correlate of DT, unilateralized noema, determined unilaterally by DT; its function of affection and empirical activation of PhD transforms into that of a simple support.

The noetico-noematic correlation is unilateralized under the radical form that we already know. We will no longer speak of this unilateral duality in the manner of phenomenological intentionality, as though a correlation always in the state of folding and surveying itself, but as a uni-lation, as an intentional (re)lation, ecstatic and not horizontal. The "dual" noema is itself simplified as NAP/G objectivity having its own identity, and consequently never in a parallel state or face to face with the noesis. Noesis is the identity (aprioristic here) of the directed, as mode (NAP/G) of FT, and in particular of its infinite dimension of ecstatic pure transcendence (however inserted into the duality). This intentional uni-lation brings about the reduced given, extracted from materials, as being the new experience of the noema. As for the object or the "support = X" to which Husserl said the noema would relate, but as an undifferentiated identity for the multiplicity of noematic meanings and sketches, it is no longer what closes the horizon on itself and blocks the aim, but is now radicalized as "support" but unilaterally, without the ecstatic aim or the various noematic a priori still determining one another reciprocally with this new identity that is support. There is a "non-phenomenological" intentionality that excludes the sufficiency of auto-reflection or auto-position, etc. The relation of objectification lets itself dualyze in a noetic uni-lation, a simplified noema or NAP/G, and a marginalized support as factor and mode of sufficiency. This identity-in-the-last-instance of noesis and noema, of uni-lation and noematic uni-late substitutes itself for philosophical syntheses, whether local or global, and represents a new economy of the field of philosophical and scientific objects.

As for the "support" function, it claims to be of the complete empirical given (not only of the being-object) and its relative autonomy. It belongs to non-philosophy rather than to philosophy of which it is a function after reduction; it is transcendental rather than itself empirical; it introduces an FT operation to the aspect of induction. What is its scope? The a priori as mode of FT claims to be a diversified philosophical matter (unlike FT). It has the dual structure of FT but its relation to the empirical is stricter, it is inseparable from the content it claims and within which it claims to be or which envelopes it. Is there then a philosophical support within the constitution of FT? FT is transcendental by virtue of its constitution originally in-One even if the essence of transcendence, Distance or Exteriority, is the empirical core, moreover first at the same time as the sufficiency of the mixture-form to which this act relates as to its first object. It is therefore transcendental for an reason older than transcendence which is only its *occasion* but not at all, from this transcendental point of view, a support. Nevertheless if FT is transcendentally indifferent to the empirical, by its real cause, it is not indifferent as transcendence or through its a priori aspect and assumes an empirical object to which it relates. This aimed-for object no longer conditions it and is reduced anyhow to the state of a simple unilateral support, no matter what its nature or its role within PhD. In PhD, transcendence (Being) and objective given (beings) reciprocally support one another on the basis of their relations. On the other hand, in

FT transcendence frees itself from a reciprocal relation with beings, transforming beings and even transforming its philosophical form into support. We will say that the mixture-form (which envelopes transcendence) is, through its auto-presentation, the *occasion* of the putting to work of the transcendental or DLI, so of the constitution of the a priori order around the FT as organon and the mixture-form as materials, but not transcendence or its essence, Distance, which is strictly speaking its support. We will only speak of the occasion as an empirical support with regard to the proper acting of FT understood this time as operation of DT or of a relation that does not unilateralize without calling for a support. The support function is what remains of the empirical in a transcendental induction such as that the FT practices. Nevertheless if the Real becoming cause—DLI—needs an occasion but does not need a support, as FT as transcendence presupposes itself (without auto-posing itself), it already includes an empirical support but a support that remains within the limits of the occasion. In a general way philosophy is not a *support* of DLI, which is not a transcendence, but only its *occasion*.

We will no longer confuse the support and materials, two functions fulfilled by philosophy. If the support designates the necessary, indestructible presence of the given of philosophy and regional knowledges once invalidated and the "passage" to the effectuated a priori, if it belongs to the noetico-noematic structure, the function of the "materials" is larger and must not be confused with that of the support; is wholly given material for FT whose philosophical sufficiency has been raised by the transcendental essence of FT, but which is conserved within its structure of the mixture, now sterilized. So it is from the materials themselves as effect of a transcendental reduction brought about by the FT and correlatively its own reduction (that of AP/G transcendence in its NAP/G essence), that the constituted FT extracts the various non-philosophical a priori. The identity of the materials or the identity-(of)-mixture of mixture—implying the raising of philosophical sufficiency—is itself a noema and it is from this noema that FT frees the most local a prioris. Once constituted, the sphere of the materials all of the variety and conditions all the a priori; but in order to be constituted itself as a non-philosophical "category", it needs a proper support that it recreates after the fact. In other words, materials and supports seem to mutually envelop one another. But in reality the material is in priority a transcendental function and derives from FT as indifference which originally and globally affects philosophical sufficiency (the first obstacle to overcome), whereas the support is also a function of transcendental origin but considered rather from the perspective of the a priori. There are two reductions in the relation identity-in-the-last-instance: one is (aprioristic-) transcendental, the other is aprioristic (-transcendental). The material is transcendentally constituted first; the support is the function the material assumes when it is aprioristically reduced or dualyzed.

Nevertheless its dualyzation does not exhaust all empirical functions. Philosophy effectively assigns it a third function, that of universal language or "metalanguage" of the structures of PhD, a function still distinct from the previous ones. It conserves itself, but by losing every constituent function within non-philosophy such that we will say that not only empirical language, but the totality of philosophical language serves as "metalanguage" for non-philosophy. But this metalanguage can no longer claim to be constitutive and fundamental nor even normative: it is reduced to the functions of overdetermination of all non-philosophy's structures, including FT. Language itself does not especially serve as support but it is included within the supports.

Except to say—this would be the means—that the a prioris are the mode of existence of FT, not of its essence or its manifestation in-One but of its auto-manifestation as DT; the philosophical, linguistic and scientific empire does not return as its direct and necessary condition of existence, that which to the contrary demands the a priori which make it return beyond its function as support and as overdetermination. The passage from FT to the "unilateral" a priori manifests *as such* its support function and that of overdetermination fulfilled by philosophy. The empirical given of non-philosophy in effect contains the symbols to "mark" structures and terms, a symbolic representation in the material-signifier sense which continues or reproduces philosophy's invariant within non-philosophy, even if from its aspect of semantics or sense, language is evidently non-philosophically worked, work which moreover affects the signifier itself to the point of creating a "non-philosophical writing". The function of overdetermination is that function where language is reduced when it ceases to reciprocally determine itself with the structures that self-autonomize in relation to it and when it is shared between the functions of support and noematic correlate. The invariant non-philosophical structures, like the philosophical ones, are modalized according to the detail of the structures of PhD and of "vocabulary", but a symbolic residue always remains which unites non-philosophy with philosophy even outside their dual relations linked to knowledge (signal, materials, support). Hence the impression, owing to the presence of the "same" language on either side, that the philosophical circle is in the process of a reconstitution of the a priori level, an illusion which breaks the support function that belongs to the general structure of DLI. This function is explicitly included within the aspect of "unilateral duality" that is the element of the a priori.

The empirical given of philosophy thus fulfills several functions within non-philosophy: those of occasion or signal, of materials then of support, and finally that of overdetermination.

# Economy of the transcendental and the a priori: Real critique of pure reason

Science and philosophy meet within the universality of the synthetic a priori. Mathematical sciences of nature for example indicate the presence of the a priori within experience, or of a connected ontological knowledge in ontic knowledge. The a priori is, as we have seen, the philosophical point of science and philosophy's undecidable or indiscernible and it is for this articulation that it will be necessary to rediscover the identity, *transcendental identity* of the a priori such that they apply equally from now on for "unified" science and philosophy but without any longer being the specular duplication of them.

A priori knowledge has a well-known history. From conceptual and analytic knowledge, it receives with Kant a more vast (intuitive and intellectual) content, and above all a more fundamental status as organon with regard to the transcendental, a new function, less as knowledge of the suprasensible than as condition of knowledge of the sensible or having validity only within the limits of experience. Non-philosophy brings about new changes. It is of a real-transcendental origin or condition: it is in effect a mode of FT; of qualitative extension: it is radically universal or expresses identity-in-the-last-instance: it is a knowledge *to* explain and (theoretically) use philosophy, science and other regions of experience. Unlike FT, a prioris directly apply to the concrete or the variety of philosophy. Let us return to what is important in these indications.

We call pure-transcendental a thought which does not occupy so much philosophy and/or science as the knowledge of their relations (epistemology) insofar as the knowledge is a priori possible. We owe to Kant the elucidation of the a priori within the philosophical frame of the empirico-transcendental doublet, as ontological relation to beings, through an analogy with the mathematical sciences of nature, an analogy guided and anticipated by the authority of philosophy. Non-philosophy on the other hand elucidates the a priori in a pure-transcendental manner, outside philosophical closure and in equal reference to science and philosophy. It infers it and deduces it as a mode of FT and on the basis of the complex experience of epistemological Difference. Actually, it is then less an eluci- dation than a manifestation. All the more so if the reality content (or rather the *real* content) of the philosophical a priori, left to its sufficiency, is by definition useless, that of the non-philosophical a priori confuses itself with the cause that determines-it-in-the-last-instance as applying equally to the philosophy/science relation or as that which establishes something of an a priori knowledge touching those relations that form the web of our experience. So, FT is (*real*) transcendental cause of the possibility of a priori knowledges for epistemo-logical Difference, rather than possibi- lizing grounding of the possibility of "synthetic a priori judgments" on "experience".

In a general way PhD is deprived of its transcendental dimension by FT as it had conceived it, meaning deprived of its claim to be applicable for the Real. The philosophical equation: transcendental = Real, equation more or less of circle, of difference, etc., is abolished by the real-One, this amphibology invalidated, and it is FT that now assumes the transcendental in a new more "pure" sense than strictly orders the only Real. Deprived of this dimension, PhD so reduced is now no longer only an a priori *for itself*- and-experience. But this a priori, as non-philosophy must still call it, changes its status in turn. The philosophical a priori prolongs itself more or less circularly, with more or less leap and continuity, within the transcendental as an instance either positive (transcendental subject), or of re-traction or retreat (Unthought, Difference *as* Difference, etc.) When the transcendental instance loses its claim to the Real, the a priori in turn loses its claim to the transcendental and the (neo-)Kantian expression of the *transcendental a priori* changes meaning. From now on the a priori can only be called "transcendental" in the genetic and heteronomous because immanent manner, if it receives this trait of the FT whose essence is the radically auton- omous and indifferent Real, and if the circle of the philosophical a priori is broken. Undoubtedly FT is the organon *par excellence* and contains the a priori dimension (essence of Being, NAG/P-Distance) but this is ordered by its real cause and does not prolong itself more or less circularly in it. Every a priori generally comes under a transcendental identity that gives it its status and its function and without which it would fall again into the empirical: if philosophy can only offer the a priori some logical form and its auto-position in the guise of identity in order to save it, non-philosophy offers it this radical identity that is FT. But just as the transcendental no longer forms a circle with the Real, the a priori no longer forms a circle with the transcendental.

If the philosophical transcendental takes as its object the rational a priori, the non-philosophical transcendental relates itself to the *identity* of Reason that applies inseparably for science and philosophy. FT marks the passage from the unitary or authoritarian power of auto-positioning Reason to the power of thought that determines-in-the-last-instance the forms of philosophical and scientific rationality. Reason ceases to be auto-examiner and auto-limiter, tribunal for its claims, in order to be examined from a heteronomous instance (by heteronomous by immanence). With this theme of the non-philosophical a priori *for* metaphysics, it is thus ontology as general metaphysics which becomes a simple object and ceases to be auto-legislating. The problem of the essence of transcendence or Being is then ruled under the form of the FT and the problem of its various a prioris is ruled by the manifestation of "unilateral" a prioris that apply equally to philosophy.

# Discovery and non-specularity: Non-Copernican mutation within truth

Non-philosophy does not just extend our knowledge: it is an understanding of philosophy outside of philosophy, the passage to another plane or an order that is no longer a synthesis, but the order of discovery or invention beyond science and philosophy themselves. The non-philosophical a prioris are the a-prioris-(of)-*discovery*. They discover the foreclosed *and thus* repressed identity of philosophy and science, their theory being unified-without-synthesis. This identity is not at the base, at the grounding of philosophy. Precisely the a priori, that which is only *before*, is not *at the base* or *at the peak*: just as priority is no longer primacy, the anteriority of the a priori is of a new order. We abandon the question: "how are synthetic a priori judgments possible?" for this one: "what can we discover of the new, the non-synthetic, with the help of synthetic a priori judgments, i.e. with philosophy?" This is the whole problem for non-philosophy, if we can summarize it and present it with Kantian material.

The labor of the FT as organon is thus not to clarify the given knowledges and statements from their logical point of view, or to supplement a priori the punctual knowledges equally given elsewhere, but rather to produce *philosophically uninterpretable and yet pertinent* statements. Neither (analytic) clarification nor synthesis, neither difference nor retraction nor subtraction. All these operations are interior to the mixture, forming the life of Philosophical Decision and contenting themselves to modify, vary, eventually to repress and displace already given representations. FT identically invents and discovers new presentations or still inexistent knowledges which do not respond to any epistemo-logical paradigm. A fortiori it cannot concern *judgments* of which the matrix ultimately still is the predicative dyad, but instead it concerns unilateral dualities where the "predicate" is neither locatable within the 'subject" nor addable to it according to any combination ruled by the mixture and its capacity to survey and redivide itself. In particular and to resume, DLI substitutes itself at once for the principle of contradiction and the principle of sufficient reason. These assume that "discovery" has *already taken place* while DLI opens a space of a priori discovery to which it is necessary to oppose to judgment as a posteriori "discovery", and which is neither locatable within philosophy nor addable to it (or subtractable, etc.): non-philosophy *has not taken place*. FT is not a judge-reason forcing "nature" to respond to his questions; FT is a phenomenalizing reason that manifests in the mode of discovery and makes a usage, a simple usage, out of philosophy in full, science of nature included. There is reason in philosophy and the sciences, but this *quid facti* does not legitimate it and says nothing about its essence, except to confuse the occasional cause with a fact (*factum*).

From a *purely* transcendental origin (that which does not exclude, to the contrary of transcendence, every relation to an experience except empirical *co*-determination alone), the a priori of the NAG/P type is itself "pure" in a non Kantian sense of this word since Kant's "pure" a priori must still here confess its impurity almost as much as the metaphysical concept must denounce it, even though abstraction is always a source of impurity. Only an a priori manifested by the FT is no longer bilaterally co-determined by experience within the mixture's general law. Undoubtedly it is inferred by the induction—and deduction—of the experience of the philosophical a priori, but this process is no longer specular; transcendental FT only returns to the philosophical a priori as to an occasional cause. Non-philosophy draws the content of its "first names" and their quasi-axiomatic validity from the sole power of FT and only calls on experience for 'structural" functions per occasion, materials and support, whose thematization "philosophies of immanence" have not come to thematize. The non-rational identity of Reason puts an end to the impurity of the *Ratio pura* because the identity of the a priori is not itself a priori and is not contained there in a latent or "originary" manner.

One such possibilization of philosophy does not result from a specular or first splitting into two (to which we oppose cloning) but forms a heteronomous instance, though immanent (and because immanent). No science or even PhD, no epistemo-logical cut can give the model of

FT, precisely because the FT is not like Reason, it does not specularly mire itself in the materials of its works. The specular splitting into two of metaphysical and philosophical Reason is particularly evident in the simultaneous identity and difference of the metaphysical method with that of the natural sciences, of which philosophy, Kant says, receives a "luminous indication" or readable sign: "Reason has insight only into what it itself produces, according to its own designs … it must take the initiative with the principles that determine its judgments." If the manifestation of Reason or the philosophical a priori is intrinsically specular or mostly an auto-alienation and a projection (certainly not psychological but objectifying), non-philosophy's task is to elaborate a concept that is from the outset transcendental, not aprioristic, of the a priori, and a concept of the transcendental that is from the outset real and not logico-reflexive or autopositional. Non-philosophy then ensures the priority of the emergent or the new over philosophical authority and keeps something that philosophy is unable not see, which is not there to see or which has not taken place, that it has not yet produced or already apprehended in an implicit manner. Let us translate Kant into the non-philosophical: the issue is to "penetrate little by little through thought into a system that does not pose any given as fundamental, even Reason, except FT as the identity of Reason, and looks therefore to develop experimentally, but without identifying itself with *any fact*, the knowledge from its original cause." In place of presupposing the *validity* of science and above all that of philosophy, or more generally that of Reason, FT infers undoubtedly from experience but reduced and without pertinence, the modes of this identity of Reason, which applies to and for all forms of knowing.

The "Copernican revolution" is subjected here to its most radical critique. Let us formulate it in its own terms: FT is not, according to its a priori non-philosophical presentations, the cause of the object—philosophy and science—just as this object is not a real cause of its presentations. The first terms, axiomatically pure or abstract, of FT, are no longer philosophically abstract from philosophy and from science or received from them, no more than the first terms produce them. The problem concerns knowing how their adequation or their accord is possible if it tolerates an emergence of these presentations in relation to what is given as an object and if these presentations cannot produce them. How can FT a priori make presentations of its objects with which the objects accord non specularly; pure presentations but not without accord to experience? FT neither treats its presentations as empirical givens in relation to philosophy, nor claims to determine its object or produce the philosophical from the non-philosophical. But what about these a prioris presentations, not produced by philosophy: how can they apply to philosophy? In any case, the most precise non-philosophical position, not negative, on the problem is no longer precisely Kantian. Rather the hypothesis is this: will we be happier in our relation to metaphysics by assuming that metaphysics is only an object for the force-(of)-thought insofar as it will infer from it those a priori over which rules no longer metaphysics but the knowledge *of* metaphysics, and which will be capable of explaining metaphysics? This non-Kantian, non-Copernican hypothesis assumes an experience—unilateral—of adequation as the essence of truth.

The solution that non-philosophy provides for this problem is of course the force-(of)-thought. FT is the capacity for discovering/inventing this philosophically impossible agreement with philosophy. It is the phenomenal content of the subject as capable of manifesting the a prioris of philosophy itself, of freeing "its" *Being*, what it will be necessary to call Being-without-ontology of ontology-as-theory-of-Being in a restrained sense; so of possessing an explication and a critique of the pretensions of philosophy and science as regards the Real. Philosophy is not accessible to man as FT without the non-philosophical a priori, in particular that of the mixed form or PhD. This prior constitution of the Being of philosophy is no longer simply a "different" mode of philosophy, for example an a priori synthetic judgment or a horizon of Being, but a Being of a dual/unilateral constitution. To translate Kant non-philosophically: "Up to now we have accepted that all our thoughts must orient themselves according to philosophy and science, but this hypothesis only leads to the principle petitions within the elucidation of the knowledge *of* philosophy and *of* science themselves. Considering that if we will not succeed better in this task of the knowledge of metaphysics and other formations of knowledge by admitting that the latter must not regulate themselves on these knowledges—by a simple inversion—but only being the occasional cause of these non-philosophical knowledges. The a prioris instead turn around objects—philosophy and science, their blends—these are those objects which, without inversely turning around these a prioris, are dualyzed and unilateralized by them and reduced to their function as materials for a theoretical usage." These "unilateral" a prioris express the radical subject that the FT is and are defetishized and defactualized by it. The problem is no longer that of knowing if philosophy can, in order to exert itself in a valid way within its spontaneous order, *contradict* non-philosophy—but at the very most, resist it—and consequently if they must be the reproduction of one another: we have opposed cloning to this specular mimesis. At the very most this resists non-philosophy or represses it. The transcendental "reduction" by FT thus signifies the abandonment of the illusion and the possibility of a relation finally adequate-(to-the)-Real. The pure transcendental truth such as it finds its site within FT and is ordered by the vision-in-One that precedes it, defines the truth as adequation though unilateral (or *cloning*) of the second term to the first, not as bilateral or metaphysical adequation. Truth is the order not even of the first to the second—an order that would claim to englobe the Real—but the dual or unilateral order of the Real-without-order and of thought which can only determine it as first under the form of a clone. The essence of the pure transcendental or non-philosophical truth understands itself as performation from one aspect and cloning from the other, these being the ultimate phenomenal content of every adequation. This is to say that the philosophical or "thinking" critique of *adequation* and *certitude* is abstract and that non-philosophy substitutes for this critique the real critique of philosophical truth as *veritas transcendentalis*.

# SECTION III: FUNDAMENTAL APRIORISTIC STRUCTURES

## Table of fundamental structures

Beyond the vision-in-One or the Real, but under its condition, how is the problem of thought posed? It is posed first under the form of FT itself. On what condition? On the condition that there is something other than the Real: that there is thought, a project of "thinking" the One. This project at first gives itself always enveloped within philosophy and its sufficiency. It is thus necessary that it apparently self-constitutes a duality by reciprocity, a dyad. But this duality (One ↔ philosophy) is not a duality from the point of view of the One, which does not form a whole [*ne fait pas nombre*] or does not enter into a set; and is not even a duality in the sense of a dual or a unilateral duality as there will soon be one. There is only a duality between the One and philosophy from philosophy's point of view and from that of its transcendental appearance, which can only integrate the One by crossing it out and lining it up with Being through "resistance". The One is itself indifferent to philosophy, but philosophy can always from its point of view persist in thinking the One. Simply, and this is neither contradictory nor does it give place to a synthesis but rather to a cloning, the One can always—nothing within it opposes this—manifest, as transcendental or in-One, the most universal element that philosophy assumes in order to be able to exist, to pose itself and to think: Being or transcendence. The

One thus manifests the essence of Being but such that it tolerates it or reduces it through its own proper mode. It clears the residue of a unilateral duality: not that of FT and the One itself, but more exactly that of FT and its transcendental essence, i.e. the clone of the One.

We call this duality FT. Its essence is identity-without-synthesis and unilaterality-without-negation. The One is an identity immanent (to) itself by definition and, on this basis, immanent *and so heteronomous* (to) a duality that, from its perspective, resolves the problem by including it under the form of transcendental essence without forming a circle or auto-position with it, deducing itself rather than including itself here. We will describe this unilateral duality, without convertibility or reciprocity, by the distinction of two vectors: FT = Essence (One)→/←DT-NAP/G. The first vector indicates the principle cause or cause by immanence which brings about the real or phenomenal manifestation; the second indicates the "motivation" of an occasional or empirical origin (hence freeing the a priori from DT produced by transcendental cloning). The One and duality, still less than Essence (One) and DT-NAP/G in the interior of this duality, do not form a whole or set, do not reconstitute the philosophical matrix in 2/3 terms. The matrix of FT does not fall within the empirical and/or transcendental arithmetic; nor even the fractional, this is why it is non-fractal and would be able to engender a "generalized fracticality". If we choose a single trait in order to characterize FT, it would be better to call it "pure-transcendental" than "real". Although it is real by its manifestation in the mode of the vision-in-One, it is transcendental by the essence that it receives and which then frees up the a priori, forming a duality with it and its support.

Concerning FT we can now say that it is, by its constitution from one side (DT-NAP/G) and by its essence from another side, a "transcendental a priori" (in order to take up again the transformed term from Kant). This designation always reflects respectively duality and its origin (the aprioristico-empirical) and transcendental identity and unilaterality, but it is going to slide by stages or orders of the Real toward philosophy and equally to the simply a priori or "nearest" instances of philosophy. Philosophy is present from the beginning of thought, albeit it under the form of spontaneous resistance to the One-in-One, and every sense of this double operation of induction and deduction of non-philosophy's moments consists in exhausting the philosophical given according to FT—under the "negative" condition of the One—and in transforming the bilateral philosophical set (One ↔ philosophy), which is a transcendental appearance, by a series of unilateral dualities captured one after the other on this dyad or on philosophical illusion. These dualities *acquired* as and by the FT and manifested in-One in-the-last-instance themselves progressively manifest the core of reality included within this illusion or establish a rigorous usage of philosophy. This is the non-philosophical "equivalent" of a philosophical "deduction" of "categories". But here it concerns scientific induction and deduction as much as philosophical.

FT is then "transcendental" by its essence qua identity and unilateral duality, but aprioristic by its DT component that motivates the existence of duality. More exactly, so that it does not reconstitute a fallacious continuity, the duality which is already FT by itself is enveloped within a second duality or taken in this duality which will be one of its modes: not the primitive and universal (One ↔ philosophy) or transformed (FT ↔ philosophy) dyad which undoubtedly subsists as the most general empirical horizon with its effect of transcendental appearance, but the new duality that FT now extracts or manifests from transcendental appearance and from its variants, which it exhausts a little more. With transcendence as essence of PhD, which is it that in effect presents itself to FT? The mixture of Other-as-One or the transcendental a priori proper to philosophy: this is what dualyzes FT. But FT, precisely as FT, has just subtracted its pure transcendental *essence*. It remains then to dualyze, within the Other-as-One, the aspect of the Other—this is DT—and the aspect of Identity: the FT frees an a priori: One-NAP/G distinct from itself. Finally the transcendental One or One-as-Other of PhD becomes the materials for the transcendental essence of FT proper to non-philosophy; and the Other-as-One, its transcendental a priori, becomes the materials for an a priori of transcendence (DT) and now of unity or identity. It thus reduces to the state of a simple non-philosophical a priori not the philosophical transcendental in general, but its double aspect of Other-as-One. Exhausting the philosophical given a little more in this way, here still duality (DT←One) which is what models FT qua a priori and transforms it by noesis should not be understood as set or two, the a priori O-NAP/G being from now on only a mode of the FT without autonomy. It does not form a circle in any way with FT but constitutes some sort of dimensional a priori, itself complex, which comes from philosophy specifying FT and its component of DT-NAG/P. "Dimensional" or 'specific" of course change meaning by passing from philosophy to non-philosophy.

The originary acquisition qua a priori, through FT, of the O-NAG/P still does not exhaust the various possibilities enveloped within PhD in the state of materials even if these possibilities are progressively restrained under the effect of FT. a) From the duality-set (FT ↔ philosophy) which is not still exhausted and in particular the a priori moments of PhD empirically anterior to the Other-as-One, FT extracts or manifests as such two dimensional a prioris of position in general, the a priori of Transcendence or Alterity, T-NAP/G and the a priori of the position properly so-called or the plane, P-NAP/D. Let us return to philosophy: its proper transcendental a priori, we have said, itself extracts the a priori from the empirical, or manifests it *as such* by an inversion of hierarchy; the empirical generality ceases to dissimulate the universal a priori and the universal a priori affirms its irreducibility to an a priori thanks to this transcendental origin—this concerns the *metaphysical* a priori. And yet this a priori is itself decomposable by two more elementary and more abstract functions, which are position in the restrained sense or the plane, the posing-in-plane or presenting-in-horizon; and the decisive dimension, although ignored in general as a priori, of alterity, cut or transcendence, let us say the Other, which was included within the transcendental a priori and which is the hidden essence or organon of the *meta*-physical a priori. Strictly speaking the plane does not belong to the transcendental a priori itself but accompanies it as its envelope within which it empirically exists, the Other-as-One never manifesting itself in the abstract or isolated state but at the heart of the plane which is instead provided to it by the Dyad which, as such, is universal position. More generally it is true that none of these a prioris are isolated from their relation to the others and that the form of PhD penetrates all their relations. Whatever the case, we use an a priori essential by its intra-philosophical status (O-NAP/G) and abstract or specific a prioris (P- and T-NAP/G), but all three or their new forms are only specific within non-philosophy. b) From the same duality-set but from its dyad-aspect of givenness or universal a priori, the FT extracts dimensional a priori that will come to modalize and specify its duality as more abstract or dependent a prioris. The dyad, as opening to the extra-philosophical and seized from this extra-philosophical, we have globally called "Intuition" and have decomposed as a function of "Affection" (by "material" exteriority) and a function of "Reception", passive receiving and reuptake of Affection, Intuition being the synthesis of preceding moments: Reception of Affection and of Reception, of the object and objectification, Auto-reception which implies the moment of Affection and which is the motor of givenness in general. All these a prioris are symmetrical two by two between the ideal or objectifying position and empirical givenness:

- to T-NAP/G corresponds real alterity, Affection or NAG/P
- to P-NAP/G corresponds the taking and receiving, the putting in place of the affected, Reception or R-NAG/P
- to O-NAP/G corresponds Intuition or I-NAG/P.

This is not "window dressing" [*fausses fenêtres*] but the deployment of possibilities of the structural field of PhD (and thus of non-philosophy) between which the philosophers choose or decide to privilege this or that operation and so to create, equally "arbitrarily", this philosophy rather than that other one.

# Internal structure of the force-(of)-thought

Let us take up the problem of FT again. It brings to every component of PhD a modification that we will not call "phenomenological" but phenomenal and transcendental because it has for as an effect delivering the phenomenal core, within each of the philosophical determinations, from its envelope more rigorously from its pertinence, its operations and its philosophical structures (phenomenological ones, dialectics, metaphysics, differential ones, etc.), meaning in general from the ultimate form of auto-givenness and auto-position. These determinations, to reiterate, subsist as materials but are invalidated as an operative "point of view" in the non-philosophical sense. In effect FT contains, beyond the One but in-One, a force-(of)-decision—rather than an infinite decision-of-decision, meaning a mixture of decision and undecidable—within which decision is force in-One and the essence of the decision force in-One. We can describe this ingredient and go deeper into it through opposition to the essence of PhD which is its non-philosophical "equivalent":

1) If the philosophical essence of philosophy in its form is the Auto-, being the identity (of difference and identity), real identity but mixed (transcendental also), the non-philosophical essence meaning FT will be called "in-One" rather than Auto-. It will then be in this very general sense *non-auto*(-positioning and giving) or will lose this "superior" identity first, in favor of the real One through-and-through and without transcendence. Within "non-auto", the "non" here designates the positivity of the One and consequently the real or absolute indifference, not yet transcendental (unilateral), of FT to the philosophical sphere of the "Auto-".

2) If the philosophical essence is also moreover, within its content, a dyad of identity and difference, then what non-philosophical structures will it give place to? This analysis must be pursued further: the mixture of identity and difference, which is the aspect or transcendental content of the essence of PhD can understand itself—we have already remarked on this—as One-as-Other (the transcendental One in the philosophical sense)

or as Other-as-One (the transcendental a priori). The first then the second serve as occasional materials and allow for the preceding descriptions to be refined according to FT.

a) The One-as-Other: at the transcendental level of PhD's essence, the One serving as the principal but not unique pole will correspond, transforming it under the condition of the real One, to the transcendental essence (of FT and the a priori) for which philosophical identity and difference thus serve as materials and indications. We will not dismember them within this process into identity → transcendental essence, and into difference → a priori (DT), but we will extract the pure transcendental dimensions such as they claim to be of DT: identity and unilaterality. This essence implies that FT or that its component of decision is called non-autopositioning/giving. *Non-auto-* no longer designates the real or absolute indifference but a transcendental identity and unilateralization (this is the transcendental itself), which together form not the residue but the transcendental essence of the decision's residue and, with the residue, the entity of FT. So this dualysis has the effect of no longer maintaining the two aspects (real and transcendental) of identity (Auto) of philosophical structure in their mixture state or simultaneously, but of reducing the aspect assumed as "real" to the effectively real or immanent identity of the One; and reducing the other aspect, assumed as "transcendental", to the state of identity and unilaterality which are therefore only but purely transcendentals.

b) To the Other-as-One or at the level of the transcendental a priori, the Other now serving as the principal but not unique pole (the occasional cause), will correspond, transforming it under the same conditions, the DT which a priori, with its transcendental essence, forms FT. From this perspective of difference-as-identity or the threshold of pure transcendental essence crossed and passed, nothing that belongs to PhD (identity, difference, alterity, etc.) can be transformed into pure-transcendental or nothing corresponds to the sphere of transcendental essence of DLI. Because DLI is of a radically different real origin than that of the philosophical transcendental, everything present in PhD is simple materials, given-by-transcendent-givenness, and transformed at best into a priori. Consequently the difference-as-identity or the Other-as-One only subsists, its phenomenal core now cleared away, in the state of the a priori reduced from PhD. It gives place and occasion to a "simplified" (NAP/G) residue, delivered from its mixed structure and taking the form of a unilateral duality. The aspect of "difference" is what is selected in a priority manner because transcendence is the essence of philosophy and it gives place to a pure distance, un-enclosed, to an ecstasy without external or internal limits, infinitely open—the essence-(of)-noesis of noesis—because intrinsically finite or received-in-One. It is radically infinite, simplified in relation to "indivisible" philosophical distances (Leibniz) or indeed "phenomenological" distances which conserve in them a residue of auto-reflection of their terms or of synopsis.

As for the aspect of philosophical identity that can be seen in the dyad (identity of difference and *identity*), and which should not be forgotten in favor of difference alone, it leaves, as we have said, the transcendental residue of aprioristic and noetic identity, without auto-reflection and which consequently does not limit noesis or close it upon itself. From its empirically given aspect, transcendence (which comes to enter into the totality of the Other-as-One, of the transcendental a priori), extracts from the One the clone of the transcendental, and it is then lived-in-One. But when it has passed to the state of the NAG/P a priori, and forms a new duality no longer with the One but with the transcendental itself, it extracts from this an identity, aprioristic this time, that transfers the noesis (DT) or gives it its undivided simplicity and its unilaterality. If effectively the transcendental rejects the essential a priori (DT), casts it outside of the Real, all the while submitting it to the Real or inserting it in-One, it also distinguishes it from itself in its way (which is no more distinction than the transcendental is). In a complementary way, the a priori is already relatively autonomous in general by its *sui generis* constitution of transcendence but the transcendental sphere does not (necessarily) relate itself to it except as to a simple or non-specular mirror which serves as vehicle.

The real One substituted for the One of the philosophical triad has thus sparked the production of the first transcendental residue, not of "*Philosophy*" or of PhD in totality, but of the essence of the latter. It is obvious that the doublet and hierarchy as circularity are excluded from FT. Can we not say however that there are still three terms within FT? Rather than 2/3 it strictly contains one and two terms according to a non arithmetic structure. If identity is present several times, it is so under absolutely heterogeneous forms. These forms are, if we want to put it this way—a philosophical appearance—the "same" identity, they are in reality incommensurable (real, transcendental, aprioristic), or even in-different; in fact the first is indifferent to the others and determines them by cloning. But this indifference is no longer that of the thing and its reflection, the philosophical mirror in reality shattering indifference to the benefit once again of the blend. Let us recall a preceding analysis: within philosophy the mirror is the synthesis of the thing and its reflection: before this dyad there is then the thing and the mirror. On the other hand, within FT a priori distance does not pre-exist continually in its essence (identity and unilaterality) and its initial empirical givenness does not capture it from the One by reflection (divided or philosophical). This is not a mirror-thing. So, transcendental identity and unilaterality are not constituted by a process of reflection redoubling the One; they are not real or detached parts of the Real discharged alongside transcendence; they are *purely* transcendental and can liberate DT from all closure and reflection. Once constituted, we can undoubtedly regard these clones from the exterior as transcendent doubles of the One. But the difference between real identity and transcendental identity is a difference without name, neither "real", nor "transcendental" since it is the radical difference of the Real (*and*) of the transcendental, that which cannot come about on the ground of their blend but within the abyss of the Real's radical indifference—the condition of cloning. Two terms and one term? No such thing: a non-term, a term and a term-clone of the non-term, and not 2/3 or a system of dyads reflecting and multiplying themselves one in the other. When there are only effectively two terms (this is unilateral duality) there is no longer any dyad.

So NA(P/G) does not designate a transcendental identity and unilaterality assumed to be separated by abstraction of their vehicle of difference or distance; they are transcendental insofar as, extracted from the One, they claim to be of distance and transmute the old "difference". So FT, if it always transmits to the materials a transcendental identity-unilaterality, transmits this with and by this NA(P/G) distance which is the essence of Being. There is not on the one hand the transcendental *and* on the other, distance, a universal NA(G/P) trait *and* the essence of Being: everything "sticks to" the shortest route. The NA(G/P) index applies to DT and hence it will apply universally for all the non-philosophical a prioris to which FT communicates at once its essence and its particular form: these will be the "modes" of DT-NAP/G. The description of FT in its component of Being as simple, non redoubled, non specular, radically undivided, etc., will now go for itself and will apply equally to the a prioris considered from the point of view of their essence.

FT is what the very essence of PhD "becomes" when this essence is taken as materials and offered to the One—in reality offered to… FT itself (the One transforms nothing) which presupposes itself (without positing itself) insofar as, if there are materials, there is already Being, transcendence, decision and, consequently, force-(of)-decision. The first work of FT, is FT itself, without giving place to an auto-production or a *causa sui*.

According to regional *data*, which specify non-philosophy, the organon will be also specifiable as force-(of)-thought, force-(of)-creation, force-(of)-law, etc. So the knowledges produced by it are not the only things that are produced. However, this specification leaves intact a certain priority of the essence of Being over the other a prioris which are the concrete dimensions of this essence. A priority which holds that within philosophy, ontology is fundamental, and holds that the unified theory is always that of philosophy... and of philosophy, and first aims for the essence of Being as an object. This priority is limited, not absolutely destroyed by non-philosophy which only prohibits that the essence of Being *unilaterally subordinate itself* along with the a priori within which it concretely exists. The transcendental theorem of FT is universal and applies for all the regionally determined species of unified theory: but on the condition that FT is specified each time, as determinant, no longer by the essence of Being but by one of its a prioris treated from now on as specific essence and as content of the organon. The essence of Being is not then suppressed since it is issued from the "philosophy" aspect, it subsists but without still being determinant or giving its determinant force to the organon.

# The non-philosophical a prioris of philosophy as materials

We formalize philosophy under the form of *Philosophical Decision* (PhD). But this term is ambiguous. It can be understood philosophically, as a concept, and consequently it is not yet *grounded theoretically*, being only hermeneutic and Decision *partially excepting* itself from the law that it announces for experience and subtracting its supposed universality. But it can be, as is the case here, already treated as a first name or a non-philosophical symbol. It is then the object of a rigorous theoretical usage; it applies universally from and for philosophy (whether in its "totality" or its "detail" matters little for now). We distinguish theoretical equality and hierarchical exception. "PhD" has some descriptive equivalents touching the essence of philosophy, and we utilize them indifferently, for example, with the same initial ambiguity: 1) the "mixture": the same thing as circularity or the empirico-transcendental doublet. This is not a property of PhD but its auto-positioning/giving essence or nature, and also the way in which it presents itself to FT, precisely *auto*-presenting itself within its sufficiency in an already non-philosophical respect. 2) The axiom: every philosophy is structured *as* a metaphysics, thus as an undecidable Decision or a structure in 2/3 terms (two sciences into a unique science), the "as" indicating the gap by which a philosophy carries out metaphysics, in general a gap of a science or a knowledge with which it identifies itself in order to distance itself from its metaphysical grounding however inexpugnable. This axiom is also either a philosophical thesis, or already an a priori proper to non-philosophy.

DLI seems to oppose PhD. The form of determination-in-the-last-instance, "the unilateral duality('s)-identity", is the essence of non-philosophy. These two essences are of equal importance within their respective fields, but we are above all unable to oppose them and place them face to face, substituting the latter for the former as if it were without reality. DLI works precisely on the materials of philosophical mixture to which it transcendentally relates; it is capable of suspending its pertinence regarding the Real and freeing the NAG/P identity of mixture itself. How does it work?

The force-(of)-thought is a transcendental reduction rather than an ontic or ontological negation of the given, not at all a "phenomeno-logical" reduction. It is a (non-)One rather than a non-Being, a unilateralization rather than a doubt or an *epoché*. Consequently it cannot choose between the sides of whatever philosophical antinomy there may be, for example the "material" rather than the philosophical "form". In effect the latter is already not simply formal and purely sartorial, but penetrates its material through-and-through. And the reduction of its side is no longer a philosophical decision or a division within a mixture, but a cloning and a performation that is addressed to identity and "produces" identity. The mixture cannot be wiped out in a blow or dismembered in its terms and aspects—followed by a new philosophical decision that would reconstitute it under another figure. The mixture and PhD are treated as identities.

PhD is then the identity for (of) the formalized transcendental structure and it is an a priori which applies to all the antinomies, for example that of auto-position and auto-givenness which for that matter only an intra-philosophical abstraction or decision can separate from one another. The identity *of* this antinomic total affects and permeates all the local concepts of every thought which presents itself as philosophy. It sterilizes philosophical sufficiency which exercises itself as unilateral choice, partial decision and auto-exception of philosophical discourse in its practice. Only metaphysics abstractly and subjectively understood as a regional "object", repressed in its aspect of antinomy and repetition can allow the belief in the possibility of its "supersession". Precisely non-philosophy, by positing an a priori identity *for* philosophy, prohibits every intra-metaphysical belief in a real supersession of metaphysics and shows that every philosophy is always structured *as*, excepting some gaps, a metaphysics. The unified theory not being a specular image of philosophy and science, either in their blend or assumed separated and in themselves (still an artifact resulting from their blend), it takes epistemo-logical Difference as simple materials and a field of quasi-objective givens, which is only possible through a prior suspension of its claimed validity. It thus frees the *non-philosophical* a priori *of philosophy*, an operation that philosophy itself self-prohibits by comprehending—and repressing—its identity as simple sameness or repetition.

In particular the identity-(of)-mixture no longer allows for dividing between position (idealism, Fichte, Marx) and givenness (phenomenology) without however leading to a Kantian synthesis (intuition *and* understanding). This a priori is identically "posing" and "giving" but without a unilateral duality. On the other hand it no longer allows for dividing between identity and multiplicity (in the numerical or metaphysical sense which always includes or interiorizes arithmetic). The transcendental non-philosophical identity of philosophy, from this point of view, has two modes: that of radical identity, identity only a priori *for* philosophy; and that of its radical multiplicity, not the multiplicity of philosophies understood in a more or less factual historico-philosophical sense, but a priori multiplicity *for* philosophy. These a prioris are precisely no longer theses on philosophy, on its essence in itself; they are forms of givenness and position for "inert" philosophical materials, and these forms no longer specularly reflect materials as if they were derived from a "superior" philosophy or a meta-philosophy, but are determined by the force-(of)-thought. Therefore they are of the force-(of)-thought type and derived from identity and unilateral duality. This is the condition whereby these a prioris are able to explain the properties under which philosophy auto-presents itself and to impose on it, not "in itself" through a claim to intervention within its effectivity, but for its entering into the transcendental order of non-philosophy, a radical identity and multiplicity which no longer mutually end one another.

There is still the example of distinctions which go from Kant to Heidegger, between: 1) the auto-grounding of the ontic and regional sciences; 2) the Kantian re-grounding (*Grundlegung*) or grounding repetition of regional ontologies and that fundamental science that is metaphysics as "ontology" or "transcendental philosophy"; finally 3) "fundamental ontology", de-grounding or Heideggerian un-grounding of metaphysics as the question of the Being of beings. Decided under the authority of philosophy, these are three heterogeneous conceptions, more than articulated, and which cannot be reduced to a unique type. Nevertheless, philosophy itself, in the words of the most lucid authors, already thinks itself as a regime of "mixed" economy and knows that the differences between philosophies are discernible *and* indiscernible, manifested *and* veiled; that every decision assumes another in order to unveil it but this other is also held within the undecidable, etc. However this law, being exerted at the same time as thought, but circularly, is only half-thought by philosophy itself which always excepts itself somewhat from one moment or another. The mixture cannot be posed as law of philosophy's radical essence except by the force-(of)-thought that constitutes it in an a priori identity *for* philosophy and which philosophy at once misunderstands or forgets through a repression, the essence of which is, at least, a true foreclosure. Auto-Position/Givenness (of the circle, mixture, etc.) is therefore brought or lived to a state of a priori identity which applies *from* and *for* the different forms or species of grounding, these forms no longer affecting it circularly. If every philosophy poses itself also as philosophy-of-philosophy or meta-philosophy, non-philosophy on its part blocks the pertinence of the circle and avoids the divisions and antinomies proper to philosophical style.

# On philosophy as generalized transcendental aesthetic and logic

From PhD, what offers itself to FT after essence as Auto (G/P), are the dimensions of givenness and position; PhD qua PhD is given and gives itself at once, it is posited and posits itself, it is Auto-Givenness and Auto-Position. This characteristic cannot be abolished or dissolved. It is instead transformed into simple materials of FT or receives a radical transcendental sense. FT transmutes philosophical Auto-Givenness and position, giving them a generalized form and, in philosophy, a new function.

Reasons linked to the universality of non-philosophy under the common name "ontology" obligate us then to think a *materiel*[2] *ontology* or theory of something in general *qua it being given* without any particular "object" being given; and a *formal ontology* or theory of something in general qua it being *posited* meaning posited as an *object* without any particular object being posited. These two halves of ontology or aprioristic theory, although from a transcendental origin, are *transcendental generalized* "Aesthetic..." and "Logic..."

The FT point of view requires a "non-philosophical generalizing" of the transcendental Aesthetic and Logic (under its sole analytic aspect, but also, as we have seen, its dialectical one) beyond their modern forms (Kant, Fichte, Husserl). Generalizing them and putting them in the charge of FT rather than requiring a "transcendental subject" still submerged in philosophical transcendence. For example we can call *chôra* the a priori of materiel givenness of the philosophical and extra-philosophical relations, extending the sense of *chôra* to all operations of givenness in general, which concern the extra- or pre- of the philosophical itself. But it is because we consider philosophy as containing this essential and universal relation to pre- and extra-philosophical experience that we now speak of givenness rather than position with regard to it, and in general we can speak of non-philosophy as a unified theory. From this perspective non-philosophy transforms philosophy into a universal transcendental aesthetic or *materiel* a priori (which gives a priori philosophical and extra-philosophical materiality) and a universal transcendental logic or *formel* [formal] a priori (which a priori poses philosophical and extra-philosophical formality or objectivity).

These generalized a prioris are called "materiel" and "formel" rather than "material" and "formal". Why? They are "simplified" or identified in an immanent way or NAG/P. Each of them frees itself thus from a contrasted couple (form/matter, for example) that it forms with another of with itself, from a more or less continuous blend that divides it, folds over on itself and on the other, splits it into two and hinders it. From now on T-, P-, O-, Other-, R-, I- all claim to be equally, without hierarchy and without blending, without "communication", of the materials or more exactly of the noetico-noematic relation that identifies the materials in an immanent way. FT then introduces democracy into the interior of transcendental Logic and Aesthetic or the two aspects of ontology.

One of the particular effects of this transcendental "democratization" and generalization is that Logic, as elsewhere the Aesthetic itself, escapes the disjunction of intellectual or sensible forms. Both contain the two types of forms (hence already indissolubly sensible and ideal in a finer philosophical examination). Characterized by position, Logic is generalized even in the intuitive forms of "transcendence" or "position" as ontologico-topological categories, provided that they, grasped as NAP, are destined for a work of formalization and position, meaning objectification in the NAP mode. Moreover it contains not only the NAP extracts of the categories and philosophical intuitions, but above all those of the transcendentals (the One itself, Being, Other, the Multiple, Unity, Beings, etc.). Generalized Logic contains in this way the theory not of the "object" in the philosophical sense, but something in general as posited or as object in the NAP mode. It will then be more *de jure* universal than "ontology" or "transcendental philosophy", which Kant says "considers the understanding and reason even within the system of all the concepts and from all the principles which relates itself to objects in general without admitting any particular given objects"; and more than "formal ontology" which Husserl says is "the essential science of the object" and which he designed as aprioristic and formal doctrine of pure modes of something in general. And the generalized transcendental Aesthetic, characterized by the axis of givenness, contains in its turn, with respect to materials or data, and designed for givenness, intellectual and philosophical forms, for example of categories or every other form assuming more or less strong idealizations. Non-philosophy reorganizes the givenness/position antinomy, dualyzes it and makes it its guiding thread in the invention of the most general a prioris (the positionals are even constituted from ancient transcendentals and "great kinds" of philosophy, as philosophy represents a change of scale as much as a new treatment of philosophy). It dualyzes a fortiori the sensible-intellectual couple (which remains at any rate in philosophy's interior and whose frontiers are labile and porous).

"Formel" and "materiel" look to generalize "formal" and "material" and their internal folding in the non-philosophical mode, their critical and Kantian projection, for example, in the "intuitive sensible form" and "intellectual form". On the one hand by reducing Aesthetic and Logic to the philosophical dyad of givenness/position, which formalizes philosophy at a higher degree and no longer takes the type of material-object of philosophy into account. On the other hand by giving them, as we have said, an immanent transcendental, and so heteronomous, cause. Couples like sensible/intellectual and givenness/position, even when they are no longer understood "metaphysically" but "transcendentally" in a neo-Kantian manner and when the logical form a priori conditions the material, remain "restrained" and circular, the "transcendental" being understood here as a superior doublet (auto-position). It is possible to generalize the "formal" in "formel" and the "material" in "materiel", to break the circle of their correlation or reciprocal determination and to posit *relatively autonomous* (with regard to FT) and unilaterally independent orders. Only FT produces an Aesthetic and a Logic that are generalized and consequently sufficiently autonomous to no longer maintain relations except of identity-in-the-last-instance. This generalization is only acquired when the "transcendental subject" and its circle cede their place to FT—the phenomenal core of every possible "subject"—capable of determining the a prioris of form and matter, of position and givenness, with their universal and equal validity for philosophy. The usage of Kantian and Husserlian terms must not be misleading: the transcendental corresponds here to FT and comes to the a priori or manifests it in some heteronomous, although immanent, way. And thus the circle which affects the Kantian and Husserlian concepts of aesthetics and logic is broken.

Finally philosophy is the aesthetic form and transcendental logic that posits and gives the World. Not the "form" in general of the World, but its materiel or donor a priori, formel or positing. Without this determination, the "World" is still an empirico-philosophical concept, metaphysical or cynical rather than transcendental, and does not really belong to non-philosophy, even in order to describe its data. We therefore no longer utilize this or that empirical theory, this regional discipline (frequently a science) as a priori giver of phenomena, but each and every philosophy, each and every region as one such transcendental aesthetic and logic of phenomena.

# SECTION IV: THEOREMS FOR A PRAGMATIC OF PHILOSOPHY

## The style and objects of non-philosophy as theoretical pragmatic

Non-philosophy is the matrix of disciplines of the type called "unified theory" which each time manifest the "simple" a priori correlation of philosophy and a region. They are specified by the regional materials whereas their designation as "first" (in the sense of a priority-without-primacy) designates the place for philosophy within the materials and that of the transcendental within non-philosophy: First Science, First Ethics, First Technology or Aesthetics, etc. First Science is the "first" discipline or the discipline universal in relation to the others, in terms of the privileged place that philosophy gives to science; and it is under its form that non-philosophy concretely realizes itself for the first time. Philosophy, by means of ontology, in effect presents itself as absolute science for two connected reasons: because it maintains a privileged relation to the "science" region rather than to art or ethics, up to the point of identifying itself there in part, a level or an operation of itself; and because it "raises" this relation to the absolute by the operation of auto-position and can then present itself, thanks to this support of that with which it identified, as being itself a science, but higher or more autonomous than the science that it has called for—as an absolute science. It is only such on condition of requesting and repressing, interiorizing and excluding, a regional science, or even the "science" region. Non-philosophy returns from this First Science as absolute in the philosophical sense of auto-position/givenness, to move to First Science as radical or non-auto-giving/positioning. It does not destroy the philosophy/science correlation—decisive for thought—but transforms it as materials of a relation of simple priority-without-primacy. It has a multiplicity of realizations, the immanent unification applying for the mixture of philosophy and whatever empirical theory. But it can and must first form itself between the former and the invariants of *Science* that the latter can claim to epistemologically clear from various practices and theories. We have undertaken a sketch here of the unified theory of philosophy and the most general procedures and operations that the sciences require (induction and deduction, theorization, experimentation and axiomatics); and incidentally, the unification of Philosophical Decision and a determined theory but which possesses a value for thought and transregional mutation within the field of the sciences (the non-Euclidean, -Gödelian, -Mandelbrotian, etc. paradigms).

The titles of "First Science", "First Aesthetics", etc., specify non-philosophy by its materials; but these materials are not indifferent and affect the progress of non-philosophy itself since FT in a sense itself brings no *concrete* instrument into the work on materials, and it is the latter that brings them under the a still philosophical form. In what measure then does non-philosophy *participate in* science, art, ethics, in terms of the transcendental effects it draws from FT? If FT, in its essence at least, is purely transcendental, without empirical co-determination (but not without a given), the concrete form of its syntax depends on materials. Yet these being primarily the philosophical, and the philosophical being *de jure* connected to science and in particular to logic, it is inevitable that this form would be that of the axiom and hypothesis, induction and deduction, but to the extent that these instruments and these operations are determined by FT and acquire a transcendental or "real" bearing in-the-last-instance. A first science thus elaborates the *hypothesis* (anhypothetical-in-the-last-instance) capable of producing a knowledge of the philosophy/science mixture. A hypothesis that is itself non-mixed, expressing FT which in one is sense the matrix of axioms. We can say of FT that it defines the pragmatico-theoretical style of non-philosophy, it is transcendental although in a scientific style, thought as inferred/deduced. Non-philosophy invents an identically pragmatic and theoretical style, called "theoretical usage". The philosophical antinomy of these formulas is raised, non-philosophy can only be the *synthesis* (dialectic, encyclopedia, etc.) of the pragmatic (which *is*, *de jure*, philosophy) and science. Neither synthesis nor resolution of this antinomy; it is indeed the identity, but in-the-last-instance, of the pragmatic of philosophical extraction and the theory of scientific extraction.

In this sense, the expression of "unified theory" is an import under non-philosophy of the theoretical vocabulary of science. The "unified" derives from the One-cause and "theory" derives from the universal presence of philosophy and science within philosophy. So "theory" returns to "philosophy" in every case a second time, within "First Science", to science. "Unified theory" defines the task of every species of non-philosophy, this never being non-"philosophy" but a unified theory of philosophy and a region of "empirical" phenomena, philosophy never intervening alone since it is by essence, even as metaphysics, explicitly or in a repressed manner connected to regional experience. Complementarily, non-philosophy is neither theoretical nor practical nor aesthetic, etc., in the sense whereby philosophy defines separated regions of experience. Similarly the transcendental universality of non-philosophy includes regional data but not in the sense where philosophy is universal *over* such data and manifests a claim of totality.

The conditions are brought back together in order to respond to an objection addressed to non-philosophy: *if the One is non-philosophy, why is it not also non-science*? The principle of response resides precisely in the undivided or immanent connection of the philosophical and scientific, in their non-separability: non-philosophy prohibits every philosophical hypothesis on the essence of science "in itself", and this is so precisely because it posits that philosophy is the universal a priori for itself-and-science. Hence the conclusion: thought-(of-the)-One (and not the One itself) is non-philosophy and consequently *non-philosophy-of-science* (non-epistemology, etc.) but it prohibits itself from presenting directly as non-science and thus from making a hypothesis on science. More profoundly still, the One is not in reality "non-philosophy", which would ultimately be a philosophical decision, of the neo-Platonic kind; it is absolutely indifferent to philosophy as much as to science, a real and not a transcendental indifference. On the other hand the thought-(of-the)-One, non-philosophy, is *transcendentally indifferent to philosophy*—to philosophy, not to science, the problem does not pose itself—and consequently to philosophy-of-the-sciences.

A particular point concerning the objects of non-philosophy can then be clarified in a principle [*principielle*] manner. What is the noema that corresponds to the noesis of philosophical extraction? This cannot be science "in itself" or some object = X assumed "pure" and "outside-philosophy", meaning still philosophically autoposited. One such object is precisely only the materials from which the corresponding noema must be extracted. Here still we move from any X-object philosophically interpreted as an object in an AG/P state to its "simplification" or to its NAG/P "identification".

Non-philosophy only works within the limits of the necessary correlation of philosophy and experience; and cannot, concerning science for example, imagine a "first" science or a science "in itself" that it would need to think. Philosophy removes [*prélève*] a theory and raises [*élève*] it by auto-position to the state of the essence of *Science*. But non-philosophy does not follow this way, does not take a theory assumed in itself to be "purely scientific" or "neutral"; it takes for its materials this theory, for example the fractality such as it is already grasped by philosophy, explicitly developing its philosophical dimensions and extracting the *essence-(of)-fractality* that is the object of a unified theory said to be of "generalized fractality"; or respectively the non-Gödelian essence of (for) Gödelism. A unified theory in general bears on a particular theory; if it bears more on the philosophical extension of this theory under the form of the essence of *Science*, then it also has the right, in this measure and with these materials, to produce an *essence-(of)-science*, but it knows the limits of this concept which will be more exactly formulated: *essence-(of)-essence of science*, which rather describes an effect accompanying philosophical materials. In reality, as it precisely suspends the AG/P of empirical theory (or of this artistic practice, or that ethical action, etc.), we can consider that unlike philosophy, it is a unified theory of this theory or of that regional object rather than of science or of ethics. These last formulas infer a risk of confusion with the pretension of philosophy to elucidate the essence-*of...* in the sense of a generality/totality. It rather concerns, even with keywords like "thought-science" or "thought-music", etc., a return to the locality and the finitude of singular or differentiated practices. Through its organon, non-philosophy is a *thought without models*, scientific models, artistic or ethical ones, etc.; through its materials it relates itself to these models in their philosophical usage; through the knowledges produced by it, it is a unified theory of such a model that it causes to move from the philosophical state to the state of a NAG/P state (in this way or under this form, non-philosophy is a theory and a pragmatic of models).

In order to turn them into objects of a universal thought, non-philosophy seems to modify fractal theory, or that of Gödel, or that of non-Euclidian geometry, etc., but it does not modify them in their empirical nature, their technical and scientific nature. It does not even intervene there as philosophy does—philosophy which, without being able to modify the content of knowledge, which is to say to produce new contents, shuts them into enclosures, signification and teleologies that abstract these from the process of knowledge. On the other hand, being identically a theory and a pragmatic, it uses them freely. But it does not use them like empirical theories, for the end of producing new knowledges of the same order or a neighboring empirical-regional order. It only uses what it has the right to use: their interpretation or their philosophical capture. "Non-Mandelbrotian fractality" does not claim to be a rival theory to that of Mandelbrot, but its usage-of-thought and only it which "deconstructs" its philosophical fetishization. Equally, "non-Gödelism" is certainly not a critique or a refusal of Gödelism.

From the moment when it admits that science, art, ethics or technology are autonomous practices, and that it itself cannot participate in them for various *de facto* and *de jure* reasons, being neither a science nor an art, etc., its only function is of making a rigorous and pure-transcendental usage of these practices, always with the goal of thinking democratically; thus of moving from their philosophical falsification to their "thought" that is now only thought-science, thought-art, etc., a means of establishing peace within the relations of thought, science, art, etc. Even within thought, there is a democracy problem. And the conditions of democracy are those of an apparent minimalism linked to the radically of immanence and the non-philosophical rigor of thought.

# Theorems for philosophy

## The identity-of-the-last-instance of the fundamental and the regional

We have declared here and there three "axioms" touching on the role of philosophy within non-philosophy and could have appeared heterogeneous, not in the same way limiting the *Principle of Sufficient Philosophy*:

1 "equivalence of all philosophical decisions, with regard to the Real or the One";

2 "everything is virtually philosophizable";

3 "philosophy is transcendental appearance and simple *doxa* of superior form".

Nevertheless these are precisely not yet true axioms or theorems but disguised philosophical theses, decisions on the in-itself of experience ("everything") and advanced without any justification other than an empirical one. Non-philosophy cannot be rigorously constituted from the exterior through the accumulation of theses. Through their final aspect of philosophical "sufficiency", the latter are symptoms or indications for a priori knowledges, axiomatically deduced, touching on philosophy and are designed for a transcendental legitimation of philosophy's role through FT alone. For example non-philosophy cannot give itself an assumed empirical state "in itself" of philosophy, of the region X and their relation "in general", but a certain a priori form of them and their resistance to the Real, a form manifested through FT. It does not only introduce data other than the philosophical data and under the ultimate authority of these as it is the case, for example, in deconstruction, but transforms and generalizes the philosophical on the occasion of this data under real or non-philosophical conditions. Then there is the thesis: "Everything is virtually philosophizable." It must be generalized and inferred as a theorem, freed from its philosophical form and signification ("Everything"), and philosophy transformed into a universal a priori of givenness and position of mixed phenomena, consequently understood as transcendental a priori or from a real origin. Not: "everything" is philosophizable, but: *if* one or some phenomena present themselves, they necessarily do so through and within philosophy.

We use elaborated regional forms of knowing (sciences, arts, technologies, ethics, etc.) and fundamental forms of knowing (philosophies). Traditionally the task of thought is defined by their blend under the authority and through the means of these fundamental forms: to realize a more or less open encyclopedic form is the final end of philosophy. Let us assume that we substitute for these solutions another form of combination of knowings: that philosophy ceases to be judge and party, that philosophy is simply a "party" or a term of the combination but not the law of it, that we define the condition of a unified-theoretical usage of all these knowings without according a primacy to the fundamental ones. Each of these, the regional knowings and in contrast even philosophy, are treated equally as a prioris equally valid for the explication of experience. This kind of generalized Kantianism will cause philosophical exception to cease and will introduce a certain democracy or peace into "the sciences". In place of arbitrarily and in a contingent way choosing the physical mathematics of Newton or Cantor's set-theory in order to raise them to the state of the sole ontological a priori of experience, all regional knowings in an equivalent way, all philosophies also will posited as such a prioris, without this "equalization" whether a leveling (except for a certain *de jure* disjunction of the regional and the fundamental) of sciences, arts, philosophy, or whether negated therein. It will be necessary that this distinction recover itself, under a form to be determined, within the common status of simple a priori knowledge, and necessary that the old primacy of philosophy resolve itself at best into a simple priority attached to the qualitative nature of philosophy and to its distinction with that of science.

We know how one such *theoretical usage* of the regional *and* the fundamental as simple a priori is possible. A thought which relates itself to the a priori of experience rather than to the objects of it, and which makes a certain usage of thought from these knowings, is in general called "transcendental". But it relates itself here to Being, to the One, to the Other, to the Multiple, etc., to the transcendentals themselves of ontology or even of its deconstruction, to the fundamental as much as to the regional and generic idealities, as being in turn a prioris, rather than directly to objects aimed at by them. If philosophy already claims to fulfill a transcendental task, the issue now is to define a generalized transcendental thought, equally "for" philosophy itself reduced to the state of a priori, deprived of its proper "real" claim by a more "powerful" thought, capable precisely of a "transcendental reduction" of the philosophical posture itself. What is the point of "non-philosophy"? Philosophy postulates that it can transform the empirical while it only transforms the relation to the empirical, leaving the empirical to science and "life". Furthermore, non-philosophy has no effect *within* the empirical, and none *within* philosophy and only transforms our relation to philosophy and to regional knowings, bringing about the passing of this relation from self-belief or the illusion of philosophical sufficiency to a theoretical usage *of* philosophy.

Non-philosophy, an anti-encyclopedic and anti-unitary project, thus realizes itself by the positing not of a synthesis of the fundamental and the regional, but of a transcendental identity and aprioristic duality having as content the regional and the fundamental, rather than a duality of two terms. We will conclude that it is neither formal-logical nor transcendental-logical: how do we equalize philosophy and science, philosophy and art, philosophy and ethics outside of every hierarchy and its last avatar (anarchist and nihilist leveling)? For this it is necessary to suppress the fundamental *claim* of one and the regional limitation of the others, without though positing their A = A identity, identity without thought, nor their difference which brings this formal identity into the interior, but instead must conserves from their difference a *de jure* priority, priority-without-primacy, not of philosophy over them, but of their identity over their duality, identity which is in effect only identity in-the-last-instance. This is to universalize them within the common layer of an a priori of a new style, rendering regional knowings more universal than they spontaneously are, or rendering them co-extensive with philosophy; and rendering philosophy more empirical than it now is, and so more aprioristic than transcendental. We aprioristically universalize the regional knowing, giving it a bearing irreducible to the experience of origin; on the other hand we empiricize philosophy by reducing it to functions of the simple universal "plane", so strictly and necessarily tying the empirical and the philosophical together in this new definition of the a priori. Depriving the regional of its empirical transcendence and its exteriority that it draws from its origins in facticity, restoring it within the immanence of the a priori universal, this operation only conceives itself as forming a system with the reduction of complementary philosophical transcendence, to this common immanence of the universal. So much so that philosophy—under the form of the non-philosophical a prioris which are cleared from it—can only be said to be reduced to the status of simple a priori of experience if the regional too is treated with such a qualitative extension. The whole of the operation demands a non-philosophical re-definition of the a priori in terms of the FT, a distinction which deals with a priority of the noetico-noematic type *without convertibility* between terms that are equal in a certain manner, these terms having for support each time the mixture of the fundamental and the regional. The theorem: "Philosophy is now included in the simple non-philosophical a priori of itself and of experience", only describes a component of the a priori, the other side being constituted by whichever regional which enters into this function with equal rights. The correlation fundamental/regional is conserved, but de-hierarchized, de-enveloped of its auto-position, reduced to the state of simple support of an a priori relation, without convertibility, of a noesis and a noema both funda-mental in *origin* (and in *supports*). It is evidently the force-(of)-thought as transcendental organon which frees up this identity proper to this new noetico-noematic a priori, an identity without any confusion or difference.

Two capital consequences arise for the signification of philosophical activity.

1) Philosophy knows regional and fundamental equations. But these are equations excepting a difference or precisely a Philosophical Decision, whether this decision is explicated as: mathematical physics = philosophy, critique, analytic geometry, or whether it is implicit, truncated and repressed: set theory = ontology of the void, etc. They combine the two principal traits of the philosophical: a) a particular regional knowing, chosen arbitrarily and posited in an exclusive manner but b) raised to the state of the essence of science of… by the transcendental power of philosophy which uses this knowing for the proper ends of claims over the Real. Non-philosophy instead generalizes the *de jure* reference of philosophy to *a* region or *a* theory, whatever it may be, which is to say *de jure* to each and every experience, and complementarily transforms whatever regional knowing into support of a purely universal a priori. It deprives philosophy of its operation on the Real and gives it, as its sphere of validity, experience alone. It is thus a purely transcendental and empirical

discipline, its "purity" excluding blends with logic or linguistics but never, on the contrary, the relation to the empirical which now contains, among other things, logic and linguistics. It is the opening of thought beyond philosophy and even, in a sense, of philosophy beyond itself, beyond any philosophical "beyond" of metaphysics.

2) It assures rigorously and in reality the connection of the philosophical and the regional by giving them the form of a certain identity which still annuls here the two traits of their philosophical relation. This is in effect traditionally: a) an alleged relation, a supposed or demanded reference, but without assurance of realization, precisely a simple will to relation to experience but never the *identity manifested as such* of this relation; b) a relation which offsets its precariousness or weakness by the force of its claim to dominate the regional and to authoritarianly legitimate between the philosophical and the arts, sciences, technics, ethics. Non-philosophy poses rather a necessary and objective connection as an a priori; intelligible or manifest as an identity that is perfectly capable of being elucidated as being of-the-last-instance, never left in the state of indetermination of or repression it has in its abstract philosophical solutions and "unilateral" decisions. Non-philosophy thus has no meaning for a datum assumed to be pure, but for a factum of experience *and* of philosophy, indissolubly blended. Philosophy itself *claims* or *wants* a mixture but for all that even it lets itself think that it is not absolutely necessary, that pure experience enjoys a certain relative autonomy, that it is even susceptible to correspond to a certain essential "in-itself": it operates the mixture *without being able to make it the necessary object of a theory*. Non-philosophy definitively ties this floating relation of philosophy and experience to an identity and a duality; it posits and elucidates this identity that philosophy has exercised without being able to thematize it and make a rigorous theory of it. The datum of philosophy and its regions finds itself, under these conditions, transformed into a true factum but one which, unlike that of Kant, does not supersede a certain empirical contingency it recognizes and does not determine the very essence of (non-philosophical) thought.

The ordinary attempts, that is to say philosophical attempts, to limit the reach of philosophy have moreover tried to postulate a relative autonomy of regional spheres of experience and to make this count against philosophical authority: an absolute and purely moral drive in itself, an artistic practice in itself, a science in itself, etc., recovered by philosophy in a more or less exterior manner, or penetrated inside and out by it (deconstruction). To the contrary, non-philosophy postulates the identity itself not of but *for* philosophy and regional experience and does not claim to submit an experience assumed to be pure to a new thought. Against this claim, we must in fact say: either the question is of acting morally, practicing science, etc., without forming hypotheses on their alleged "in-themselves"; or if such hypotheses are made, they are already philosophical in nature. There are not phenomena "in-themselves" outside of philosophy, if this is not by a supplementary thesis which comes under philosophy. It concerns either an autonomous regional practice, a production effective for example for moral acts or objects of knowledge—and here there is no problem that can solicit philosophy as such, its intervention in qualities, and so non-philosophy—or it concerns a more or less explicit philosophical reprisal of this experience. We neither think nor know anything about an innocent moral practice, absolutely a-philosophical; Kant seemingly posited such an innocence but admitted that it had to be critically protected against metaphysical speculation, and that it thus was continuously affected by this speculation and by critique.

We gather all these effects in the concept of unified theory. It excludes the set of philosophical solutions of the "encyclopedic" type; it speaks neither of the unitary synthesis in process, teleologically oriented, of a variety under a horizon of unity, nor of the logical identity A = A, which is to say the "arithmetic" equality of philosophy = science, philosophy = art, etc., an apparently absurd solution as such, but in reality assumed and interiorized by all of philosophy; nor of the transcendental identity of isolated generalities, without correlation, precisely assumed in themselves, like *Philosophy*, *Science*, etc. More concretely, the unified theory is not the more or less exterior or transcendent unification of the two disciplines by philosophy as a third term to its benefit. Philosophy is a necessarily invited part but an invariant part; it is one of the sides to be unified along with a supposedly "regional" experience, rather than the agent of an ultimate synthesis. The unification sought is internal or immanent itself even if it is operated by the force-(of)-thought, an instance heteronomous to the variety to unify and *for* it but not transcendental like philosophy is. In philosophy itself, in the element of Auto-Position/Donation, the disciplines are posited, as we have said, as in-themselves to reunite in an external and internal manner, philosophy being this ringleader and master of the game: this is the *unitary* or philosophical theory of knowing, with its modes ("encyclopedia", "unified science", the "totalization of culture", the "acceptance of truths", etc.). In non-philosophy, the transcendental organon begins by reducing this position in itself, this auto-position of philosophy and the regions, without destroying the regional and philosophical variety, now available. FT is a transcendental identity (neither real nor transcendent or irreal, but determined-in-the-last-instance by the Real) which establishes an equality of the philosophical and the regional within an a priori relation that we have described. This is the identity of a duality, an identity of a transcendental origin, operating in turn under the form of a determination-in-the-last-instance. In this manner, the hierarchy is broken and democracy is instated in the relations of philosophy and… art, ethics, science, etc. The synthesis "philosophy-of-science" or "epistemo-logos" is replaced by their unified theory. Hence, to abridge the complete formulation, the expressions "unified theory of ethics", of man, science, art or thought-art, etc., which always signify "of philosophy and of ethics", etc.

We call unified theory, then, the concrete form of non-philosophy when it is given as real object of identity and duality (a priori, of transcendental origin) of (for) philosophy and of whatever regional datum = X. Its product always has the form "essence (of) X", "X" designating a variable region of data, "(of)" designating the identity-of-the-last-instance; "essence" desig-nating the stratified architecture of a prioris which are the knowledge of the essence (of) X.

## *The universality of the non-philosophical* a priori *and the unification of experience*

If the essence of Reason is no longer rational, if it is "non-rational" in this phenomenally positive sense, its a priori field and its object expand beyond science and philosophy assumed as separately given and/or in a mixture. This concerns a qualitative extension: the non-philosophical a prioris no longer apply for "primary" or intra-philosophical objects nor even for "philosophy" in the historico-vulgar sense of the term, but for this new object for a more complex discipline, the *mixture* or *philosophy-form*. The change of content, form and function is just as much that of beings as that of Being or of the a priori to which these relate: the intra-ontological beings are replaced by the mixture, which is not a physical and/or metaphysical thing but *Metaphysics* itself, thus *the* philosophical (as epistemo-logical Difference mainly, but not exclusively). The a priori then applies to science and philosophy taken in a mixture, without however giving place to their reassembly or totalization. The totality is always a re-sharing according to the dyad, the reconstitution of an antinomy or an exterior and interior remainder, but the non-philosophical identity includes the antinomy, the remainder and the supplement in the simple materials: for example the rational/empirical antinomy to which non-rational identity applies. The philosophical system of hierarchization and auto-exception, totalization in a dyad, is transformed by a new transcendental "logic", the a priori and the empirical included together in a relation of unilateral duality which at the same time narrows them down to identity and frees them from any synthesis.

Precisely because they are liberated from any transcendental claim, the a prioris only apply now, at best, more universally, *for* philosophy itself and its relation to experience. Torn from the legislation of PhD by FT, FT gives them a universality that is qualitatively superior to the one they possess. Those ordered by the Auto-Position that limits them are ordered by the FT which liberates them *for* philosophy itself. Those that are intra-philosophical, limited by PhD which partially excepts itself from them, are generalized to philosophy *and* experience to which they in fact give an identity. Thanks to these a prioris of a new force, non-philosophy is a sphere into which philosophy enters again along with experience or democracy too, outside of any hierarchy of worth, reality, dignity. Thought is then said to be thematically "raised" by a degree: if philosophy relates to beings qua beings, non-philosophy relates to this more complex object which is the philosophical itself or, in other words, relates to inhuman metaphysical man.

In a sense FT "transforms" PhD to the state of a priori itself, but this is on the condition of substituting for its proper philosophical essence, transcendental essence or identity, and the NAG/P index. Under this form, we can say that philosophy, in its non-philosophical form, becomes the universal a priori *for* itself-and-experience. This is really always about its givenness and position "by itself". But this "by itself", this auto-, ceases to be an auto-reflection. It changes meaning, ceasing to be a Same in order to be a transcendental identity. "Philosophy gives itself" only means "under its own form", and this formula ceases to make claims over the Real in order to be a simple a priori trait. It is indicative of itself but not by its own force; it continues to give itself to itself (*and* experience), it is always the universal form of its own givenness and position, but these a prioris are only universal at this point because they change internal form, abandoning *their* auto-position and division, acquiring NAG/P essence.

So it is the theoretical and pragmatic global status of philosophy that changes, but it is not destroyed like an idealism of radical immanence, insufficiently understood, would have wanted. What is suspended? The Principle of Sufficient Philosophy, the *Auto* (D/P) or the philosophical essence of philosophy, which limited philosophy and prevented it from accomplishing itself as absolutely universal, which is to say non-philosophical. Non-philosophy is only the most universal form of philosophy but outside of it and so *for* it, a universality which corresponds to the suspension of its closed and restrained character. This is not linked to the content of philosophy's a priori but to the mechanism of auto-givenness/

position that paralyzes it and, closing it in on itself, gives it a transcendental claim, and to the transcendental gives a claim to the Real. The (Auto-) givenness/position of philosophy is thus conserved but under a regime other than its own. This is not a question of brutally suppressing this mechanism in the name of the One, at least, as we have said, its content of identity and difference then donation and position with their a prioris—all this given changes syntax, worth and essence. In a sense even the real claim of philosophy and the transcendental claim of the a prioris are not simply annulled but transformed into an entirely other experience which separates the first of the Real and the second of identity, to which it admittedly relates but in a heteronomous though immanent manner—since immanence itself is precisely always heteronomous to philosophy and determines a thought *for* it.

Reduced in this way and posited as simple a priori form of phenomena, the philosophical gives and poses phenomena that are not pure or in themselves, but precisely already in the state of blending with philosophy. This is not a simple formal or material a priori (Husserl): this would be to still philosophically *decide* between form and matter, or posit their identity under a still transcendent form, not moving out of the logic of Auto-Position/Giving. The *data* of science, art, language, morality, etc., are not dressed up again in formal clothing that would never find its necessary connection to them, but are indissolubly or intrinsically of science (and) of philosophy, of art (and) of philosophy, etc. In these identities, posited as such and not simply naively exercised by philosophy as mixtures, philosophy is as much matter as form, science or ethics as much form as matter. The a priori is an organon *for* philosophy, no longer a *form* or a *condition* that is intra-philosophical (Kant, Husserl). One last clarification: we cannot say—precisely because we refuse to dismember the philosophical mixture by isolating its sides from one another—that philosophy assumes the noetic side and science or any other region the noematic side of dualities. In reality, whether it concerns noesis, noema or object-support, the mixture is always present under different angles in each of its functions—hence a work of particularly complex and combinatory dualysis if we are to be absolutely rigorous or complete. Distance or noetic aim is assumed and qualified as identity-of-the-last-instance of science and philosophy, the noema as their reduced duality, and the support as their difference or the mix-form itself.

# On philosophy as transcendental doxology: Philosophical resistance

In *doxa*, opinion, belief and appearance are reconciled. In a still philo-sophical and naive manner, we would say that philosophy is the superior or transcendental form of the doxa—of opinion, belief and appearance ("transcendental appearance" such as it is conceivable by philosophy itself). But philosophy as opinion opposed to the *episteme*, as (rational) belief opposed to truth, is still a positivist reduction of philosophy prolonging and generalizing that of metaphysics; still a thesis on philosophy's essence in itself—still a philosophy of philosophy. This thesis is thus ambiguous—in a certain sense, contradictory. To say that philosophy is the "superior form" of doxa is undoubtedly a first step toward the solution. But if the doxa is opposed to the episteme, the problem of non-philosophy as that of their unified theory, not of a domination of science over whatever opinion and/or philosophy, or a reversal of this to the benefit of philosophy, but of their equivalence without hierarchy, through identity-of-the-last-instance.

FT overcomes these difficulties by making philosophy the universal a priori form which without a doubt gives the materiality of phenomena, but which gives them in the mode of transcendence in general which is the real content of "belief" in the non religious sense or of *doxa*. As a priori doxological or of appearance, it *gives* the phenomena in the form of an opinion, a belief and an appearance, all objective. The question is no longer of making philosophy the superior form of *doxa* (with these three determinations and the concepts of collective consciousness, popular consciousness, quotidian, vulgar, etc. which accompany it) but of making philosophical *doxa* a universal and necessary a priori. Philosophical consciousness not as superior form of collective consciousness, but as universal consciousness-form, other-than-collective, within which every experience is given in the mode of belief. In this manner, philosophy becomes the materiel organon, "our" new non-empirical sensibility. Its "aesthetic" and "logical" functions are enveloped in a transcendental doxology. The non-philosophical ceases to take a science or theory as a model of sensibility or a priori or ontological logic, and to fetishize it as givenness and position of Being. It is all of philosophy, by means of whatever system, that is subject to a non-philosophical generalization as the medium of access to beings, in whatever way that philosophy—its alleged "essence"—can no longer except it from philosophy.

Non-philosophy is not then a *popular philosophy* (Fichte). This term is understood as form or the type of exposition of philosophy adapted to consciousness that is not philosophically educated, but more profoundly as setting philosophical technique in service of the defense of "life", the "heart", "true Christianity" or "collective consciousness" and its famous "facts" (*Tatsache*). Hence a usage of philosophy against itself, a dialectic against the transcendent metaphysical speculation on this consciousness. The first gesture of such a philosophy is to widen its field of phenomena and to transcendentally legitimate not science's "judgments on experience" but collective consciousness's "judgments on perception" and rational beliefs. But this distinction of science and doxa is restrictive and falls into philosophy; it is a new "decision" between logic and *doxa*, incapable as such of bringing the philosophy of the doxa, however transcendental, to the state of widened doxa itself, of positing and thematizing the identity-of-the-last-instance of doxa and philosophy for a more powerful transcendental thought than philosophy. All nineteenth and twentieth century continental philosophy, whence the Fichtean critique of speculation, finds its original site in the rift of the real and logic prized open by Kant, never closed up again but never radically affirmed either, without reserve, reticence or resistance, ultimate and "unconscious". Since philosophy in general, even "existential" and of the essence of Being, even of the deconstruction of Being, is the thought that prohibits the unilateral duality of the Real (radical autonomy) and logic (relative autonomy) in favor of their simple "dis-location" as last residue of their circularity.

It remains to specify the status of resistance-philosophy. Philosophy spontaneously presents as resistance to the One when it interprets it "itself" in its mode to philosophy, whether it intends or not to "speak" for the first time. But this is a misunderstanding "over" the One: *if* philosophy knows it adequately as One foreclosed to itself, it could have no motive for opposing its concept and/or appropriating it. If it resists something then, it is a false One, a One-in-Being already interpreted by philosophy and falsified. Resistance proves nothing "over" the One which does not redoubt it, does not need it, does not devote itself to anything but indifference and imposes its own being-foreclosed to every thought. Resistance only demonstrates itself and expresses philosophical sufficiency. This misunderstanding regarding the Real is also radical and without solution, this core of resistance has no reason to cede.

On the other hand, the problem of resistance is diversified in relation to *thought*-(of)-the-One: it can be "worked" and limited, it ceases to be a pure illusion without reason in its object if not the foreclosure of the One that the One imposes, and acquires a function in relation to FT. Philosophy being reduced in its sufficiency and deprived of its transcendental claim to the Real, its resistance finds reasons or motives in FT. With regard to FT, which is to say the essence of Being included in it, resistance takes a sense and a reality precisely by finding itself limited by its transcendental reduction by FT. A sense in relation if not to the One, at least to Being such as its essence is included in FT. We could say that like the philosophical a prioris, it is a material and does not cease to be resistance, but loses the spontaneity of its "transcendental" belief, a belief that it has a sense and an efficacy (a *validity*) against FT itself. It continues to announce itself as resistance—it is not destroyed by definition, nor is it a radical misunderstanding in relation to the One—but under its proper form only as simple a priori of some sort, without "believing" itself to have some pertinence beyond its simple existence. It is *known*, rather than it knows itself as resistance, which renders it universal and sterile at once.

From the first state to the second, it passes from an illusory "primary" claim, though invincible in its last cause, to a "secondary" reality (to take up Freudian concepts out of context), but object of a possible elaboration. Finally, it passes through two essential states: 1) that of a resistance which believes itself to be constitutive, itself *real* to the very point of denying itself as resistance, and which claims itself to be, for the One, an absolute illusion of reality, motivated by philosophical narcissism and sufficiency alone and "negatively", if we can put it this way, by the radicality with which the One gives itself as immanent and foreclosed; 2) that of a resistance which is manifested as not being real but only effective in its origin and reducible to an a priori without claim, as an inert state of things under the form of which philosophy gives itself.

Non-philosophy does not annul philosophy but regards it philosophically, it manifests philosophy as phenomenally sterile state-of-things, leaves it "in state" as if it were without-philosophy. It accomplishes this outside of metaphysics. This is to say that it continues or still uses the All, the Mix as mechanism of the All, their infinitely varied modes, but in a manner that relieves them of their theoretically naive claim, now in terms of the contingency of relative autonomy of experience which the One indirectly frees. This no longer concerns its death by realization or its suppression by dissolution, but the transcendental recognition of its relative autonomy or resistance. This is the end of its claim of universal authority and of its auto-limitation carried out by confusion of the Real and the empirical. Correlatively, its extension to the contingent given, to "all" givens, does not come back to a new philosophical decision. To the contrary: having become an a priori deprived of its proper transcendental dimension, it instead has a limitation which forbids it from functioning as decision over the empirical. For the empirical, it is only a dominating "form" which can no longer enclose, exclude, decide, or subordinate it to other layers of the real.

The texture of the "philosophical" is always the mixture, the gentle antinomy, the dyad as more or less narrow or wide, harmonious or dislocated, but it is deprived of its force of auto-position or auto-determination because it is paralyzed by an identity which does not destroy its proper form but deprives it of any impulse by rejecting it as support; the mix-form, freeing an a priori in this way, loses its philosophical claim and motor but never its reality or its being-given. The non-philosophical prevents concluding from the effectivity of philosophy to its ultimate theoretical pertinence, but it is indeed the recognition of its unsurpassable nature —of its *identity-(of)-mix* that is posited and thematized. If, on the other hand, we give, at the end of the chain, a radical immanence that is still a transcendent *quasi-object*, we must admit then, at the other end, the dissolution of the mix without remainder, the incapacity to afford philosophy under a reduced form—a relative autonomy; to recognize its status as a priori; and the impossibility of undertaking a differentiated analysis of philosophical resistance. Inversely, in order to have under-estimated philosophical resistance *because of it, by an effect of resistance itself*, philosophy continues to makes its most archaic claims over the Real prevail, and leads to a semi-radical conception of immanence. Sometimes the One is pulled down over Being, sometimes Being is pulled down over the One: it is sufficiency that prolongs its effects in this double solution

We will not confuse this real critique of philosophy with a philosophical critique of the real. Philosophy is spontaneously dogmatic and skeptical in an evidently widened sense of these words, since they apply now to critical philosophy itself. Dogmatic: every philosophy is dogmatic insofar as it claims to accede to the Real (under the name of "Being") and co-constitute it *de jure* or implicitly when in fact this would only be to posit it as a "thing in itself". Skeptical: every philosophy is skeptical insofar as it *auto*-limits this claim or undertakes *by itself, which is to say not constrained by the force of thought*, to restrain its legislation. This is why non-philosophy begins by suspending the Principle of Sufficient Philosophy (of which the tribunal of Reason is a mode) and reducing philosophy to the state of a simple a priori of phenomenal existence, an a priori under which it gains a sound necessity.

# From the philosophical resolution of antinomies to theory and the explication of mixtures

We can distinguish two levels of problems touching on philosophy considered from the perspective of non-philosophy.

1) The relation of philosophy to experience; philosophy as form-for… the not-yet-philosophical. Hence the problem of non-philosophy as unified and not unitary theory of philosophy and experience.

2) The relation of philosophy to itself, its auto-presentation, which is to say the Philosophical Decision with its forms of antinomy both hard and soft. We will include in the mix all the inverted, deconstructed, intensified and possibilized forms of the philosophical dyad. *Hence a theory of antinomies or mixtures which is no longer their simple "philosophical resolution".*

We have dealt with the first problem, so let us examine the second. Philosophy proceeds with regard to its own antinomies and, in general, its contradictions, oppositions, amphibologies and differences—all the modes of the dyad—by dissolution and conciliation; destruction and synthesis—all the modes of the dialectic as economy of contraries or essence of the dyad. But the dissolution and synthesis, resolution, differentiation, dialectic and becoming, dissemination and "games", etc., are operations which evidently lead back, some nuances (though circular) aside, to the problem they had needed to address. These are not theoretical operations; they do not claim to know and to explain the amphibologies, or more precisely to turn them into a *theoretical usage*. They are their auto-philosophical fetishizing usage, displacing them by a mimetic or specular process, by prolonging, diversification, relaxation of their most massive or indicted forms. When he claims to resolve the philosophical antinomies through a transcendental dialectic and to use the logical organon, in spite of everything, against itself, Fichte gives the pure formula of general process of philosophy. If the dialectic (even "transcendental" in the limited sense philosophy gives to this word) is only an auto-interpretation of the dyad, it does not suffice to extend and weaken the antinomies ("difference", "passage", "becoming"), to pass from contradictions in logical structure to the logos of "combat" of opposites. It is necessary to change the terrain, to cast a new non-philosophical eye over these phenomena, perhaps honed by science, in order to explain, which is to say, really resolve rather than dissolve-and-reproduce, the uninterrupted flux of antinomies that philosophy carts along.

*To resolve* an antinomy, in effect, is always to seek in the shorter or longer term an identity under the form of a "unity of synthesis" which in reality circularly reproduces or displaces it. Theoretically using an antinomy, explaining it in an immanent manner, is to require an identity-without-synthesis, a transcendental identity of a "unilateral duality", capable of explaining it, rather than a bilateral dyad. The true "solution" to philosophical antinomies, under whatever form they present themselves, does not consist in interiorizing them or imploding them, but in making them into a *problem* regarding which we discover a hypothesis that is at once a priori and experimental and designed to explain and critique them in an immanent manner. For this, non-philosophy uses hypotheses or axioms which express the pure transcendental organon and no longer a logico-transcendental organon, which thus do not themselves have the antinomical form but which are modes of the "dual". First, it goes right up to positing a *non-antinomical identity for the antinomy*. Non-philosophy is rather an ergodic theory (of blends, those of philosophy and those of philosophy and experience), a transcendental ergodism which transforms these into simple a prioris of experience. As though this concerned an immanent generalization, without redoubling, but by identification-in-the-last-instance, of the Transcendental Dialectic (Kant, Fichte) or indeed the Onto-Theological Constitution of Metaphysics (Heidegger) etc.

To the philosophical solution (dialectic, differentiating or decon-structing) of antinomies, which requires the logico-transcendental organon, its doubles and its antidotes—transcendental imagination or indeed an affect of alterity—non-philosophy thus opposes their pure-theoretico-transcendental solution. If philosophy seeks the resolution and accord, in transcendence, of the Other assumed as determinant, non-philosophy seeks the explication and validation of the philosophical dyad, of all dyads, even distended up to the Other, in immanence as deter-minant-in-the-last-instance. From the one to the other, the determinant instance changes the mode of determination in this way. Determination passes from the dyad or the mix, from transcendence which is their essence, to the identity-in-the-last-instance that is the immanence of FT. The dyad no longer represents the Real or an ingredient thereof, its essence or an organon, but only a "secondary" instance, determined, which is now only determinant "occasionally". This is its displacement: no longer of a philosophical decision into an other, by interiorization of the antinomy in a more powerful and more enveloping system, but of an essential or deter-minant function into a function of simple support and "occasional cause". The quasi-experimental and theoretical explication of mixtures supposes a consistence of them. A philosophy that would dissolve the mixture or cause it to evaporate, cloudlike, into the limits of radical immanence or real identity would still make a usage of real identity, not as *real* but as mixture, real and transcendental, an antiscientific and nearly metaphysical usage, a thought which deprives itself of its own object in the name of its still badly understood cause, a reconstitution of a certain simultaneity of the real-One and thought. The relative autonomy of instances other than the One: of Being, beings (of philosophical resistance more generally and first of all), is reason, we know this, for which an organon is necessary; an organon which does not confuse itself with its object or its materials, and which avoids the circle of object and thought through a certain unilaterality. So FT permits us to "save" the relative autonomy of philosophy—no longer of philosophy brought to the spontaneity of its sufficiency but as simple a priori giver of phenomena. The World and philosophy are not negated in this purely transcendental reduction by FT and their reality as mixed is not simply dissolved. While philosophy "implodes" the antinomy, non-philosophy transforms it by non-antinomical means, without claiming, though—a typically philosophical gesture—to annul all its reality. It determines the antinomy through the Real-in-the-last-instance and renders its aspect of antinomy inoperative; this becomes a simple philosophical material. In a general sense, a science or a discipline unifying philosophy and science does not destroy its object but destroys only the claims to the Real of its spontaneous knowing of itself. Moreover, it explains its nature and function on the basis of a hypothesis which is irreducible to it, and of a material that is experimentally prepared. Philosophical violence claims to intervene directly in the Real, and even in philosophy itself, to the point of dissolving it—and so it reproduces the state of things it intends to change. Non-philosophy removes from the dyad just its sufficiency or its alleged power of real determination. This does not concern, then, immediately negating the reality and relative autonomy of mixtures and amphibologies by claiming to free up a pure material of its philosophical form; but rather using a transcendental identity which suspends or unilateralizes the *determinant* or allegedly real function of the dyad. FT is a *solution* to the problem of antinomies, a solution producing knowledges, not a new philo-sophical decision.

# NOTES

## Cloning the untranslatable

**1** See A. P. Smith, "Philosophy and Ecosystem: Towards a Transcendental Ecology", *Polygraph* 22 (2010), pp. 65–82 and A. P. Smith, "Thinking from the One: Science and the Ancient Philosophical Figure of the One", *Laruelle and Non-Philosophy*, (eds). J. Mullarkey and A. P. Smith (Edinburgh: Edinburgh University Press, 2012), pp. 28–30. For a more general and synoptic introduction see also Smith's translator's introduction to F. Laruelle, *Future Christ: A Lesson in Heresy* (London and New York: Continuum, 2010) entitled "The Philosopher and the Heretic: Translator's Introduction" as well as the other essays that make up *Laruelle and Non-Philosophy*.

## Preface

**1** In French both the physical sense of "objectivation" (converting an abstraction or concept into an object) and the everyday social and political sense of objectification (turning a subject or person into an object) are covered by the French word *objectivation*. Laruelle appears to be playing on both in setting it against "performation", with its relation to speech-act theory or a "performative" (i.e. when a judge *says* something he also *does* something) and the emphasis, theoretically important for what follows, on form rather than an object as such. [Translators' note.]

**2** This announced book was never released, though arguably Laruelle's *Philosophie non-standard. Générique, quantique, philo-fiction* (published in France by Kimé in 2010) constitutes just such a realization of non-philosophy through rethinking all its major themes in a "matrix" or "conceptual collider" bringing together quantum mechanics with philosophy in a unified theory. [Translators' note.]

# Chapter One

1 François Laruelle, *Philosophie et non-philosophie* (Liège/Brussels: Mardaga, 1989) forthcoming in English as *Philosophy and Non-Philosophy*, translated by Taylor Adkins (Minneapolis: Univocal Publishing, 2013).

2 The French *à cause* typically is translated as "because". [Translators' note.]

3 Non-philosophy also distinguishes itself from the europanalysis (Serge Valdinoci). If one takes non-philosophy as a measure of the most radical suspension of philosophy, europanalysis situates itself, from this point of view, on the vector which goes from non-philosophy to philosophy, where it occupies an original and fertile "attached" place. [Author's footnote.]

# Chapter Two

1 Rocco Gangle explains in his translation of Laruelle's *Philosophies of Difference: A Critical Introduction to Non-Philosophy* that Laruelle makes use of the two French words for "dual" that exist *duel* and *dual*. The former has a sense of opposition that is lacking in the latter, which is properly non-philosophical. [Translators' note.]

2 Laruelle here marks a difference between *la mystique* and *le mystique*, the latter taking the male definite article, which has the effect of forming a neologism in French. The difference follows that of *la politique* and *le politique* in French, which marks the philosophical difference between "politics" and "the political". We have tried to capture this by translating *la mystique* as "mystique", since he also distinguishes this from what we would call mysticism (*le mysticisme*, another French neologism), and *le mystique* as "the mystical". [Translators' note.]

# Chapter Four

1 Laruelle uses quotes here since precession [*précession*], despite being an English word, is a French neologism playing on precede and cession. [Translators' note.]

# Chapter Six

1 Laruelle is making a play on words here that is theoretically important but impossible to capture in translation. In short he is making reference to the double *apport*, meaning provision, but this plays off of the *rapport* above where Laruelle drops the "re", meaning the recursive element, self-reflexive element. [Translators' note.]

2 Here Laruelle uses the term "materiel", which translates the French neologism *matérial*, differing from both "material" [*matériel*] (the common adjectival form) and the "materials" [*matériau*] used by non-philosophy (like "building materials") as well as the "matter" [*matière*] of philosophical materialism. The model for the construction of this neologism is found in Heidegger's differentiation between what is translated in the Macquarrie and Robinson translation of *Being and Time* as existentiel and existential. [Translators' note.]

# OTHER WORKS BY FRANÇOIS LARUELLE

## Philosophy I

*Phénomène et différence. Essai sur Ravaisson* (Paris: Klincksieck, 1971)
*Machines textuelles. Déconstruction et libido-d'écriture* (Paris: Le Seuil, 1976)
*Nietzsche contra Heidegger* (Paris: Payot, 1977)
*Le déclin de l'écriture* (Paris: Aubier-Flammarion, 1977)
*Au-delà de principe de pouvoir* (Paris: Payot, 1978)

## Philosophy II

*Le principe de minorité* (Paris: Aubier, 1981)
*Une biographie de l'homme ordinaire. Des autorités et minorités* (Paris: Aubier, 1985)
*Philosophies of Difference: A Critical Introduction to Non-Philosophy*, trans. Rocco Gangle (New York and London: Continuum, 2010 [1987])
*Philosophie et non-philosophie* (Liège-Bruxelles: Mardaga, 1989)
*En tant qu'Un* (Paris: Aubier, 1991)
*Théorie des identités* (Paris: PUF, 1992)

## Philosophy III

*Théorie des Étrangers* (Paris: Kimé, 1995)
*Principles of Non-Philosophy*, trans. Nicola Rubczak and Anthony Paul Smith (London: Bloomsbury, 2013 [1995])
*Éthique de l'Étranger* (Paris: Kimé, 2000)
*Introduction au non-marxisme* (Paris: PUF, 2000)

# Philosophy IV

*Future Christ: A Lesson in Heresy*, trans. Anthony Paul Smith (New York and London: Continuum, 2010 [2002])

*L'ultime honneur des intellectuels* (Paris: Textuel, 2003)

*Struggle and Utopia at the End Times of Philosophy*, trans. Drew S. Burk and Anthony Paul Smith (Minneapolis: Univocal Publishing 2013 [2004])

*Mystique non-philosophique à l'usage des contemporains* (Paris: L'Harmattan, 2007)

# Philosophy V

*Introduction aux sciences génériques* (Paris: Petra, 2008)

*Philosophie non-standard* (Paris: Kimé, 2010)

*The Concept of Non-Photography*, trans. Robin Mackay (Falmouth and New York: Urbanomic-Sequence, 2011)

*Anti-Badiou: On the Introduction of Maoism into Philosophy*, trans. Robin Mackay (London: Bloomsbury, 2013 [2011])

*Thérorie générale des victimes* (Paris: Mille et Une Nuits, 2012)

*Photo-Fiction, A Non-Standard Aesthetics*, trans. Drew S. Burk (Minneapolis: Univocal Publishing, 2013)

# INDEX